Webster's
Legal
Dictionary

Webster's
Legal
Dictionary

by James E. Clapp
Member of the New York and
District of Columbia Bars

RANDOM HOUSE
REFERENCE

Originally published as *Random House Webster's Pocket
Legal Dictionary, Second Edition*

Copyright © 1996 by Random House, Inc.

Printed in the United States of America

ISBN-13: 978-0-307-29073-1
ISBN-10: 0-307-29073-5

10 9 8 7 6 5 4 3 2 1

CONTENTS

To Mom and Dad
who passed their love of
language on to me

PREFACE

The law touches almost every aspect of life, and the language of law is accordingly as broad and complex as human experience itself. Defining, refining, debating, interpreting, and applying the words of constitutions, statutes, contracts, wills, judicial opinions, and other legal writings is a major preoccupation of the law.

It is, in fact, a fundamental preoccupation: to question the meaning of a term in a legal context is often to question the scope of the law itself. To define the word "murder," for example, is to articulate just what it is that distinguishes one of the most heinous of crimes from a lesser offense such as manslaughter, or for that matter from a heroic act of justifiable homicide. Even a seemingly insignificant word can make a crucial difference in the interpretation of a legal writing. One standard legal reference work—a 90-volume compendium entitled *Words and Phrases*—cites almost 50 judicial opinions discussing the meaning of just the first word listed: "a."

Because law, like the society whose rules it expresses, is constantly evolving—and also because the United States does not have a unified legal system, but instead has more than fifty separate systems of state and federal law—legal terms are seldom susceptible of a precise definition upon which everyone can agree. But lawyers, legislators, and judges could not even carry on discussions about nuances and variations in legal concepts if there were not a large body of specialized vocabulary whose central meaning is understood and shared by all. The objective of this dictionary is to provide a basic understanding of the core of that vocabulary— a few thousand of the most common and most important terms used in contemporary American law.

A great many of these legal terms have considerable currency in popular usage as well and are at least vaguely understood by almost everyone. The intent here is to go beyond such superficial understandings, enabling the user to come away with some grasp of the current scope and significance of these legal concepts. This is done through:

1 definitions that include enough detail to avoid being simplistic. (See, for example, MURDER; HEARSAY.)

2 examples of sentences and phrases showing how a term is used. (See IMPRESS; UNDERWRITE.)

3 subentries that flesh out the meaning of the main entry term. (See the categories of property listed under PROPERTY, or the two branches of the concept of due process listed under DUE PROCESS.)

4 historical information, summaries of recent cases, or other commentary. (See SEPARATE BUT EQUAL; LACHES.)

5 division of certain terms into separate entries to avoid confusion between unrelated or easily conflated meanings. (See ACQUIT[1] with its noun form *acquittal,* versus ACQUIT[2], and its noun form *acquittance.*)

6 copious cross references to related or contrasting terms that help to place an entry in context and clarify its scope.

7 an appendix summarizing all of the amendments to the United States Constitution, which are the source of so many of the most fundamental principles in American law.

Much of the specialized vocabulary of the law consists of everyday English words used in specialized senses. By and large, this dictionary gives only the specialized meanings.

GUIDE TO THE DICTIONARY

Entries and Subentries

Main entries, printed in large **bold** type, are alphabetized word by word, in "telephone-book" style. For example, the various Latin phrases beginning with the word "per" (such as "per curiam," "per se," and "per stirpes") are grouped together before such words as "percentage lease," "perjury," and "person."

Many entries include a number of related terms and phrases as subentries, shown within the entry in normal-sized **bold** type. Most of these are specific phrases using the main-entry term, grouped together for ease of comparison; these phrases are shown alphabetically under the main entry at their own numbered definitions. See, for example, *adhesion contract, bilateral contract, contract under seal,* and the other types of contract listed and defined at defs. 4–10 under CONTRACT.

In addition, as also exemplified in the entry for CONTRACT, subentries may be

1 incorporated into the text of a definition, where they are defined implicitly. See the terms *oral contract* and *written contract* in def. 7 and, in def. 9, where *third-party beneficiary contract* is defined, the related term *third-party beneficiary.*

2 included as variants or alternate terms for a main entry or a subentry, preceded by "Also" or "Also called." See *contract of adhesion* at def. 4.

3 shown at the end of an entry as a related grammatical form—usually another part of speech—derived from the main entry term. See *contractual* following def. 11.

Note that definitions and numbered subentries for a one-word main entry are grouped by part of speech. For example, in the entry for CONTRACT, all of the definitions of "contract" as a noun and the phrases using that term as a noun are grouped together, followed by the definition of "contract" as a verb.

Cross References

The grouping of related phrases by subject matter under a main-entry term (as just illustrated for the term "contract")—instead of scattering them alphabetically throughout the dictionary—is one of the primary ways in which this book seeks to facilitate understanding of the legal concepts represented. Another is the inclusion of extensive cross references directing the reader to additional entries for further information.

Kinds of cross references

The cross references have three broad functions:

1 When a term is dealt with in an entry in another part of the alphabet, a cross reference directs the reader who has looked for the term alphabetically to the entry where it is discussed. These cross references are usually signaled by such words as "see," "see under," or "same as." See ADHESION CONTRACT (directing the reader to see under CONTRACT), PRIME CONTRACTOR (noting that this is the same thing as a *general contractor*, as defined in the entry for CONTRACT), and CONCURRENT (directing the reader to the appropriate entries for defininitions of *concurrent jurisdiction* and *concurrent sentences.*)

2 Cross references also call attention to related entries containing additional information on

the subject just discussed, entries for various legal phrases containing a particular word, and entries for contrasting terms, all of which provide context and additional understanding for the specific term under discussion. These cross references are typically introduced by such signals as "see," "see also," or "cf." (meaning "compare"). See CONSTRUCTIVE (citing numerous entries for phrases employing the term "constructive," and calling attention to the entry for the contrasting term "actual") and FREEDOM OF RELIGION (directing attention to the entry for the related concept of SEPARATION OF CHURCH AND STATE).

3 Many definitions depend upon an understanding of certain key legal terms that are defined elsewhere. Cross references to such terms are indicated simply by highlighting them typographically, as discussed directly below. See REPLY (defined as a PLEADING in response to a COUNTERCLAIM akin to an ANSWER) and BURDEN² (citing EASEMENT and *covenant running with the land* as the kind of thing that gives rise to this kind of burden).

Type styles for cross references

As the foregoing examples illustrate, all cross references (whether or not preceded by a signal such as "see" or "cf.") are highlighted by the use of a distinctive typeface.

Whenever a main entry is specifically referred to elsewhere in the dictionary, the term is printed in SMALL CAPITAL LETTERS. When the reader's attention is being directed to a specific subentry, *italics* are always used, in one of the following three ways:

1 Usually the subentry being referred to is given in full in italics, followed closely by a parenthetical reference to the main-entry term (in small capitals) under which that

subentry will be found. See def. 4 under DEFENSE, with its cross references to *burden of pleading* and *burden of proof,* both of which will be found under BURDEN[1].

2 Often a list of cross references to phrases all beginning with the same word is shortened by writing, e.g., "See also *indecent* ASSAULT, SPEECH under those words" instead of "See also *indecent assault* (under ASSAULT); *indecent speech* (under SPEECH)." See PERSONAL for a more extensive example.

3 When the cross reference is simply from one subentry to another under the same main entry, the small-capital reference to the main entry is omitted. See the "cf." cross references back and forth between *bilateral contract* and *unilateral contract* under CONTRACT.

Plural forms in cross references

Occasionally a sentence containing a cross reference uses the plural form of the term being referred to, even though the actual entry is in the singular. See def. 7 under ANSWER (referring to COUNTERCLAIMS), and def. 4 under TRUST (referring to CONFLICTS OF INTEREST).

Labels

Terms or definitions that are significantly more casual in tone than is typical of legal discourse are labeled *Informal* or *Slang.*

Words and phrases in *Latin, French,* or *Law French* (a dialect of French, quite different from modern French, used extensively by English lawyers in the 14th and 15th centuries) are so labeled, and unless their current definition is substantially the same as their original meaning, a more literal translation is added in parentheses to show how the actual Latin, French, or Law French words relate to the current use of the term in American law. See PARENS PATRIAE; FORCE MAJEURE; CY PRES.

Parts of speech are indicated in italics for all one-word main entries and any related forms listed at the end of such entries. (For abbreviations used, see list following this Guide.)

Examples

Many definitions include examples of how the term is used in phrases or in sentences, typically signaled by a colon. See CONTRACT (def. 1); APPROPRIATION (defs. 1–2).

These examples are normally italicized. In some cases, the phrase used as an example is also specifically defined elsewhere in the dictionary. In these cases, the sample phrase is also a cross reference, and so is either accompanied by a parenthetical reference in small capitals to the appropriate main entry or is itself printed in small capitals. See the entry for SPECIFIC, with sample phrases exemplifying each of its meanings, each of which is itself a main entry or subentry elsewhere in the dictionary.

Typefaces

As noted above, all main entries and subentries appear in bold print. This makes them easy to find when looking up a cross reference. For example, the entry for ORAL includes a reference to *oral contract* (under CONTRACT). That subentry actually appears in def. 7 under CONTRACT (in the definition of *express contract*), not between defs. 8 and 9 as it would if it were a numbered subentry; but because it is in bold print it should be easily located upon a quick perusal of the entry for CONTRACT.

Small capitals always denote a cross reference to a main entry.

Italics are used for cross references to subentries, for labels, for examples, and occasionally to highlight a key word. (See the italicized word "state" in the second sentence of the entry for INCORPORATION DOCTRINE.)

Personal Pronouns

The approach taken in this book to the perennial problem of masculine and feminine pronouns (he/she, him/her, etc.) is to use them interchangeably and randomly. Unless the context clearly indicates otherwise, each should be read as including the other. Obviously, no suggestion should be read into any use of such a term that one sex is more likely than the other to sue or be sued, commit a crime or a tort, be a lawyer or a judge, or the like.

ABBREVIATIONS USED IN THIS BOOK

abbr.	abbreviation
adj.	adjective
adv.	adverb
cf.	compare (Latin *confer*)
cap.	capitalized
def., defs.	definition, definitions
e.g.	for example (Latin *exempli gratia*)
i.e.	that is (Latin *id est*)
interj.	interjection
l.c.	lower case (not capitalized)
lit.	literally
n.	noun
n.pl.	plural noun
pl.	plural
prep.	preposition
v.	verb
v.	versus (in case names)
vs.	versus (other than in case names)

ab initio, *Latin.* from the beginning; see, for example, *void ab initio* (under VOID)

abandon, *v.* **1.** to give up a right, claim, or interest without specifically transferring it to someone else **2.** to desert a child or spouse See also DESERTION —**abandonment,** *n.*

abate, *v.* **1.** to reduce or eliminate *to abate taxes, to abate rent; to abate a nuisance* **2.** to diminish or be extinguished· *The action abated because the plaintiff failed to serve the defendant with a summons.* —**abatable,** *adj* —**abatement,** *n*

abduction, *n.* **1.** KIDNAPPING, especially of a child, ward, or spouse. **2.** the tort of luring away, carrying off, or concealing another's spouse or child. When no force is involved, also called **enticement.** The tort has its origins in a man's ownership of his wife and children and his right to compensation for being deprived of their services The modern scope of the tort varies from state to state

abet, *v.* to incite, encourage, instigate, or support, especially something bad In legal contexts, used almost exclusively in, or as short for, the phrase AID AND ABET —**abettor, abetter,** *n.*

abide, *v.* **1.** to await. For example, see *costs to abide the event* (under COSTS) **2.** to accept and obey *a law-abiding citizen*

abnormally dangerous activity, an activity, such as blasting, that is regarded as so inherently dangerous that anyone who engages in it should be held strictly liable for any damage it causes to person or property. Also called **ultrahazardous activity.** See also *strict liability* (under LIABILITY).

abortion, *n.* the intentional termination of a pregnancy other than by live birth A limited right of a woman to decide for herself whether to seek an abortion is included in the RIGHT TO PRIVACY protected by *substantive due process* (see under DUE PROCESS).

about. See ON OR ABOUT

above, *adv.* previously in the same document *the authorities cited above.* See also SUPRA

abridge, *v.* to restrict or diminish a legal right. *The First Amendment prohibits Congress from abridging freedom of speech.* —**abridgment,** *n.*

abrogate, *v.* to annul, repeal, overturn, supersede, or cancel by some legally effective means. *to abrogate a statute, an order, a contract, a will* —**abrogation,** *n.*

abscond, *v.* to depart from a jurisdiction or secrete oneself in order to avoid arrest, service of a summons or other process, or action by creditors —**absconding, abscondence,** *n.*

absolute, *adj.* unrestricted; unencumbered; unconditional A term used to distinguish an unqualified right, interest, duty, privilege, order, transaction, document, or the like from one that is qualified in some way. See, for example, *absolute discretion* (under DISCRETION); *absolute immunity* (under IMMUNITY); *absolute privilege* (under PRIVILEGE); *fee simple absolute* (under FEE¹).

abstention, *n.* the act of a federal court in refusing to exercise its jurisdiction over a case on the ground that the issues would be better dealt with by a state court or an administrative agency. —**abstain,** *v.*

abstract of title, a summary of the history of ownership of a parcel of land, with a list of encumbrances on the land. An abstract of title is typically prepared in connection with a proposed sale of land by a company in the business of ferreting out such information from public records.

abuse, *n.* **1.** mistreatment of a person: *physical abuse; psychological abuse;* SPOUSAL ABUSE; CHILD ABUSE. **2.** wrongful or unwarranted exercise of a right or power. ABUSE OF DISCRETION; ABUSE OF PROCESS.

abuse of discretion, an unsound or illogical ruling by a court or administrative body on a matter within its DISCRETION. A discretionary ruling will not be reversed simply because the reviewing court would have decided the matter differently, but only if the decision is found to be so unreasonable as to constitute an "abuse of discretion." The phrase does not imply wrongdoing; it simply indicates that the tribunal committed an error. Also called **improvident exercise of discretion.**

abuse of process, the tort of instituting a judicial proceeding or otherwise using judicial PROCESS for an improper purpose. Essentially it is the use of an otherwise justifiable judicial procedure as a form of extortion to gain some advantage or benefit unrelated to the legitimate objective of the judicial proceeding. This tort differs from MALICIOUS PROSECUTION in that there may have been a legally sufficient basis for instituting such a proceeding, but the actual purpose to which the proceeding is put is wrongful.

accelerate, *v.* **1.** to cause a legal right, duty, or interest that was to arise or vest in the future to do so immediately. **2.** in particular, to cause a debt that was to be repaid in the future to become immediately due. *Under the terms of the automobile loan, his failure to pay one installment accelerated the entire debt.* —**acceleration,** *n.*

acceleration clause, a clause in a credit agreement providing that upon the occurrence of specified events the party extending credit may declare the entire outstanding balance immediately due. The purpose of such clauses is to enable the creditor to take immediate legal action to recover the amount loaned if it appears that the debtor is in financial difficulty.

accept, *v.* to manifest satisfaction with or assent to a transaction, proposal, or state of affairs, thereby becoming legally bound. For example: (a) in property law, to take delivery of property or otherwise give formal assent to becoming the owner; (b) in contract law, to agree to an offer (this is the final step in forming a legally binding contract); (c) in the case of a bank or other entity upon which a check or other draft is drawn, to indicate on the instrument that it will be paid; for example, to certify a check. —**acceptance,** *n.*

accessory, *n.* **1.** one who assists a criminal in connection with a crime, especially a felony, without being present when the crime is committed. **2. accessory after the fact,** one who knowingly assists a person who has committed a felony to avoid or hinder capture, prosecution, conviction, or punishment. This conduct is usually treated as an offense of less severity than the felony itself, often under the name **hindering.** See also OBSTRUCTION OF JUSTICE. **3. accessory before the fact,** one who encourages or assists in the planning or commission of a felony without being present. An accessory before the fact is an *aider and abettor* (see under AID AND ABET) and is ordinarily regarded by the law as equally culpable with the person who directly commits the felony.

accommodation, *n.* **1.** something done as a favor rather than for consideration, especially acting as a SURETY: *The mother signed the car loan as an accommodation to her son.* **2. accommodation party,** a person who adds her name to a negotiable instrument or credit agreement as an accommodation to the principal obligor and so becomes liable on it. This is often done when the person taking the instrument or extending the credit is not satisfied with the creditworthiness of the principal obligor. See also PUBLIC ACCOMMODATION.

accomplice, *n.* one who, for the purpose of promoting or facilitating a crime, solicits or encourages another to commit it, assists or attempts to assist in its planning or commission, or in some situations simply fails to make an attempt to prevent it. An accomplice is normally equal in culpability to the person who directly commits the crime.

accord, *n.* **1.** an agreement to settle a claim for a sum of money to be paid in the future, or occasionally for some other performance. **2. accord and satisfaction,** an accord that has been satisfied by rendering the promised payment or performance. A claim that is the subject of an accord and satisfaction can never again be raised in court.

account, *n.* **1.** a list of financial transactions between two parties, typically a buyer and seller of goods or services, showing amounts of money paid and to be paid as a result of their business with each other. **2.** Also called **bank account.** a deposit of money in a bank, pursuant to an agreement with the bank as to services it will provide (such as payment of checks), interest to be paid by the bank for the use of the money, and fees to be paid by the depositor **3. individual account,** a bank account held by one person only. **4. joint account,** a bank account held by two or more people, each of whom may withdraw funds without the consent of the other. Such an account usually entails a RIGHT OF SURVIVORSHIP, so that any balance in the account when one holder dies becomes the property of the surviving holders. See also *Totten trust* (under TRUST).

account stated, 1. a statement of account upon which

the parties agree; typically it is prepared by the party to whom money is owed and submitted to the debtor, who indicates assent. **2.** a common law action for the balance due upon such an account.

accounting, *n.* **1.** a detailed description of how the assets in an estate or trust fund have been managed and disposed of. **2.** an action, which originated in courts of equity, to compel a FIDUCIARY to account for all assets handled in a fiduciary capacity and to turn over any profits received.

accrue, *v.* **1.** (of a financial right or obligation) to come into existence, mature, or accumulate. *accrued interest.* **2.** (of a legal claim) to arise; to come into existence or mature so that it can be sued upon: *The statute of limitations begins to run when the cause of action accrues.* —**accrual,** *n.*

accusatorial system, the Anglo-American system of criminal prosecution, in which the government, having accused the defendant, must prove its allegations by the adversary process, with the judge acting only as a neutral referee. Same as ADVERSARY SYSTEM, except that the latter term applies to both civil and criminal cases. Cf. INQUISITORIAL SYSTEM.

accusatory instrument, a formal document accusing a person of a crime and initiating a criminal prosecution, such as an INFORMATION or INDICTMENT.

accused, *n.* a person arrested, indicted, or otherwise formally charged with a crime; the defendant or prospective defendant in a criminal case: *The Sixth Amendment guarantees the accused the right to a speedy and public trial.*

acknowledgment, *n.* **1.** an admission of the truth of a fact or the existence of an obligation, by which one accepts civil legal responsibility. This may be by words ("I am the father of that child") or by action (e.g., signifying acknowledgment of a debt by making a partial payment). **2.** an individual's declaration that she is the one who executed a particular deed or other instrument, and that she did so for the purposes stated in the instrument. Such an acknowledgment is made before a notary public or similar officer, who is responsible for confirming the individual's identity, and who puts a formal notation of the acknowledgment on the instrument. —**acknowledge,** *v.*

acquaintance rape. See under RAPE.

acquit¹, *v.* to release a criminal defendant from a charge, either upon a finding of NOT GUILTY by the jury or because the court or the prosecution determined that the case should not go forward after the trial was commenced. So far as the law is concerned, an acquitted defendant is innocent. —**acquittal,** *n.*

acquit², *v.* to release a person from a contractual obligation (especially an obligation to pay money) or acknowledge that the obligation has been fulfilled, as by giving a receipt. —**acquittance,** *n.*

act, *n.* **1.** a statute: *act of Congress; legislative act; the Civil Rights Act of 1964.* **2.** something done (an **affirma-**

tive **act** or **act of commission**) or under some circumstances not done (a **negative act** or **act of omission**) by a person. See also ACTUS REUS, OMISSION; OVERT ACT; VERBAL ACT.

act of God, a natural event such as lightning, a hurricane, an earthquake, or some other natural catastrophe beyond human causation or control. Sometimes such events provide an excuse for nonperformance of an obligation, either because a contract specifically so provides or as a matter of law.

act of state, an official act of a foreign government. Under the **act of state doctrine,** American courts will not question the validity of such an act (for example, the expropriation of American property) by a recognized foreign government within its own territory.

action, *n.* **1.** any conduct; an act or series of acts by a person or entity. See also STATE ACTION **2.** a court case, especially a civil case; the procedure by which a legal dispute, claim, or accusation is resolved **3. civil action,** an action brought for any purpose other than punishment of a crime. This is the usual meaning of the word "action." **4. class action,** an action brought on behalf of, or occasionally against, a class of persons having a common interest but too numerous to be conveniently joined as individual parties in the case. **5. criminal action,** a case brought by the government to punish a person or entity for a crime; more often called a criminal case, a criminal proceeding, or a prosecution. **6. damage action.** See under DAMAGES. **7. derivative action,** an action brought on behalf of a corporation by one of its shareholders, to protect a right of the corporation. Also called **shareholder derivative action** or **stockholder derivative action. 8. equitable action,** an action of a type traditionally maintainable only in courts of EQUITY. Also called **action in equity** or, more traditionally, SUIT in equity. **9. in personam action** or **action in personam,** an action in which the plaintiff seeks damages or other relief against a specific person or entity It must be based upon *in personam jurisdiction* (see under JURISDICTION[1]) over the defendant. Most lawsuits are of this type. See also IN PERSONAM. Cf. *in rem action; quasi in rem action.* **10. in rem action** or **action in rem,** an action in which the plaintiff seeks judgment declaring the status or disposition of property or a relationship within the jurisdiction of the court. For example, see *in rem jurisdiction* (under JURISDICTION[1]). See also IN REM. Cf. *in personam action; quasi in rem action* **11. legal action, a.** broadly, any court case. **b.** Also called **common law action** or **action at law.** An action of a type traditionally maintained in courts of LAW as distinguished from courts of EQUITY See also FORM OF ACTION, CAUSE OF ACTION, EX CONTRACTU, EX DELICTO, and MERGER OF LAW AND EQUITY. **12. quasi in rem action** or **action quasi in rem,** an action against an out-of-state defendant, typically commenced by ATTACHMENT of property of the defendant located within the state, in which the plaintiff seeks judgment on a claim unrelated to the property and seeks to use the seized property to satisfy that judgment if payment is not made. This was formerly a device by which a claim could be litigated against a defendant who was not personally subject to the jurisdiction of the court, but the modern view is that the court must have *in personam jurisdiction,* not just *quasi in rem jurisdiction* (see both under JURISDICTION[1]), to render such a judgment. See also QUASI IN REM. Cf *in personam action; in rem action.* **13. third-party action.** See under THIRD PARTY.

actionable, *adj.* describing an act or situation that could be the basis for a lawsuit: *Defamatory speech is actionable, but not speech that is merely offensive*

actual, *adj.* real; existing in fact: a word used to distinguish something known to have happened or to exist from something that the law simply deems to have happened or to exist. The opposite of CONSTRUCTIVE, IMPUTED, APPARENT, and *implied in law* (see under IMPLIED). See *actual* AUTHORITY[1], DAMAGES, EVICTION, FRAUD, KNOWLEDGE, MALICE, NOTICE under those words.

actus reus, *Latin.* (lit. "guilty act") a voluntary act or omission to which criminal responsibility can attach. Without such an act there can be no crime, for a fundamental principle of Anglo-American law is that one cannot be punished for bad thoughts alone. See also MENS REA.

ad damnum, *Latin* (lit. "to the loss") the amount of money sought as damages in a complaint. The **ad damnum clause** is the part of a complaint in which that amount is specified. If judgment is obtained by default, it cannot exceed that amount; if the defendant does not default, then the judgment will be for whatever amount of damages the plaintiff proves at trial, whether higher or lower than the ad damnum.

ad litem, *Latin.* (lit. "for the case") for purposes of a particular case. Used primarily in the phrase GUARDIAN AD LITEM.

ad testificandum, *Latin.* for the purpose of testifying. See *subpoena ad testificandum* (under SUBPOENA).

ad valorem, *Latin.* (lit. "according to the worth") **1.** in proportion to the value of something. **2. ad valorem tax,** a tax or duty calculated as a percentage of the stated or assessed value of the thing taxed.

additur, *n. Latin.* (lit. "it is added") an order increasing the amount of damages awarded by a jury. The defendant must either agree to the higher figure or submit to a new trial. Cf. REMITTITUR.

ademption, *n.* the reduction or extinguishment of a legacy because, by the time of the testator's death, some or all of the money or property needed to satisfy the legacy has been destroyed, disposed of, or already given to the legatee. Cf. ADVANCEMENT. **—adeem,** *v.*

adequate remedy at law. See under REMEDY.

adhesion contract. See under CONTRACT

adjective law. Same as PROCEDURE (def 2)

adjourn, *v.* to suspend or postpone a proceeding, either temporarily or indefinitely —**adjournment,** *n.*

adjudge, *v.* to render a judicial decision or judgment to a certain effect *The will was adjudged void. It is adjudged that the plaintiff shall recover the sum of $3,500*

adjudicate, *v.* to hear and resolve a case in a court or administrative agency· *The matter was adjudicated in the Court of Common Pleas.* —**adjudication,** *n.*

adjudicated, *adj.* determined by adjudication *an adjudicated incompetent; an adjudicated matter.*

administer, *v.* to take charge of the estate of a decedent, marshal and manage the assets, see to the paying of the estate's debts and taxes, and distribute whatever is left in accordance with the terms of the will or, if there is no will, the laws of INTESTATE SUCCESSION See also ADMINISTRATOR, EXECUTOR. —**administration,** *n*

administrative, *adj.* pertaining to an ADMINISTRATIVE AGENCY or to the work of such agencies in general. *administrative officer; administrative order; administrative function.* See also *administrative procedure* (under PROCEDURE); *administrative review* (under REVIEW)

administrative agency, a federal, state, or local governmental unit with responsibility for administering and enforcing a particular body of law; for example, the Internal Revenue Service, a state power commission, or a city human rights department Also called **agency.** See also REGULATORY AGENCY

administrative law, 1. the body of law that deals with the duties and operations of administrative agencies. **2.** a body of law on a particular subject created by an administrative agency through its regulations and decisions

administrative law judge, an official of an administrative agency who hears, weighs, and decides on evidence in administrative proceedings In some states called a **hearing examiner** or **hearing officer.**

administrator, *n.* a person appointed by a court to ADMINISTER the estate of a person who dies without a will. It is still common to refer to a female administrator by the archaic term **administratrix.** Cf. EXECUTOR.

admiralty. See under MARITIME

admissible, *adj.* **1.** (of evidence) permitted by the rules of evidence to be considered by the judge or jury in a case Evidence that is admissible may nevertheless not be admitted by the judge if, for example, it is CUMULATIVE or unduly inflammatory. See also PREJUDICIAL EFFECT. **2. admissible for a limited purpose,** describing evidence that may be considered for one purpose or on one issue, but not another. —**admissibility,** *n*

admission, *n.* **1.** any words or acts of a party to a case offered as evidence by that party's opponent Admissions are usually allowed into evidence as an exception to the *hearsay rule* (see under HEARSAY) on the ground that the party whose admission is being offered can take the stand and explain or dispute it if it is misleading. **2.** a defendant's failure to deny an allegation in a complaint, counter-claim, or *request for admissions*. The usual consequence is that the allegation in question is deemed true and may no longer be contested in the case **3.** the act of a judge in allowing proffered evidence to be considered by the jury See also RECEIVE. Cf. EXCLUSION. **4. admission to the bar,** the granting or obtaining of a license from the state, or permission from a court, to practice law in that state or before that court. When an out-of-state lawyer, or a lawyer not admitted to the bar of a particular court, is given special permission to appear in a particular case, that is called **admission pro hac vice.** See also PRO HAC VICE. **5. request for admissions,** a paper served by one party upon another in a case, demanding that an adversary admit or deny certain facts; often served shortly before a trial to narrow the issues and eliminate the need to spend court time proving things that are not in dispute. —**admit,** *v.*

admonition, *n.* a judge's courtroom direction, advice, or warning to a jury, witness, lawyer, or even spectator, regarding any matter arising during a case. —**admonish,** *v*

adoption, *n* the legal procedure by which an adult acquires the rights, duties, and status of a parent with respect to a child who is not the adult's natural offspring. —**adopt,** *v*

adultery, *n.* sexual intercourse by a married person with someone other than that person's spouse. This was traditionally regarded as a crime, at least when committed by a woman, and as a ground for divorce. Most states have abolished the crime and eliminated the requirement of an accusation of wrongdoing in order to obtain a divorce. Cf CRIMINAL CONVERSATION; FORNICATION.

advance directive, a LIVING WILL, a HEALTH CARE PROXY, or a combination of the two.

advancement, *n.* an advance payment or transfer of a portion of one's estate to an heir (usually a child) while one is still alive, with the understanding that this is in place of a share of the estate after death The effect is to extinguish, to the extent of the advancement, that heir's claim to a share of the estate under the laws of INTESTATE SUCCESSION. Cf ADEMPTION

adventure. See JOINT VENTURE

adversary system, the Anglo-American method of adjudication, in which the responsibility for ferreting out the truth in a case rests almost exclusively on the opposing parties and their lawyers, through examination and cross-examination of witnesses of their choosing. With reference to criminal cases, also called ACCUSATORIAL SYSTEM Cf. INQUISITORIAL SYSTEM

adverse possession, a method of acquiring title to real estate, accomplished by openly occupying the property to the exclusion of everyone else and in defiance of the rights of the real owner for a period of time set by statute, typically ten to twenty years. If the owner fails to take appropriate action to oust you within that time, the property is yours.

adverse witness. Same as *hostile witness* (see under WITNESS)

advisory opinion, an opinion by a court on a hypothetical legal question posed by a legislative or executive body or official, as distinguished from a question arising in an actual case; for example, a question about the constitutionality of a proposed law or the legality of a proposed transaction. The Constitution bars federal courts from issuing advisory opinions, but some state courts are authorized to render such advice in certain circumstances.

affiant, *n.* the person who makes an AFFIDAVIT.

affidavit *n.* **1.** a formal written statement affirming or swearing to the truth of the facts stated, signed before a notary public or similar officer Dishonesty in an affidavit is FALSE SWEARING or PERJURY. In a narrow sense, "affidavit" refers to a sworn statement (see SWEAR) and so is distinguished from AFFIRMATION (def. 2); in a broader sense it includes affirmations. **2. affidavit** (or **affirmation**) **of service,** an affidavit or affirmation stating the time and manner in which a summons or other court paper was served in a case.

affirm¹, *v.* **1.** to declare solemnly that certain statements are true, or that one will testify truthfully. **2.** to make a solemn promise, particularly to carry out one's duties as a citizen or officeholder and to obey or uphold the law. See also SWEAR; SWEAR OR AFFIRM; OATH —**affirmation,** *n.*

affirm², *v.* to uphold the judgment of a lower tribunal in a case that has been appealed. Cf REVERSE; REMAND; VACATE. —**affirmance,** *n.*

affirmation, *n.* **1.** the act of affirming something (see AFFIRM¹), or the words recited in doing so An affirmation has exactly the same legal effect as an OATH. **2.** a formal written statement affirming certain facts subject to the penalties for false swearing and perjury, sometimes required to be executed before a notary public and sometimes not. This is substantially the same in form, and exactly the same in legal effect, as an AFFIDAVIT See also *affirmation of service* (under AFFIDAVIT); OATH; OATH OR AFFIRMATION.

affirmative act. See under ACT.

affirmative action, any step by a public or private employer, school, institution, or program, beyond the mere cessation of intentional discrimination, to promote diversity, provide opportunities, and alleviate the effects of past discrimination on the basis of race, sex, national origin, or disability.

affirmative defense. See under DEFENSE.

affirmative easement. See under EASEMENT.

affirmative relief. See under RELIEF

affirmative warranty. See under WARRANTY.

after-acquired property, property acquired by a debtor after the debtor's existing property has been pledged as collateral for a loan. The security agreement with the lender may provide that any after-acquired property will automatically become part of the collateral.

against the weight of the evidence. See *verdict against the weight of the evidence* (under VERDICT).

age, *n.* **1. age of consent, a.** the age below which one may not get married without a parent's consent. **b.** the age below which a person is deemed incapable of consenting to sexual intercourse. Sexual intercourse with a person below that age is *statutory rape* (see under RAPE) In many states the age of consent depends upon the age of the other party to the sexual act; for example, a 14-year-old might be regarded by the law as capable of consenting to intercourse with a 17-year-old but not with an 18-year-old **2. age of majority,** the age at which an otherwise competent person acquires the power to make binding contracts, along with most of the other legal rights and responsibilities of adulthood. Traditionally 21, the age of majority has generally been reduced to 18 in the wake of ratification of the Twenty-Sixth Amendment (see Appendix). Also called **majority; full age.** See also *legal age.* **3. age of reason,** the age below which a child cannot be found guilty of a crime or, in some states, liable for a tort; most commonly, the age of seven. **4. legal age,** the age at which a person becomes legally capable of exercising certain rights or assuming certain responsibilities. For most purposes, same as *age of majority;* but it may be younger (e.g., driving age) or older (e.g., drinking age). See also UNDERAGE.

age discrimination, discrimination on the basis of a person's age. Federal law protects most workers between the ages of 40 and 70 from age discrimination in employment; other federal and local laws provide varying degrees of protection from age discrimination in such areas as credit, housing, and public accommodations. See also BONA FIDE OCCUPATIONAL QUALIFICATION; SENIORITY SYSTEM.

agency, *n.* **1.** a relationship between two people or entities whereby one (the AGENT) is authorized to act on behalf of the other (the PRINCIPAL). For legal purposes, the acts of the agent within the SCOPE OF AUTHORITY are generally deemed to be acts of the principal, and the agent is a FIDUCIARY of the principal. **2.** Short for ADMINISTRATIVE AGENCY.

agent, *n.* a person or entity authorized to act on behalf of another in some matter or range of matters. For example, an insurance agent is authorized by one or more insurance companies to sell their insurance; an ATTORNEY IN FACT is an agent. See also AGENCY.

aggravated, *adj.* (of a crime) characterized by some element that makes the crime more serious, such as the use of a deadly weapon, the seriousness of the injury caused or intended, or the youthfulness of the victim: *aggravated assault, aggravated rape.* Aggravated offenses are subject to more serious penalties than unaggravated forms of the same offense.

aggrieved, *adj.,* adversely affected by an act or a situation, or perceiving oneself to be so affected: *A party aggrieved by a trial court's judgment may appeal.*

agreed case. See under CASE[1]

agreement, *n.* **1.** a manifestation of assent by two or

(See IMPERTINENT; INFANT.) This does not mean that lawyers never use such terms in their ordinary meanings; even in legal discourse, impertinent can mean rude, and an infant is sometimes just a baby.

Many individuals have been instrumental in bringing this project to fruition. Particular thanks go to my friends William H. Roth and Nancy S. Erickson, who provided support and assistance in many ways; to Paul Hayslett, whose programming wizardry solved a number of computerization problems; to Georgia S. Maas, who handled computer keyboarding and coding tasks with uncommon skill and intelligence; to my copyeditor Robert L. Cohen, for his perceptive suggestions; and above all to my editor, Enid Pearsons, whose guidance and assistance in every aspect of the project made this book possible.

JEC
New York
February, 1996

more people to a course of action. An agreement is normally enforceable only if it meets the requirements of a CONTRACT, in which case the terms "agreement" and "contract" are interchangeable. **2. agreement to agree,** a preliminary agreement that the parties will enter into a contract along certain lines, the exact terms of which have not yet been entirely worked out. Whether the agreement to agree is itself a contract, and thus enforceable, depends upon how definite or INDEFINITE it is. See also *collective bargaining agreement* (under COLLECTIVE BARGAINING); GENTLEMEN'S AGREEMENT.

aid and abet, 1. to order, encourage, or knowingly assist or attempt to assist a person who commits a crime. Aiding and abetting a crime is normally punishable to the same extent as committing the crime directly. **2.** to assist another in the commission of a tort. Ordinarily this results in joint liability with the primary actor. See also *joint tortfeasor* (under TORTFEASOR). —**aider and abettor** (or **abetter**). —**aiding and abetting.**

alibi, *n.* in a criminal case, a defense that the accused was somewhere else when the crime was committed. In the federal and most state systems, the defendant must notify the prosecution in advance if she intends to use such a defense.

alien, *n.* **1.** a person who is not a citizen or national of the United States. **2. nonresident alien,** an alien whose permanent residence is in another country; for example, a tourist or seasonal worker. **3. resident alien,** an alien who has lawfully established a permanent residence in the United States. Such persons are entitled to full constitutional protection, and may not be discriminated against in employment on the basis of citizenship See also ALIENAGE **4. undocumented alien,** an alien who has entered or remained in the United States without government authorization. Also called **illegal alien.** Although it is illegal for an employer to hire such a person, the Supreme Court has held that the public schools may not exclude children for being undocumented.

alienage, *n.* the state of being an alien. For EQUAL PROTECTION purposes, alienage is a SUSPECT CLASSIFICATION, so that laws and public policies discriminating between citizens and *resident aliens* (see under ALIEN) are subject to STRICT SCRUTINY.

alienate, *v.* to transfer property to another by gift, sale, or will. See also RESTRAINT ON ALIENATION. —**alienation,** *n.*

alienation of affections, a tort consisting of conduct by a third party intentionally causing one spouse in a married couple to become disaffected with the other The tort has been abolished in many states.

alimony, *n.* money that one divorced spouse must pay to the other for support during or after the divorce, pursuant to a court order or an agreement between the parties. Also called **maintenance; spousal support.**

all the world, everyone in the world. Often referred to simply as **the world.** Whereas an IN PERSONAM action normally determines only the relative rights of the particular parties before the court, an IN REM action, being directed at a piece of property rather than a particular person, typically seeks to establish the plaintiff's rights with respect to that property as against "(all) the world "

allegation, *n* an assertion that one intends to prove at trial, especially such an assertion as set forth formally in a complaint, indictment, or the like —**allege,** *v.*

Allen charge. See under CHARGE

allocution, *n* **1.** the process by which a guilty plea is made and accepted in a criminal case, typically involving a series of questions and answers through which the judge seeks assurance that the defendant understands the charges, understands the consequences of the plea and the rights that are being given up, and is pleading guilty of his own free will **2.** the procedure by which a criminal defendant who is about to be sentenced is given an opportunity to make a personal statement to the judge Typically, the judge, having heard argument from both the prosecution and the defendant's lawyer, addresses the defendant by name and says, "Is there anything that you would like to say before I pronounce sentence?" **3.** a similar procedure by which the victim of a crime is sometimes given an opportunity to address the court personally before sentence is pronounced on the person convicted of the crime

alternative pleading. See under PLEADING

ameliorating waste. See under WASTE

amenable, *adj* reachable; subject to the court's power *amenable to suit; amenable to process* —**amenability,** *n.*

amend, *v.* to revise, correct, add to, or subtract from a document of legal significance such as a constitution, a legislative bill, an executive order, a tax return, or a corporation's bylaws Virtually any paper submitted to or issued by a court may be amended if prompt action is taken and no undue prejudice results *amended complaint; amended offer of proof; amended reply; amended order.*

amendment, *n* **1.** the act or process of amending something **2.** the words added to, or other changes made in, a document that has been amended, especially, an addition to the Constitution of the United States The term is usually capitalized when referring to a specific amendment to the Constitution: *the Fifth Amendment; the Prohibition Amendment* For a summary of all U S constitutional amendments to date, see Appendix

amicus curiae, *pl* **amici curiae.** *Latin.* (lit. "friend of the court") a nonparty that volunteers or is invited by the court to submit its views on the issues presented in a case, because it has an interest in or perspective on the matter that may not be adequately represented by the parties Usually the amicus curiae (or **amicus** for short) only submits a BRIEF (called a **brief amicus curiae** or **amicus brief**), but sometimes the amicus is also allowed to participate in oral argument Also called **friend of the court,** but only by nonlawyers or by lawyers addressing nonlawyers.

amnesty, *n.* a government's forgiveness of past offenses for a class of people, as when a state or city declares that for a period of time anyone who turns in an illegal weapon will not be prosecuted for illegal possession, or when President Ford declared an amnesty for Vietnam War deserters and draft evaders on the condition that they perform alternative public service. Amnesties may be granted either by executive decree or by legislative act, and have the effect of a PARDON for each individual covered. Cf. COMMUTE; REPRIEVE. See also CLEMENCY.

amortize, *v.* **1.** to pay off a debt in regular installments over a specific period of time. **2.** to write off or deduct for income tax purposes a portion of the cost of an intangible asset each year until the entire cost has been used up. —**amortization,** *n.*

amount, *n.* See JURISDICTIONAL AMOUNT.

ancillary jurisdiction. See under JURISDICTION¹.

annotated, *adj.* describing a compilation of statutes to which ANNOTATIONS have been added for the benefit of legal researchers; a typical title is *United States Code Annotated.* Cf. UNITED STATES CODE

annotation, *n.* **1.** Also called **case note.** a one-paragraph summary of the holding of a case applying or interpreting a particular statutory provision, appended to the statute in question by the editors of a set of ANNOTATED statutes. An important statute may have hundreds, even thousands, of annotations in such a book. **2.** a COMMENT.

annuity, *n.* **1.** a regular income paid out at fixed intervals for a certain period of time, often beginning at a certain age and continuing for the life of the recipient (the **annuitant**), usually in consideration of a PREMIUM paid by the annuitant either in a lump sum or in installments. **2.** the right to receive such income.

annulment, *n.* **1.** a judicial declaration that something is legally VOID, either as of the date of the declaration or AB INITIO. **2.** in particular, a judicial declaration that a marriage is void because of some defect dating back to the time of the marriage, such as the fact that one of the partners was already married. —**annul,** *v.*

answer, *v.* **1.** to respond to a complaint, motion, discovery request, or other procedural step in a case. **2.** to account for one's actions; put up a defense: *We will answer the allegations in court.* **3.** to assume responsibility or liability: *to answer for the debt of another.* **4.** to suffer the consequences for: *answer for one's crimes.* **5.** to respond to a question: *The witness is directed to answer.* —*n.* **6.** a response to a procedural step, allegation, or question: *Our answer to the motion will be filed on Friday.* **7.** in particular, the pleading filed in a civil case in response to the COMPLAINT. In the answer, the defendant must admit or deny each allegation in the complaint except for those as to which she lacks sufficient information to respond. The answer must also contain any *affirmative defense* (see under DEFENSE) that the defendant wishes to raise, and may contain COUNTERCLAIMS, to which the plaintiff must then file a REPLY

answering brief. See under BRIEF.

antenuptial agreement. Same as PRENUPTIAL AGREEMENT.

anticipatory breach (or **repudiation**) See under BREACH. See also REPUDIATION

antilapse statute, a statute that protects the family of a person named in a will from losing the legacy if that person dies before the will takes effect. For example, if a testator names his sister in his will but then the sister dies before the testator, at common law the bequest to the sister would LAPSE and the sister's family might end up with nothing. Under antilapse statutes in most states, the bequest to the sister would remain valid and be distributed to her own heirs.

antitrust, *adj.* relating to the body of law—primarily federal law—intended to foster vigorous competition among businesses by outlawing such practices as price fixing and monopolization. The principal antitrust laws are the SHERMAN ANTITRUST ACT and the CLAYTON ACT See also TRADE REGULATION.

apparent, *adj.* **1.** obvious, or at least deducible from the facts available: *It is apparent from the record that the defendant failed to exercise due care.* **2.** seeming, but not ACTUAL; for example, see *apparent authority* (under AUTHORITY¹).

appeal, *n.* **1.** the process by which one obtains review of a judicial decision by a higher court, or of an administrative decision by a court or by a higher authority within the administrative agency: *The case is on appeal.* **2. appeal as of right, a.** an appeal that the higher tribunal is required by law to consider. **b.** to file or pursue such an appeal: *The defendant appealed as of right to this court.* **3. appeal by permission, a.** Also called **discretionary appeal.** an appeal that may be pursued only if specific permission is granted by a court. **b.** to file or pursue such an appeal. **4. interlocutory appeal,** an appeal from an interim order in a case that is still proceeding in the lower tribunal. Most jurisdictions permit interlocutory appeals only under limited circumstances. —*v.* **5.** to seek or pursue review by a higher authority· *If we lose, we will appeal. They are appealing the order.* —**appealable,** *adj.* —**appealability,** *n.*

appeal bond. See under BOND².

appealable order. See under ORDER¹.

appear, *v.* **1.** (of a person) to come before a court or file a formal paper announcing that one will participate in a case: *The defendant appeared voluntarily; the attorney appeared on behalf of the defendant; the witness appeared pursuant to subpoena.* For many purposes a party need not appear personally but may send a lawyer instead (**appear by counsel**). **2.** (of a fact) to be found in or deducible from the record in a case, so that it can be considered by an appellate court: *The defendant's age does not appear in the record.*

appearance, *n.* **1.** the act of coming before a court or of formally notifying the court that one will participate in a case as a party, lawyer, or witness. **2. general appearance,** an appearance in which a party consents to the court's jurisdiction and agrees to participate in a case for all purposes. **3. special appearance,** an appearance for the limited purpose of contesting the court's jurisdiction. Also called **limited appearance.**

appellant, *n.* the party who files an appeal

appellate, *adj.* relating to appeals or an appeal: *appellate judge; appellate decision.* See also *appellate* BRIEF, JURIS-DICTION¹, REVIEW under those words.

appellee, *n.* the adversary of the party who files an appeal.

appoint, *v.* to designate who shall receive property that is the subject of a POWER OF APPOINTMENT

appraisal rights, the rights of corporate shareholders, granted by statutes which vary from state to state, to dissent from certain extraordinary corporate actions such as a merger, have the value of their stock prior to such an action appraised in a judicial proceeding, and compel the corporation to buy the stock back at the appraised value.

appraise, *v.* to determine the MARKET VALUE of something. Cf. ASSESS. —**appraisal,** *n.*

appropriation, *n.* **1.** the taking of anything; for example, the government's TAKING of private property for public use: *appropriation of land for construction of a school.* **2.** the act of a legislative body in setting aside a sum of money from public funds for a particular use. *appropriation of $1,000,000 for construction of a school.* —**appropriate,** *v.*

appurtenant, *adj.* describing a right or thing attached to or associated with a parcel of land in such a way that it normally passes with title to the land. For example, buildings on land are appurtenant to it, and an easement to pass over a neighbor's land to reach one's own land is appurtenant to one's own land.

arbitrary, *adj.* completely unreasonable; lacking a rational basis. Often used in the phrase **arbitrary and capricious,** which means the same thing.

arbitration, *n.* **1.** a process for resolution of disputes without resort to the courts, through submission of the dispute to a private individual (the **arbitrator**), or a panel of arbitrators, selected jointly by the parties. Arbitration can sometimes be cheaper and quicker than litigation and have the advantage of utilizing arbitrators who are specialists in the field involved in the dispute. It can also be amazingly expensive and time-consuming, and result in decisions biased in favor of the industry with which the specialist arbitrators are associated. Cf. MEDIATION. **2. compulsory arbitration,** arbitration required by law, rather than submitted to by mutual agreement. —**arbitrable,** *adj.* —**arbitrate,** *v.*

arguable, *adj.* capable of being supported by respectable argument, though not necessarily a winning argument.

argue, *v.* to present an ARGUMENT on a matter: *argue the motion; argue the appeal; argue the issue;* or simply *argue.*

arguendo *Latin.* (lit. "in arguing") hypothetically; for purposes of argument; a term used in assuming a fact for the purpose of argument without waiving the right to question its truth later: *Assuming arguendo that the plaintiff's allegations are true, the complaint nevertheless fails to state a claim.*

argument, *n.* **1.** the reasons supporting a conclusion or proposed conclusion, or the formal presentation of such reasons to a person or body that one hopes to convince **2.** the section of a BRIEF in which a party presents its analysis of the law pertaining to a motion or appeal. This follows a section in which the pertinent facts are outlined, and explains why the party contends that, upon those facts, the law requires a particular decision. **3.** Also called **oral argument. a.** an oral presentation to a court of the reasons—both legal and factual—why a party contends that the court should reach a particular conclusion or take a particular action. **b.** the procedure in which a court hears such arguments from both sides on a motion or appeal, often questioning the lawyers on various details as they argue. Cf. *take on submission* (under SUBMIT). **4.** Also called **closing argument.** a SUMMATION.

argumentative, *adj.* (of a statement or question) suggesting that the facts support a particular inference or conclusion. See also *argumentative question* (under QUESTION[1]).

arm's length, referring to dealings between unrelated parties, each motivated solely by its own self-interest: *The parties dealt at arm's length. It was an arm's-length transaction.* See also MARKET VALUE.

arraignment, *n.* the proceeding in which a criminal defendant is brought before the court, formally advised of the charges, and required to enter a PLEA. —**arraign,** *v.*

array. Same as VENIRE.

arrest, *n.* **1.** any significant deprivation of an individual's freedom of action, especially the taking of an individual into custody for the purpose of transporting him to a police station and charging him with a crime. Cf. STOP. **2. citizen's arrest,** an arrest made by a private citizen rather than a law enforcement officer, as when bystanders tackle a purse-snatcher. Such arrests are lawful only under narrow circumstances. **3. false arrest.** See under FALSE IMPRISONMENT. **4. warrantless arrest,** an arrest made without a warrant (see WARRANT[1]). As a general rule, a police officer may arrest a person for a felony without a warrant if she has PROBABLE CAUSE and the arrest is made in a public place, but a warrant is required to enter a person's home. —*v.* **5.** to make an arrest of a person.

arrest warrant. See under WARRANT[1].

arson, *n.* the crime of intentionally causing a dangerous fire or explosion, especially for the purpose of destroying a building of another or of damaging property in order to collect insurance.

articles of impeachment, the formal written instrument that forms the basis for an IMPEACHMENT proceeding against a public officer, listing the charges against the officer.

articles of incorporation, a document setting forth the basic structure of a corporation, including its name and purposes and the number of shares of stock that it will be authorized to issue, which must be filed with a state government in order to bring the corporation into existence See also CERTIFICATE OF INCORPORATION; CHARTER[1].

artifical person. See under PERSON.

as a matter of law, (of a legal conclusion) compelled by principles of law and justice; said particularly of factual findings that a court takes out of the hands of the jury: *The judge directed a verdict for the defendant in the personal injury case because the plaintiff deliberately ignored a warning sign and therefore assumed the risk of injury as a matter of law* See also BY OPERATION OF LAW.

as applied. See *unconstitutional* (or *invalid*) *as applied* (under UNCONSTITUTIONAL)

as is, without any express or implied warranty. The words "as is," "with all faults," or the like in a contract for sale of goods mean that the buyer assumes the risk of any defects or malfunctions

assault, *n.* **1.** in tort law, an act putting another person in apprehension of imminent BATTERY, done either with intent actually to cause a battery (as by taking a swing at someone) or simply with intent to cause the apprehension (as by shaking your fist under someone's nose). If in either case the act results in physical contact, then there has been both an assault and a battery **2.** in criminal law, a term used in different states to mean one or more of the following crimes **a.** BATTERY **b.** attempted battery. **c.** conduct inducing a reasonable fear of battery or immediate bodily harm **3. assault and battery.** Another term for the crime of battery **4. sexual assault,** the crime of intentionally touching another person in a sexual way without that person's consent, or when that person lacks the capacity to give legally effective consent. Also called **indecent assault.**

assembly. See FREEDOM OF ASSEMBLY; UNLAWFUL ASSEMBLY

assess, *v* **1.** to set the amount of, and impose, a tax, fine, or damages: *Damages were assessed at $1.5 million. The Liquor Authority assessed a fine of $10,000.* **2.** to establish the value of real estate for property tax purposes (the **assessed value**). Typically the assessed value is lower than the MARKET VALUE. Cf APPRAISE **3.** to require stockholders to make additional contributions to the corporation, or partners to make additional contributions to the partnership, to fill a need for additional capital. See also *assessable stock* and *nonassessable stock* (under STOCK). —**assessment,** *n.*

assessable stock. See under STOCK.

asset, *n.* **1.** any property or right of a person or entity that has monetary value, such as land, an automobile, stock, a copyright, money, or a right to payment for goods sold (if payment is a realistic possibility). Cf LIABILITY (def 3). **2. assets,** all such property and rights collectively, or their total value; the total resources of a person, estate, business, etc. If assets exceed liabilities, the excess is the entity's **net assets:** *The company has assets of $1,000,000, liabilities of $900,000, and net assets of $100,000* **3. capital asset,** for income tax purposes, virtually all property except certain business assets and certain other property excluded by the Internal Revenue Code *The tax treatment of a sale or exchange of property depends in part upon whether the property was a capital asset.* **4. liquid asset,** an asset readily convertible into cash, such as shares of publicly traded stock.

assign, *v.* **1.** to transfer an interest, right, or duty; to substitute another person for oneself in a contract *The company assigned its accounts receivable to the bank. I assigned my lease to someone else and moved to San Francisco.* **2.** to appoint: *The judge assigned counsel for the defendant.* **3.** to identify, point out. *The appellant assigns numerous alleged errors by the trial judge.* —n. **4. assigns,** persons to whom an interest, right, or duty might be assigned. Used principally in the phrase *heirs and assigns* (see under HEIR); in most other contexts, and whenever the singular is called for, the term used IS ASSIGNEE. —**assignment,** *n.*

assignable, *adj.* capable of being assigned. Some rights and most duties are not assignable, at least without the permission of other parties involved; for example, an opera star cannot unilaterally assign her contract to sing in an opera to an inferior performer But a right to receive a payment is normally freely assignable.

assigned counsel. See under COUNSEL

assigned risk, a risk that, under state law, is assigned to an insurer chosen from a pool of insurers who otherwise would not accept it.

assignee, *n.* the person or entity to which an interest, right, or duty is assigned.

assignment for the benefit of creditors, an assignment, by an entity overwhelmed with debts, of substantially all of its assets to a trustee, to be liquidated and used to satisfy the debts to the extent possible.

assignment of error, a specification, in appellate papers, of a ruling by the court below that the appellant contends was improper and requires reversal

assignor, *n.* the person or entity that assigns an interest, right, or duty to another.

Assistant United States Attorney. See under UNITED STATES ATTORNEY.

assisted suicide. See under SUICIDE.

associate, *n.* the usual title for an attorney in a law firm who works on salary but does not share in the firm's profits Most attorneys in large law firms are associates rather than partners or owners.

association, *n.* **1.** Also called **unincorporated association.** any group of people organized for a common purpose and not formed as a corporation. **2.** for income tax purposes, an unincorporated organization having characteristics that make it more like a corporation than like a partnership or trust. Such an association is taxed as a corporation. **3. joint stock association.** The name used in some states for *joint stock company* (see under COMPANY). **4. professional association.** The name used in some states for *professional corporation* (see under CORPORATION). See also *cooperative association* (under COOPERATIVE).

assume, *v.* to take on or accept responsibility for; especially, to take over an obligation of another. For example, the purchaser of a house with a mortgage may assume the mortgage; the purchaser of a business may assume the debts of the business. —**assumption,** *n.*

assumption of risk, the doctrine that one who voluntarily enters into a situation known to be dangerous may not recover from someone else for any resulting injury; the injured party is said to have "assumed the risk" of being injured. The defense of assumption of risk has been modified or abolished in many states. Cf. *comparative negligence* (under NEGLIGENCE).

assure, *v* to provide INSURANCE, act as a SURETY, or put up collateral (see COLLATERAL¹) —**assurance,** *n.* —**assured,** *adj., n.*

asylum, *n.* refuge granted by a country to a person who is wanted for prosecution in another country; especially, such refuge for a person wanted for exercising political, civil, or human rights such as speaking or running for office (**political asylum**) Cf EXTRADITE.

at, *prep.* **1.** the word customarily used instead of "in," "under," or "by" in referring to modern or ancient COMMON LAW (often shortened to "law"). *Commercial bribery was not a crime at common law, but is a crime under modern criminal statutes. We are seeking relief in equity because we do not have an adequate remedy at law.* **2.** the word usually used by lawyers to refer to a page number: *You'll find the citation at page 33, Your Honor, and the discussion begins at 35.*

at bar. See under BAR.

at will, describing or referring to a status or relationship that can be terminated at any time for any reason: *tenancy* (or *estate*) *at will* (see under TENANCY); *employee at will.*

attach, *v.* to effect an ATTACHMENT· *The plaintiff attached the defendant's car and bank account.*

attachment, *n.* **1.** the seizing or freezing of property by court order in order to subject the property to the jurisdiction of the court, either so that a dispute as to ownership of it can be resolved or so that it will be available to satisfy a judgment against the owner. **2.** the writ or other document authorizing or effecting such a seizure.

attachment bond. See under BOND².

attack. See *direct attack* (under DIRECT¹); *collateral attack* (under COLLATERAL²).

attainder. See BILL OF ATTAINDER

attempt, *n.* the taking of a substantial step toward the commission of a crime, beyond mere preparation. Attempt is itself a crime, sometimes punishable to the same extent as the crime that was attempted, sometimes (especially in the case of more serious crimes such as murder) treated as a slightly lower grade of offense. In a prosecution for attempt, it does not matter whether the attempt was successful or not. **—attempted,** *adj.*

attest, *v.* **1.** to sign a document as a witness to its execution by someone else. **2.** to CERTIFY the authenticity of a document or the accuracy of a copy. **3. attested copy.** Same as *certified copy* (see under CERTIFY). **—attestation,** *n.*

attesting witness. See under WITNESS.

attorney, *n.* **1.** Also called **attorney at law.** A slightly pretentious word for LAWYER. **2.** Also called **attorney in fact.** A person who acts on behalf of another pursuant to a POWER OF ATTORNEY. **3. attorney of record,** the attorney or law firm listed in court records as representing a particular party in a case. All papers and communications in a case intended for that party must go to the attorney of record. Cf. PRO SE.

attorney-client privilege. See under PRIVILEGE.

Attorney General, 1. the chief legal officer of the federal government or of a state; the head of the United States Department of Justice or of a state's legal department. Cf. *Solicitor General* (under SOLICITOR); UNITED STATES ATTORNEY. **2. private attorney general,** *Informal.* a private person who brings a civil case to draw attention to unlawful conduct and force compliance or punish noncompliance with a law, not only for personal satisfaction or compensation but also in the hope that the public at large will ultimately benefit. The term is rather subjective; what one person might hail as the action of a private attorney general another might condemn as a *strike suit* (see under SUIT).

attorney work product. Same as WORK PRODUCT

attorney's lien. See under LIEN.

attractive nuisance, a condition existing on private property, but in a place where children are likely to trespass, that poses an unreasonable danger to such children. In general, property owners will be held liable to children injured by such conditions if the danger could have been prevented by reasonable measures For example, a homeowner would be expected to take strong precautionary measures to make sure that children cannot get in and play near his uncovered swimming pool without supervision.

authenticate, *v.* **1.** to introduce evidence to show that a document or other item offered as evidence in a case is in fact what the proponent claims it to be Some authenticating evidence is ordinarily required before an exhibit can be admitted into evidence. **2. self-authenticating,** showing on its face that it is authentic, or otherwise presumed to be authentic, so that no other authenticating evidence is required unless the authenticity of the item is called into question; for example, a certified copy of a public document. —**authentication,** *n.*

authority[1], *n.* **1.** the legal power of a public official or body to act in an official capacity **2.** the power to act on behalf of another and bind the other by such actions; the power of an AGENT to act on behalf of the PRINCIPAL. See also SCOPE OF AUTHORITY. **3. actual authority,** authority intentionally granted by a principal to an agent. Such authority may be granted explicitly (**express authority**) or simply understood as necessary or proper in order to carry out expressly authorized tasks (**implied authority**). **4. apparent authority,** authority of an agent reasonably inferred from conduct of the principal, even if the principal did not intend the agent to have such authority.

authority[2], *n.* a source of information or insight on how to interpret and apply the law in a particular situation. The term includes judicial decisions, legislative history, and scholarly writing. A clearly applicable HOLDING by a higher court in the same jurisdiction must be followed by a lower court (**binding authority**); all other authority is at best **persuasive authority,** which need not be followed by a court.

automatic stay. See under STAY.

automobile guest statute, a statute providing that a nonpaying passenger in an automobile (a "guest" of the driver) who is injured in an accident caused by the driver's negligence may not recover damages from the driver, and hence from the driver's insurance company, unless the driver's negligence was extreme. At one time over half the states had such statutes, largely as a result of insurance industry lobbying. In recent years the tide has turned, and now only a few states still have such statutes.

avoid, *v.* to nullify, upon some legal ground, an obligation or transaction to which one is a party; especially, in a situation where one party to a contract lacked the capacity to contract (e.g., because of infancy), to render the contract void by disaffirming it. See also VOIDABLE. Cf RATIFY. —**avoidance,** *n.*

award, *n.* **1.** a grant of damages or other relief by a court, jury, or administrative tribunal. —*v.* **2.** to grant such relief: *The plaintiff was awarded $5,000.*

B

bad, *adj.* generally, not favored by the law or acceptable in the marketplace. The specific legal meaning varies from phrase to phrase; see the entries directly below and *bad* CHECK, DEBT, TITLE under those words.

bad faith, absence of GOOD FAITH; lack of overall fairness and honesty in a transaction; especially, an intent to deceive others or to evade one's own obligations

bad law, 1. a judicial opinion or decision that misconstrues or misapplies a legal principle, producing erroneous or misleading results. **2.** any statute or ruling regarded by the speaker as unwise. Cf. GOOD LAW

bail¹, *n.* **1.** money or other property pledged to a court by or on behalf of a person accused of a crime to assure her appearance in court. Cf. PREVENTIVE DETENTION; RELEASE ON OWN RECOGNIZANCE. **2. bail bond,** the document in which bail is pledged by the accused. Typically a third party acceptable to the court (traditionally called a **bail bondsman**) must also sign as a SURETY, so that the court will not have to try to collect forfeited bail from a missing defendant. **3. cash bail,** bail posted entirely in cash. If the accused satisfies all bail conditions, the cash is eventually returned. **4. excessive bail,** bail set in an amount higher than is reasonably necessary to secure the defendant's presence at trial. The Eighth Amendment (see Appendix) prohibits the government from demanding excessive bail and thereby keeping people not convicted of a crime in jail unnecessarily. **5. jump bail,** to flee while free on bail. **6. make bail,** to secure one's own release from custody by posting the required bail or having someone else do so. **7. on bail** or **out on bail,** free from custody because bail has been posted. **8. post bail,** to provide the required cash or bond for bail, either for oneself or for someone else **9. stand bail,** to post bail for someone else —*v.* **10.** to secure the release of a person by posting bail (usually with *out*): *My sister bailed me out*

bail², *v.* to transfer possession of personal property temporarily. See also BAILMENT.

bailable offense, a charged offense for which the accused may be released on bail. Cf. PREVENTIVE DETENTION

bailiff, *n.* a court officer charged with managing the courtroom and taking care of the jury.

bailment, *n.* an arrangement in which one person (the **bailor**) transfers possession (but not ownership) of personal property to another (the **bailee**) for storage, use, or some other temporary purpose The legal rights and duties of the parties depend upon the purpose and terms of the bailment. The bailee may be storing the bailor's goods for a fee **(bailment for hire),** or working on them, as in the case of a car in a repair shop **(bailment for mutual benefit),** or simply borrowing them **(gratuitous bailment);** in each case, the bailor and bailee may be referred to according to type of bailment: *gratuitous bailee, bailor for mutual benefit,* etc. If one person is renting property from the other, the arrangement is usually referred to as a LEASE rather than a bailment.

bait and switch, the practice of drawing customers into a store by advertising a product at a low price and then inducing them to purchase a more expensive product by disparaging the advertised product or saying that it is not available. This is usually a crime. See also FALSE ADVERTISING.

balancing of the equities, a court's weighing of all factors favoring each side in order to determine the overall fairness of granting or denying an injunction or other equitable relief. Also called **balancing of the hardships.**

balancing test, any decision-making process that involves the weighing of competing values and interests.

banc. See EN BANC.

bank account. See under ACCOUNT

bank check. See under CHECK.

bankrupt, *n.* a person or entity that is the subject of BANKRUPTCY proceedings.

bankruptcy, *n.* **1.** a judicial proceeding under federal law (the **Bankruptcy Code**) by which a person or corporation unable to pay its debts can have the debts adjusted and get a fresh start. The entity that is the subject of such proceedings is referred to as the DEBTOR or the BANKRUPT, and is said to be "in bankruptcy." The proceedings are often identified by the chapter of the Bankruptcy Code under which they are brought: **Chapter 7 bankruptcy** (also called **straight bankruptcy**), in which most of the debtor's remaining assets are sold outright, the court distributes the proceeds among the creditors, and the debts are extinguished; **Chapter 11 bankruptcy** (also called REORGANIZATION), in which the debtor, usually a corporation, is allowed to continue operating its business in the hope of making more money with which to pay creditors, and a plan **(reorganization plan** or **plan of reorganization)** is worked out under which creditors agree to reduce the amount of the debts or extend the payment schedule; **Chapter 12 bankruptcy,** a proceeding analogous to Chapter 11, designed specifically for farmers going through hard times to enable them to keep their farms and keep farming; **Chapter 13 bankruptcy** (also called REHABILITATION), a proceeding analogous to Chapter 11, designed specifically for individuals with a steady income and involving a plan **(wage earner's plan)** under which they agree to pay off at least a specified portion of their debts over time. **2. involuntary bankruptcy,** a bankruptcy proceeding initiated by a creditor. **3. voluntary bankruptcy,** a bankruptcy proceeding initiated by the debtor. See also *bankruptcy estate* (under ESTATE²); *bankruptcy trustee* (under TRUSTEE); *discharge in bankruptcy* (under DISCHARGE).

bar, *n.* **1.** the legal profession generally, or all lawyers whose practice shares a common element· *the Houston bar; the plaintiffs' bar; the Tax Court bar.* See also *admis-*

sion to the bar (under ADMISSION); DISBAR. Cf BENCH. **2.** a legal impediment or barrier, especially to the formation of a valid contract or the pursuit or defense of a case **3. at bar,** currently before the court· *the case at bar; the plaintiff at bar.* **4. in bar,** as a bar to an action: *Because the defendant in the contract action was a minor when she signed the contract, she pleaded legal incapacity in bar* —*v.* **5.** to prohibit or act as a bar to. *The statute of limitations bars the action.*

bare. Same as NAKED

bargain, *v.* **1.** to negotiate terms of a contract; to haggle. —*n.* **2.** a negotiated contract Cf *adhesion contract* (under CONTRACT).

bargained for, 1. describing a contract term that was subject to negotiation or for which some concession or return benefit is deemed to have been given If placed before the noun, requires a hyphen: *The term was bargained for; a bargained-for term.* Cf. BOILERPLATE. **2. bargained-for exchange,** a classic definition of CONTRACT, reflecting the ideal that a contract represents a mutually satisfactory exchange of benefits resulting from genuine bargaining between parties of equal BARGAINING POWER. The reality is often very different Cf. *adhesion contract* (under CONTRACT).

bargaining. See COLLECTIVE BARGAINING.

bargaining power, the ability of a party to a proposed contract to influence the terms of the contract. Two successful corporations negotiating a joint venture typically have equal bargaining power; an individual seeking coverage from an insurance company typically has no bargaining power at all.

barratry, *n.* persistently stirring up litigation or quarrels. This was an offense at common law. Initiating groundless litigation may still be an offense in some states. See also CHAMPERTY; MAINTENANCE; ABUSE OF PROCESS; MALICIOUS PROSECUTION.

barrister, *n.* **1.** in England, a lawyer who is a courtroom advocate. Cf. SOLICITOR. **2.** in America, occasionally and informally, another word for lawyer.

barter, *n.* **1.** an exchange of goods or services without using money. Such transactions are normally subject to the same income and sales taxes as money transactions, but are sometimes employed to avoid taxes because they are difficult to trace —*v.* **2.** to effect or engage in a barter

basis, *n.* the amount of money that one has invested in a piece of property. The gain or loss on sale of the property is calculated for tax purposes as the amount by which the value received for the property exceeds or falls short of the basis.

bastard, *n.* formerly the standard legal term for a child born out of wedlock.

bastardy action (or **proceeding**), the older legal term for a PATERNITY SUIT.

battered person syndrome, a psychological condition

said to result from persistent physical abuse, regularly invoked in recent years as a proposed JUSTIFICATION for homicide. The argument has had a mixed reception from courts and scholars, but often finds favor with juries. Also called **battered woman syndrome, battered child syndrome,** etc., according to the circumstances.

battery, *n.* harmful or offensive touching of another person, either intentionally or as a byproduct of some other intentional wrong. The touching may be either direct or indirect, as by grabbing clothes, using a stick, or launching a projectile. Battery is usually both a tort and a crime. Cf. ASSAULT.

battle of the experts, *Informal.* a trial whose outcome depends in large part on a choice between the conflicting opinions of expert witnesses hired by the opposing sides In the federal courts and in most states the court can appoint a neutral expert, but this is seldom done.

bearer, *n.* a person in possession of a negotiable instrument or other document, especially an instrument or document made out or indorsed to "bearer" or in some other way that does not designate a specific payee or person entitled to enforce it, such as a check made out to "cash" or indorsed IN BLANK. Such a document is called a **bearer instrument, bearer bond,** or the like, depending upon its nature; and if it is an instrument for the payment of money, such as a check or note, it is **payable to bearer.** Bearer paper must be carefully safeguarded, since anyone who comes into possession of it may NEGOTIATE it. Cf. *order instrument* (under ORDER²).

below, *adv.* **1.** in the lower court from which an appeal was taken (the **court below**): *The decision below should be affirmed.* **2.** later on in the same document: *As we will explain below, the decision should be affirmed.* See also INFRA.

bench, *n.* **1.** the judge's seat and desk in a courtroom: *Instead of issuing a written opinion, the judge ruled from the bench.* **2.** the judicial profession; judges collectively, as distinguished from practicing lawyers: *The conference provided an opportunity for the bench and the bar to meet informally.* **3. bench conference.** Same as SIDEBAR. See also *bench trial* (under TRIAL); *bench warrant* (under WARRANT¹). Cf. BAR.

beneficial, *adj.* referring to rights that derive from something other than legal title to property, particularly rights of a trust beneficiary. See *beneficial* ESTATE¹, INTEREST¹, OWNER under those words. See also EQUITABLE.

beneficiary, *n.* **1.** a person for whose benefit a trust is established, and for whose benefit the trustee must manage the trust property. **2.** the person to whom benefits are to be paid under an insurance policy. **3. third-party beneficiary.** See under CONTRACT.

bequeath, *v.* **1.** to give personal property by will. Cf. DEVISE. **2.** broadly, to give any property by will.

bequest, *n.* **1.** a gift of personal property by will, or the property so given. Also called **legacy,** especially in reference to gifts of money. Cf. DEVISE. **2.** broadly, any testamentary gift of property, whether real or personal. *Legacy* is also used in this broad sense. **3. general bequest** (or **legacy**), a bequest to be paid out of the general assets of the estate, that is, out of whatever is left after payment of debts and expenses and distribution of specific bequests. **4. residuary bequest** (or **legacy**), the final bequest in a typical will, disposing of any assets left over after payment of all debts and expenses and satisfaction of all other bequests. **5. specific bequest** (or **legacy**), a bequest of a specific item or items of property.

best evidence rule, the principle that in order to prove the contents of a writing, photograph, or the like, one must produce the original unless it is unavailable through no serious fault of one's own. Modern evidence rules, however, permit the use of a duplicate, such as a photocopy, in most circumstances.

best use or **best and highest use.** See under USE.

beyond a reasonable doubt, the highest STANDARD OF PROOF; the degree of certainty necessary to convict a defendant of a crime. It does not mean beyond all possible doubt, but beyond any doubt based upon reason and common sense.

beyond the scope. Short for **beyond the scope of the direct (cross, redirect, recross) examination.** The objection raised at a trial or hearing when a person examining a witness (other than on direct examination) attempts to delve into matters that were not asked about in the immediately preceding examination. See also EXAMINATION; SCOPE OF EXAMINATION; OPEN THE DOOR. Cf. SCOPE OF EXPERTISE.

BFOQ. See BONA FIDE OCCUPATIONAL QUALIFICATION.

bias crime. Same as HATE CRIME.

bilateral contract. See under CONTRACT.

bill, *n.* **1.** a formal document, often one containing a list of items. **2.** a proposed statute filed in Congress or a state or local legislature by one or more members for consideration by the whole body. **3.** the initial pleading in courts of EQUITY. In modern practice this has been replaced by the COMPLAINT. **4. no bill,** the outcome of a grand jury's deliberations when it refuses to issue a proposed INDICTMENT. **5. true bill,** words endorsed on a proposed indictment to indicate that the grand jury has approved of it; hence, an INDICTMENT.

bill of attainder, a law imposing a punishment on someone, or on a class of people, without a trial. Bills of attainder are prohibited by the Constitution.

bill of exchange. Same as DRAFT.

bill of lading, 1. a document issued by a person or entity in the business of transporting or forwarding goods, identifying goods received for shipment and designating who is entitled to delivery of them. **2. order bill of lading,** or **order bill,** a bill of lading stating that the goods are to be delivered to the order of a named party. This is a *negotiable document of title* (see under DOCUMENT OF TITLE). **3.**

straight bill of lading, or **straight bill,** a bill of lading stating that the goods are to be delivered to a specific named party. This is a *nonnegotiable document of title* (see under DOCUMENT OF TITLE). **4. through bill of lading,** or **through bill,** a bill of lading issued by the first of a series of connecting carriers, assuming responsibility for the entire shipment.

bill of particulars, a written statement setting forth the details of a civil claim or a criminal charge.

Bill of Rights, 1. the first ten amendments to the Constitution, added to the Constitution shortly after its adoption as a formal statement of fundamental rights of Americans. See Appendix for summary. Originally intended only as a limitation on the powers of the federal government (not state governments), most of the Bill of Rights has now been extended to the states, so that, for example, a law restricting freedom of speech would be unconstitutional whether adopted by Congress or by a state legislature See INCORPORATION DOCTRINE. **2.** (*sometimes l.c.*) by extension, a name given to any formal list of rights of a group, enacted as a law or adopted by an organization or institution· *patients' bill of rights; victim's bill of rights; consumer bill of rights.*

bill of sale, a document transferring title in personal property from seller to buyer.

bind, *v.* to put under a legal obligation. See also *binding authority* (under AUTHORITY²).

bind over, to order that a person accused of a crime be subjected to a trial, as a result of a finding of PROBABLE CAUSE at a *bindover hearing* (see under HEARING): *The defendant was bound over to the Superior Court for trial.*

binder, *n.* a document granting a person who has applied for an insurance policy temporary coverage until the policy is issued or the application is rejected.

black letter law. Same as HORNBOOK LAW.

blackmail, *n.* **1.** EXTORTION, especially extortion by means of threats to reveal injurious truths about a person. —*v* **2.** to extort money from a person, especially by threatening to reveal an injurious truth.

blank indorsement. See under INDORSEMENT.

blind trust. See under TRUST.

blockbusting, *n.* inducing people to sell their homes by spreading stories about ethnic minorities moving into the neighborhood. This once common device used by real estate agents to induce panic selling by white homeowners—generating commissions for the agents—was outlawed in 1968 by the federal Fair Housing Act.

blue law, a law of Puritan origin or inspiration regulating conduct for essentially religious reasons, especially a SUNDAY CLOSING LAW.

blue sky law, any of the state statutes, which exist in all fifty states, regulating the issuance of securities within the state; the state counterparts of the federal SECURITIES ACTS

Bluebook, The The most commonly used reference work

on how cases, statutes, and other authorities are cited in legal writing. Formerly titled, and now subtitled, **A Uniform System of Citation.**

board of directors, the governing body of a corporation, elected by the shareholders to set policy, select officers to carry it out, monitor the corporation's operations, and make major decisions regarding the corporation's business and finances.

boiler room sales, high-pressure selling of securities by telephone.

boilerplate, *n.* standardized language usually included in legal documents of a certain type, such as contracts, wills, or deeds, or in a particular class of such documents, such as apartment leases or bank loan agreements. In a printed contract, boilerplate often appears in fine print and represents terms that are either noncontroversial (such as a clause specifying which state's law governs the contract) or nonnegotiable. See also *adhesion contract* (under CON-TRACT).

bona fide, *Latin.* (lit. "in good faith") **1.** describing a thing done or a person acting in GOOD FAITH: *bona fide purchaser.* **2.** genuine: *bona fide occupational qualification.*

bona fide occupational qualification (BFOQ), a qualification reasonably necessary to the normal operation of a particular business or enterprise. The federal civil rights laws outlawing discrimination in employment provide exceptions for situations in which a particular religion, sex, national origin, or age range (but not race or color) is a bona fide occupational qualification. In addition, a special exception allows religious organizations and schools to discriminate on the basis of religion even when hiring people for positions for which religion is not a bona fide occupational qualification, such as janitor in a church-owned building in which no religious activities take place.

bona fide purchaser or **bona fide purchaser for value.** Same as GOOD FAITH PURCHASER

bona fides, *Latin.* good faith: *His bona fides was proved at trial.* Because the *s* in this Latin phrase makes it look like an English plural, one occasionally sees it with a plural verb (*"His bona fides were proved"*); more often the phrase is used in a way that avoids the issue· *He proved his bona fides at trial* In modern legal writing, the phrase is usually rejected entirely in favor of the English GOOD FAITH.

bond¹, *n.* a kind of security (see SECURITY²) issued by a corporation or governmental body in order to borrow money from the public It is in the form of a certificate evidencing the issuer's obligation to repay the debt in full on or by a specific date, and usually to make regular interest payments until then. Unlike a stockholder, the owner of a bond (the **bondholder**) has no ownership interest in the issuing corporation, but is simply a CREDITOR of the issuer See also *bearer bond* (under BEARER); DEBENTURE.

bond², *n.* **1.** a written obligation to pay or forfeit a sum of money, or occasionally to perform some other act, upon the occurrence of a specified event—particularly some default by the person or entity by or for which the bond is issued. The bond may be issued by the person or entity whose default is being guarded against (**personal bond**), but in most situations it is provided—for a fee—by a third party such as an insurance company (**surety bond** or **suretyship bond**). See also SURETY; SURETYSHIP. **2. appeal bond,** a bond required of a losing party in a civil case who wishes to appeal, to assure that the winning party's costs will be paid if the appeal is dropped or is unsuccessful. **3. attachment bond,** a bond posted by a person whose property has been attached, as a substitute for the attached property. This frees the property while providing the same protection for the attacher. See also ATTACH; ATTACHMENT. **4. bail bond.** See under BAIL[1]. **5. completion bond,** a bond posted to provide money to complete a construction project if the construction contractor fails to do so in accordance with the terms of the contract. Also called **performance bond. 6. fidelity bond,** insurance against loss due to embezzlement or other dishonest conduct by an employee, particularly one whose position deals with the employer's financial affairs. **7. fiduciary bond,** a bond issued to protect against misappropriation or misapplication of property under the control of a FIDUCIARY such as a trustee, a guardian, or the executor or administrator of an estate. **8. payment bond,** a bond issued to guarantee that funds will be available to pay workers, subcontractors, and suppliers of materials for a construction project if the general contractor fails to pay them, so that their claims will not be a lien on the property. **9. supersedeas bond,** a bond required of a losing party in a case as a condition for obtaining a delay in execution of the judgment while the judgment is appealed. The purpose is to assure that there will be money available to satisfy the judgment if the appeal is unsuccessful. See also SUPERSEDEAS.

bondholder. See under BOND[1]

border search. See under SEARCH.

boycott, *n.* **1.** concerted action by two or more people or entities not to buy from, sell to, work for, or in some other way deal with a company, or an effort to induce others to engage in such conduct. The legality of a boycott depends upon the circumstances. **2. group boycott,** concerted action by a group of business competitors to boycott a business that they otherwise might do business with, for example a boycott of a supplier to pressure it into lowering its prices. Group boycotts are a violation of the SHERMAN ANTITRUST ACT. **3. primary boycott,** a union-organized boycott of an employer with which the union is engaged in a labor dispute; for example, urging shippers to refuse to ship the employer's goods or consumers not to buy them. Primary boycotts are permitted by the National Labor Relations Act. **4. secondary boycott,** a boycott or other coercive tactics directed at an employer other than the one with which a union has a grievance, for the purpose of inducing that employer to refrain from dealing with the one with which the union does have a grievance. Secondary boycotts are forbidden by federal law. —*v.* **5.** to engage in a boycott directed against a particular company, group of companies, or product: *to boycott a store; to boycott grapes.*

Brady material, any evidence known to the prosecution that is favorable to the defendant in a criminal case. Under a rule laid down in the 1963 Supreme Court case of Brady v. Maryland (the **Brady rule**), such evidence must be disclosed to the defendant if requested; a later modification of the rule requires it to be disclosed even if not requested, if it is obviously helpful to the defendant's case.

brain death, irreversible cessation of brain functioning. In an age when heart and lung functioning can often be maintained indefinitely by machines, this is increasingly used as the legal definition of death, though the details of the definition vary from state to state.

breach, *n.* **1.** a violation of a legal duty. Usually the term refers to wrongful conduct viewed as the basis for a civil remedy rather than a criminal penalty: *Embezzlement is both a crime and a breach of the employee's duty of loyalty to the employer.* **2. anticipatory breach,** a statement or action showing that a party to a contract does not intend or will not be able to perform when the time comes to do so. Most jurisdictions allow the other party to treat that as a *breach of contract* even though, technically, no obligation has yet been breached because the performance is not yet due. Also called **anticipatory repudiation. 3. breach of fiduciary duty,** an intentional or unintentional failure by a FIDUCIARY to live up to the duty of utmost care and loyalty in dealing with matters that are the subject of a FIDUCIARY RELATIONSHIP. See also FIDUCIARY DUTY. **4. breach of contract,** any failure, without legal justification, to perform as promised in a contract, or any act hindering another party from performing as promised; for example, after contracting for certain repairs to your house, not allowing the contractor in to do the work. **5. breach of promise.** Short for **breach of promise of marriage** or **breach of promise to marry;** the breaking off of an engagement to be married. The common law action for damages for breach of promise has been abolished in many states. **6. breach of the peace, a.** broadly, any conduct, especially criminal conduct, tending to provoke violence or disrupt public tranquility. **b.** in some jurisdictions, a specifically defined offense; see under DISORDERLY CONDUCT. **7. breach of trust,** a *breach of fiduciary duty,* especially by a TRUSTEE and especially if it is intentional: *It was a breach of trust for the guardian of the child's property to borrow money from the child's bank account to pay a personal debt.* **8. breach of warranty,** any falsehood in a WARRANTY; any failure of a product, instrument, or transaction to conform to a warranty made with respect to it. **9. immaterial** (or **partial**) **breach,** a minor breach of contract, entitling the aggrieved party to damages or some other appropriate remedy, but not entitling that party to cancel the contract. **10. material** (or **total**) **breach,** a breach of contract so serious that it destroys the value of the contract for the other party, entitling that party to call off the deal and refuse any further performance of its own obligations under the contract. —*v.* **11.** to violate a legal duty: *By driving when he was too tired, he breached the duty of due care.*

breaking and entering, two of the elements of the crime of BURGLARY. At common law, breaking and entering required forcible entry into the premises of another; under modern statutes, it is usually enough simply to enter or remain without authorization, as by crawling in an open window or hiding in a store until it closes. See also *criminal trespass* (under TRESPASS).

bribery, *n.* **1.** the crime of giving or receiving, or offering or requesting, something of value to influence the official conduct of a public official. **2. commercial bribery,** the giving or receiving of something of value to influence the business conduct of an employee or agent of a company This is usually both a crime and a tort against the company, as well as a form of UNFAIR COMPETITION. See also COMPOUNDING A CRIME; KICKBACK.

brief, *n.* **1.** a written argument submitted to a court, outlining the facts and presenting the legal authorities upon which a party relies in a case. In addition to briefs stating the parties' overall positions on a case, submitted at major stages (**trial brief** often submitted just before a trial, **appellate brief** submitted when the case is on appeal), briefs are submitted in connection with motions, evidentiary issues, and other matters as they arise during the course of a case. On most motions and on appeal, three briefs are normally submitted: a **brief in support** or **main brief** by the party making the motion or taking the appeal; a **brief in opposition** or **answering brief** by the opposing party; and a **reply brief** by the first party. Occasionally a court will give special permission for the opposing party to put in a **surreply brief** responding to new arguments made in the reply brief. In some courts, a brief is customarily referred to as a **memorandum of law, memorandum of points and authorities,** or simply **memorandum:** See also *brief amicus curiae* (under AMICUS CURIAE). **2.** a digest of a judicial opinion, prepared by a law student or junior lawyer. —*v.* **3.** to prepare or submit a brief on a matter: *The judge asked us to brief the issue* (or *brief her on the issue*) *of the plaintiff's standing to sue. Beginning law students are required to brief each case they read.*

bring, *v.* **1.** to initiate; file in court: *to bring suit; bring a complaint; bring a motion.* **2. bring on,** to call a case or motion for trial, hearing, or argument, or cause it to be called: *The motion for a preliminary injunction was brought on by order to show cause. After several months of discovery, the case was brought on for trial.*

broad construction. See under CONSTRUCTION.

broker, *n.* a middleman; a person or entity that puts together a buyer and seller of property or services, acting as an AGENT for one or both of the parties and taking a COM-

MISSION on the transaction. Examples include a broker who arranges insurance coverage for people or companies (**insurance broker**), a broker who arranges sales of real property (**real estate broker**), and a broker who arranges purchases and sales of stocks and bonds (**securities broker** or **stockbroker**).

broker-dealer, *n.* a company that acts both as a securities broker, taking commissions on securities transactions in which it is merely a middleman, and as a securites dealer, buying and selling securities in its own name and taking a profit, or occasionally a loss, on the change in price.

brother, *n., pl.* **brethren.** a traditional term by which one lawyer or judge referred to another. The customary use of the archaic plural "brethren" (instead of "brothers") shows how up-to-date this terminology is.

burden[1], *n.* **1.** an obligation to take some action to protect one's own rights: *The burden was on the insurance company, as drafter of the policy, to make sure that the language was unambiguous; therefore the ambiguous clause will be construed against the company.* **2. burden of persuasion,** the requirement that a party to a case introduce sufficient evidence of a fact to persuade the jury (or judge in a bench trial) of it by the applicable STANDARD OF PROOF. Also called **risk of nonpersuasion.** See also *burden of proof.* **3. burden of pleading,** the requirement that a party seeking to raise a particular issue in a case include allegations about it in the pleadings. **4. burden of producing evidence,** the requirement that a party to a case introduce evidence to support a claim or defense in order to have that issue considered by the judge or jury. Also called **burden of going forward (with evidence), burden of introducing evidence, burden of proceeding, burden of production.** See also *burden of proof;* PRIMA FACIE CASE. **5. burden of proof, a.** usually, same as *burden of persuasion.* **b.** occasionally, same as *burden of producing evidence.* In most situations, the same party will have both the initial burden of producing evidence and the ultimate burden of persuasion on a particular issue, so that *burden of proof* can be used to refer to both simultaneously. **6. burden shifting,** the shifting of the *burden of producing evidence* on a particular issue from one party to another as the evidence unfolds at trial. See also *affirmative defense* (under DEFENSE) (for defs. 2–5).

burden[2], *n.* **1.** a restriction upon the uses that an owner may make of a piece of land, resulting from an EASEMENT, a *covenant running with the land* (see under COVENANT), or the like. It is not the owner, but the land itself, that is said to be under a burden. —*v.* **2.** to impose or constitute a burden upon a piece of land; for example, if Jones has an easement to walk across Smith's land in order to reach his own land, Smith's land is "burdened" by the easement.

burglary, *n.* the crime of BREAKING AND ENTERING with intent to commit a crime in the place entered.

business. See DOING BUSINESS; TRANSACTION OF BUSINESS.

business corporation. See under CORPORATION.

business judgment rule, the rule of corporate law that directors and officers cannot be held liable to investors for business decisions that turn out to have been bad for the corporation, so long as the decisions were within their power to make, were made in good faith, and had a reasonable basis.

business record. See under RECORD.

business trust. See under TRUST.

buy-sell agreement, an agreement among shareholders in a *close corporation* (see under CORPORATION) that if any one of them leaves the business or dies, her shares will be sold to, and bought by, the remaining shareholders or the corporation itself, so as to keep the business in the hands of the original group

buyer in the ordinary course of business, a buyer of some product who buys it in the normal way from a person in the business of selling goods of that kind and buys it in good faith, without knowledge that the sale is a violation of someone else's rights in the goods Such a buyer will get good title to the thing bought even if the thing was in fact pledged to a lender as security for a loan

by operation of law, as a result of application of legal rules, rather than the action or intent of a person *Upon her death, the property that she did not dispose of by will went to her children by operation of law.* See also AS A MATTER OF LAW

by the entirety, words used to describe ownership of an interest in real property granted to a married couple as a unit, with each spouse having RIGHT OF SURVIVORSHIP. *estate by the entirety; ownership by the entirety; tenants by the entirety.* At common law the husband had exclusive control over all property held by the entirety so long as he lived, on the theory that "the husband and wife are one, and that one is the husband." This form of ownership has been abolished in the majority of states; where it still exists, the husband and wife now have equal rights with respect to the property, making ownership by the entirety substantially identical to joint ownership Cf JOINT; IN COMMON, IN SEVERALTY. See also COMMUNITY PROPERTY.

bylaw, *n.* any rule in the set of rules **(bylaws)** adopted collectively by an association, corporation, or other entity to govern itself

C

©, copyright; a symbol giving notice that COPYRIGHT protection is claimed for the work upon which it appears. If the copyright is valid, the work may not be copied without permission of the copyright owner, whose name ordinarily appears with this symbol, along with the year from which the copyright runs.

calendar, *n.* **1.** a court's list of cases scheduled for argument, hearing, or trial on a particular day or over a certain time period. Sometimes called a DOCKET. **2. calendar call,** a courtroom procedure in which a court officer calls out the names of cases on the calendar and lawyers or litigants respond by saying whether they are ready to proceed or desire an adjournment. The officer is said to **call the calendar.**

call, *n.* **1.** a demand for payment, or for delivery of a bond (see BOND¹) or other instrument in exchange for payment, by one having a right to make such a demand. —*v.* **2. call the calendar.** See under CALENDAR.

callable security. Same as *redeemable security* (see under SECURITY²).

camera. See IN CAMERA.

canon, *n.* a rule or principle, particularly one regarded as fundamental: *a canon of statutory construction; the canons of ethics.*

canon law, the internal rules of the Roman Catholic Church, or a similar body of religious rules in certain other Christian denominations.

capacity, *n.* the legal ability to perform an act having legal consequences, such as entering into a contract, making a will, suing or being sued, committing a crime, or getting married. Also called **legal capacity.** See also DIMINISHED CAPACITY.

capita. See PER CAPITA.

capital¹, *n.* **1.** broadly, any form of wealth used or capable of being used for the production of more wealth **2.** money and property owned or employed in business by a corporation or other enterprise Sometimes refers to a company's total *assets,* sometimes to *net assets* (see both under ASSET). See also *capital stock* (under STOCK). **3. capital gain** (or **loss**), the GAIN or LOSS incurred by a taxpayer upon the sale or exchange of a *capital asset* (see under ASSET) **4. capital gains tax,** income tax on a capital gain, such as an investor's profit on sale of stock; often this is taxed at lower rates than wages and other ordinary income. See also *holding period* (under HOLDING)

capital², *adj.* punishable by death, or involving the death penalty: *capital case; capital crime*

capital asset. See under ASSET

capital punishment, the killing of a person by the government as punishment for a crime Also called **death penalty.**

capital stock. See under STOCK.

capricious, *adj.* arbitrary; unreasonable. Usually used in the phrase *arbitrary and capricious* (see under ARBITRARY).

caption, *n.* the heading on a court paper, containing such information as the name and number of the case, the name of the court, and the nature of the paper The exact form of the caption in each court is a matter of local custom.

care, *n.* **1.** the exercise of caution and prudence in one's conduct so as to avoid causing injury or loss **2. ordinary care,** the degree of care that a person of ordinary intelligence and prudence would exercise under the given circumstances. This is the standard of care expected of virtually everyone at all times; a failure to exercise ordinary care is NEGLIGENCE. Also called **due care** or **reasonable care.** See also MALPRACTICE. **3. utmost care,** the standard of care that must be exercised by a trustee or other FIDUCIARY in matters relating to her fiduciary responsibilities; also called **extraordinary care** or **highest degree of care.** A fiduciary's failure to exercise such care is a *breach of fiduciary duty* (see under BREACH)

carnal knowledge, an old term for sexual intercourse

carrier. See COMMON CARRIER.

case[1], *n.* **1.** all proceedings with respect to a charge, claim, or dispute filed with a court *criminal case; civil case; contract case.* **2. agreed case,** a civil case in which the parties stipulate to the facts and submit them to the judge for a ruling upon their legal effect instead of having a trial. Also called **case stated. 3. case in point,** a previously decided case involving facts or issues that are similar or analogous to those currently under consideration, cited as a precedent. **4. case of first impression,** a case raising a significant legal issue that has not previously been ruled upon by any court. **5. companion case,** one of a pair or group of separate cases raising related issues, dealt with at the same time by a court, especially the Supreme Court. **6. consolidated case,** two or more separately filed cases involving common issues, combined into a single case for efficient treatment **7. diversity case,** a federal civil suit between citizens of different states. See also *diversity jurisdiction* (under JURISDICTION[1]) **8. federal case,** a case filed in federal court, especially one involving FEDERAL LAW. A federal case is not necessarily big or important, and you cannot "make a federal case out of" a case that does not fall within the *limited jurisdiction* (see under JURISDICTION[1]) of the federal courts. **9. landmark case,** a case whose decision established a new legal principle of historic importance; a case viewed as representing a great stride forward for the law. For example, Marbury v Madison (the 1803 decision establishing the doctrine that courts may strike down laws as unconstitutional) or Brown v. Board of Education (the 1954 decision holding racial segregation of public schools unconstitutional). **10. leading case,** a case that is generally regarded as the first example of a particular legal principle, or whose decision is an especially influential early exposition of a principle; for example, the 1863 English case of Byrne v. Boadle, in which the phrase RES IPSA LOQUITUR was first used. **11. test case,** a case instituted or continued for the purpose of testing the constitutionality of a law or establishing a new legal principle.

case², *n.* the totality of evidence presented by a party in support of its position in a case· *plaintiff's case; defendant's case; prosecution case.* In a typical trial, the plaintiff or prosecution first presents what it regards as sufficient evidence to prove its claims (the **case in chief**), then the defendant puts on its case, then the plaintiff responds with further evidence (the **rebuttal case,** or simply **rebuttal**). Sometimes the defendant then puts in still more evidence (a **surrebuttal case,** or **surrebuttal**) to rebut the rebuttal, but the alternation seldom goes beyond this. The party that ultimately prevails is said to have "proved (or sustained) its case." See also *prima facie case* (under PRIMA FACIE).

case law, 1. law created by judicial decision rather than by statute, including decisions interpreting statutes. **2.** the body of published judicial opinions in cases dealing with a particular point or kind of issue: *The case law under this statute generally adopts a narrow construction.* Also called **decisional law.**

case method (or **system**), the general method by which most legal subjects are taught in most law schools today, in which students' primary reading material consists of judicial opinions in actual cases, which are analyzed in class by use of the SOCRATIC METHOD. See also CASEBOOK.

case note. Same as ANNOTATION (def. 1).

case or controversy, an actual dispute over legal rights. Under the Constitution, the federal courts may consider only cases or controversies, not hypothetical questions. See also ADVISORY OPINION.

casebook, *n.* a collection of judicial opinions in a particular area of law, edited, organized, and supplemented with questions and commentary for use in the CASE METHOD of legal instruction.

cash bail. See under BAIL¹.

cashier's check. See under CHECK

casual, *adj.* occasional; irregular; out of the ordinary. *casual employee; casual sale.*

casualty, *n.* harm to person or property caused by a sudden, unexpected, or unusual event such as an automobile accident or a natural disaster.

causa mortis, *Latin.* (lit. "because of [impending] death") describing something done by a person in the belief that she is about to die. See also *gift causa mortis* (under GIFT).

causation, *n.* the fact that a certain action or event produced a certain result. This is an essential element to be proved in many kinds of cases; for example, to convict a defendant of murder the prosecution must prove that the victim's death actually resulted from the defendant's conduct; to recover damages in a tort or contract action the plaintiff must prove that the claimed loss was actually caused by defendant's wrongful conduct (**causation of loss** or **loss causation**).

cause, *n.* **1.** an action or event that brings about or contributes to a particular outcome See also PROXIMATE CAUSE. **2.** a reason for taking certain action, especially a good or legally sufficient reason. See also FOR CAUSE; GOOD CAUSE; INSUFFICIENT CAUSE; PROBABLE CAUSE. **3.** a somewhat formal or flowery term for case (see CASE¹), especially a civil case *The cause was tried in Superior Court, County of Los Angeles.*

cause of action, 1. facts which, if proved, would entitle a party to relief in a lawsuit on some legal theory. *The complaint was dismissed for failure to state a cause of action* In the federal courts and many states, this terminology has been replaced for many purposes by *claim for relief* (see under CLAIM). **2.** a right of recovery arising from such facts. *The seller has a cause of action for breach of contract against the purchaser, who failed to pay for the goods.*

cautionary instruction. See under INSTRUCTION.

cease and desist order, an order of an administrative agency directing a person or entity to refrain from specified unlawful conduct. If issued by a court, such an order is more often called an INJUNCTION.

censure, *n.* **1.** a formal statement issued by a body such as a legislature or a bar disciplinary committee condemning the behavior of one of its own members or a member of a group whose conduct it is legally charged with monitoring. —*v.* **2.** to issue such a statement

cert. See under CERTIORARI.

certificate, *n.* **1.** a formal document, typically a single sheet of paper, evidencing some right, interest, or permission granted to the person or entity to which it was issued. **2.** Also called **certification.** a written statement confirming that certain facts are true, that certain acts have been performed, or that something is authentic.

certificate of deposit (CD), an acknowledgment by a bank of receipt of money with a promise to repay it upon specified terms as to interest rate and time of repayment.

certificate of incorporation, 1. in some states, same as ARTICLES OF INCORPORATION. **2.** in most states, a document issued by the state certifying that articles of incorporation have been filed and the named corporation has come into existence; essentially a fancy receipt for the articles and the filing fee.

certificate of title, 1. an official certificate that a certain person is the owner of a particular motor vehicle. **2.** in jurisdictions with a TITLE REGISTRATION SYSTEM for land, a certificate issued by the state or local government identifying the owner or owners of interests in specified real estate and listing any easements, mortgages, covenants, or other encumbrances on the property. **3.** a certificate issued by a title insurance company expressing its professional opinion, after diligent examination, that a person has good title to certain land, except as specifically noted. This does not constitute a guarantee or insurance of good title

certification, *n* **1.** the act of certifying or issuing a certificate **2.** the fact or state of being certified **3.** CERTIFICATE (def. 2) **4.** the word for CERTIORARI in some state court systems

certify, *v.* **1.** to make a written representation or guarantee that something is authentic, acceptable, or true, or that certain acts have been or will be performed. **2.** to issue a CERTIFICATE **3. certified check.** See under CHECK. **4. certified copy,** a copy of a document to which a statement has been affixed swearing or affirming that it has been compared with the original and is a true copy Also called **verified copy** or **attested copy. 5. certified question,** under procedures permitted in some jurisdictions, a question of law posed by a lower court to a higher court, or a question of state law posed by a federal court to the appropriate state court, so that the answer can be applied in resolving a pending case **6. certify the record,** to transmit documents constituting the record in a case to a higher court for appellate review, with a certification that this is in fact the record

certiorari, *n. Latin.* (lit "to be informed," "to be assured") a writ issued by an appellate court as a matter of discretion, directing a lower court to *certify the record* (see under CERTIFY) in a case that was not appealable as of right. The usual route by which a case reaches the Supreme Court of the United States is by a petition for certiorari from the party on the losing end of a decision of a United States Court of Appeals or a state's highest court, the Supreme Court grants only about one percent of such petitions In informal speech, certiorari is typically referred to by its abbreviation· **cert.**

cestui que trust, *Law French* (lit. "the one who trusts") the BENEFICIARY of a trust. Often shortened to **cestui;** more often not used at all, since "beneficiary" means the same thing and is pronounceable

chain of custody, the sequence of places where, and persons with whom, a piece of physical evidence was located from the time of its gathering to its introduction at a trial Establishing the chain of custody is essential to proof of authenticity of the evidence.

chain of title, the sequence of owners and transfers of a parcel of real property. Any gap in the recorded chain of title casts doubt upon the validity of a present claim of title to the property.

challenge, *n.* **1.** a party's rejection of a potential juror, either because of an obvious bias or interest in the case **(challenge for cause)** or simply because of a belief that the juror may not be receptive to that party's arguments **(peremptory challenge).** In selecting a jury, each party is allowed unlimited challenges for cause and a limited number of peremptory challenges. **2. challenge to the array,** a party's objection to the manner in which the entire array of potential jurors was selected from the population at large

chambers, *n.pl.* a judge's office Depending upon the court, it may be a single room or a suite of two or three rooms for the judge, one or more law clerks, and a secretary. See also ROBING ROOM.

champerty, *n* an agreement to finance someone else's lawsuit in return for a share of the proceeds Prohibitions on champerty are the reason that lawyers working for a **contingency fee** (see under CONTINGENCY) usually insist that filing fees and other expenses of a suit be paid by the client See also MAINTENANCE; BARRATRY. —**champertous,** *adj.*

chance verdict. See under VERDICT

Chancellor, *n* the traditional title of judges in courts of EQUITY or CHANCERY

chancery, *n* the traditional name for a court of EQUITY Also called **chancery court** or **court of chancery.**

Chapter 7, 11, 12, or **13.** See under BANKRUPTCY

character, *n.* the general disposition of a person, particularly with respect to some trait that is relevant in a case, such as honesty or propensity for violence. See also **character evidence** (under EVIDENCE), **character witness** (under WITNESS).

charge, *n* **1.** a formal allegation that a person has violated a specific criminal law; a COUNT in an indictment or information **2.** a judge's INSTRUCTION to the jury on a particular point of law, or her *instructions* collectively (see under INSTRUCTION) **3. Allen charge,** a charge to a jury that has declared itself unable to reach a verdict, urging it to try harder The Allen charge is prohibited in some states because of its tendency to coerce holdout jurors to go along with the majority despite genuine doubts. —*v* **4.** to make or deliver a charge

charter¹, *n.* **1.** a formal grant of rights and powers from a sovereign, or the document embodying such a grant; for example, the MAGNA CARTA, or **Great Charter. 2.** the basic set of governing principles of an organization the *United Nations Charter* **3.** Also called **corporate charter. a.** a legislative act establishing a corporation and setting forth its purposes and basic structure **b.** a CERTIFICATE OF INCORPORATION or other document issued by the state granting corporate status to an entity **c.** a corporation's ARTICLES OF INCORPORATION —*v.* **4.** to establish, or grant a corporate charter to, an entity. *The United Nations was chartered in 1945.*

charter², *n* **1.** the rental of a ship, airplane, or bus. **2.** Also called **charter party.** A written contract for the hire of such a vessel, especially a ship —*v* **3.** to rent such a vessel to or from someone *We chartered a bus for the company picnic*

chattel, *n.* an item of personal property, especially tangible personalty

chattel mortgage. See under MORTGAGE

check, *n.* **1.** an instrument by which a person (the drawer) directs a bank (the drawee) to pay a specified sum of money to the order of another person (the payee), or to the bearer of the instrument, upon demand Normally the payment is made out of funds that the drawer has on deposit with the bank A check is a special kind of DRAFT **2. bank check,** a check drawn by a bank upon another bank **3. bad check,** a check that is forged, drawn upon insufficient funds, or in some other way defective, so that payment is properly refused by the drawee bank. **4. cashier's check,** a check drawn by a bank on itself; it amounts to a promise to pay if the payee makes a proper demand. **5. certified check,** a check on which the bank has written a notice (usually just the word "certified") signifying that the funds necessary to pay it have been set aside so that payment will definitely be made upon proper demand by the payee. **6. NSF check,** a check that the drawee bank may refuse to pay because the drawer does not have sufficient funds on deposit to cover it when it is presented to the bank for payment. NSF stands for "not sufficient funds" or "non-sufficient funds." See also KITE.

child, *n.* **1.** a person deemed by the law to require special protection or treatment because of youth. The age below which one is regarded as a child depends upon the particular statute or legal doctrine at issue. **2.** an offspring or a person treated as such Depending upon the context, the term may or may not include an illegitimate child or a stepchild, but would almost always include an adopted child.

child custody. See under CUSTODY

child neglect. See under NEGLECT.

child pornography. See under PORNOGRAPHY

chilling effect, a tendency to inhibit the exercise of constitutional rights, especially those protected by the First Amendment (see Appendix). Statutes that unnecessarily create such an effect are often held unconstitutional.

choice of evils. Same as NECESSITY.

choice of law, the problem of deciding which law to apply when an action involves events that took place or have an impact in two or more jurisdictions having different laws. This is the central concern of the field of CONFLICT OF LAWS.

chose in action, a right to obtain money or personal property by bringing a legal action; a claim for such a thing For example, a right to recover a debt. "Chose" (pronounced "shows") is Law French for "thing," and the entire phrase is sometimes rendered in English as **thing in action.**

churning, *n.* a stockbroker's excessive and inappropriate trading of securities in a customer's account for the purpose of generating extra commissions for the broker. This is made illegal by the securities laws

circuit, *n.* a geographic division established by some states or by the United States for purposes of judicial administration, with a court in each circuit. At the federal level, the United States is divided geographically into twelve circuits for appellate purposes, with the United States Court of Appeals for each such circuit handling appeals from all federal district courts within its area. In addition, a special circuit covering the entire country, called the **Federal Circuit,** has been established in order to funnel all appeals on a number of subjects, such as patents and international trade, to a single specialized court, the **United States Court of Appeals for the Federal Circuit.** See also UNITED STATES COURT OF APPEALS. Cf. DISTRICT.

circumstantial evidence. See under EVIDENCE

citation, *n.* **1.** a written notice to appear in court (or sometimes to respond by mail) to answer a charge; for example, a traffic ticket. Citations are a substitute for arrest in minor offenses. **2.** a reference to a statute, previous judicial decision, or other writing as authority for a fact or legal proposition. Standard abbreviations and formats for citing common sources minimize the space required and are recognized by all lawyers. See also BLUEBOOK.

    —**cite,** *v*

citizen, *n.* **1.** a person who owes allegiance to a government and is entitled to its protection. Under the Fourteenth Amendment (see Appendix), virtually all persons born or naturalized in the United States are citizens of the United States and of the state where they reside. In addition, by statute, persons born in Puerto Rico, the U.S. Virgin Islands, Guam, and the Northern Mariana Islands are citizens of the United States See also NATIONAL; NATURALIZE. **2.** for purposes of determining whether a suit by or against a corporation or a resident alien falls within the *diversity jurisdiction* (see under JURISDICTION[1]) of the federal courts, an alien admitted to the United States for permanent residence is deemed to be a "citizen" of the state where the alien is domiciled, and a corporation is deemed to be a "citizen" both of the state where it was incorporated and of the state where it has its principal place of business.

citizen's arrest. See under ARREST.

civil, *adj.* **1.** pertaining to all aspects of law other than those dealing with criminal or military matters *civil court; civil case.* See also *civil* ACTION, COMMITMENT, CONTEMPT, LIABILITY, PENALTY, PROCEDURE, PROSECUTION under those words Cf. CIVIL LAW. **2.** pertaining generally to the rights, duties, and status of people as members of society. See CIVIL RIGHTS; CIVIL DISOBEDIENCE.

civil disobedience, open and nonviolent refusal to obey certain laws, and acceptance of punishment, for the purpose of influencing public opinion, legislation, or governmental policy.

civil law, the prevailing system of law in continental Europe, derived from Roman law. In contrast to the traditional COMMON LAW system of England and America, the basic source of law in the civil law system is organized codes rather than case-by-case judicial decisions. In the United States, Louisiana stands out as the state whose law is most heavily influenced by civil law, because of its origins as a French territory. See also COMMUNITY PROPERTY; INQUISITORIAL SYSTEM.

civil liberties. See under CIVIL RIGHTS.

civil rights, 1. Also called **civil liberties.** governmentally recognized and legally protected rights and liberties of people in areas of personal autonomy, personal welfare, and participation in the political, business, and social life of the nation. In the United States, these include political and personal liberties protected by the Constitution (see FUNDAMENTAL RIGHT) and freedom from private and governmental discrimination on the basis of characteristics such as race, sex, religion, or disability. **2.** more narrowly, the phrase "civil rights" is sometimes distinguished from "civil liberties," with the former phrase referring to freedom from discrimination, especially on the basis of race, and the latter referring to rights of personal autonomy and political expression and participation.

Civil War amendments, the Thirteenth, Fourteenth, and Fifteenth Amendments to the Constitution (see Appendix), adopted in the wake of the Civil War to bring a permanent end to slavery and extend basic rights of citizenship and equal treatment to people of color Unfortunately, the Supreme Court construed these amendments so narrowly (see SEPARATE BUT EQUAL) that legally endorsed public and private discrimination were permitted to continue for almost a century more, and became so entrenched that the nation is still struggling with the consequences.

claim, *n.* **1.** an assertion that one is entitled to something. **2.** Also called **claim for relief.** in the federal courts and many states, an assertion of facts that, if true, would legally entitle the claimant to judgment in a civil case. A plaintiff's complaint must allege such facts or suffer dismissal for "failure to state a claim." See also CAUSE OF ACTION. **3.** an apparent or actual right to receive something by way of a lawsuit: *The person injured in the automobile accident has a tort claim against the negligent driver.*

claim joinder. See under JOINDER

claimant, *n.* one who has a claim; one who asserts a claim.

class action. See under ACTION.

classification, *n.* **1.** in a regulation or statute, a division of people into different classes subject to different legal treatment This may occur intentionally and explicitly, as when a legislature decrees that only citizens (not aliens) shall receive certain benefits, or simply as a practical consequence of application of the law, as when a fee requirement effectively excludes the poor (but not the wealthy) from some opportunity. For the purpose of assessing the constitutionality of such laws under the EQUAL PROTECTION clause, the Supreme Court has created two special categories of classifications, known as SUSPECT CLASSIFICATION and QUASI-SUSPECT CLASSIFICATION **2.** in modern criminal codes, the categorizing of offenses according to severity, with a specified range of punishments for each class of offense.

Clayton Act, a federal ANTITRUST law prohibiting a range of business activities that may substantially lessen competition, such as a corporate merger between two dominant companies in the same business, where the effect would be to eliminate competition between them and enable them to use their combined strength against smaller competitors.

clean hands, the quality of having acted fairly and properly in a matter over which one is suing someone else. Cf. UNCLEAN HANDS; see also *clean hands doctrine* and *clean hands defense* (under UNCLEAN HANDS).

clear and convincing evidence, an intermediate STANDARD OF PROOF, more stringent than PREPONDERANCE OF THE EVIDENCE but less than BEYOND A REASONABLE DOUBT. It requires that the factfinder be persuaded that the fact to be proved is highly probable. This standard is used in various types of noncriminal proceeding in which public policy requires an extra level of proof, such as a deportation hearing.

clear and present danger, an imminent risk of harm of a type that the government may legitimately protect against; a phrase sometimes used to describe the circumstances under which the government may prohibit or punish SPEECH.

clear title. Same as *marketable title* (see under TITLE).

clearly erroneous, the STANDARD OF REVIEW by which a trial judge's findings of fact are normally tested in the appeal of a civil case that was tried without a jury. The appellate court may not reverse simply because it would have reached a different conclusion on the same evidence, but it may reverse a judge's findings more easily than a jury's

clemency, *n.* the exercise by a President or governor of the power to grant an AMNESTY, PARDON, or REPRIEVE, or to COMMUTE a sentence Also called **executive clemency.**

clergy-communicant privilege. See under PRIVILEGE.

clerk, *n.* **1.** Also called **court clerk.** a court official charged with the overall administration of the court's operations or with some aspect of administration, particularly the processing and maintenance of court papers and records. **2.** Also called **law clerk.** a recent law graduate employed as an assistant to a judge for one or two years —*v.* **3.** to serve as a law clerk

close (or **closely held**) **corporation.** See under CORPORATION.

closing, *n.* **1.** the completion of a transaction, especially a real estate transaction or major corporate transaction, usually at a meeting attended by counsel for all parties. A detailed written summary of the financial aspects of the transaction being closed is called a **closing statement. 2.** Also called **closing statement** or **closing argument.** a SUMMATION.

cloud on title, a claim with respect to land that casts doubt on the validity or completeness of the owner's title to the land. The legal mechanism for removing such a cloud is an action to QUIET TITLE.

co-conspirator. See under CONSPIRACY

code, *n.* **1.** an organized compilation of statutes or rules *Code of Federal Regulations;* UNITED STATES CODE **2.** a coherent and comprehensive statute dealing with a major area of law· INTERNAL REVENUE CODE; UNIFORM COMMERCIAL CODE

codicil, *n.* an addition to or amendment of an existing will. To be valid it must be executed with all the formalities of a will.

codify, *v.* **1.** to enact a statute embodying a principle of common law or a particular judicial interpretation of the law. **2.** to organize existing statutes or an existing body of law into a CODE. —**codification,** *n*

coercion. Same as DURESS

cognizable, *adj.* **1.** within the jurisdiction of a court; capable of being considered· *Divorce actions are not cognizable in federal court.* **2.** describing a claim for which a court could provide relief· *Mere disagreement by a taxpayer with the way tax revenues are spent does not give rise to a cognizable claim.*

cognovit, *n. Latin* (lit "he has recognized") an instrument containing a CONFESSION OF JUDGMENT See also *cognovit note* (under NOTE[1])

cohabit, *v* **1.** of unmarried couples, to live together in an intimate relationship similar to that of husband and wife Viewed until recently as a crime or at least evidence of a crime (see FORNICATION), cohabitation has begun to emerge as a legally protected relationship (see PALIMONY). See also DOMESTIC PARTNERSHIP Cf. *common law marriage* (under MARRIAGE). **2.** of unrelated people generally, to live together Zoning ordinances may restrict the number of unrelated people who can cohabit in single-family residential areas. —**cohabitation,** *n*

coinsurance, *n.* a form of insurance in which the insurance company pays only a certain percentage of any loss, the balance being paid by the policyholder personally or by other insurance purchased by the policyholder; for example, medical insurance under which the insurer pays 80% of covered expenses and the policyholder pays 20%

collateral[1]**,** *n.* property in which someone has a *security interest* (see under INTEREST[1]), especially property pledged as security for a loan (see PLEDGE).

collateral[2]**,** *adj* **1.** indirect; off to the side Often used in contrast to DIRECT[1] **2. collateral attack,** an attack on a judgment or judicial proceeding that is made in a different proceeding. For example, if A obtains a default judgment against B in New York and then attempts to seize B's property in California to satisfy the judgment, B might attack the New York judgment in California on the ground that the New York court did not have jurisdiction over him. Cf *direct attack* (under DIRECT[1]) **3. collateral estoppel.** See under ESTOPPEL. **4. collateral heir,** an heir who is not a direct ancestor or descendant of the deceased, but is descended from a common ancestor, for example, a sister, cousin, uncle, or nephew Cf. *direct heir* (under DIRECT[1]).

5. collateral source rule, the principle of tort law that compensation for an injured party from a source other than the tortfeasor (e.g., from the injured party's insurance company) does not reduce the amount that can be collected from the wrongdoer. See also SUBROGATE.

collective bargaining, 1. negotiation between an employer and a union representing employees with regard to wages and other conditions of employment. **2. collective bargaining agreement,** a contract between an employer and a union representing employees with regard to the terms and conditions of employment

colloquy, *n.* discussion among lawyers, or between the lawyers and the judge, in the course of a judicial proceeding.

color, *n.* **1.** appearance; especially, appearance without reality: *color of authority; color of title.* See also UNDER COLOR OF LAW. **2.** skin complexion. Constitutional provisions and civil rights statutes prohibiting discrimination on the basis of RACE customarily add "color" as well, to eliminate legalistic arguments over the exact basis upon which someone is wrongfully discriminating.

color of law. See UNDER COLOR OF LAW.

colorable, *adj.* **1.** superficially, and perhaps actually, valid; possibly valid **2.** seemingly, but not actually, valid or authentic; deceptive

combat zone. See under ZONE.

comity, *n.* the principle under which the courts of one jurisdiction will recognize and defer to the decisions, proceedings, and laws of another jurisdiction, not out of obligation but out of mutual respect. For example, American courts will ordinarily extend comity to a decision of a court in another country if it is convinced that the procedures in the other country were fundamentally fair. Cf. FULL FAITH AND CREDIT.

comment, *n.* an article, usually written by a student and published in a law review, analyzing a particular judicial decision and placing it in a larger legal context. Sometimes called an **annotation.** Cf. NOTE².

commerce, *n.* trade, business, and travel, especially across state lines (**interstate commerce**) or between the United States and other countries (**foreign commerce**). The powerlessness of the new national government to prevent trade wars between the states following independence from Britain was a principal motivating factor behind the adoption of the Constitution, with a clause (the **Commerce Clause**) giving Congress the power to regulate interstate and foreign commerce (the **commerce power**). This power forged the United States into a powerful economic unit and has also enabled Congress to adopt laws in such diverse fields as guaranteeing civil rights, protecting the environment, and attacking organized crime, since these are matters seen as affecting interstate commerce.

commercial bribery. See under BRIBERY.

commercial paper, NEGOTIABLE INSTRUMENTS, especially short-term promissory notes (see NOTE¹) issued by corporations to investors and traded among investors as securities. Also called **paper.**

commercial speech. See under SPEECH.

commission, *n.* **1.** compensation for services rendered in facilitating a transaction, or for acting as a trustee, executor, or the like, calculated as a percentage of the value of the transaction or of the property involved. See also KICKBACK. **2.** authority to hold an appointive office or perform delegated duties. **3.** the act of committing a crime. **4.** a name sometimes given to an administrative agency. *Interstate Commerce Commission.*

commissive waste. See under WASTE

commit, *v.* **1.** to do something wrong: *The witness committed perjury. The judge committed error by admitting hearsay testimony.* See also COMMISSION. **2.** to place a person in a prison, hospital, or other institution, especially by court order. See also COMMITMENT.

commitment, 1. imprisonment or institutionalization of a person, especially by order of a court **2. civil commitment, a.** commitment of a person to a mental hospital or other treatment facility upon a court's finding that the person poses a danger to himself or others **b.** the jailing of a person for *civil contempt* (see under CONTEMPT) to induce compliance with a court order. **3. voluntary commitment,** commitment to a treatment facility upon the request or with the consent of the person in need of care.

committee, *n.* **1.** a small group of members of a larger organization, established to carry out specific duties delegated ("committed") to it by the organization. Virtually all bills in Congress or a state legislature are considered by a committee before being voted on by the entire legislative body. **2.** the word used in some states for a GUARDIAN of an incompetent adult (the person into whose care the incompetent is committed). See also CONSERVATOR

common. See IN COMMON.

common carrier, a company in the business of transporting people or goods, or sometimes messages or information, and offering this service to the public at large.

common law, 1. the legal system that evolved over many centuries in England and is the foundation of law in Great Britain and many of its former possessions, including the United States. In contrast to the CIVIL LAW system of continental Europe, the basic source of common law is judicial decisions rather than codes, with judges seeking in each new case to adapt the principles worked out in previous cases to new facts and circumstances in such a way as to achieve justice. See also ADVERSARY SYSTEM. **2.** judge-made law, as distinguished from STATUTORY law. Although large areas of earlier common law have now been codified, including criminal law and commercial law, there remain other large areas, notably tort law, contract law, and property law, that are still predominantly governed by common law rather than statutes. See also *common law crime* (under CRIME). **3.** Often shortened to **law.** legal principles that originated in the procedures and decisions of England's

LAW courts as distinguished from its courts of EQUITY *Damages are a common law remedy* (or *remedy at law*), whereas *the injunction is a form of equitable relief* See also AT; MERGER OF LAW AND EQUITY **4.** all of the law of England at the time when America achieved its independence That law, whether judge-made or statutory, was generally regarded as the common law of the United States after independence. **5. federal common law,** law made by federal court judges with respect to subjects of uniquely federal concern under the Constitution, such as admiralty law and law pertaining to rights of action under the Constitution. With respect to matters of general law traditionally regulated by the states, such as torts and contracts, the federal courts may not develop a uniform national body of common law, but instead must follow state law. See also FEDERAL LAW.

common law action. See under ACTION

common law crime. See under CRIME

common law marriage. See under MARRIAGE

common law state or **common law property state.** See under COMMUNITY PROPERTY.

common stock. See under STOCK.

community property, a system of property ownership and distribution for married couples, derived from Spanish civil law and followed in California and a few other western and southwestern states (called **community property states;** all other states, having property systems derived from English common law, being referred to for this purpose as **common law states** or **common law property states**). Under this system, most income or property obtained by either spouse during marriage belongs to the "marital community." Each spouse may distribute half of the community property by will; in the event of divorce, the community property is divided either equitably (in certain states) or equally (in certain states, including California) See also EQUITABLE DISTRIBUTION Cf. BY THE ENTIRETY

commute, *v.* to reduce a convicted criminal's sentence by executive action: *The governor commuted the death sentence to life imprisonment* Cf. PARDON, REPRIEVE See also CLEMENCY **—commutation,** *n.*

compact, *n.* a contract or treaty, especially an agreement between two states **(interstate compact)** to resolve a dispute or cooperate in a matter of mutual concern.

companion case. See under CASE[1]

company, *n.* **1.** a business enterprise, especially one owned or carried on by a group of people; an association, partnership, or corporation. **2. holding company,** a company, usually a corporation, formed to hold stock in other companies, and often to control those other companies through ownership of large amounts of their stock. **3. joint stock company,** an unincorporated company with ownership interests represented by shares of stock, in which owners share the profits in proportion to their holdings of stock but, unlike corporate stockholders, are personally liable to the company's creditors if the company's assets prove insufficient to pay its debts. Also called **stock association** or **joint stock association**. See also PARENT COMPANY.

comparative negligence. See under NEGLIGENCE.

compelling interest, an extremely important governmental interest, important enough to justify a law that limits a FUNDAMENTAL RIGHT or treats people differently on the basis of a SUSPECT CLASSIFICATION Also called **compelling governmental interest** or, in the case of a state law, **compelling state interest.**

compensation, n. **1.** payment for services rendered **2.** payment for injury or loss sustained See also *compensatory damages* (under DAMAGES); JUST COMPENSATION

competent¹, *adj.* possessing sufficient mental capacity to make rational decisions about a legal matter and understand the consequences, so that the law will permit one to proceed and will give legal effect to one's actions: *competent to make a will; competent to stand trial; competent to act as one's own lawyer.* —**competency;** occasionally **competence,** n.

competent², *adj* **1.** (of a person) possessing the legal or other qualifications necessary to perform a task For example, to be competent to serve as a witness to the execution of a will one must ordinarily be over a certain age and not a beneficiary under the will **2.** (of a court or other official body) possessing jurisdiction or authority to deal with a matter. Such a court is often referred to as a "court of competent jurisdiction." **3.** (of evidence or of a witness in a proceeding) admissible, or possessing information that would be admissible. A person whose only knowledge about an issue is hearsay would ordinarily not be competent to testify on that issue —**competence;** (for defs 1,3) sometimes **competency,** n

competent evidence. See under EVIDENCE

complaint, n. **1.** the initial PLEADING in a civil case, in which the plaintiff states the facts that she contends entitle her to relief and states what relief she seeks. See also *verified complaint* (under VERIFY) **2.** the initial instrument charging a person with a crime, sworn to by a witness or police officer (the **complainant**) and describing the alleged crime.

completion bond. See under BOND².

compound question. See under QUESTION¹.

compounding a crime, the offense of accepting something of value from a person known to have committed a crime, and agreeing in return not to report or prosecute the crime. If the crime in question is a felony, this offense is also called **compounding a felony.** In some states an exception is made for victims who agree not to prosecute if the criminal restores what was taken or compensates them for their injury or loss. Cf. MISPRISION OF FELONY

compromise verdict. See under VERDICT

compulsory arbitration. See under ARBITRATION

compulsory counterclaim. See under COUNTERCLAIM.

compulsory joinder. See under JOINDER

concealed weapon. See under WEAPON

conclusion of law, in a nonjury trial, a judge's decision on a legal issue (e.g., whether the court has jurisdiction or which state's law applies to the case) or conclusion based upon the application of law to the facts (e g , that the defendant is or is not liable for negligence) See also FINDING OF FACT; FINDINGS OF FACT AND CONCLUSIONS OF LAW

conclusive presumption. See under PRESUMPTION

conclusory, *adj.* stating a conclusion without supporting facts· *a conclusory allegation; a conclusory affidavit.*

concur, *v* **1.** (of one or more judges on a panel) to agree with the decision being made by the court; to agree with the conclusion, though not necessarily with all of the reasoning, of the majority or plurality opinion. **2. concurring in the result** or **concurring in the judgment,** a phrase used to emphasize that a particular judge on a panel agrees with the outcome in a case but in no way endorses the reasoning in the majority or plurality opinion See also *concurring opinion* (under OPINION) —**concurrence,** *n*

concurrent, *adj* **1.** occurring or existing simultaneously *concurrent jurisdiction* (see under JURISDICTION[1]); *concurrent sentences* (see under SENTENCE) **2.** acting together *concurrent causes, concurrent tortfeasors* —**concurrently,** *adv*

condemn, *v* **1.** to take property for public use, exercise the power of EMINENT DOMAIN **2.** to order something destroyed because it is illegal or poses a hazard to the public **3.** to adjudge a person guilty or impose sentence, especially a very severe sentence such as death or life imprisonment —**condemnation,** *n*

condition, 1. a future event which is possible but not certain, upon the occurrence of which a right, interest, or obligation under a contract, deed, will, or other instrument is made to depend **2. condition precedent,** (pronounced preSEEdent), a condition that must occur in order for such a right, interest, or obligation to arise **3. condition subsequent,** a condition whose occurrence extinguishes such a right, interest, or obligation —**conditional,** *adj*

condition of bail. See under BAIL[1]

conditional fee. Same as **fee simple defeasible** (see under FEE[1])

conditional privilege. See under PRIVILEGE

condominium, *n.* a form of ownership of real property in which several owners each own a separate residential or commercial unit within the property and all of them together own the common areas, such as lobbies and recreational areas, as tenants in common Cf COOPERATIVE (def 2)

confession, *n* **1.** a statement admitting that one has committed a crime **2. involuntary confession, a.** narrowly, a confession obtained by physical or psychological coercion. **b.** broadly, a confession obtained by such coercion or in violation of the MIRANDA RULE A confession that is involuntary in this broad sense may not be used in a criminal case against the person who makes it. **3. voluntary confession,** a confession that is not involuntary.

confession of judgment, an acknowledgment by a defendant that the plaintiff is right and that judgment should be entered in favor of the plaintiff Transactions in which a party is required to provide such a confession in advance, so that in the event of any default by that party the other one can go straight into court and get a judgment without allowing any opportunity for presentation of a defense, are restricted or prohibited in many states For example, see *cognovit note* (under NOTE¹). See also COGNOVIT

confidentiality stipulation, a STIPULATION by the parties in a case, usually SO ORDERED by the judge (turning it into a **confidentiality order**), that information obtained during pretrial discovery, or the terms of a settlement, will be kept confidential. Sometimes the purpose is to protect legitimate confidential information, such as trade secrets or employee medical records; sometimes it is simply to prevent public access to damaging information that might assist other injured parties in seeking justice.

conflict of interest, 1. a situation in which one has both a personal interest in a matter and some duty to another, or to the general public, with respect to that same matter, so that one's personal interest could potentially influence the way one carries out the duty. For example, a judge presiding over a suit against a company in which she owns stock, or an office manager asked to hire the best candidate for a position for which his brother is one of the applicants, would have a conflict of interest **2.** a situation in which one owes duties to two different people whose interests in a matter may not be compatible, as when an attorney undertakes to represent two different defendants in the same case, or both the husband and the wife in an uncontested divorce The law tolerates some conflicts of interest if the interested parties are informed of them and have no objection; in other situations, the law requires a person with a conflict of interest to withdraw from the matter.

conflict of laws, the field of law that deals with the problems arising from application of the laws of different states or countries to events and transactions affecting two or more jurisdictions. These problems include CHOICE OF LAW and the question whether a judgment rendered in one jurisdiction will be recognized in another. In most countries this conflict of laws is primarily a branch of INTERNATIONAL LAW, but because law in the United States is a patchwork of more than fifty independent legal systems, it is a subject that pervades all areas of American law. See also COMITY; FULL FAITH AND CREDIT; UNIFORM LAWS.

conformed copy, a copy of a document on which changes or insertions have been made to make it an accurate copy of the original. When a proposed order is submitted to a judge, the judge typically writes in various changes before signing it; then the party who submitted it "conforms" a copy of the proposed order by copying in the judge's changes and writing the judge's name on the signature line, and serves that conformed copy on the person to whom the order is directed The original piece of paper signed by the judge stays on file with the court. See also /s/.

conforming use. See under USE.

confrontation, *n.* the right of a criminal defendant, under the Sixth Amendment (see Appendix), to be confronted in open court by the witnesses against him so that they can be cross-examined and the jury can evaluate their demeanor. The Supreme Court has held, however, that a child may be permitted to testify by closed circuit television upon a finding that face-to-face confrontation with an alleged abuser would cause the child serious emotional distress.

congressional intent. See under LEGISLATIVE INTENT.

connect up, to introduce evidence showing that previously offered evidence was admissible. A judge may permit evidence to be presented to a jury "subject to connection" or "subject to connecting up"; if the necessary connection to the case is never shown, the jury will be instructed to disregard that evidence

conscientious objector, 1. a person whose religion or sincere personal belief system forbids participation as a combatant in any war By statute, conscientious objectors may provide an alternative form of service to the country if drafted in time of war. **2. selective conscientious objector,** a person opposed not to all wars, but only to those he regards as unjust. The law does not give such a person the status of a conscientious objector.

consecutive sentences. See under SENTENCE.

consent, *n.* **1.** acquiescence in a course of action. **2. age of consent.** See under AGE. **3. informed consent,** consent given after receiving sufficient information about the nature, costs, risks, and benefits of a proposed course of action to make an intelligent decision. In the absence of such information, one's "consent" may not be legally valid. For example, surgery upon a person who was not informed of the nature of the procedure may make the surgeon liable for the tort of BATTERY. **4. on consent,** describing a judicial action taken because all parties agree to it, or at least none objects. *The injunction was entered on consent.* —*v.* **5.** to give consent or manifest acquiescence: *The defendant consented to the entry of a preliminary injunction.* —*adj.* **6.** describing action taken with the consent of those affected· *consent decree; consent order.* See also *consent search* (under SEARCH).

consequential damages. See under DAMAGES.

conservator, *n.* the term used in some states for a court-appointed GUARDIAN for an incompetent adult. See also COMMITTEE. —**conservatorship,** *n.*

consideration, *n.* **1.** that which is given or promised by a party to a CONTRACT in exchange for the other's promise. Unless something is given up by the promisee or some benefit is conferred on the promisor in exchange for the promise, the promise is merely GRATUITOUS and ordinarily will be unenforceable for *want of consideration* (see under WANT). See also FAILURE OF CONSIDERATION **2. nominal consideration,** consideration recited in the contract but of no meaningful value, as in a contract to sell a parcel of land for one dollar Although under traditional contract law courts do not pass judgment on the fairness of consideration, a court today might conclude that such a contract is unenforceable because of UNCONSCIONABILITY, or on the ground that the transaction is not a contract at all, but merely an unenforceable promise of a gift **3. past consideration,** conduct in the past that is recited as "consideration" for a new promise; for example, "In consideration of the years of faithful service that you have given me, I promise to leave you my house." In most situations, traditional contract law regarded such a promise as unenforceable because nothing was actually demanded or given in exchange for it, but in sympathetic cases modern courts sometimes find a way to enforce such promises despite the lack of real consideration

consign, *v.* to place goods into the hands of a carrier for delivery to another person (the **consignee**), or to place goods in the hands of a merchant (the **consignee**) for sale to others. In both cases, the original owner (the **consignor**) retains title to the goods until the ultimate delivery or sale occurs. Goods that have been consigned to a merchant and are awaiting sale are said to be "on consignment." —**consignment,** *n*

consolidate, *v.* to put two or more things together; particularly, to combine two or more cases into one for administrative convenience See also *consolidated case* (under CASE¹). Cf SEVER. —**consolidation,** *n.*

consortium, *n.* **1.** the companionship, affection, services, and sexual attention of a spouse In some states, for some purposes, the concept has been extended to include the affection and companionship between parent and child. **2. loss of consortium,** the loss of such companionship by reason of wrongful conduct of another. This is commonly an element of damages for which recovery is sought in a tort action, usually an action against someone who has negligently or intentionally injured or killed one's spouse See also SERVICES.

conspiracy, *n.* an agreement among two or more persons (each referred to as a **conspirator** or **co-conspirator**) to do an unlawful act, or to achieve a lawful end by unlawful means; often described informally as a "partnership in crime." Conspiracy is a separate offense from the one it is formed to accomplish, and is a crime even if the contemplated acts are never performed, although in most states the agreement itself is not a crime until there has been some OVERT ACT by one of the conspirators in furtherance of the conspiracy

constitution, *n* **1.** the fundamental law of a nation or state, providing a framework against which the validity of all other laws is measured, the system of fundamental principles according to which the nation or state is governed **2. Constitution,** a particular constitution Unless the context indicates otherwise, in American legal writing this always refers to the **Constitution of the United States**

constitutional, *adj* **1.** (of a law, policy, or action) in harmony with or not forbidden by a constitution, especially the Constitution of the United States Cf. UNCONSTITUTIONAL **2.** pertaining or pursuant to a constitution, especially the Constitution of the United States **3. constitutional issue** (or **question**), an issue in a case that requires resort to the Constitution and cases interpreting it for resolution See also *constitutional right* (under RIGHT); *constitutional tort* (under TORT)

constitutionality, *n* the quality or state of being CONSTITUTIONAL. *A case was instituted to test the constitutionality of the statute.*

construction, *n.* **1.** the process of determining the meaning of a constitution, statute, or instrument and its legal effect in a particular situation, or the meaning and effect so determined. Often interchangeable with **interpretation,** although "construction" is the more common term with respect to constitutions, rules, and statutes **(statutory construction),** and "interpretation" is more commonly used with respect to private instruments such as contracts, wills, and deeds **2. liberal construction,** construction of a statute or constitutional provision that considers the overall purposes for which it was enacted and interprets it in such a way as to further those purposes. This approach, also called **broad construction,** recognizes that words are always an imperfect tool and that not all possible circumstances to which a provision might apply can be anticipated and specifically addressed by the language used. As a general rule, statutes granting rights, benefits, and protections are construed liberally. **3. strict construction,** construction of a statute or constitutional provision that focuses on the specific words used and tends to reject application to circumstances not clearly within the ordinary meaning of those words. Also called **narrow construction.** Criminal statutes are usually construed strictly, on the ground that no one should be punished for conduct that the legislature has not clearly and specifically made a crime See also LEGISLATIVE HISTORY; LEGISLATIVE INTENT, ORIGINAL INTENT; PLAIN MEANING. —**construe,** *v.*

construction warranty. See under WARRANTY

constructive, *adj.* having the legal effect of; deemed by the law to exist or to have occurred even though that is not actually true For example, a person who says "I'm giving you the contents of my safe; here's the key," would probably be held to have made "constructive delivery" of the contents of the safe (or to have "constructively delivered" them) by delivering the key, even though the contents have actually not been moved. See also *constructive* EVIC-

TION, FRAUD, NOTICE, SERVICE, TRUST, TRUSTEE under those words Cf ACTUAL. —**constructively,** *adv*

construe. See under CONSTRUCTION

consumer, *n.* a person who purchases or leases goods, services, or real property primarily for personal, family, household, or other nonbusiness purposes See also *consumer goods* (under GOODS)

contemnor. See under CONTEMPT

contemplation of death. See *gift in contemplation of death* (under GIFT)

contempt, *n* **1.** a judicial or legislative finding of willful disobedience of an order, or other willful conduct disrupting the procedures of a court (**contempt of court**) or legislature (e.g., **contempt of Congress**) Unless otherwise specified, "contempt" alone usually means contempt of court The person or entity guilty of contempt is called a **contemnor.** See also CONTUMACIOUS; CONTUMACY. **2. civil contempt,** continuing contempt for which the court imposes a sanction that is to be lifted as soon as the contempt ends. The usual case is refusal to comply with a court order, for which the court places a person in jail or imposes a daily fine with the understanding that the fine or jailing will end as soon as steps are taken to comply with the order. **3. criminal contempt,** contempt that is not continuing, for which a fixed sanction is imposed as a penalty. For example, in a courtroom proceeding a judge may impose an instant fine upon a lawyer who does something in front of the jury that the lawyer was told not to do, or even send a disruptive person directly to jail.

contingency, *n.* **1.** a future event or circumstance that may or may not arise, upon the occurrence of which something else depends See also CONTINGENT **2.** Short for **contingency fee,** also called **contingent fee.** An arrangement under which the amount of an attorney's fee in a civil case will depend upon the outcome of the case, usually being a percentage of the amount recovered: *The law firm took the case on contingency.*

contingent, *adj* uncertain; subject to future events Said of something that will or will not occur, come into existence, or become definite, depending upon circumstances in the future See *contingent* ESTATE¹, INTEREST¹, LIABILITY under those words, and *contingent fee* (under CONTINGENCY). Cf VESTED.

continuance, *n.* an order suspending or postponing a proceeding· *The defendant's new attorney moved for a 30-day continuance to allow her time to become familiar with the case.*

continue, *v.* to grant or order a CONTINUANCE of. *The judge refused to continue the case, and instead ordered the parties to proceed as scheduled*

continuing jurisdiction. See under JURISDICTION¹.

continuing objection. See under OBJECTION.

contraband, *n.* illegal goods; goods that it is illegal to possess, sell, or transport; e g , illegal drugs, smuggled goods

contract, *n.* **1.** broadly, any legally enforceable promise: *A bank's signature on a check that it has certified represents its contract to honor the check when it is presented for payment.* **2.** in its usual sense, an agreement among two or more persons or entities (the parties to the contract; see PARTY) whereby at least one of them promises to do (or not to do) something in exchange for something done or promised by the others Such a contract typically comes into existence when one party accepts (see ACCEPT) another's OFFER, provided that there is CONSIDERATION for the promises in the agreement See also *breach of contract* (under BREACH), *option contract* (under OPTION); QUASI CONTRACT; SUBCONTRACT **3.** a document embodying such an agreement **4. adhesion contract,** a preprinted contract that is not subject to negotiation, offered to a consumer on a "take it or leave it" basis; e.g., an automobile rental agreement or apartment lease Also called **contract of adhesion.** If the terms are extremely oppressive, enforcement may be denied on the ground of UNCONSCIONABILITY. **5. bilateral contract,** a contract in which promises are made on both sides The consideration for each party's promise is the return promise made by the other. Cf. *unilateral contract.* **6. contract under seal,** an old form of contract in which the promise is embodied in a *sealed instrument* (see under SEAL[1]) delivered to the promisee. At common law such a promise was enforceable even if there was no consideration for it. In most states the role of the contract under seal has been modified or eliminated by statute. **7. express contract,** a contract expressed in words, whether spoken **(oral contract)** or reduced to writing **(written contract). 8. implied contract, a.** Also called **contract implied in fact.** a contract manifested by conduct For example, if you sit down in a barber's chair and allow your hair to be cut, it is understood that this amounts to an agreement to pay for the haircut, even though nothing is said about it **b.** Also called **contract implied in law.** a contract-like obligation imposed by law to do justice in a situation where there is no enforceable contract. For example, if a doctor provides necessary care to an unconscious accident victim, the law will "imply" an obligation to pay a reasonable amount for those services, even though the patient obviously never agreed to do so See also QUASI CONTRACT **9. third-party beneficiary contract,** a contract made for the purpose of conferring a benefit on someone other than the parties to the contract (the **third-party beneficiary**). For example, suppose A and B agree that A will plow B's field, in return for which B will permit C to grow his own crops on a portion of the field. If A plows the field but then B refuses to let C plant on it, C, as a third-party beneficiary, has an action against B for breach of the contract even though C was not a party to the contract **10. unilateral contract,** a contract in which there is a promise on only one side, the considera-

,tion for which is not a return promise but the doing of some act For example, an offer of a reward for return of a lost dog is an offer of a unilateral contract if someone who has seen the offer returns the dog, the offeror is contractually obligated to pay the reward Cf *bilateral contract* —*v* **11.** to enter into a contract, make a contractual promise —**contractual,** *adj*

contractor, *n* **1.** a party who contracts to provide goods or services, especially on a large scale **2. general contractor,** a company that undertakes contractual responsibility for completion of a large project, especially a construction project, by hiring and coordinating the work of specialized *subcontractors* (see under SUBCONTRACT) for different facets of the project Also called **prime contractor. 3. government contractor,** a company, or occasionally an individual, hired by the government to furnish goods (such as airplanes or toilet seats for the military) or services (such as construction or consulting) **4. independent contractor,** an individual who contracts to provide services to others but, unlike an employee, retains significant autonomy in deciding how to carry out the work; e g , a plumber, a management consultant, a freelance editor

contribution, *n.* **1.** the principle that when one of several people liable for the same judgment or obligation is called upon to satisfy it, the others may be required to reimburse her ("make contribution") to the extent of their share of the total liability The principle is often applied in tort cases, where it is called **contribution among joint tortfeasors. 2.** a payment or reimbursement under the principle of contribution, or the amount paid, or a claim or cause of action for such reimbursement.

contributory negligence. See under NEGLIGENCE.

controlled substance, a drug whose addicting, intoxicating, or mood-altering qualities have led Congress and state legislatures to make its production, possession, importation, and distribution for all but very limited purposes a crime. Examples include narcotics, amphetamines, barbiturates, tranquilizers, hallucinogens, and marijuana America's traditional addictive and intoxicating recreational substances—tobacco and alcohol—are not included

controversy. See CASE OR CONTROVERSY

contumacious, *adj.* describing behavior that would justify a finding of CONTEMPT, or a person who engages in such behavior. *The lawyer's conduct was contumacious The lawyer was contumacious*

contumacy, *n.* disruptive or disrespectful behavior that would justify a finding of CONTEMPT

conversation. See CRIMINAL CONVERSATION

conversion, *n.* **1.** the tort of intentionally depriving another of the use or benefit of her personal property, as by taking it, seriously damaging it, or exercising control over it One who does this is said to "convert (the property) to his own use " **2.** the exchange of a *convertible security* (see under SECURITY²) for another security in accordance with the terms of the convertible security —**convert,** *v*

convertible security. See under SECURITY²

conveyance, *n.* **1.** a transfer of an interest in property, especially real estate, by means of a deed or other instrument other than a will. **2.** the instrument by which a conveyance is accomplished. **3. voluntary conveyance,** a GRATUITOUS conveyance. —**convey,** *v.*

convict, *v.* to prove or officially declare someone GUILTY of an offense, especially after a trial. —**conviction,** *n.*

cooperative, *n.* **1.** a jointly owned enterprise carrying out purchasing, distribution, management, or other activities on behalf of its members, not for profit but to achieve economies of scale and other benefits of combined rather than individual efforts and resources. A cooperative may be organized as an association (**cooperative association**) or a corporation (**cooperative corporation**). **2.** an apartment building owned by a cooperative corporation whose shareholders are the building's tenants, all of whom lease their apartments from the corporation. Cf. CONDOMINIUM.

copy. See *certified copy* (under CERTIFY); conformed copy; courtesy copy; examined copy.

copyright, *n.* **1.** the exclusive right, granted by federal statute to the creator of a written, musical, artistic, or similar work, to control the reproduction and exploitation of the work for a considerable period of time, usually the life of the author plus 50 years. It is not the ideas and facts in a work that are protected, but the way in which they are expressed. See also ©; FAIR USE; WORK MADE FOR HIRE —*v.* **2.** to take such steps as are necessary to secure or register a copyright. —**copyrightable,** *adj.* —**copyrighted,** *adj.*

coram nobis, *Latin.* (lit "before us," "in our presence") a writ under which a court may review one of its own judgments for errors of fact and, if necessary, change the judgment in light of facts that were not and could not have been known when the judgment was rendered.

corporate, *adj.* **1.** pertaining to a corporation, to corporations generally, or even, in some broad contexts, to business matters generally **2. corporate law,** broadly, the area or type of legal practice that deals with business organizations and transactions rather than personal legal matters; sometimes the term includes corporate LITIGATION, and sometimes it refers only to counseling and assistance with business matters rather than court-related work **3. corporate veil,** the legal distinction between a corporation and its owners; the recognition of a corporation as a distinct legal entity for whose acts and debts its owners (the shareholders) are not personally responsible In rare cases, a court may find that a corporation is essentially a sham or that the corporate form is being used for improper purposes, and will therefore disregard the corporate form (**pierce the corporate veil**) and hold the owner or owners (often a PARENT COMPANY) liable for its debts. See also *corporate* CHARTER¹, INCOME TAX, SEAL¹, SECURITY² under those words.

corporation, *n.* **1.** a legally recognized entity formed by legislative act, or by individuals pursuant to general legislative authorization, with ownership ordinarily represented by shares of stock owned in varying quantities by anywhere from one to millions of stockholders. Corporations are typically characterized by LIMITED LIABILITY of stockholders, separation of ownership and management (in that the stockholders usually have no day-to-day role in management of the company, but merely vote once a year for directors), and treatment for most legal purposes as a distinct entity or "person" separate from its owners. **2. business corporation,** a corporation organized to carry out activities for profit. Also called **for-profit corporation.** Cf. *nonprofit corporation.* **3. close corporation,** a corporation owned by a single shareholder or a small group of shareholders, who typically are all personally active in the business of the corporation or are related to each other, and ordinarily are not allowed to sell their shares to anyone else without approval of the group. Also called **closely held corporation; privately held corporation.** See also *private corporation.* Cf. *publicly held corporation.* **4. domestic corporation, a.** usually, a corporation incorporated in one's own state. **b.** sometimes (e.g., for federal income tax purposes), any corporation incorporated within the United States. Cf. *foreign corporation.* **5. foreign corporation, a.** usually, a corporation incorporated in another state. For example, in a Maryland court or a discussion of Maryland law, a Delaware corporation would be referred to as a "foreign corporation." **b.** sometimes (e.g., for federal income tax purposes), a corporation or similar entity organized under the laws of another country. Cf. *domestic corporation.* **6. nonprofit (or not-for-profit) corporation,** a corporation organized for charitable, religious, educational, cultural, or similar purposes, and not to generate profits for the shareholders. Cf. *business corporation.* **7. nonstock corporation,** a corporation that does not issue stock. **8. parent corporation.** Same as PARENT COMPANY. **9. private corporation, a.** a corporation established for nongovernmental purposes. Cf. *public corporation.* **b.** sometimes, a *close corporation.* **10. professional corporation (P.C.),** a form of business organization allowed to individuals or groups practicing professions such as law or medicine, having some characteristics of corporations but not affording LIMITED LIABILITY to the members. In some states, called **professional association (P.A.). 11. public corporation, a.** a corporation established by legislative act to carry out specified governmental purposes. Cf *private corporation.* **b.** sometimes, short for *publicly held corporation.* **12. publicly held corporation,** a corporation owned by a diverse group of shareholders, with stock freely traded among members of the public. See also *public corporation.* Cf. *close corporation* **13. S corporation,** a small business corporation whose shareholders have elected, under Subchapter S of Chapter 1 of the Internal Revenue Code, to have the corporation's income treated as personal income to them and taxed as part of their personal income taxes, thus avoiding normal corporate income taxes. **14. shell corporation,** a corporation having no business or ongoing activity of its own, and sometimes lacking any substantial assets as well. **15. sister corporations,** corporations that are subsidiaries of the same parent corporation. **16. subsidiary corporation.** Same as SUBSIDIARY. See also *cooperative corporation* (under COOPERATIVE); MUNICIPAL CORPORATION.

corpus, *n. Latin.* (lit. "body") **1.** the property of a trust; all of the assets under administration by a trustee pursuant to a particular trust instrument. See also PRINCIPAL; RES. **2.** any collection of things viewed as a unit.

corpus delicti, *Latin.* (lit. "the body of the crime") the fact that a crime under discussion did occur—that there was in fact a crime. In general, American law does not allow a person to be convicted of a crime solely on the basis of his own confession, absent some independent evidence of the corpus delicti, that is, some evidence that the crime for which he claims responsibility actually happened.

corroborate, *v.* to provide support or confirmation from an independent source for testimony or other evidence already introduced; to back up independently —**corroborating, corroborative,** *adj.*

costs, *n.* **1.** filing fees and certain other expenses necessarily incurred in pursuing or defending a civil case The losing party is usually required to pay the winner's costs Since "costs" does not include attorneys' fees, this is often a rather insignificant amount. Also called **court costs. 2. costs to abide the event,** a phrase appearing in appellate decisions indicating that a decision on which party must pay the other's costs must await the outcome of further proceedings, usually a new trial.

counsel, *n.* **1.** a lawyer or lawyers, particularly in the role of advisor to or representative of a particular client: *Upon the advice of counsel, he cancelled the interview.* **2.** a collective term for the lawyers representing parties in a case or present for a proceeding: *Copies of the scheduling order were sent to all counsel. Will counsel please approach the bench?* **3. assigned counsel,** counsel appointed by a court to represent a criminal defendant who cannot afford to hire a lawyer See also RIGHT TO COUNSEL. **4. general counsel,** a company's chief legal officer. **5. house counsel, a.** a company's regular lawyer or law firm **b.** Also called **in-house counsel.** a lawyer or lawyers who are employees of a company and do legal work only for that company. **6. independent counsel,** counsel hired or appointed to handle a matter because the lawyers who would normally do so have a CONFLICT OF INTEREST. **7. local counsel,** an attorney admitted to practice in the court in which a case is pending, who assists an attorney not so admitted (usually from out of state) in representing a client in the proceeding. See also PRO HAC VICE. **8. outside counsel,** any counsel performing services for a company other than *in-house counsel.* **9. special counsel,** counsel hired or appointed to assist in a matter because of special expertise, or to act as *independent counsel.* **10. standby coun-**

sel, counsel appointed by a court to stand by and lend such assistance as she can to a criminal defendant who insists on representing himself, and to take over the representation if the defendant changes his mind. See also OF COUNSEL

counselor, *n.* a lawyer. The word is used only in two contexts (a) in letterheads, usually in the form **counselor at law** or the plural **counselors at law.** The British spelling **counsellor** is also seen. (b) as a form of oral address in a judicial proceeding: *Counselor, please sit down.* For the plural, only COUNSEL is used in this context, never "counselors."

count, *n.* each of several distinct claims or causes of action in a civil complaint, or charges in a criminal information or indictment.

counterclaim, *n.* **1.** a CAUSE OF ACTION or *claim for relief* (see under CLAIM) asserted by a defendant against the plaintiff in a civil case. It is asserted in the ANSWER to the complaint. **2. compulsory counterclaim,** any claim that the defendant has against the plaintiff arising out of the same events that are the subject of the plaintiff's complaint. As a general rule, failure to assert such a counterclaim constitutes a waiver of it. **3. permissive counterclaim,** any other claim that the defendant has against the plaintiff, regardless of what it relates to. The defendant may assert such a claim as a counterclaim or hold it for a separate action, as she chooses.

counteroffer, *n.* a response to an OFFER of a contract that does not accept the offer as stated, but instead proposes different terms.

course of business. See ORDINARY COURSE OF BUSINESS

course of dealing, a sequence of previous dealings between the parties to a particular transaction, to which courts will refer, in the event of a dispute about the latest transaction, as evidence of how the parties intended it to be carried out. Cf. COURSE OF PERFORMANCE; USAGE

course of performance, the carrying out of some recurring contractual obligation, such as the making of installment payments, in substantially the same way several times without objection from the other party to the contract. In the event of a dispute over a subsequent performance of that obligation, the previously established course of performance will normally be taken by the court as showing how the parties intended that step to be performed. Cf. COURSE OF DEALING; USAGE.

court, *n.* **1.** an institution of government whose function is to interpret and apply the law to specific cases within its jurisdiction. Within a judicial system, a court is referred to as a **lower court** or **higher court** in relation to others, as determined by the fact that decisions of the lower courts are subject to review by those above, and decisions of the higher courts are binding upon those below. In the basic three-tier judicial system of the United States and most states, the first level is primarily a trial court and the next two are primarily or exclusively appellate courts; the middle level is thus the lowest appellate court for most cases, but is usually referred to as the **intermediate appellate court.** See also CHANCERY; *court below* (under BELOW); INFERIOR COURT; INTERNATIONAL COURT OF JUSTICE; KANGAROO COURT; STAR CHAMBER; SMALL CLAIMS COURT; SUPERIOR COURT; SUPREME COURT; UNITED STATES COURT OF APPEALS; UNITED STATES DISTRICT COURT **2.** the judges, collectively, of a court **3.** the judge or panel of judges sitting on a particular case **4.** (*cap.*) **a.** a particular court, especially the Supreme Court of the United States or the court in which a specific case is pending. **b.** a form of address commonly used in addressing or referring to the judge or panel of judges in a case. *May it please the Court .. As the Court will recall...* **5. court of law** or **court of record,** phrases that formerly had specialized meanings but now are rather formal ways of referring to almost any court, especially a trial court.

court clerk. See under CLERK.

court costs. Same as COSTS.

court-martial, *n.* **1.** a military court; a court of military personnel convened to try a member of the military for an offense against military law **2.** a trial or conviction in or by such a court —*v.* **3.** to charge, try, or convict a person in such a court

court reporter, a person who makes a word-for-word record of what is said in a trial or similar proceeding, and if requested (and paid) by the litigants, produces a typed or printed transcript.

court rules. See under RULE.

courtesy copy, an extra copy of a motion, brief, or other document being filed in a case, delivered directly to the judge's chambers "as a courtesy." Some judges find the extra copy so convenient that they require it; some find the extra paper such a nuisance that they forbid it.

covenant, *n.* **1.** a legally enforceable promise, especially a promise that a particular state of affairs will be maintained during the term of a contract or that certain actions will or will not be taken with respect to land **2.** a WARRANTY, especially in connection with a transfer of land **3. covenant not to compete,** a promise in an employment contract or contract for the sale of a business, that the employee or seller will not subsequently go into competition with the employer or buyer. Such covenants are enforceable only if limited in duration and geographic scope. **4. covenant not to sue,** in an agreement settling a claim, dispute, or lawsuit, a promise not to pursue the matter in court. **5. covenant running with the land,** a promise with respect to land that survives transfers of the land; it is binding on and enforceable by subsequent owners. Also called **running covenant. 6. covenants** (or **warranties**) **of title,** a set of covenants, including the *covenant of quiet enjoyment* or *covenant of warranty* (see under QUIET ENJOYMENT), usually insisted upon by a buyer of real estate as assurance that she will receive good and unencumbered title to the property. Often referred to in negotiations as the

usual covenants. Cf *warranty of title* (under **WARRANTY**) **7. restrictive covenant, a.** a covenant limiting the use or disposition that an owner may make of land. A covenant forbidding transfer of property to anyone of a particular race or ethnic group **(racially restrictive covenant)** was formerly a tool for maintaining segregated housing; such covenants are no longer enforceable. **b.** Another term for *covenant not to compete.*

covenantee, *n.* one to whom a covenant is made or who has a right to enforce it.

covenantor, *n.* one who makes or is bound by a covenant.

cover, *v.* **1.** (of a buyer of goods) to buy substitute goods from another source when a seller under contract to provide certain goods fails to make delivery If the reasonable cost of "cover" exceeds the original contract price, the buyer may recover the difference from the original seller as part of the damages for breach of the contract **2.** (of an insurer or insurance policy) to protect a certain person or protect against a certain risk: *My health insurance policy covers my children but does not cover cosmetic surgery* —*n.* **3.** the purchase of substitute goods elsewhere when a seller fails to deliver as promised

craft union. See under **UNION**

credible, *adj.* worthy of belief· *credible testimony, credible evidence; a credible witness; a credible defense* —**credibility,** *n.*

credit, *n.* **1.** trust in the ability and intention of a person or entity to repay a loan or to pay for goods or services provided without immediate payment, or the quality of a person or entity that inspires such trust: *to extend credit to a purchaser; to make a purchase on credit.* **2.** the amount of money loaned or made available, or of payments deferred or that a vendor is willing to defer, by reason of such credit: *We have used $1,500 of credit on our credit card and have $500 of credit left for additional purchases.* **3.** a reduction in an amount owed, by reason of a payment or correction or for some other reason. See also **TAX CREDIT. 4.** respect; deference. See also **FULL FAITH AND CREDIT.** —*v.* **5.** to believe *The jury credited the witness's testimony on the issue of self-defense.*

creditor, *n.* **1.** a person to whom money is owed. Cf **DEBTOR. 2. judgment creditor,** a person who obtained a money judgment in a civil case which has not yet been fully paid. See also *secured creditor* (under **SECURE**).

crime, *n.* **1.** an act or omission contrary to laws established for the welfare of the public at large, for which the law provides a punishment. Especially, an act or omission punishable by a sentence of incarceration; a **FELONY** or **MISDEMEANOR**. See also **INFRACTION; OFFENSE; VIOLATION. 2. common law crime,** an offense that was a crime at common law, before criminal laws were generally written into statutes. Most acts that were crimes at common law are also crimes under modern statutes Because of the constitutional problem of vagueness (see **VAGUE**), it is doubtful that any common law crime not embodied in a statute could now be enforced. **3. statutory crime, a.** an act that was not a crime at common law, but has been made a crime by statute. **b.** broadly, any crime defined by statute, whether or not it was a crime at common law. See also *crime against nature* (under UNNATURAL ACT); HATE CRIME; HIGH CRIMES AND MISDEMEANORS; VICTIMLESS CRIME; WHITE-COLLAR CRIME.

criminal, *adj.* **1.** constituting an offense or an element of an offense. See CRIMINAL CONVERSATION, and *criminal* CONTEMPT, HOMICIDE, NEGLIGENCE, TRESPASS under those words. **2.** pertaining to crime and criminal law· *criminal case; criminal law.* See also *criminal* ACTION, LIABILITY, PROCEDURE, PROSECUTION under those words. —*n.* **3.** a person who commits a crime.

criminal conversation, the tort of engaging in sexual intercourse with another person's spouse Like many legal concepts having their origin in the concept of wife as chattel, this tort has been abolished in many states. Cf. ADULTERY.

criminalist, *n* a specialist in the collection and scientific analysis of physical evidence of crimes (**criminalistics**).

criminally negligent homicide. See under HOMICIDE

criminologist, *n.* a person engaged in the sociological study of crime and criminals (**criminology**).

cross, *Informal.* —*n.* **1.** Same as *cross examination* (see under EXAMINATION). —*v.* **2.** Same as *cross-examine* (see under EXAMINE).

cross-appeal, *n.* **1.** an appeal filed by the appellee in a case in which an appeal has already been filed, challenging the same judgment that is the subject of the first appeal but on a different ground For example, a losing defendant might appeal a decision on the ground that the damage award was too high, then the plaintiff might cross-appeal on the ground that the damage award was too low —*v.* **2.** to file a cross-appeal.

cross-claim, *n.* in a civil action against two or more defendants, a CLAIM or CAUSE OF ACTION asserted by one of the defendants against one or more of the other defendants For example, in a tort case against several people alleged to have harmed the plaintiff jointly, the defendants often assert cross-claims against each other, each claiming a right of CONTRIBUTION from the others In rare cases, a cross-claim might be asserted by one plaintiff against another in the same case.

cross-complaint, *n.* the pleading in which one asserts a CROSS-CLAIM.

cross examination. See under EXAMINATION

cross-examine. See under EXAMINE

cruel and unusual punishment, punishment of a person convicted of a crime in a manner that fails to meet minimal contemporary standards of decency, or that is grossly disproportionate to the crime The Eighth Amendment (see Appendix) forbids such punishments.

cruelty, *n.* a traditional ground for divorce, consisting of a pattern of physical or psychological abuse by one spouse rendering married life intolerable for the other The level of abuse that a married woman was formerly expected to tolerate from her husband is illustrated by the names given to this ground for divorce ("cruelty," "extreme cruelty," "cruel and inhuman treatment," and the like), and the fact that a single instance of cruelty was normally not considered sufficient to entitle one to a divorce

culpable, *adj.* blameworthy; meriting imposition of liability or punishment. —**culpability,** *n.*

cumulative evidence. See under EVIDENCE.

cumulative sentences. See under SENTENCE.

cumulative zoning. See under ZONING.

curative instruction. See under INSTRUCTION.

custodial interrogation. See under INTERROGATION.

custody, *n.* **1.** immediate possession and control over a thing, with responsibility for its care **2.** any significant restraint on a person's freedom of action imposed by law enforcement authorities **3.** Also called **child custody.** the right and responsibility of determining the residence, care, and education of a minor child. **4. joint custody,** an arrangement whereby divorced parents continue to share responsibility for raising their children **5. sole custody,** custody of a child by one adult only. This is the most common arrangement for custody of a child following divorce of the parents

custom, *n.* **1.** in older law, a traditional business practice of such ancient origin and universal application as to have acquired the status of a legal requirement. **2.** Also called **custom and usage.** in modern contexts, same as USAGE

customs, *n.* **1.** taxes imposed by the federal government on goods imported into or exported from the country. Also called **duties,** except that "duties" has a singular form (see DUTY) but "customs" does not. **2.** the agency or procedure by which, or the place where, such taxes are collected.

cy pres, *Law French* (lit "as near") the doctrine under which a court confronted with a deed or will whose terms cannot be carried out exactly may modify it so as to carry out the intent of the maker as nearly as possible, especially in the case of charitable bequests and trusts

D

damages, *n.pl.* **1.** a sum of money asked for by a plaintiff or awarded by a court in a civil action, to be paid by the defendant because of the wrong that gave rise to the suit An action seeking an award of damages is called a **damage action. 2.** sometimes, the injuries for which the plaintiff seeks an award of damages **3. compensatory damages,** damages awarded to compensate for the harm resulting from the defendant's wrong, including actual financial loss and intangible harm such as pain and suffering These are the damages to which a plaintiff is normally entitled upon proving her case Also called **actual damages.** For some purposes, compensatory damages are subdivided into **general damages,** which compensate for losses of a sort that would normally be expected to follow from the nature of the wrong, and **special** (or **consequential**) **damages,** which arise from the unique circumstances of the case **4. liquidated damages,** damages for breach of contract in an amount stated in the contract, where the parties agreed at the time of contracting on a reasonable figure or formula for determination of the compensation to be paid in the event of a breach Also called **stipulated damages.** Unlike the payment provided for in a *penalty clause* (see under PENALTY), agreements for payment of liquidated damages are normally enforceable **5. nominal damages,** an award of a token amount, such as $1 00, indicating that the defendant did do the wrong alleged but that no significant measure of damages was established by the plaintiff. In certain kinds of DEFAMATION action, such an award can be made to vindicate the honor of the plaintiff. **6. punitive damages,** damages awarded in excess of actual damages in tort cases in which the defendant's conduct is deemed especially egregious Punitive damages are awarded to punish the defendant, discourage repetition of such conduct, and set an example for others who might be tempted to engage in similar conduct Also called **exemplary damages. 7. speculative damages,** claimed damages for injury or loss that may occur in the future but cannot be predicted or evaluated on any reasonable basis. Speculative damages are not allowed **8. treble damages,** damages in an amount equal to three times the *actual damages,* awarded in cases under certain statutes specifically providing for such an award, notably the ANTITRUST laws and the RACKETEER INFLUENCED AND CORRUPT ORGANIZATIONS ACT

dangerous weapon. See under WEAPON

date rape. See under RAPE

de facto, *Latin* (lit "arising from that which has been done") existing in fact, without regard to legal requirements or formalities; said of things that came into being without legal blessing, but that the law chooses to take cognizance of for practical reasons: *de facto segregation; the de facto government of a foreign country* Cf. DE JURE.

de jure, *Latin.* (lit "arising from law") existing by reason of law; brought into existence and maintained in accordance with legal requirements and formalities Sometimes the existence is more theoretical than real, as in the case of a *de jure government* that has been ousted by war or revolution; sometimes it is all too real, as in the case of *de jure segregation* in the old South. Cf. DE FACTO

de minimis, *Latin.* (lit. "concerning trifles") insignificant; too small to merit attention: *The plaintiff suffered only de minimis damages. The chilling effect on speech, if any, is de minimis.* The phrase comes from the maxim **de minimis non curat lex** ("the law does not concern itself with trifles").

de novo, *Latin.* (lit "anew") from the beginning; all over again. See *de novo review* (under REVIEW); *de novo trial* (under TRIAL).

deadly weapon. See under WEAPON.

dealer, *n.* a person who buys and resells things as a business. See also BROKER-DEALER

death. See BRAIN DEATH.

death penalty. Same as CAPITAL PUNISHMENT

death warrant. See under WARRANT[1]

deathbed declaration. See under DECLARATION.

debenture, *n.* a corporate debt obligation, usually a long-term bond or note, that is not secured or guaranteed, but depends solely upon the company's continued financial well-being for payment.

debt, *n.* **1.** an unconditional obligation to pay a sum of money, either at present or in the future **2. bad debt,** a debt owed to a taxpayer that the taxpayer will be completely unable to collect The taxpayer usually may deduct all or part of a bad debt for income tax purposes in the year in which the debt becomes worthless

debt security. See under SECURITY[2]

debtor, *n.* **1.** a person who owes money Cf CREDITOR. **2.** a person or entity that is the subject of a bankruptcy action **3. debtor in possession,** a debtor in bankruptcy who is allowed to continue to control his business during REORGANIZATION **4. judgment debtor,** a person who owes money pursuant to a judgment entered against him in a civil case **5. principal debtor.** See under PRINCIPAL

decedent, *n.* a person who has died This is the term used in the law of trusts, wills, intestate succession, administration of estates, and the like; in a murder case or wrongful death action, "deceased" would be the more common term. See also *decedent's estate* (under ESTATE[2])

deceit, *n.* an older, but still often used, term for FRAUD

decision, *n* **1.** the determination of a court, jury, or administrative tribunal on how a case should come out **2.** a judicial or administrative OPINION

decisional law. Same as CASE LAW

declarant, *n.* the person who makes a DECLARATION; particularly, in discussions of the *hearsay rule* (see under HEARSAY), the maker of an out-of-court statement whose admissibility is under discussion.

declaration, *n.* **1.** an oral or written assertion; a statement. **2.** a formal announcement: *Declaration of Independence; declaration of war.* **3.** a word used in some jurisdictions for AFFIRMATION (def. 2). **4.** an old word for the initial pleading in a case at law; now called a COMPLAINT. **5. declaration against interest,** a statement that is so strongly contrary to the interests of the declarant at the time it is made that a reasonable person in the declarant's position would not have made it unless he believed it to be true; e.g., "I owe her $1,000," "I shouldn't have been driving so fast " Such statements are generally admissible under an exception to the *hearsay rule* (see under HEARSAY). **6. declaration of trust,** a document in which a property owner declares that she holds the property in trust for the benefit of someone else, thereby creating a TRUST with herself as trustee. Cf. DEED OF TRUST. **7. dying** (or **deathbed**) **declaration,** a statement made in the belief that one is about to die, particularly about the circumstances of the impending death; e g., "Joe shot me." Such statements are often admitted into evidence as an exception to the *hearsay rule* (see under HEARSAY), on the quaint assumption that no one would dare "go to his death with a lie upon his lips." **8. spontaneous declaration.** Same as EXCITED UTTERANCE

declaratory judgment. See under JUDGMENT.

decree, *n.* **1.** a JUDGMENT Before the MERGER OF LAW AND EQUITY, the final order disposing of a case was called a "judgment" at law but a "decree" in equity Now "judgment" is the usual term for most cases, but "decree" is often used as a synonym and is the usual term in certain contexts. *bankruptcy decree, divorce decree.* **2. consent decree,** a court order entered by agreement between a federal agency and a party accused of illegal conduct in the field regulated by the agency, resolving the case and typically including a promise by the party not to engage in certain activities in the future —*v.* **3.** to ORDER or ADJUDGE.

decriminalize, *v.* to repeal a criminal law or otherwise make conduct that previously was a crime no longer a crime; sometimes distinguished from LEGALIZE in that conduct that has been "legalized" might still be subject to extensive special regulation, whereas conduct that has been "decriminalized" would be regulated primarily by the general laws applicable to all conduct For example, to "legalize" prostitution might mean to require prostitutes to have special licenses and practice in specific areas; to "decriminalize" prostitution might mean to remove the government from involvement with exchanges of money for sex except for enforcement of general rules regarding fraud, public decency, exploitation of minors, and the like

dedication, *n.* a gift or abandonment of an interest in land, in a copyrightable work, or in some other property, by the owner or creator to a governmental entity or to the public at large

deductible, *adj.* **1.** qualifying as a DEDUCTION for income tax purposes: *a deductible contribution to charity; a deductible trip to a business conference in Hawaii.* —*n.* **2.** the amount for which the insured is liable on covered losses before the insurance company must begin paying under a policy *a medical insurance policy with a $500 annual deductible.*

deduction, *n.* **1.** a portion of income or an item of expense that a taxpayer may subtract from income for purposes of calculating income tax Cf TAX CREDIT. **2. itemized deduction,** any of a number of specific types of expense that must be specifically listed on a tax return to be claimed as deductions; e.g., medical expenses, mortgage interest. **3. standard deduction,** a fixed amount that may be claimed as a deduction instead of claiming separate itemized deductions.

deed, *n.* **1.** a formal instrument by which a living person or an entity conveys an interest in property, especially real property. **2. quitclaim deed,** a deed conveying to someone else whatever interest one has in a piece of real property, without any promise that the title one is purporting to convey is any good Typically used for gifts of property. **3. warranty deed,** a deed conveying title to real property and containing *covenants of title* (see under COVENANT), making the grantor liable to the grantee for losses caused by undisclosed defects in the title. —*v.* **4.** to convey property by deed

deed of trust, 1. an instrument by which the owner of certain property conveys it to another to be held in trust for the benefit of someone, thereby creating a TRUST with the person receiving the property as trustee Cf *declaration of trust* (under DECLARATION) **2.** specifically, in some states, a deed conveying title to real property to a trustee to hold as security until the transferor repays a loan; similar to a MORTGAGE except that the mortgage is given directly to the creditor to hold Also called **trust deed**.

defalcation, *n.* **1.** misuse, misappropriation, or loss of funds over which one has fiduciary responsibility as a trustee, a corporate or public official, or the like. **2.** the sum taken or lost.

defamation, *n.* the communication to a third person of a falsehood that is injurious to the reputation of a living individual, or of a corporation or other organization. Defamation is the basis for the torts of libel (see LIBEL[1]) and SLANDER —**defamatory,** *adj.* —**defame,** *v.*

default, *n.* **1.** failure to fulfill a legal obligation, such as performing a contract, paying a debt, or responding to a properly served summons. —*v* **2.** to fail to perform a legal obligation

default judgment. See under JUDGMENT

defeasance, *n* the termination or nullification of a fee interest in real property See *fee simple defeasible* (under FEE[1]).

defeasible fee. Same as *fee simple defeasible* (see under FEE[1]).

defeat, *v.* to cause to be void or ineffective; to bar· *The original owner's title was defeated by adverse possession The statute of frauds defeats the plaintiff's contract claim.*

defect, *n.* **1.** a flaw in design or manufacture that renders a product ineffective or dangerous **2.** a circumstance that defeats a legal transaction, claim, or right See also *defective title* (under TITLE) —**defective,** *adj.*

defendant, *n.* **1.** the person against whom a lawsuit is brought. **2.** a person against whom a criminal COMPLAINT or other charging instrument has been filed with a court in a criminal case

defendant in error, the APPELLEE in a case where the appeal is commenced by *writ of error* (see under WRIT).

defense, *n.* **1.** the facts and legal theories relied upon, or the evidence and argument presented, in opposition to a civil claim or criminal charge **2.** a legal justification for conduct that otherwise appears to be wrongful, or a legal principle that renders one immune from liability for wrongful conduct: *the defense of duress; the defense of statute of limitations.* See also TWINKIE DEFENSE. **3.** the defendant and attorneys representing the defendant in a case. **4. affirmative defense,** a defense that, rather than simply showing that a claim or charge is untrue or arguing that it is legally insufficient, presents additional facts to defeat the claim or charge For example, the defense of RES JUDICATA in a civil case; the INSANITY DEFENSE in a criminal case; or the defense that one was acting in SELF-DEFENSE in a tort case or criminal case In most situations the defendant who relies upon such a defense has the *burden of pleading* and *burden of proof* (see under BURDEN[1]) regarding the facts necessary to establish it. **5. equitable defense,** in a civil suit, a defense based upon principles that originated in courts of EQUITY; e.g , *fraud in the inducement* (see under FRAUD) or UNCLEAN HANDS

deficiency judgment. See under JUDGMENT.

defined-benefit plan. See under PENSION PLAN.

defined-contribution plan. See under PENSION PLAN

definite failure of issue. See under ISSUE[2]

defraud, *v.* to obtain money or property from a person by FRAUD.

degree, *n.* the GRADE of an offense

degree of care. Same as STANDARD OF CARE

degree of proof. Same as STANDARD OF PROOF

dehors, *prep. Law French.* outside; beyond the scope of· *facts dehors the record; evidence dehors the contract*

delegated power. See under POWER

delict, *n.* a civil or criminal wrong, especially a tort

delinquent, *n.* Same as *juvenile delinquent* (see under JUVENILE)

delivery, *n* the voluntary transfer of possession of property, or handing over of a piece of paper with intent thereby to consummate a legal transaction For example, a conveyance of land by DEED normally requires delivery of the deed Delivery may be ACTUAL or CONSTRUCTIVE; see discussion under CONSTRUCTIVE. See also GIFT, *personal service* (under SERVICE)

demand, *n.* **1.** a call for someone to perform a legal obligation. **2.** a request for payment of a check or other instrument for the payment of money **3.** an assertion of legal right in a complaint or lawsuit **4. demand deposit,** money deposited with a bank which can be withdrawn at any time. An ordinary checking or savings account is a demand deposit Cf *time deposit* (under TIME) **5. demand for relief.** Same as PRAYER FOR RELIEF **6. demand letter,** a letter making a formal demand for payment of money owed, or for satisfaction of some other legal obligation. A demand letter is sent partly to lay the groundwork for a lawsuit, and partly in the hope that the recipient will perform as requested or work out a settlement so that a suit will not be necessary **7. due demand,** demand that must be made before it can be said that a party has failed to perform a legal obligation. Usually this is made by means of a *demand letter.* For example, before suing to evict a tenant for nonpayment of rent, a landlord normally must make a formal demand for payment. Complaints seeking performance of a contract or remedy for breach typically recite that the defendant failed to perform "despite due demand," "due demand having been made," or the like **8. on demand,** upon request; whenever requested A negotiable instrument that does not specify a time for payment, such as a check, is **payable on demand,** and is referred to as a **demand instrument, demand note,** or the like Cf. TIME.

demise, *n.* **1.** the transfer of an estate in land, especially one for a limited time, particularly by lease or by will or intestacy. **2.** death. —*v.* **3.** to bring about a demise of real property, especially by renting out the property *The tenant is required to maintain the demised premises*

demonstrative evidence. See under EVIDENCE.

demur, *v.* **1.** to file a DEMURRER **2.** broadly, to raise any objection to a claim or procedure, especially on the ground that it is legally irrelevant or insufficient.

demurrer, *n.* a motion or pleading in response to a complaint or counterclaim, taking the position that the facts alleged, even if true, would not entitle the claimant to relief on any theory of law In most American jurisdictions the demurrer has been replaced by the motion to dismiss for failure to state a claim (see discussion under CLAIM), but "demurrer" is sometimes used as an informal term for such a motion.

deny, *v.* **1.** to assert, in response to a complaint, counterclaim, or *request for admissions* (see under ADMISSION), that a particular allegation is untrue, or that the party responding lacks sufficient knowledge or information to form a belief as to its truth or falsity. All allegations not denied in one of these manners are deemed admitted and, absent special circumstances, can no longer be contested in the case. **2.** (of a court) to refuse to grant a motion, petition, or other request for judicial action. Opposite of GRANT —**denial,** *n.*

dependent, *n.* an individual who depends upon another for financial support For income tax purposes, a taxpayer may claim an EXEMPTION for each dependent who meets certain tests, including receiving over half of his support from the taxpayer and either being a close relative of the taxpayer or living as a member of the taxpayer's household.

deponent, *n* a person who makes a written statement or gives testimony under oath or affirmation, especially the witness in a DEPOSITION.

deportation, *n.* the expulsion of an ALIEN from the country. DUE PROCESS requires that a person believed to be subject to deportation be allowed a hearing before an impartial tribunal before being deported

depose, *v.* **1.** to give a sworn statement or testimony **2.** to say under oath or affirmation **3.** to ask questions of the deponent in a deposition; also referred to as "taking the deposition": *The lead attorney for the defense will depose the plaintiff.*

deposit. See CERTIFICATE OF DEPOSIT; *demand deposit* (under DEMAND); *time deposit* (under TIME).

deposition, *n* **1.** a DISCOVERY procedure in which a witness testifies under oath in response to questions from the lawyer for one of the parties to a case It is usually conducted much like a regular courtroom proceeding, complete with a court reporter and cross examination by the opposing lawyer, but it normally takes place outside the courtroom and without a judge present The purpose is partly to discover information and partly to have the testimony available on record in case the witness is no longer available when the trial is finally held **2.** the testimony, or the transcript of the testimony, given at a deposition. **3. deposition in aid of execution,** a posttrial deposition of a party against whom a money judgment has been entered, for the purpose of identifying assets that could be seized to satisfy the judgment

depreciation, *n* **1.** the gradual decrease in the value of tangible property that occurs because of wear and tear and obsolescence **2.** a DEDUCTION allowed for income tax purposes because of depreciation in the value of property used in business or held for production of income. Ordinarily, a portion of the original cost of the property may be deducted each year for a number of years, until all or most of the original cost has been deducted.

derivative action. See under ACTION.

derogation, *n.* limitation on the scope of something; partial repeal. Statutes on subjects that traditionally were governed by common law are said to be "in derogation of the common law"

descend, *v.* **1.** (of property of a decedent, especially real property) to pass to one's heirs by INTESTATE SUCCESSION. **2.** loosely, to pass by intestate succession or by will, especially if the person who takes by will is a child or other relative who would have received property by intestate succession if there had been no will —**descent,** *n.*

descent and distribution, 1. the principles by which the property of a person who dies without a will is distributed Also called INTESTATE SUCCESSION. **2.** broadly, the principles by which the property of a decedent is distributed, whether by intestate succession or by will See also DISTRIBUTION.

desertion, *n.* **1.** the breaking off of marital cohabitation, unprovoked by any wrongdoing by one's spouse, with the intent not to return and not to fulfill marital responsibilities Desertion is one of the traditional grounds for divorce **2.** the military crime of abandoning one's post to avoid danger or of leaving one's unit with the intent of staying away permanently

desuetude, *n* the state of being no longer used or enforced Statutes that have not been enforced for a great many years, or that linger on the books even though the subject they address or the reason for their enactment no longer exists, are said to have "fallen into desuetude " Nevertheless, if they are on the books and circumstances arise to which they are applicable, they can be enforced See the case discussed under SODOMY

detain, *v* **1.** to keep a person in CUSTODY for a limited time for an official purpose. *detain for questioning.* See also PREVENTIVE DETENTION **2.** to retain possession of another's property —**detention,** *n*

detainer, *n* **1.** a WRIT calling for continued detention of a person about to be released from custody, as when a prisoner is wanted for another crime **2.** Also called **unlawful detainer.** Wrongfully retaining possession of property of another, as by refusing to vacate an apartment upon expiration of the lease **3.** any detention of person or property (See DETAIN)

detention, *n* See under DETAIN See also PREVENTIVE DETENTION

determinable, *adj.* See *fee simple determinable* (under FEE[1])

determinate sentence. See under SENTENCE.

determine, *v.* **1.** to reach a DECISION on a matter See also *hear and determine* (under HEAR) **2.** (of an interest in real property) to terminate; come to an end; expire

detrimental reliance. See under RELIANCE.

devise, *v.* **1.** to dispose of real property by will Cf BEQUEATH, GRANT —*n.* **2.** a gift of real property by will, or the property interest so given. Cf. BEQUEST Note that although the very influential Uniform Probate Code uses *devise* in reference to personal as well as real property, that broader usage does not appear to have caught on among practicing lawyers generally

devisee, *n* the recipient of a DEVISE Cf LEGATEE

devisor, *n* one who makes a DEVISE

devolve, *v.* to pass from one person to another, especially BY OPERATION OF LAW· *Upon President Lincoln's death,* the Presidency devolved on Vice President Johnson When the corporations merged, their debts devolved upon the successor corporation. —**devolution,** n

dictum, n., pl. **dicta.** Latin. (lit "a remark") short for OB- ITER DICTUM; a legal assertion in a court's opinion that is peripheral to its main argument and unnecessary to the actual HOLDING Because it may not have received the court's fullest consideration, dictum is regarded as less persuasive in a precedent than a fully considered holding Note that "dictum" is used to refer either to a single such assertion or to a number of them collectively, "dicta" can properly be used only if two or more discrete passages are being referred to: In support of its position, plaintiff cites only dictum. The defendant points to several dicta in older cases, but we find them unpersuasive

digest, n a book or series of volumes in which HEADNOTES or other summaries of the holdings of cases are collected and arranged by subject matter for ease of reference by lawyers or others doing legal research

diligence, n. serious and persistent attention and effort In many contexts the law requires people to exercise dili- gence in regard to a matter in order to preserve their rights or avoid liability. —**diligent,** adj

diminished capacity (or **responsibility**), mental retar- dation or other mental condition, sometimes including in- toxication, that is not the kind or degree of impairment necessary to establish the INSANITY DEFENSE, but that calls into question whether a defendant could have had the nec- essary STATE OF MIND to commit a particular crime In some jurisdictions this may be considered as a factor reducing the degree of the crime for which a defendant may be con- victed

diplomatic immunity. See under IMMUNITY

direct¹, adj **1.** proximate; straightforward; without inter- vening events. Often distinguished from collateral; for ex- ample, a **direct attack** on a judgment is one made in the same case, as by an appeal or motion for a new trial, and a **direct heir** is a direct descendent or ancestor (compare collateral attack and collateral heir, under COLLATERAL²) See also direct examination vs cross examination (under EXAM- INATION); direct evidence vs. circumstantial evidence (under EVIDENCE). —n. **2.** Short for direct examination (see under EXAMINATION).

direct², v. (of a judge or court) to instruct or order some- one to do something; a gentle way of saying "order": The jury is directed to disregard the answer. The plaintiff is di- rected to produce the documents requested by the de- fendant forthwith. Would Your Honor please direct the wit- ness to answer the question? In such contexts, "direct" is interchangeable with INSTRUCT. See also directed verdict (under VERDICT). —**direction,** n.

director, n. one of the persons elected by the stockhold- ers of a corporation to manage its affairs. The directors to- gether constitute the BOARD OF DIRECTORS Cf. OFFICER.

disability, n. **1.** for purposes of insurance, unemployment compensation, social security, and the like, a disease or injury that renders one unable to perform one's usual occupation, or a physical or mental condition making it impossible to engage in any substantial gainful employment. **2.** for purposes of the federal law against DISABILITY DISCRIMINATION, a physical or mental impairment that substantially limits one or more of the major life activities of an individual. **3.** Also called **legal disability.** Same as INCAPACITY.

disability discrimination, discrimination against, or failure to provide reasonable accommodation for, people with disabilities or people who have been disabled or are perceived as being disabled, in such areas as employment, public accommodations, transportation, and communications Such discrimination is prohibited by the federal Americans with Disabilities Act of 1990.

disbar, *v.* to take away an attorney's right to practice law, usually for criminal or unethical conduct

discharge, *v.* **1.** to release a person from an obligation, or to satisfy or extinguish an obligation —*n.* **2.** the release of a person from an obligation or the satisfaction or extinguishment of an obligation. **3. discharge in bankruptcy,** the discharge of all or most of a bankrupt's remaining debts at the conclusion of a BANKRUPTCY proceeding.

disclaim, *v.* **1.** to renounce or disavow a right, interest, or claim. **2.** to renounce or disavow a duty or liability. —**disclaimer,** *n.*

disclosure. See under DISCOVERY

discontinuance, *n.* DISMISSAL of a suit, especially *voluntary dismissal* (see under DISMISSAL), which is also called **voluntary discontinuance. —discontinue,** *v.*

discovery, *n.* the set of procedures by which each side in a case may obtain pertinent information from the other. The most common discovery techniques are the DEPOSITION, *interrogatories* (see under INTERROGATORY), and PRODUCTION OF DOCUMENTS Modern practice permits liberal discovery in order to prevent TRIAL BY AMBUSH. Discovery is primarily of use in the period leading up to the trial, and thus is often referred to as **pretrial discovery;** but in some situations it is also conducted during or even after a trial. In some jurisdictions discovery is usually referred to as **disclosure,** which is just the same thing from the point of view of the giver of the information rather than the receiver. Information, documents, or other things that may be obtained through discovery are said to be **discoverable.** See also FISHING EXPEDITION

discredit, *v.* to introduce evidence, by cross examination or otherwise, casting doubt upon the believability of a witness or authenticity of a document

discretion, *n.* **1.** the power to exercise one's own judgment in a matter and choose among various options in dealing with it **2. absolute discretion,** theoretically unlimited discretion, so that any choice among available options, however unreasonable it might appear, would be immune from challenge. For example, a will might give the executor "absolute discretion" to decide how certain property should be distributed among the testator's children. Even so, a court might set aside a distribution upon a showing that the decision was not made in good faith. **3. judicial discretion,** the power of a judge to make any reasonable ruling on matters with respect to which there is no single "right answer." A court's decision on such a matter may be reversed only for ABUSE OF DISCRETION. **4. prosecutorial discretion,** the discretion of prosecutors in choosing cases to prosecute and accepting or rejecting plea bargains. Not every violation of law can be prosecuted, and prosecutors have wide discretion in deciding which to pursue and which to drop, so long as their decisions are not discriminatory or vindictive

discretionary appeal. See under APPEAL.

discrimination, *n.* **1.** treating some people differently from others for reasons that are extraneous to the matter at hand, especially because of some group membership or characteristic such as race, sex, religion, or national origin **2.** Also called **illegal discrimination.** discrimination in violation of a state or federal constitution, statute, or regulation. **3. invidious discrimination,** illegal discrimination, especially discrimination on the basis of a SUSPECT CLASSIFICATION. See also AFFIRMATIVE ACTION; AGE DISCRIMINATION; DISABILITY DISCRIMINATION; PREGNANCY DISCRIMINATION, RACIAL DISCRIMINATION; SEPARATE BUT EQUAL; SEX DISCRIMINATION; SEX-PLUS DISCRIMINATION.

dishonor, *v.* **1.** to fail or refuse to HONOR an instrument for the payment of money when presented for payment or acceptance —*n.* **2.** the act of dishonoring an instrument

disinterested, *adj.* lacking in bias or interest (see INTEREST⁴) in a case. The judge and jurors in a case must be disinterested. Cf. INTERESTED

dismissal, *n.* **1.** an order or judgment in favor of a defendant, throwing a case out of court without a trial, or without completing a trial **2.** the act of issuing such an order or judgment. **3. dismissal with leave to replead,** dismissal of a civil case because of some inadequacy in the complaint, with permission to file an amended complaint to try to cure the defect Plaintiffs are normally given at least one chance to replead when their first complaint is inadequate. **4. dismissal with prejudice,** a dismissal barring the plaintiff or prosecution from ever reinstituting the case. **5. dismissal without prejudice,** a dismissal leaving the plaintiff or prosecutor free to try again later if circumstances change. For example, a dismissal for lack of personal jurisdiction would normally be without prejudice to the filing of a new case upon the same claims if jurisdiction can be obtained over the defendant. **6. involuntary dismissal,** dismissal upon motion of the defendant or upon the court's own motion, without the consent of the plaintiff **7. voluntary dismissal,** dismissal at the request of the plaintiff, or with the plaintiff's consent —**dismiss,** *v*

disorderly conduct, a term used in some states for such minor offenses as public drunkenness, public fighting, making too much noise, urinating in public, or other conduct that is mildly dangerous or disturbing to the public The particular conduct covered by the term must be clearly defined by statute; otherwise the statute making it an offense would be *void for vagueness* (see under VAGUE) Other terms sometimes used for the same general range of offenses include **breach of the peace** and **disturbing the peace.**

disparagement, *n.* the communication to third parties of false and derogatory information about a person's property, products, or business, such as to discourage others from doing business with the person or otherwise cause economic and personal injury Disparagement, also called **injurious falsehood,** is a tort akin to DEFAMATION.

dispossess, *v* to put someone out of possession of real property; for example, to evict a tenant Cf QUIT.

dissent, *v* **1.** to declare formally that one disagrees with a course of action being taken by a body of which one is a member, as when a stockholder dissents from a corporate action in order to pursue her APPRAISAL RIGHTS **2.** specifically, of one or more members of a panel of judges, to put on record the fact that they voted against the decision of the majority —*n* **3.** the act of dissenting or the fact that one dissents **4.** a *dissenting opinion* (see under OPINION)

dissolve, *v.* to terminate a legal relationship or bring the legal existence of an entity to an end *dissolve a marriage; dissolve a partnership, dissolve a corporation* —**dissolution,** *n*

distinguish, *v* to recognize or point out differences between a previous case and a case currently under consideration that make it appropriate to reach a different result in the current case A precedent that can be distinguished in this manner is said to be **distinguishable:** *The cases cited by the plaintiff are distinguishable in that they all involved fiduciary relationships rather than arm's-length contracts.*

distrain, *v* to seize a person's goods as security for an obligation, as when a landlord changes the locks on property upon which the rent has not been paid so that the lessee cannot remove the things inside until the rent has been paid, and if necessary they can be sold for back rent Distraint is now regulated by statute in all or nearly all states.

distress or **distraint,** *n* the act of distraining, or the state of being distrained *The landlord resorted to distraint The goods are under distress.* The terms are interchangeable

distributee, *n.* **1.** a person entitled to share in the DISTRIBUTION of an intestate's estate or, more broadly, of any decedent's estate **2.** generally, anyone who shares in any DISTRIBUTION of money or property

distribution, *n* **1. a.** the parceling out of the property (especially the personal property) of a person who died without a will, to those entitled to it under the rules of INTESTATE SUCCESSION **b.** more broadly, the parceling out of any decedent's estate, whether by the rules of intestate succession or under a will. See also ADMINISTER, ADMINISTRATOR, EXECUTOR. **2.** generally, any allocation and dispensing of money or property in which a number of people are entitled to share, e.g., a distribution of corporate profits to shareholders in the form of dividends, or the distribution of a bankrupt's assets to creditors. **3.** the total amount of money subject to such a distribution. **4.** Also called **distributive share.** the portion of an estate or other aggregate of property received by a particular DISTRIBUTEE. —**distribute,** v

district, n. **1.** generally, any geographic division established by a government for administrative convenience *school district; election district* **2.** Also called **judicial district.** a geographic division established for purposes of organizing a court system. For federal judicial purposes, the United States is divided into over ninety such districts, with at least one for every state or other federal political subdivision, and from two to four in each of the larger states: *District of Delaware; District of Guam; Western District of Texas.* See also UNITED STATES ATTORNEY; UNITED STATES DISTRICT COURT. Cf. CIRCUIT.

district attorney, the public official responsible for managing the prosecution of criminal offenses under state law in a particular locality.

disturbing the peace. See under DISORDERLY CONDUCT.

diversity case. See under CASE[1].

diversity jurisdiction. See under JURISDICTION[1]

diversity of citizenship, the situation that exists when a plaintiff and defendant in a federal case are citizens of different states. Often called **diversity** for short Diversity is one of the two major grounds upon which a federal court can exercise jurisdiction over a case See *subject matter jurisdiction* and *diversity jurisdiction* (under JURISDICTION[1]).

dividend, n. a portion of the earnings and profits of a corporation distributed to the shareholders in proportion to their holdings: *The company paid a year-end dividend of $1.25 per share.*

divorce, n. **1.** the termination of a marriage other than by death. This can be accomplished in the United States only by obtaining a judgment (typically called a **divorce decree**) from a court in accordance with state law. The divorce decree typically includes provisions regarding division of property, custody of children, and alimony and child support. **2. no-fault divorce,** a divorce obtained without assessing blame on either party for the breakdown of the marriage. Traditionally, divorce was permitted only if one party proved wrongdoing by the other, such as ADULTERY, CRUELTY, or DESERTION. Now most divorces are granted without any showing of fault, and many states have completely abolished the concept of fault as a basis for divorce. —v. **3.** to obtain a divorce.

docket, n. **1.** a chronological record of steps taken in a case—papers filed, orders entered, trial days held, etc

—maintained by a court clerk **2.** sometimes, a court CAL-ENDAR. —*v.* **3.** to record on a docket.

doctrine, *n.* a legal principle The term sometimes connotes a firm rule, sometimes a general guideline to be applied flexibly and judiciously

document, *n.* anything upon which information is recorded; most often a writing (including telephone message slips, checks, grocery lists), but also, in some contexts, photographs, audio tapes, computer files, or any other form in which information can be preserved See also PRODUCTION OF DOCUMENTS

document of title, 1. a document, such as a BILL OF LADING or WAREHOUSE RECEIPT, issued by or addressed to a person or entity entrusted with goods for storage or shipment, identifying the goods and serving as evidence of the right of the person with the document to receive the goods or direct their delivery **2. negotiable document of title,** a document of title stating that the specified goods are to be delivered either to the order of a named person or simply to whoever presents the document. Title to the goods covered by such a document can be transferred from a seller to a buyer simply by indorsing and handing over the document The buyer then presents the document to receive the goods **3. nonnegotiable document of title,** a document of title that provides for delivery of the goods covered by it only to a specific named person, who need not present the document to receive the goods.

documentary evidence. See under EVIDENCE.

doing business, (of a corporation) conducting regular activity within a particular state, of a nature sufficient to justify holding the corporation subject to suit in the state even on causes of action that are unrelated to any particular business transacted there An out-of-state corporation found to be "doing business" in the state is deemed to be present in the state and subject to the jurisdiction of its courts for all purposes. Cf. TRANSACTION OF BUSINESS

domain. See EMINENT DOMAIN; PUBLIC DOMAIN.

domestic, *adj.* pertaining to the internal workings of the United States, a particular state, or a family. See, for example, *domestic corporation* (under CORPORATION); *domestic relations* (under FAMILY LAW).

domestic partnership, a committed relationship between two unmarried people, of the same or opposite sex, analogous to a marriage. Some municipalities and some private companies formally recognize such relationships, particularly for same-sex couples, granting them the same status and employment benefits as married couples.

domicile, *n.* the place where one has one's permanent and primary home, or where a corporation has its headquarters or principal place of business; the place with which one is associated for taxing and voting purposes. One can have many residences, but only one domicile One whose domicile is in a particular place is said to be **domiciled** there or to be a **domiciliary** of that place: *a*

person domiciled in Paris; an Idaho domiciliary. See also
RESIDENCE, RESIDENT

donee, *n* **1.** the recipient of a gift **2.** the person designated to exercise a POWER OF APPOINTMENT

donor, *n.* **1.** a person who makes a gift **2.** one who confers a POWER OF APPOINTMENT **3.** the SETTLOR of a trust

double jeopardy, being put in JEOPARDY twice for the
same offense. This is prohibited by the Fifth Amendment
(see Appendix), so that a defendant who has been acquitted may not be tried again in the hope of a conviction, a
defendant who has been convicted may not be tried again
to increase the punishment, and the government, seeing
that a trial is going badly, may not ask for a mistrial in the
hope of doing better with a new jury and a fresh start On
the other hand, a defendant may be retried if a conviction
is overturned on appeal, if a mistrial is declared at the request of the defendant or because of a hung jury or other
circumstance beyond the control of the prosecution, or if
the same conduct also constitutes an offense in another
jurisdiction.

doubt, *n.* See BEYOND A REASONABLE DOUBT

draft, *n.* **1.** an instrument by which one person (the
drawer) orders another (the drawee) to pay a specified
sum of money to the order of someone else (the payee),
or to the bearer. Also (but no longer commonly) called a
bill of exchange. The most common form of draft is an
ordinary check See also NEGOTIABLE INSTRUMENT **2. time
draft,** a draft that is not payable until a specified time in
the future. **3. sight draft,** a draft payable on demand

draw, *v.* **1.** to prepare a legal instrument. *draw a contract;
draw a will.* **2.** to prepare and sign an instrument for the
payment of money, especially a DRAFT. The person who
draws a draft is called the **drawer,** the person ordered by
the draft to pay money (often a bank) is the **drawee,** and
the person designated to receive the money is the PAYEE,
the draft is said to be drawn "on" the drawee and "to" or
"payable to" the payee. Cf. MAKE. **3.** to withdraw money
from a fund or account.

driving while intoxicated (DWI), the offense of driving a motor vehicle while intoxicated by alcohol or other
drugs that impair driving ability. Also referred to in various
jurisdictions as **driving under the influence (DUI), driving while impaired (DWI),** or **driving while ability impaired (DWAI),** and commonly known everywhere as
drunk driving. In some jurisdictions several such terms
are used to designate varying degrees of intoxication.

drug, *n.* **1.** a substance intended to affect the structure or
function of the body of humans or animals, or intended for
use in the diagnosis, treatment, or prevention of disease in
humans or animals. Such substances are subject to regulation by the federal Food and Drug Administration **2.** a
CONTROLLED SUBSTANCE

drunk driving, *Informal.* Same as DRIVING WHILE INTOXI-
CATED.

duces tecum, *Latin.* (lit. "you will bring with you") See *subpoena duces tecum* (under SUBPOENA).

due, *adj.* **1.** appropriate to the circumstances; such as is required to fulfill legal obligations or satisfy legal standards: *due care* (see under CARE); *due diligence; due demand* (see under DEMAND); *due delivery;* DUE PROCESS. **2.** owing; supposed to be paid or performed now; to be paid or performed at the time specified. *The rent is due. The account is past due. Payment is due upon delivery.*

due process, 1. fair administration of law in accordance with established procedures and with due regard for the fundamental rights and liberties of people in a free society The concept is embodied in the Fifth and Fourteenth Amendments to the Constitution, which prohibit the federal government and state governments, respectively, from depriving any person "of life, LIBERTY, or PROPERTY, without due process of law." These provisions are interpreted as dealing primarily with the PROCEDURE by which law is administered (see *procedural due process*), but also as having some smaller and less well defined role in assessment of the SUBSTANCE of laws whose effect would be to deprive people of FUNDAMENTAL RIGHTS (see *substantive due process*). **2. procedural due process,** the concept that in administering a system of justice, and in taking any official action aimed at depriving a particular person of life, liberty, or property, the government must follow, and require individual litigants to follow, established and known rules, and that those rules must be fundamentally fair. At a minimum, the persons directly affected must be given NOTICE and an OPPORTUNITY TO BE HEARD; at the maximum, in criminal cases, a wide array of due process protections comes into play, from the MIRANDA RULE to proof BEYOND A REASONABLE DOUBT. **3. substantive due process,** the concept that there are some freedoms so fundamental that any law taking them away, absent a COMPELLING INTEREST, must be struck down as a deprivation of liberty without due process. Some such freedoms, notably the First Amendment freedoms of speech, press, religion, and assembly, are specified in the Constitution (see INCORPORATION DOCTRINE); others, including the RIGHT TO TRAVEL and the RIGHT OF PRIVACY in areas of marriage and childbearing, are regarded as inherent in the concept of LIBERTY. See also SCRUTINY

durable power of attorney. See under POWER OF ATTORNEY.

durable power of attorney for health care. Same as HEALTH CARE PROXY.

duress, *n.* the use of force, or the threat of force or of other unlawful acts, to induce someone to do something that she otherwise would not do, such as sign an instrument or commit a crime. Conduct that is induced by duress of such a nature that a person of reasonable firmness would not have been able to resist it is usually relieved of its normal legal effect; for example, a will signed under duress may be void, a contract signed under duress is usually voidable, and duress can constitute a complete defense to a criminal charge Also called **coercion.**

duty, *n.* **1.** a legal obligation, whether imposed by operation of law (e g , the duty to pay one's taxes or to exercise due care so as to avoid unnecessary injury to others) or assumed voluntarily (e g , the duty to perform a contract or repay a debt). See also FIDUCIARY DUTY; OBLIGATION. **2.** a tax on imports or exports.

dying declaration. See under DECLARATION

E

earned income. See under INCOME

easement, *n* **1.** an interest in land belonging to another, consisting of a right to use it or control its use for some purpose, but not to take anything from it or possess it. **2. affirmative easement,** an easement allowing the holder of the easement to go on the land; for example, a right to use a path across the land **3. easement appurtenant,** an easement in one piece of land specifically for the benefit of another; for example, a right to cross someone else's land in order to reach one's own, which otherwise would be inaccessible (**easement of access**) Such an easement passes automatically with any transfer of title to the benefited land. **4. easement in gross,** an easement whose benefit is unrelated to specific other land; for example, an easement granted to a public utility company to run wires over or pipes under the property burdened with the easement. **5. negative easement,** an easement whose only effect is to limit the use that the owner of the burdened property can make of that land, for example, an easement in a neighbor's property prohibiting its owner from spoiling one's view by building above a certain height **6. public easement,** an easement for the benefit of the public at large, such as a street across private land See also BURDEN² Cf PROFIT (def 2)

eavesdropping, *n* **1.** the act of listening in on conversations or activities of others without their knowledge If done without any trespass and without electronic or other artificial assistance, this in itself normally has no legal consequences **2. electronic eavesdropping,** eavesdropping by means of hidden microphones or other electronic aids This is severely restricted by law, see WIRETAP See also SURVEILLANCE

effective assistance of counsel. See under RIGHT TO COUNSEL

effective tax rate. See under TAX RATE

ejectment, *n* the traditional name for an action to obtain possession of land from another person, such as a holdover tenant or a person claiming ownership of the land, by establishing paramount title to the property

elect, *v* to make a choice in a situation where the law presents two permissible alternatives but allows only one to be selected *The couple elected to file income tax returns separately rather than jointly Since Congress does not allow immigrants to have dual citizenship, an immigrant must elect between becoming a United States citizen and retaining her original citizenship*

election, *n.* **1.** the act of making a legally required choice, or the choice made **2. election of remedies,** a plaintiff's choice among available remedies for the same wrong, e g , between return of an item of property wrongfully taken and payment for the loss **3. election under the**

will, an election by a person named in a will either to be bound by all of the terms of a will or to give up all rights under the will and pursue independent claims to property in the estate. One cannot ordinarily take what one is given under a will and also assert claims to property that the will left to someone else **4. spouse's** (or **widow's** or **widower's**) **election,** the election of a surviving spouse either to take the property left to her under the decedent's will or to take her ELECTIVE SHARE of the estate.

elective share, the share of a decedent's estate that the surviving spouse is entitled to under state law when a married person dies and leaves a will If the will leaves a different amount, the survivor may (but need not) choose to take the elective share instead of what the will provides Also called **statutory share; spouse's** (or **widow's** or **widower's**) **elective** (or **statutory**) **share.** See also *spouse's election* and *election under the will* (both under ELECTION).

electronic eavesdropping. See under EAVESDROPPING

electronic surveillance. See under SURVEILLANCE

element, *n.* a constituent part of something; especially, one of the components of a crime or cause of action that must be proved to sustain a charge or claim. For example, the usual elements of a claim for fraud are. (1) a false representation by the defendant, (2) knowledge by the defendant of the falsity, (3) intent by the defendant to induce some conduct by the plaintiff, (4) reasonable reliance by the plaintiff, and (5) resulting damage to the plaintiff.

emancipation, *n.* **1.** the freeing of slaves in the United States by the Emancipation Proclamation issued by President Lincoln during the Civil War, confirmed after the war by the Thirteenth Amendment (see Appendix) **2.** the freeing of a minor from parental control (and of parents from their duties toward the child), giving the child the right to keep and control her own earnings and make decisions with regard to such matters as her own medical care. This may occur by agreement of parent and child, by order of a court upon petition of the child, or automatically upon marriage. A minor after emancipation is called an **emancipated minor.**

embezzlement, *n* the crime of converting to one's own use property of another that is lawfully within one's possession The usual case involves the taking of money over which one gains control in the course of one's job

embracery, *n* an old word for the crime of improperly attempting to influence a jury, now usually dealt with in statutes on bribery and obstruction of justice

eminent domain, the inherent power of a government to take private property for public purposes, e.g , to build a road or reservoir See also TAKING, JUST COMPENSATION

emolument, *n* anything received as compensation for services, especially by a public or corporate official

Employee Retirement Income Security Act of 1974 (ERISA). See under PENSION PLAN

employee stock option. See under STOCK OPTION

employers' liability act. See under WORKERS' COMPENSATION.

employers' liability insurance. See under WORKERS' COMPENSATION.

employment. See SCOPE OF EMPLOYMENT.

en banc, *Law French.* (lit "as a bench") referring to consideration of a matter by all of the judges of a court together, as distinguished from a single judge or a panel. Some courts, including the Supreme Court, normally sit en banc; other courts, notably the United States Courts of Appeals, do so only in special situations. See also PANEL; REARGUMENT.

enabling, *adj.* **1.** (in reference to a statute) authorizing an official or agency to take the necessary steps to carry out a law or policy· *enabling clause; enabling legislation.* **2.** broadly, authorizing any particular conduct by anyone

encouragement, *n.* conduct by a law enforcement officer creating an opportunity for a suspect to commit a crime and encouraging the suspect to do it The fact that a crime was induced by such encouragement is not a defense in a subsequent prosecution for that crime Cf. ENTRAPMENT.

encumbrance, *n.* any interest, right, or obligation with respect to property that reduces the value or completeness of the property owner's title; for example, a mortage, lease, easement, or covenant

endorse, *v.* **1.** to show support for or approval of. *to endorse a candidate; to endorse another court's interpretation of the law.* **2.** to write something on a document, as in the margin or on the back *Instead of issuing a typed opinion regarding the motion, the judge endorsed her two-sentence decision on the notice of motion.* **3.** (in the law of negotiable instruments) to INDORSE. In this field, the spelling "indorse" has become standard in American (but not British) legal writing, although "endorse" is acceptable and is still preferred in nonlegal writing. —**endorsement,** *n.*

English-only law, a popular name for any of a variety of laws in a number of states, and of proposed federal laws, that designate English as the "official" language, require the use of English for various governmental purposes, and the like. These laws do not appear to have deterred lawyers and judges from using Latin locutions like CORPUS DELICTI, EX POST FACTO, and IN LOCO PARENTIS in official proceedings.

enjoin, *v.* to issue an INJUNCTION against; to forbid by court order: *The judge enjoined the sale of the land* (or *enjoined the parties from selling the land*).

enjoy, *v.* to possess or exercise a right or interest: *Americans enjoy the right of trial by jury in criminal cases* See also QUIET ENJOYMENT.

enlarge, *v.* **1.** to expand: *The statute enlarged the rights of judgment creditors.* **2.** especially, to extend a procedural time limit. *Defendant moved for an enlargement of the time to respond to the complaint.* —**enlargement,** *n.*

enter, v. **1.** to go onto or into real property **2.** to place formally in the record, especially a court record, as by adding to the court file or making a notation in a docket, judgment book, or the like: *enter an appearance; enter an order; enter judgment for the defendant* See also ENTRY

enticement, n. **1.** Also called **enticement of a child.** the crime of luring a child into a secluded place for sexual purposes **2.** For the meaning in tort law, see under ABDUCTION.

entirety, n. See BY THE ENTIRETY.

entitlement, n. a legislatively created right or benefit, such as a driver's license or welfare benefits, which, once granted to a person, cannot be taken away without a fair hearing to make sure that the recipient is no longer entitled to the benefit. Entitlements are sometimes regarded as PROPERTY and sometimes as a LIBERTY; either way, the Supreme Court holds that they cannot be taken away from an individual without *procedural due process* (see under DUE PROCESS)

entrapment, n. the planning of a crime by law enforcement agents and their procuring of its commission by a person who had no predisposition to do it and would not have done so but for the trickery of the officers Entrapment is a defense in a subsequent prosecution for the crime, but the police conduct must be extreme for the defense to succeed. Cf. ENCOURAGEMENT.

entry, n. **1.** the act of entering (see ENTER) **2.** a notation entered in a record.

enumerated power. See under POWER

equal protection, the principle that law should be even-handed in its application and that people should be free from irrational and invidious discrimination at the hands of the government. Under the Fourteenth Amendment (see Appendix), a state government may not "deny to any person within its jurisdiction the equal protection of the laws," and the DUE PROCESS clause of the Fifth Amendment has been interpreted as extending the principle of equal protection to the federal government as well Thus any law or governmental practice having a discriminatory purpose or effect is subject to challenge in the courts to determine whether it meets constitutional standards See also SCRUTINY; SEPARATE BUT EQUAL.

equitable, adj. **1.** pertaining to, enforceable under, or derived from principles of EQUITY as distinguished from LAW (def. 4). See, for example, *equitable* ACTION, DEFENSE, ESTOPPEL, REMEDY, RIGHT under those words **2.** in particular, describing property rights and interests deriving from something other than legal title, including the rights of a trust beneficiary with respect to the property held in trust. See, for example, *equitable* ESTATE¹, OWNER, INTEREST¹, TITLE under those words. **3.** fair; consistent with fundamental justice. See, for example, EQUITABLE DISTRIBUTION

equitable action. See under ACTION.

equitable distribution, a method of dividing property in a divorce case, authorized by statute in most states, under which the court allocates property acquired by the couple during marriage according to what seems fair, without regard to whether *legal title* (see under TITLE) is in the name of the husband or the wife The court takes into account a wide range of factors, such as the relative earning capacity of the parties and the role that each played in the family as an economic unit, including a homemaker's contribution to overall family welfare

equity, *n* **1.** one of the two systems of justice that grew up side by side in England and together gave rise to the present-day system of justice in both England and the United States Equity was a flexible system in which judges were able to fashion remedies for situations that did not fit within principles followed in the courts of LAW (def 4); it was less concerned with technicalities and more concerned with reaching a fair result—"doing equity " Its most notable power was the power to issue INJUNCTIONS. See also MERGER OF LAW AND EQUITY **2.** overall fairness; justice in a moral as well as legal sense See also BALANCING OF THE EQUITIES **3.** the net value of an owner's interest in property; the market value of the property minus amounts still owed on debts secured by mortgages or liens on the property **4.** the *net assets* (see under ASSET) of an enterprise, representing the value of the owners' interest in the business

equity of redemption, a statutory right to avoid losing one's property through foreclosure of a mortgage by paying off the mortgage in full, with interest and costs, within a specified time after default

equity security. See under SECURITY[2]

ERISA. See under PENSION PLAN.

error, *n.* **1.** an incorrect ruling by a judge in a case, as determined by a higher court on appeal In a nonjury trial, there can be error in the judge's findings of fact (see CLEARLY ERRONEOUS); however, the word is most often used in reference to rulings on matters of law, as in admitting or excluding certain evidence or giving certain instructions to the jury. **2. harmless error,** an error that did not affect the outcome of the case or prejudice a substantial right of a party. Reversal will not be granted on the basis of errors deemed to be harmless **3. plain error,** an error so obviously prejudicial to substantial rights of a party that it amounts to an affront to the judicial system Such an error will result in reversal even if the party adversely affected by it failed to object to it. Also called **fundamental error. 4. reversible error,** an error that prejudiced the appellant in a way that could have affected the outcome of the trial Such an error, if properly objected to when the ruling was made, requires modification or reversal of the judgment Also called **prejudicial error.** See also STANDARD OF REVIEW. —**erroneous,** *adj.*

escheat, *n.* **1.** the reverting of property to the state if no claimant with a right to it can be found, especially upon the death of an owner who leaves no will and no known heirs —*v.* **2.** to revert to the state by escheat.

escrow, *n.* **1.** money or a deed or other instrument deposited with a third person for delivery to a given party upon the fulfillment of some condition While in the keeping of the third party, the money or instrument is said to be "in escrow " —*v.* **2.** to place into escrow.

Esq., abbreviation of *Esquire,* a title often appended (usually in abbreviated form) to the names of American lawyers (instead of putting Mr or Ms in front of the name) in addressing letters or in certain other formal contexts

esse. See IN ESSE

essence. See OF THE ESSENCE

establishment of religion, governmental sponsorship of religion, including financial support for a religion or religions at public expense This is prohibited by the **Establishment Clause** of the First Amendment to the Constitution. Under current Supreme Court doctrine, a government program having the effect of providing public financial support for religion does not violate the Establishment Clause if it is regarded as (1) having a secular purpose, (2) having a primary effect that neither aids nor inhibits religion, and (3) not involving "excessive entanglement" of government and religion See also SEPARATION OF CHURCH AND STATE

estate[1], *n.* **1.** an interest in real property which is or may become possessory; that is, it either confers upon the owner of the interest a current right to exclusive possession of the property for some period of time or embodies at least the possibility that the owner will have such a right in the future An estate may be designated as JOINT, BY THE ENTIRETY, IN COMMON, or IN SEVERALTY, depending upon the ownership arrangement, and as either a **legal estate** or a **beneficial** (or **equitable**) **estate,** depending upon whether it is viewed from the perspective of a *legal owner* or, in the case of property held in trust, a *beneficial owner* (see both phrases under OWNER) Because an estate is a form of property interest and a tenancy is a form of estate, the words "estate," "interest," and "tenancy" are interchangeable in many contexts See INTEREST[1]; TENANCY **2. contingent estate,** an estate that is not yet possessory, and in which the owner's right of exclusive possession in the future depends upon circumstances that are not certain to occur For example, if A grants land "to B so long as the property is used for church purposes," then A retains a contingent estate in the land, called a POSSIBILITY OF REVERTER, because it is possible (but not certain) that the condition for continuation of B's estate will be violated and the land will revert to A's possession Cf. *vested estate.* **3. estate** (or **tenancy**) **in fee.** Same as FEE[1]. **4. future estate,** an estate which has not yet become possessory For example, a grant of property "to A for life, then to B" gives B a future estate (called a REMAINDER), because B's right of possession will not arise until A dies. For types of future estate, see *executory interest* (under INTEREST[1]); POSSIBILITY OF REVERTER; REMAINDER; REVERSION. Cf *possessory estate.* **5. life estate** (or **tenancy**), an estate whose duration is measured by the life of some person or group of people (the MEASURING LIFE or lives); for example, the estates granted by the words "to A for life," "to B during the life of his mother," or "to C Church so long as any of its present parishioners remain alive " Also called **estate** (or **tenancy**) **for life** or, when the measuring life is not the grantee's own, **estate** (or **tenancy**) **pur autre vie** (*Law French*. lit "for another life"). **6. possessory estate,** an estate whose owner has a current right to exclusive possession of the property, at least for a while. Also called **present estate** or **present possessory estate.** Cf. *future estate.* A possessory estate may be classified as either a **freehold estate** (same as FREEHOLD) or a **leasehold estate** (same as LEASEHOLD) For types of leasehold estate, see under TENANCY. **7. vested estate,** an estate that is either possessory or certain to become so in due course; the owner's right to eventual possession is not subject to a contingency. For example, if land has been granted "to A for life, then to B," both A's present estate (a *life estate*) and B's future estate (a REMAINDER) are vested estates: A's because it is already possessory, and B's because it will become possessory upon A's death, which is certain to occur If B is no longer alive at that point, B's heirs or other successors will possess the property. Cf. *contingent estate.*

estate[2], *n.* **1.** an aggregate of money and property administered as a unit. **2. bankruptcy estate,** the total assets of a person or entity in bankruptcy. Also called **estate in bankruptcy. 3. decedent's estate,** all money and property owned by a decedent at the time of death. **4. residuary estate,** in the case of a decedent who left a will, whatever is left of the decedent's estate after payment of debts and expenses and distribution of all bequests save the *residuary bequest* (see under BEQUEST). Also called the **residue** of the estate.

estate tax, a tax imposed on large estates left by decedents, based upon the value of the estate and required to be paid out of estate funds before the estate is distributed to heirs or takers under a will. Cf. INHERITANCE TAX.

estimated tax, an advance on income taxes that must be paid approximately quarterly by taxpayers whose income is not subject to WITHHOLDING TAX, or whose withholding will not substantially cover their tax liability for the year.

estop, *v.* to hinder or prevent by ESTOPPEL. When the doctrine of estoppel bars a litigant from taking a position at trial contrary to a prior assertion, he is said to be "estopped to deny" or "estopped from denying" the truth of the assertion.

estoppel, *n.* **1.** a bar or impediment preventing a litigant in certain situations from asserting facts or claims inconsistent with facts previously established or with his own prior assertions or conduct **2. collateral estoppel,** the doctrine that a person who has had a full and fair opportunity to litigate an issue of importance to a case and had the issue resolved against him may not relitigate the issue in a subsequent case involving the same parties. Sometimes the estoppel extends to subsequent cases against other parties as well. Also called **issue preclusion. 3. equitable estoppel,** the doctrine that one who makes an assertion (or by conduct creates an impression) upon which another relies may not turn around and assert the opposite to gain advantage in subsequent litigation against the other person. The doctrines of LACHES and *apparent authority* (see under AUTHORITY[1]) are essentially special applications of equitable estoppel. **4. promissory estoppel,** the doctrine under which a promise that is not enforceable under traditional principles of contract law (for example, for lack of consideration) may nevertheless be enforced to the extent necessary to prevent injustice if the promisor should reasonably have expected that the promisee would take substantial action in reliance upon the promise, and the promisee did so.

et al., *Latin.* abbreviation for *et alius* ("and another") or *et alii* ("and others"); used primarily as a stand-in for the names of all parties except the first on each side of a case in the CAPTION on court papers. In citations to cases, even this is usually left out, and only the last name of the first party on each side is listed unless there is a special reason for indicating that there were others involved.

et seq., *Latin.* abbreviation for *et sequentia* ("and those following"); used in citations to include a number of pages or sections beyond the one listed: *appellant's brief at page* (or *pages*) *34 et seq.*

et ux., *Latin.* abbreviation for *et uxor* ("and wife"); formerly used instead of the wife's name in case names and legal documents involving a husband and wife jointly: *Smith et ux. v. Jones.*

ethics, *n.pl.* **1.** standards of honesty and fairness in the conduct of a business or profession, often embodied in written rules adopted by professional associations See also UNETHICAL CONDUCT. **2.** moral principles generally.

eviction, *n.* **1.** a landlord's exclusion of a tenant from possession of leased premises, either by legal proceedings or by personal action. **2. actual eviction,** physically excluding a tenant, as by changing the lock while the tenant is out. **3. constructive eviction,** conduct by a landlord rendering leased premises unfit for use and thus, as a practical matter, forcing the tenant out.

evidence, *n.* **1.** information and things pertaining to the events that are the subject of a case, especially the testimony or objects (but not the questions or comments of the lawyers) offered at a trial or hearing for the judge or jury to consider in deciding the issues in the case. **2. character evidence,** evidence pertaining to the CHARACTER of a party or a witness. **3. circumstantial evidence,** evidence of a fact that makes the existence of another fact—one that actually must be decided in the case—more or less likely. Circumstantial evidence is not second-class evidence; it is as valid, as admissible, and as acceptable a basis for a verdict as *direct evidence.* Most evidence in most cases is circumstantial, and many kinds of issues, such as intent and good faith, depend upon a SUBJECTIVE

TEST that cannot be satisfied in any other way. **4. competent evidence,** evidence that is ADMISSIBLE. **5. cumulative evidence,** additional evidence introduced to prove a fact for which there has already been considerable evidence, adding little to what has already been admitted. A trial judge has discretion to draw the line at a reasonable point and preclude further evidence on a particular issue, or of a particular type, on the ground that it is cumulative. **6. demonstrative evidence,** evidence that the jury can perceive directly instead of just being told about it by a witness, including documents and objects involved in the incident giving rise to a case, lawyers' charts and diagrams admitted into evidence, courtroom demonstrations, site visits, and the demeanor of witnesses. **7. direct evidence,** evidence purportedly showing the existence or nonexistence of a fact that must be decided in a case without the need for any application of reasoning or linking of related facts; sometimes a document or other *real evidence,* most often the testimony of an eyewitness. See EYEWITNESS for discussion of reliability. Cf. *circumstantial evidence.* **8. documentary evidence,** *real evidence* in the form of a DOCUMENT. **9. extrinsic evidence,** evidence pertaining to a written instrument such as a deed, contract, or will, beyond what is contained in the writing itself. See also PAROL EVIDENCE. **10. hearsay evidence.** See under HEARSAY. **11. opinion evidence,** testimony as to what a witness believes or concludes about a situation as distinguished from what the witness personally observed Except for opinions on matters within common experience ("He sounded angry." "She acted drunk"), opinion evidence may be given only by an *expert witness* rather than a *fact witness* (see both under WITNESS). **12. real evidence,** broadly, any *demonstrative evidence;* specifically, a document or other object offered as having been involved in the events that are the subject of the case, such as a murder weapon, a ransom note, or a bloody glove See also BEST EVIDENCE RULE; *burden of producing evidence* (under BURDEN[1]); EXHIBIT; IN EVIDENCE; MATERIAL; PAROL EVIDENCE; PREPONDERANCE OF THE EVIDENCE; *prima facie evidence* (under PRIMA FACIE); RELEVANT; STATE'S EVIDENCE, SUBSTANTIAL EVIDENCE; *weight of the evidence* (under WEIGHT); WITNESS

evidentiary fact. See under FACT.

ex contractu, *Latin.* (lit "arising from a contract") based upon a contract: *a right ex contractu; an action ex contractu.*

ex delicto, *Latin.* (lit. "arising from a wrong") based upon a breach of duty other than a contractual promise, as a tort or a crime. *an action ex delicto; a trust ex delicto.*

ex officio, *Latin.* (lit "by virtue of office") describing a position or power that comes automatically with a particular office. *As chairman of the board, she sits ex officio on the executive committee.*

ex parte, *Latin.* (lit. "from a side") done by, for, or with one side of a case or dispute without notice to the other side: *an ex parte application for a restraining order; an or-*

der granted ex parte; an ex parte conversation between the judge and the plaintiff's attorney. The situations in which ex parte proceedings are allowed are very limited See, for example, *temporary restraining order* (under RE-STRAINING ORDER). Cf. ON NOTICE

ex post facto, *Latin.* (lit "from what is done afterward") retroactive; retroactively; after the fact The Constitution prohibits the states and the federal government from passing any "ex post facto Law"—that is, any law that criminalizes conduct that was legal at the time it was done, or increases the penalty for a crime after it was committed Laws affecting civil rights and duties can be made retroactive, however, as frequently occurs when tax laws are changed.

ex rel., *Latin.* abbreviation for *ex relatione* (lit. "on the proposal of"); an abbreviation appearing in the names of certain kinds of proceedings brought by a state or the United States on behalf of a private party (the RELATOR): *State of New York ex rel. Smith v. Jones* (Smith is the relator at whose request or for whose benefit the state instituted the action against Jones) Some courts and lawyers use English equivalents such as "on behalf of," "for the use of," or, most commonly, **on the relation of.** All such phrases are usually shortened to "ex rel." in citations.

examination, *n.* **1.** the questioning of a witness at a trial, hearing, or deposition Examination of a witness begins with **direct examination,** also called **examination in chief,** by the side that called the witness, followed by **cross examination** by the other side. Then each side in turn may ask follow-up questions, called **redirect examination** and **recross examination** respectively, alternating back and forth until both sides run out of questions. Informally, these stages are called **direct, cross, redirect,** and **recross,** without the word "examination." Ordinarily, only subjects that were raised on direct may be inquired about on cross. Each redirect and recross is strictly limited to follow-up on the testimony in the immediately preceding examination, so these are quite brief. See also SCOPE OF EXAMINATION; BEYOND THE SCOPE; OPEN THE DOOR; SCOPE OF EXAMINATION. **2. examination before trial,** a pretrial DEPOSITION. **3. examination in aid of execution.** Same as a *deposition in aid of execution* (see under DEPOSITION).

examine, *v* **1.** to ask questions of a witness at a trial, hearing, or deposition. *The lawyers for both sides examined the chauffeur at length.* **2. cross-examine,** to conduct the cross examination of a witness: *After Mr Jones examined the chauffeur, Miss Smith cross-examined her.* Also, very informally, **cross.** Note that there are no parallel expressions "to direct-examine" or "to direct" —**examiner,** *n.*

examined copy, a copy of a document that has been compared with the original and found to be accurate See also CERTIFIED COPY

exception, *n.* **1.** a special situation excluded from coverage of an otherwise applicable rule, principle, contract, insurance policy, etc.; e g., *hearsay exception* (see under HEARSAY). **2.** a formal objection to a judge's overruling of an objection or denial of a motion at a trial, formerly required in order to preserve the issue for appeal. Modern rules of practice do away with the tedious and silly requirement of taking exception every time a trial judge makes an adverse ruling.

excess insurance, supplemental insurance to cover a portion of potential loss in excess of the limits of other policies; essentially a policy with a large deductible. A company with large risks might have a basic insurance policy and several layers of excess insurance from different insurers, with coverage under each policy picking up where the previous one leaves off.

excessive bail. See under BAIL¹

excessive verdict. See under VERDICT

excise or **excise tax, 1.** a tax on products manufactured, sold, or used within the country; e g , a gasoline tax, liquor tax, or tobacco tax **2.** a tax paid for the privilege of carrying on certain transactions or activities; e g., a FRANCHISE TAX.

excited utterance, a statement about a startling event or condition made in the excitement caused by the situation. Such utterances are usually admitted into evidence as an exception to the rule against HEARSAY on the theory that people cannot make up lies under such circumstances. (Of course, their perceptions may be distorted) Also called **spontaneous declaration** (or **statement** or **exclamation**).

exclusion, *n.* **1.** the act of a judge in refusing to allow proffered evidence to be considered in a case Cf. ADMISSION; RECEIVE. See also EXCLUSIONARY RULE. **2.** the act of a judge in barring certain people, especially prospective witnesses in a case, from the courtroom during a trial. See also SEQUESTER. **3.** the omission of a particular class of people, property, transactions, or events from coverage of a statute or of a contract or other instrument, or a provision expressly rejecting such coverage In particular, **a.** the specification in an insurance policy of particular risks not covered by the policy. **b.** the specification in a tax law of particular kinds of income, property, or transactions that will not be subject to the tax; for example, the exclusion of most municipal bond interest from income subject to the federal income tax. —**exclude,** *v.*

exclusionary rule, the principle that the prosecution in a criminal case may not use evidence obtained in violation of the Constitution, particularly evidence derived from an illegal search and seizure in violation of the Fourth Amendment (see Appendix). In recent years the Supreme Court has created several exceptions to this rule, including the GOOD FAITH EXCEPTION and the INEVITABLE DISCOVERY EXCEPTION. See also FRUIT OF THE POISONOUS TREE.

exclusionary zoning. See under ZONING.

exclusive jurisdiction. See under JURISDICTION¹.

exclusive zoning. See under ZONING.

exculpatory statement. See under STATEMENT.

excusable neglect. See under NEGLECT.

execute, *v.* **1.** to sign a legal instrument such as a deed, will, or contract, and sometimes to take additional steps necessary to put the instrument into effect, such as delivering a deed or acknowledging a will. **2.** to carry out an obligation fully; to complete performance. **3.** to carry out a court order or judgment; especially, to seize and, if necessary, sell property of a *judgment debtor* (see under DEBTOR) to satisfy a money judgment **4.** to put a person to death pursuant to a death sentence. —**execution,** *n.*

executed, *adj.* **1.** complete; fully performed; leaving no uncertainty to be resolved. In this sense, an "executed contract" is one that has been performed by both parties, leaving nothing for either side to do. Opposite of EXECUTORY. **2.** signed; fully effective: *executed will; executed deed.*

executive, *adj.* pertaining to the branch of government charged with implementing the law, headed at the state level by the governor of each state and at the national level by the President, and operating through executive departments and administrative agencies. See also SEPARATION OF POWERS.

executive agreement, an agreement between the United States and one or more other countries, entered into by the President but not submitted to the Senate for ratification as a TREATY. Such agreements are sometimes negotiated pursuant to specific statutory authority, but even when they are not they are generally regarded as binding upon the United States so long as Congress does not specifically act to overrule them.

executive clemency. Same as CLEMENCY.

executive order, an order issued by the President or a state governor on a matter within the scope of executive authority, having the force of law. For example, the desegregation of America's armed forces after World War II came about not by any action of Congress or the courts, but by an executive order of President Truman.

executive privilege, the right of the President, founded in the constitutional principle of SEPARATION OF POWERS, to refuse to disclose to the courts or Congress confidential communications within the executive branch. This is a *qualified privilege* (see under PRIVILEGE), so that a strong need for the information can outweigh the privilege when there is no strong need to keep the information secret.

executor, *n.* a person designated in a will, or appointed by a court if necessary, to ADMINISTER the estate of a decedent who left a will in accordance with the terms of the will. The archaic term **executrix** is still often used to refer to an executor who is a woman. Cf. ADMINISTRATOR.

executory. *adj.* not yet fully performed or fully resolved. For example, an "executory contract" is one under which at least one side has not completed performance. Opposite of EXECUTED (def. 1). See also *executory interest* (under INTEREST¹).

exemplar, *n.* a typical specimen or example, especially a sample of a criminal suspect's handwriting, voice, finger-prints, hair, or other identifying information taken under controlled conditions for analysis and subsequent use as evidence. The compelled production of such exemplars does not violate the constitutional ban on compulsory SELF-INCRIMINATION because an exemplar is not a statement or testimony by the suspect.

exemplary damages. Same as *punitive damages* (see under DAMAGES).

exempt. See *exempt property* (under EXEMPTION); TAX EX-EMPT.

exemption, *n.* **1.** the relieving of a particular person or class of persons from a legal duty: *exemption of conscientious objectors from combat duty; exemption of an individual from jury duty on the ground of hardship.* **2.** statutory protection of certain property of a debtor (**exempt property**) from attachment by creditors See also HOMESTEAD EXEMPTION. **3.** an income tax DEDUCTION, in an amount fixed by statute, for each taxpayer who is not claimed as a dependent on someone else's return and for each DEPENDENT claimed by the taxpayer.

exhaustion of administrative remedies, the general rule that where the law provides an administrative procedure for dealing with a particular kind of matter, a person must pursue all possible avenues for redress within the administrative agency before resorting to the courts

exhaustion of state remedies, the general rule that a state prisoner who feels that he is being held in violation of the Constitution must pursue all possible avenues for redress in the state courts before seeking a writ of HABEAS CORPUS in federal court.

exhibit, *n.* **1.** a document referred to in an affidavit, contract, or other instrument and attached to the instrument Such exhibits are regarded as an intrinsic part of the instrument to which they are attached **2.** a document or object sought to be used as evidence at a trial. Each party's proposed exhibits are numbered or lettered sequentially ("marked") for ease of identification, and until they are admitted into evidence they are referred to as "Plaintiff's Exhibit C for identification," "Defendant's Exhibit 3 for identification," and the like. If the judge admits an exhibit into evidence, it is thereafter referred to as "Plaintiff's Exhibit C in evidence," "Defendant's Exhibit 3 in evidence," or the like.

exigent circumstances, special circumstances under which law enforcement officers who have probable cause to conduct a search may do so without waiting to get a search warrant. These include, among others, any situation involving the search of an automobile on a roadway and any situation in which the police reasonably believe that the search is necessary to protect life or prevent serious injury. See also FRESH PURSUIT.

expectancy, *n.* a property interest that may or may not come into existence in the future; a hoped-for property right but not one that exists at present *Her uncle has made a will leaving her the house, but he can always change his will, so all she has now is a mere expectancy*

expert witness. See under WITNESS See also BATTLE OF THE EXPERTS; *qualify as an expert* (under QUALIFY¹)

expertise. See SCOPE OF EXPERTISE

express, *adj.* explicit; set forth in words; oral or written. Opposite of IMPLIED. See *express* AUTHORITY¹, CONTRACT, REPEAL, TRUST, WAIVER, WARRANTY under those words. For a somewhat broader use of the term, see def b of *express warranty* (under WARRANTY)

expropriation, *n.* a TAKING of private property by a government under the power of EMINENT DOMAIN.

extortion, *n.* the crime of obtaining money or property from a person by threat of harmful conduct in the future (e.g., killing, injuring, destroying property, disclosing embarrassing information) or threat of imminent harm falling short of the kinds of threatened harm necessary for ROBBERY (e.g., a threat to destroy property other than a home) See also KICKBACK (def. 2); BLACKMAIL. —**extort,** *v.*

extradition, *n.* **1.** the handing over by one state to another of a suspect wanted for criminal prosecution in the second state The Constitution requires the states of the United States to honor each other's requests for extradition if the suspect has been formally charged with a crime in the requesting state and was in that state at the time the crime was committed. The suspect may, however, be required to serve out a current sentence in the sending state before being handed over **2.** the handing over of a criminal suspect from one country to another. Such extraditions are provided for by treaties between the United States and many other countries. Cf. ASYLUM

extrajudicial, *adj.* not part of court proceedings or not within the authority of a court

extraordinary care. See under CARE

extraordinary remedy (or **relief**) See under REMEDY

extraordinary writ. See under WRIT

extrinsic evidence. See under EVIDENCE

eyewitness, *n.* **1.** a person who saw an event under discussion. **2.** broadly, a person who directly perceived an event under discussion, whether by seeing, hearing, or otherwise. Eyewitness testimony, or the lack of it, is often viewed as crucial in a case, despite scientific studies consistently showing that such testimony is very unreliable and despite repeated accounts of people convicted on the basis of eyewitness identification who are later released from prison when the real criminal comes to light Cf *circumstantial evidence* (under EVIDENCE)

face, *n.* **1.** the front of an instrument. **2.** the obvious meaning of a statement or a writing; the explicit provisions of a writing: *The legislature's discriminatory purpose is clear from the face of the statute.* **3.** the outward appearance as distinguished from the real significance. *Although the minimum height requirement for employees is facially neutral, in practice it discriminates against women.* **4. on its face, a.** obviously and without qualification· *unconstitutional* (or *invalid*) *on its face* (see under UNCONSTITUTIONAL). **b.** apparently; superficially *The statement that one can buy bacon at a certain butcher shop, though innocent on its face, amounts to defamation when made in reference to a kosher butcher shop* —**facial,** *adj.* —**facially,** *adv.*

face amount (or **value**), the sum shown on the face of an instrument; the principal amount of an obligation, not taking into account interest, deductions, or other adjustments: *The face amount of the mortgage is $60,000, but only $25,000 remains to be paid. The face value of the life insurance policy is $100,000, but with dividends it will pay $120,000.*

fact, *n.* **1.** an event or circumstance; an aspect of reality. As distinguished from LAW, a matter ascertained by consideration of evidence; as distinguished from OPINION, a matter directly observed by a witness. **2. evidentiary fact,** a fact that is itself evidence of another fact at issue in a case; a fact providing a basis for determination of an *ultimate fact.* **3. ultimate fact,** one of the facts so basic to a claim, charge, or defense that their determination is the ultimate objective of a trial. See also *fact witness* (under WITNESS); FINDING OF FACT; *implied in fact* (under IMPLIED); *stipulated fact* (under STIPULATION); *question of fact* and *mixed question of fact and law* (both under QUESTION²); TRIER OF FACT.

factfinder. Same as TRIER OF FACT.

factor, *n.* **1.** a merchant who, instead of buying goods and reselling at a profit, receives goods on *consignment* (see under CONSIGN) and sells them for a commission. **2.** a company that lends money to merchants or manufacturers, taking an assignment of their accounts receivable as security.

fail, *v.* **1.** (of a contract) to be unenforceable—for example, because the terms are too INDEFINITE, or a party lacked CAPACITY to contract, or the contract is against PUBLIC POLICY. **2.** (of a gift or bequest) to be ineffective—for example, because the property no longer exists or the donee is deceased.

failure of consideration, a situation in which the CONSIDERATION agreed upon in a contract does not materialize or ceases to exist or becomes worthless In some cases this renders the promise or the negotiable instrument given in exchange for that consideration unenforceable, or justifies other relief. The most common example of failure of consideration is simply the failure of a party to do whatever was promised in the contract Cf. *want of consideration* (under WANT).

failure of issue. See under ISSUE[2]

failure to prosecute, in either a civil or criminal case, the failure of the plaintiff or prosecutor to pursue the case diligently once it has been commenced Also called **want of prosecution.** In extreme cases, a civil case may be dismissed for failure to prosecute; criminal cases will be so dismissed if there is a violation of the requirement of a *speedy trial* (see under TRIAL)

fair comment, the right to express one's opinion on matters of public interest, such as the conduct of a public official, the conduct of a private person in a matter affecting the community at large, or the contents of a book or other published work. As long as the comment is not completely unreasonable, the person making it may not be held liable for DEFAMATION on account of it

fair market value. Same as MARKET VALUE.

fair preponderance of the evidence. Same as PREPONDERANCE OF THE EVIDENCE.

fair use, reasonable and limited use of a copyrighted work without permission of the owner, as in quoting a few lines from a book in a review of the book Such use is not an infringement of the copyright

faith. See GOOD FAITH; BAD FAITH

false, *adj.* **1.** untrue: *false representation* **2.** misleading FALSE ADVERTISING **3.** unlawful FALSE IMPRISONMENT

false advertising, advertising that is materially misleading about the nature, origin, or quality of a product or the training or skill of a provider of service It is illegal See also BAIT AND SWITCH

false arrest. See under FALSE IMPRISONMENT

false exculpatory statement. See under STATEMENT

false imprisonment, the tort and crime of restricting a person to a particular area without legal justification, whether by means of physical restraints (as in a prison, a locked room, or a speeding automobile) or through force or threat of immediate harm to one's person or valuable property. Also called **false arrest,** especially when done by one falsely claiming to have law enforcement authority, or by a law enforcement officer who lacks probable cause or other legal grounds for detaining the arrestee.

false pretenses, the crime of obtaining title to property, especially personal property, by means of false representations, as by swindling someone out of money or tricking someone into selling something If only possession, rather than title, is obtained by trick, the crime is LARCENY.

false swearing, the crime of making a false statement under oath or affirmation, other than in the belief that what is being said is true. A broader and less serious offense than PERJURY.

falsus in uno, falsus in omnibus, *Latin.* (lit. "deceitful in one thing, deceitful in all things") the doctrine that a witness who is shown to have deliberately lied on a material issue in a case may be regarded by the jury as generally unworthy of belief

family, *n.* a group of people related by blood, marriage, or adoption, or in an analogous relationship linked by bonds of affection and commitment. The exact scope of the term varies with the context

family law, the area of law dealing with marriage, separation, and divorce; adoption, custody, and support of children; DOMESTIC PARTNERSHIP; and related matters. Also called **domestic relations.**

fatal, *adj.* causing invalidity; describing an error or legal defect that renders a transaction or interest void, an argument ineffective, a trial invalid, or the like: *A new trial was ordered because of the judge's fatal error in excluding certain evidence at the first trial.*

fatal variance. See under VARIANCE

fault, *n.* wrongfulness; blameworthiness; broadly, the doing of anything that provides a basis for a suit or criminal action against oneself; narrowly, the element—often called STATE OF MIND or MENS REA—that makes an act a tort or crime. Cf. NO-FAULT DIVORCE; NO-FAULT INSURANCE; STRICT LIABILITY.

federal, *adj.* relating to the United States, and especially to the government and law of the United States, as distinguished from a state. *federal crime; federal income tax; federal government; federal judge.*

federal case. See under CASE[1]

Federal Circuit. See under CIRCUIT

Federal Insurance Contributions Act (FICA). See under SOCIAL SECURITY

federal law, law adopted or recognized by the government of the United States with respect to matters within its constitutional powers, uniformly applicable throughout the nation. It includes the Constitution; statutes adopted by Congress; executive orders of the President; regulations and rulings of federal agencies; treaties and executive agreements to which the United States is a party; international law, at least to the extent that the courts choose to recognize it and Congress has not acted to the contrary; judicial interpretations and rulings with respect to all of the foregoing matters; and *federal common law* (see under COMMON LAW)

federal question, an issue requiring the application or interpretation of FEDERAL LAW in a case. See also *federal question jurisdiction* (under JURISDICTION[1])

federal statute. See under STATUTE

fee[1]**,** *n.* **1.** Also called **estate** (or **tenancy**) **in fee; fee estate.** a possessory interest in real estate of potentially infinite duration. (See *possessory interest,* under INTEREST[1].) If not sold or given away during the owner's life or by will, and so long as no condition specified for its continued existence is violated, a fee descends automatically to the owner's heirs upon the owner's death, and then to their heirs, and so on indefinitely. **2. fee simple,** a fee which is inheritable by any heir of the owner. Older forms of fee in which the property was restricted to certain heirs, such as male descendants only, have been abolished, so that now every fee is a fee simple, and those two terms are often used interchangeably. **3. fee simple absolute,** a fee simple that is not subject to any condition on its continuation in the hands of the present owner and his heirs so long as they do not transfer it to someone else. (Even a fee simple absolute, however, is subject to the state and federal governments' power of EMINENT DOMAIN.) Cf. *fee simple defeasible.* **4. fee simple defeasible,** a fee simple estate that is subject to termination (DEFEASANCE) upon the occurrence of some future event Upon defeasance, the current owner loses the property and the fee vests in someone else. Also called **defeasible fee; conditional fee.** Cf. *fee simple absolute.* **5. fee simple determinable,** a defeasible fee which is to continue only so long as a certain state of affairs continues, or only until a certain event occurs. Such fees are most often created in gifts to charity, as when real estate is left by will to a university "so long as the property is used for educational purposes." If the deed or will creating such a fee specifies who should get the property if the fee is terminated, that person has an EXECUTORY INTEREST in the property; otherwise the transferor and his heirs retain a POSSIBILITY OF REVERTER. In either case, if the condition for continuation of the present fee is violated, the person next in line will automatically get the property in *fee simple absolute.*

fee², *n.* **1.** compensation for services rendered by an *independent contractor* (see under CONTRACTOR), especially professional services by a lawyer, doctor, or the like See also *contingency fee* (under CONTINGENCY) **2.** a sum paid for a LICENSE or privilege, such as a fee paid to the government for a driver's license or for admission to a national park. See also *filing fee* (under FILE). Cf TAX.

felon, *n.* a person who commits a FELONY.

felony, *n.* a serious crime, usually defined as one punishable by death or by imprisonment for more than one year Cf. MISDEMEANOR. —**felonious,** *adj*

felony murder, the commission or attempted commission of a felony that unintentionally results in a death Felony murder is punishable as MURDER. The felony murder doctrine in its most extreme form holds a peripheral participant in a minor felony guilty of murder if an accidental and unforeseeable death occurs in the course of the crime, even if that participant had essentially nothing to do with the death Most states limit the doctrine in various ways, as by applying it only to serious felonies and allowing a defendant to show as an *affirmative defense* (see under DEFENSE) that she was not involved in the killing and had no reason to believe that such a thing might occur

FICA. See under SOCIAL SECURITY

fiction. See LEGAL FICTION.

fidelity bond. See under BOND².

fidelity insurance, insurance against loss due to dishonest or unfaithful conduct by an employee. A fidelity insurance contract is also called a *fidelity bond* (see under BOND²).

fiduciary, *n.* **1.** a trustee or a person in a position analogous to that of a trustee, whereby another person or persons must rely upon the fiduciary to exercise special care, good faith, and loyalty in dealing with money and property. For example, an attorney is a fiduciary of her client, a corporate director is a fiduciary of the corporation, and each general partner in a business is a fiduciary of the other partners. See also FIDUCIARY DUTY. —*adj.* **2.** pertaining to a fiduciary or a FIDUCIARY RELATIONSHIP.

fiduciary bond. See under BOND².

fiduciary duty, the duty of utmost good faith, loyalty, and care that the law imposes upon every FIDUCIARY in dealing with matters that are the subject of a FIDUCIARY RELATIONSHIP. See also *breach of fiduciary duty* (under BREACH); *utmost care* (under CARE); SELF-DEALING

fiduciary relationship, a legal relationship in which one party necessarily reposes special trust and confidence in the other, so that the other is held to be a FIDUCIARY of the first.

fighting words, words spoken directly to a person that are of a sort likely to provoke violent retaliation. Such speech may be outlawed as a *breach of the peace* (see under BREACH). See also FREEDOM OF SPEECH; *hate speech* (under SPEECH).

file, *v.* **1.** to commence an action by depositing a copy of the complaint, indictment, or other initial court paper with the court: *to file suit; file charges.* **2.** to deposit a copy of each successive court paper with the court clerk for notation on the docket, for transmittal to the judge if it is a matter requiring the judge's attention, and ultimately for placement in the court's official file on the case. *to file a motion for summary judgment.* See also COURTESY COPY. **3.** to deposit any legal document with an appropriate governmental agency: *to file a tax return; file an application for a liquor license; file a registration statement for an issue of preferred stock.* **4. file under seal,** to file papers with a court in a sealed envelope to be opened only by the judge and not made available to the public, usually pursuant to a CONFIDENTIALITY STIPULATION. **5. filing fee,** a fee that must be paid to a court in order to commence an action in that court, or a fee required by any other government office upon the filing of certain kinds of papers. Cf. IN FORMA PAUPERIS. —*n.* **6.** the complete set of documents pertaining to a matter kept by a court or other government or private office.

final order. See under ORDER¹.

financial statement. See under STATEMENT

find, *v.* to make a determination of any kind in the course of a case: *The appellate court found the cases cited by the* *appellant unpersuasive The jury found the defendant guilty.*

finding of fact, in a nonjury trial, a judge's decision on a purely factual issue (e.g., whether the light was red or green; whether the purchaser was acting in good faith). See also CONCLUSION OF LAW; FINDINGS OF FACT AND CONCLUSIONS OF LAW.

findings of fact and conclusions of law, the form in which a judge's decision is rendered in a civil suit tried without a jury in the federal courts and many state courts. This full statement of the factual and legal bases for the court's decision provides a clear record for appellate review. Also called, informally, **findings and conclusions.** See also FINDING OF FACT; CONCLUSION OF LAW.

fine, *n.* **1.** a sum of money required to be paid as a civil or criminal PENALTY. —*v.* **2.** to impose a fine upon a person; to sentence a person to pay a fine.

first impression, describing a legal issue not previously considered by the courts. *question of first impression; matter of first impression.* See also *case of first impression* (under CASE[1]).

first mortgage. See under MORTGAGE.

fishing expedition, *Informal.* a derogatory term applied to requests from an adversary for wide-ranging DISCOVERY. In general, the purpose of discovery is to obtain evidence, or information leading to evidence, pertaining to a known cause of action, not to "fish around" in the hope of stumbling upon a basis for maintaining a suit.

fitness. See *warranty of fitness for a particular purpose* (under WARRANTY).

fixture, *n.* an article that is attached to real property in such a way that its removal would damage the property, such as a furnace or a built-in bookcase. Ordinarily such fixtures are regarded as part of the real property.

flat tax. See under TAX.

floating zone. See under ZONE.

FOIA. See FREEDOM OF INFORMATION ACT

follow, *v.* (of a court) to adhere to a PRECEDENT; to apply the principles articulated or used in a particular precedent to the case at hand.

for cause, for a legally sufficient reason logically related to the action being taken, not for arbitrary, whimsical, or irrelevant reasons; for example, the firing of an employee because of inadequate performance would be a "termination for cause." See also *challenge for cause* (under CHALLENGE).

for the record. See under RECORD.

for-profit corporation. See under CORPORATION

force majeure, *French.* (lit. "superior force") an unforeseeable natural or human event beyond the control of the parties to a contract, rendering performance of a contract impossible A "force majeure clause" in a contract relieves a party from the duty to perform if performance is rendered impossible by force majeure

foreclosure, *n.* **1.** the termination of a property owner's rights in property that is subject to a mortgage or other *security interest* (see under INTEREST[1]) when the owner has failed to pay the debt secured by the property, so that the property can be sold to pay off the debt **2.** the entire procedure (normally a court action) by which foreclosure is accomplished, the property is sold (normally auctioned off), the proceeds are applied to the debt, and any money left over is refunded to the debtor —**foreclose,** *v.*

foreign, *adj.* referring to another jurisdiction—sometimes another country (see *foreign commerce,* under COMMERCE), but often just another state (see *foreign corporation,* under CORPORATION). To avoid confusion, the phrase "foreign country" is often used when that is what is meant· *a foreign country judgment; a foreign country divorce.*

forensic, *adj.* for law enforcement and courtroom purposes: *forensic medicine; forensic chemistry; forensic anthropolgy.*

foreperson, *n* a jury member selected either by lot or by vote of the jury to coordinate deliberations and render the jury's verdict in court

forfeiture, *n.* the loss of a right, license, or property as a civil or criminal penalty; e g , the loss of a fishing license as a penalty for taking fish that are too small or the loss of an automobile because it was used in a crime —**forfeit,** *v.*

forgery, *n.* the crime of making or altering a writing, recording, coin, or other document that is to be passed off as genuine and authorized when it is not, or of attempting to pass off such a document See also *uttering a forged instrument* (under UTTER). —**forge,** *v*

form, *n.* **1.** the superficial appearance of a transaction as distinguished from the underlying reality See example under SUBSTANCE. **2.** Also called **legal form.** a model or preprinted document containing standard legal language for accomplishing a particular kind of transaction Such forms can often be purchased in stationery and office supply stores.

form of action, any of the dozen or so specific categories into which every action at law traditionally was required to fit. Each form of action had a special name, could be used only in certain types of cases, had its own highly technical pleading rules, and provided only a specific kind of remedy. The rigidity of this system was the main reason for the growth of EQUITY Under modern rules of civil procedure, there is but one form of action—the civil action—and the plaintiff may request and obtain any relief warranted by the facts. The common law forms of action are still often referred to, however, because of their influence in shaping English and American law over the centuries

forma pauperis. See IN FORMA PAUPERIS.

fornication, *n.* the crime of engaging in sexual intercourse while unmarried. The crime has been abolished in most states; in the states where it has not been abolished, there are a lot of criminals. Cf ADULTERY

forum, *n.* the court or jurisdiction in which an action is pending See also LEX FORI; PUBLIC FORUM

forum non conveniens, *Latin* (lit "an inappropriate forum") the doctrine that a court in which an action has properly been filed may decline to exercise jurisdiction over it if the case has no significant relationship with that jurisdiction and would be more suitably litigated in another state or another country.

forum shopping, the choosing of a forum expected to be sympathetic to one's case; for example, the choice of a tobacco state for a suit by a tobacco company, of a nontobacco state for a suit against a tobacco company, or of a Bible Belt state for a pornography prosecution

foundation, *n* **1.** evidence establishing the admissibility of an exhibit or other evidence For example, in order to introduce testimony that the plaintiff made a certain out-of-court statement about the defendant, it would usually be necessary to "lay a foundation" by establishing that the party testifying was in a position to hear the statement, to know who was making it, and perhaps to know whom it referred to See also AUTHENTICATE; CONNECT UP **2.** an institution established, usually by means of a large donation or legacy, to support research, the arts, or charitable activities

franchise, *n* **1.** a right or license granted by a company (the **franchisor**) to an individual or group (the **franchisee**) to market its goods or services and use its trademark in a specific territory, usually pursuant to a detailed agreement requiring operation of the business in accordance with the franchisor's standards and setting forth the financial terms of the arrangement **2.** a privilege granted by the government, such as the right to operate in the form of a corporation or to operate a bus company. **3.** the right to vote.

franchise tax, a tax imposed upon a corporation for the privilege of doing business in a state

fraud, *n.* **1.** Also called **actual fraud** or **fraud in fact.** the tort of obtaining money or property by means of a false portrayal of facts, either by words or by conduct For a list of the elements of fraud, see ELEMENT. In criminal law, fraudulent conduct may be classified as larceny, forgery, theft, or other crimes depending upon the circumstances **2. constructive fraud,** conduct viewed by a court as having the same effect as actual fraud though not involving any false representation of fact This usually occurs when a FIDUCIARY abuses the trust and confidence of the person to whom she owes a fiduciary duty, profiting by keeping silent about matters that should have been disclosed to that person (In a nonfiduciary relationship, as between an ordinary buyer and seller, there is no general duty to speak about things one is not asked about) Also called **legal fraud** or **fraud in law. 3. fraud in the factum,** a misrepresentation as to the fundamental nature of a contract, will, or other instrument being signed, as in a classic case in which a wife was told that a certain legal document was just a formality for tax purposes and it turned out to be a separation agreement. Such fraud renders an instrument VOID. Also called **fraud in the execution. 4. fraud in the inducement,** misrepresentation upon which a person relies in entering into a contract, not about the terms of the contract itself but about the subject of the contract or the surrounding circumstances, as when a seller conceals a serious defect in a product with a coat of paint. Such fraud renders the contract VOIDABLE. Also called **fraudulent inducement. 5. mail fraud,** the federal crime of using the mails in connection with a scheme to defraud **6. wire fraud,** the federal crime of using interstate telephone or telegraph wires in connection with a scheme to defraud See also SECURITIES FRAUD; TAX FRAUD.

frauds, statute of. See STATUTE OF FRAUDS.

fraudulent, *adj.* **1.** pertaining to or constituting a FRAUD. **2.** intentionally wrongful; dishonest; unfair

fraudulent conveyance, a transfer of property by a debtor for less than its full value, in an effort to put it into friendly hands where it cannot be attached by creditors, or to favor one creditor over others A court will usually set aside such a conveyance.

fraudulent inducement. Same as *fraud in the inducement* (see under FRAUD).

free exercise of religion, the practice of one's religion and observance of its tenets without government interference—a right guaranteed by the **Free Exercise Clause** of the First Amendment to the Constitution This right may be limited by laws of general applicability not targeted at religion, however; for example, in the 1980's and 1990's the Supreme Court upheld military regulations preventing Orthodox Jewish servicemen from wearing yarmulkes and criminal laws barring the sacramental use of peyote in Native American religious ritual

freedom, *n.* absence of legal restraint; the RIGHT to do or not do something without governmental interference The conventional term used to describe a number of constitutional rights, including those referred to in the next few entries

freedom of assembly, the right of people to gather peacefully for political or other purposes. This is guaranteed by the First Amendment (see Appendix), subject only to the government's right to impose reasonable restrictions on the time, place, and manner of such assembly. Cf UNLAWFUL ASSEMBLY

freedom of association, the constitutional right to join with others for lawful purposes, derived primarily from a combination of First Amendment rights (assembly, religion, etc.)

freedom of contract, the name given to a now discredited constitutional doctrine, which the Supreme Court followed from 1897 to 1937, holding that the government has only very limited power to regulate contractual relationships, especially in regard to conditions of employment. It is now accepted that federal and state governments have wide powers to dictate reasonable terms for employment relationships, consumer transactions, and other contracts, which no claim of "freedom of contract" can overcome.

freedom of expression, a general term for FREEDOM OF SPEECH and FREEDOM OF THE PRESS; sometimes used broadly to include FREEDOM OF RELIGION also.

Freedom of Information Act (FOIA), a federal statute, widely imitated at the state level, requiring most government documents and records to be made available to the public on request and specifying procedures for requests and disclosure.

freedom of religion, the freedom to hold and practice one's religious beliefs and freedom from government involvement in religious matters, guaranteed by the First Amendment clauses protecting FREE EXERCISE OF RELIGION and prohibiting ESTABLISHMENT OF RELIGION. See also SEPARATION OF CHURCH AND STATE.

freedom of speech, the First Amendment right to express oneself. It covers any form or medium of SPEECH, not just speaking and writing, and generally prohibits the government from restricting expression on the basis of content or viewpoint. As interpreted by the Supreme Court, however, the degree of freedom depends upon the category of speech. It is greatest for speech conveying ideas about such matters as politics, art, religion, or science. It is lower for such categories as *commercial speech* and *indecent speech* (see under SPEECH). And some categories, most notably OBSCENITY, are completely unprotected—not regarded as "speech" at all within the meaning of the Constitution.

freedom of the press, the First Amendment right to publish books, newspapers, and magazines and otherwise distribute and broadcast information, opinion, and expression, largely free from government censorship. See also PRIOR RESTRAINT

freehold, *n.* a possessory interest in real property amounting to an *estate in fee* or *life estate* (see under ESTATE¹). Also called **freehold estate** or **freehold interest.** Cf. LEASEHOLD.

fresh pursuit, pursuit by a law enforcement officer of a suspected felon who is fleeing and may escape if the pursuit is abandoned. An officer in fresh pursuit may usually follow the suspect across jurisdictional lines to make the arrest, or pursue a suspect into a building and search for him there without a search warrant Also called **hot pursuit.** See also EXIGENT CIRCUMSTANCES.

friend of the court. See under AMICUS CURIAE.

frisk. See STOP AND FRISK

frivolous, *adj.* describing an action or procedural step that clearly has no basis in law or in any reasonable argument for a change in the law· *a frivolous action; a frivolous motion; a frivolous appeal.* A court may SANCTION an attorney or party who takes frivolous action, as by requiring him to pay the attorneys' fees incurred by his adversary in opposing it.

frolic of one's own, conduct by an employee outside the SCOPE OF EMPLOYMENT The employer is not liable for the acts of an employee under such circumstances. The classic example is a company driver who, when sent to make a delivery, makes a detour to visit his mistress and causes an accident while on the detour. The company will not be liable for the damages because the employee was on "a frolic of his own." Cf. RESPONDENT SUPERIOR.

fruit of the poisonous tree, evidence derived from information obtained through an illegal search or other illegal investigative technique. Such evidence is generally subject to the EXCLUSIONARY RULE to the same extent as the illegally obtained information that led to it

frustration, *n.* an unforeseen circumstance that destroys the purpose of a contract. Under the "doctrine of frustration," further performance of the contract is excused. For example, if an agreement is reached to rent a room overlooking a parade, and then the parade is unexpectedly cancelled, the would-be renter need not go through with the contract

full age. See under AGE.

full faith and credit, deference given by the courts of one state to the laws and judicial proceedings of another state. The Constitution requires the states to give full faith and credit to each other's laws and judgments; thus a judgment obtained in one state is generally enforceable in every other state, and may generally be attacked in another state only upon grounds that would have been allowed in the state where the judgment was rendered Cf COMITY

full partner. See under PARTNER

full warranty. See under WARRANTY.

fully paid stock. See under STOCK.

fundamental error. See under ERROR

fundamental right, any right expressly guaranteed by the Constitution, or deemed by the Supreme Court to be so basic to the concept of liberty as to be protected from government restriction (except to the extent necessary to serve a COMPELLING INTEREST) by the DUE PROCESS clause of the Fourteenth Amendment (see Appendix). Areas now deemed fundamental include voting and running for office, access to the courts, freedom of travel, freedom of association, and decision making in matters of marriage and procreation See also RIGHT OF PRIVACY; *substantive due process* (under DUE PROCESS), STRICT SCRUTINY

future estate. See under ESTATE[1]

future interest. See under INTEREST[1]

futuro. See IN FUTURO

G

gag order, a judge's order to parties and attorneys in a sensational case not to discuss the case publicly, issued in the hope of avoiding publicity regarded as damaging to the fairness and dignity of the proceedings Cf. CONFIDENTIALITY STIPULATION.

gain, *n.* the profit on a sale or exchange of property; generally, the amount by which the value received in exchange for the property exceeds the owner's BASIS in the property Ordinarily, the gain is subject to income tax See also *capital gain* and *capital gains tax* (both under CAPITAL[1]); REALIZE; RECOGNIZE. Cf. LOSS.

garnish, *v.* to serve a GARNISHMENT; to attach wages or other money or property owed to or held for a debtor, so that those assets can be redirected to the debtor's creditor

garnishee, *n.* **1.** a person or entity served with a GARNISHMENT; for example, the employer of a judgment debtor whose wages are being garnished. —*v* **2.** to GARNISH

garnisher or **garnishor,** *n* the creditor for whose benefit a garnishment is effected

garnishment, *n.* **1.** the ATTACHMENT of wages or other money or property owed to or held for a debtor, usually a judgment debtor, so that they can be used to satisfy the debtor's obligation. For example, the wages of a divorced parent who has failed to pay court-ordered child support may be subject to garnishment by the custodial parent to satisfy the child support obligation **2.** a judicial proceeding to effect such a garnishment **3.** the formal document which must be served on the employer or other person being garnished in order to effect a garnishment

general, *adj.* describing the most usual, basic, comprehensive, or undifferentiated form or application of something, as distinguished from specialized forms, which are often characterized by such terms as "specific," "special," "limited," or "qualified." See *general* APPEARANCE, BEQUEST, CONTRACTOR, COUNSEL, DAMAGES, JURISDICTION[1], PARTNER, PARTNERSHIP, POWER OF ATTORNEY, RELEASE, VERDICT under those words.

generation-skipping trust, a trust created, usually by will, in such a way that one's children will have the use and benefit (but not ownership) of certain property during their lives, and then ownership of the property will pass to their children. Formerly this saved the family one round of estate taxes because actual ownership of the property skipped over one generation. That tax loophole was plugged by the **generation-skipping transfer tax,** which is collected upon expiration of the beneficial interests of the first generation of children

gentlemen's agreement, an agreement not intended by the parties to be enforced by legal action, but expected to be performed or adhered to solely as a matter of personal friendship or honor. Sometimes this is because the agreement is in fact illegal, as to fix prices or pay a bribe

geographic jurisdiction. Same as JURISDICTION².

gerrymander, *n* **1.** a voting district of seemingly illogical shape created in order to achieve a political purpose, such as diluting the votes of the opposing political party, protecting incumbents, or increasing the chance that a member of a racial or ethnic minority group will be elected to legislative office The Supreme Court has been loath to upset gerrymanders created for the first two reasons, but has been strongly critical of "bizarre" district lines drawn in an effort to increase minority representation in Congress —*v.* **2.** to create such a district; to draw irregular district lines for such purposes.

gift, *n.* **1.** Also called **inter vivos gift** or **gift inter vivos. a.** a voluntary transfer of money or property, completed during one's lifetime, without expecting anything in return For such a gift to be effective, the DONOR must understand and intend the consequences of the act, and the property must be delivered to and accepted by the DONEE. **b.** the property so transferred. See also DELIVERY; INTER VIVOS. **2.** Also called **testamentary gift. a.** a transfer of property by will; a BEQUEST or DEVISE. **b.** property so transferred. **3. gift causa mortis,** a conditional gift of personal property by a person who is ill or injured and expects to die To be legally effective it must satisfy all the requirements of other inter vivos gifts, and in addition the donor must die of the illness or injury If the donor recovers, the property must be returned. See also CAUSA MORTIS. **4. gift in contemplation of death, a.** a *gift causa mortis.* **b.** for tax purposes, a gift made within three years of death. Ordinarily the value of the gift is included in the donor's estate for estate tax purposes

gift over, a transfer of a future interest in property to one person in connection with the transfer of a present interest in the same property to someone else. For example, if property is granted "to A for life, then to B," the grant to B is a "gift over." The word *gift* is used even if the future interest being transferred was paid for.

gift tax, a tax imposed by the federal government on very large gifts made during a person's lifetime Payment of the tax is the obligation of the donor, not the recipients.

give, *v.* to make a GIFT.

gloss, *n.* **1.** an explanation or interpretation of a statute, constitutional provision, or judicial ruling, especially one that adds or makes explicit some qualification that is not expressly stated in the statute or ruling **2. judicial gloss, a.** a court's gloss on a statutory or constitutional provision or prior court ruling, usually made in a discussion of its applicability or inapplicability to a particular case. **b.** the accumulated interpretations of a number of courts over a period of years; a judicial consensus on interpretation of a statutory or constitutional provision or a significant earlier ruling.

go forward or **go forward with evidence,** to introduce evidence on an issue in a case, thereby placing the issue before the factfinder. See also *burden of going forward* (under BURDEN[1]).

go private, to cease to be a *publicly held corporation* and become a *closely held corporation* (see both under CORPORATION) through a transaction by which most shareholders are forced to accept money for their shares and the business is left in the hands of a few officers, directors, or major shareholders. Cf. GO PUBLIC.

go public, (of a corporation) to issue shares to the general public for the first time, thereby becoming a *publicly held corporation* (see under CORPORATION) Cf. GO PRIVATE.

go to, to bear upon; be relevant to the issue of: *That evidence is admissible because it goes to the witness's credibility. Point 3 of their brief goes to the constitutionality of the statute.*

going concern, an enterprise that is carrying on its normal business and is expected to continue indefinitely. Cf WIND UP.

golden parachute, a contract between a corporation and any of its high executives promising the executive extremely generous financial compensation in the event that he loses his job or resigns because of a merger or takeover. This assures that regardless of what happens to ordinary employees who lose their jobs as a result of such corporate changes, the top executives will be amply rewarded.

good, *adj.* generally, of a type approved or favored by law, or regarded as acceptable in the marketplace or by society at large. The specific legal significance of the word varies greatly from phrase to phrase.

good cause, 1. a legally sufficient reason or excuse, especially for taking or omitting some procedural step in a case. Cf. INSUFFICIENT CAUSE. **2. for good cause shown** or **good cause having been shown,** expressions often used by a court in issuing an order, indicating that the party seeking the order has made a sufficient showing of facts warranting its issuance.

good faith, the quality of mind and heart possessed by a person who is acting with sincerity and honesty, and without intent to cheat or take unfair advantage of another. Cf. BAD FAITH.

good faith exception, an exception to the EXCLUSIONARY RULE, whereby evidence found in an illegal search may be used against a defendant if the police made the search in good faith reliance upon a search warrant issued by a neutral magistrate, which turned out to be invalid through no fault of the police.

good faith purchaser, a purchaser of property who acts in good faith in making the purchase and has no reason to suspect that someone else might have a right to the property. Unless the property was stolen, a good faith purchaser will ordinarily get to keep the purchased property even if it turns out that the seller did not have the right to sell it. Also called **good faith purchaser for value** or **bona fide purchaser (for value).**

good law, in accord with current law. The phrase is used mostly in discussing the status of past judicial decisions or statements of legal principle in light of subsequent evolution of the law· *The much criticized rule that property owners owe a higher duty of care to business invitees than to social guests is still good law in most states; but in at least thirteen states it is no longer good law.* Cf. BAD LAW.

good title. Same as *marketable title* (see under TITLE).

good will, 1. the benefit to a business of customer loyalty, brand name recognition, reputation for quality and honesty, and the like. Wrongful conduct injurious to a company's good will may be the basis of an action for damages **2.** in the purchase of an existing business, the excess of the price paid over the net asset value of the company Now often written **goodwill,** but always pronounced as if two separate words, with the stress on *will*.

goods, *n.pl.* **1.** virtually any *tangible personal property* (see under PROPERTY); movable things **2. consumer goods,** goods used primarily for personal, family, or household purposes

government, *n* **1.** the ruling authorities of a city, state, nation, or other political unit; the body of officials that makes and enforces the laws. **2.** (*sometimes cap.*) the prosecuting authority in a federal criminal case. Such cases are captioned United States v. So-and-So, but in court and in court papers the prosecution is typically referred to as "the Government" *The Government argues that the search was reasonable* Cf. STATE; PEOPLE. **3. federal government,** the national government of the United States. **4. republican form of government,** government by the people, through their elected representatives. According to the Constitution, the federal government is required to guarantee that the states will maintain a republican form of government.

government contractor. See under CONTRACTOR.

government security. See under SECURITY².

grade, *v* **1.** to categorize offenses according to their degree of seriousness, setting more serious penalties for more serious crimes; for example, criminal homicide is typically graded into several levels, such as first degree murder, second degree murder, voluntary manslaughter, involuntary manslaughter, and criminally negligent homicide. —*n.* **2.** Also called **degree.** the level of a particular offense in such a grading system.

grand, *adj. Law French.* (lit. "large") large, major, greater Used in certain phrases, usually in contrast to PETIT or PETTY; e.g., *grand jury* (see under JURY), *grand larceny* (see under LARCENY).

grandfather, *v.* **1.** to exempt a person or entity from a new law: *Existing buildings were grandfathered by the new zoning law, so they can remain even if they are nonconforming.* —*adj.* **2. grandfather clause,** a clause in a statute that exempts a class of persons or entities established and operating under prior law from new requirements

grant, *v.* **1.** broadly, to transfer or bestow property or a right of any kind· *The inventor granted his patent to a university The Fifth Amendment grants to all property owners the right of just compensation if the government takes their property.* **2.** specifically, to convey an interest in real property. **3.** to accede to a motion, petition, or other request for judicial action, by issuing the requested order or taking the requested action; opposite of DENY: *The judge granted our motion for a protective order* —*n* **4.** the act of granting something. **5.** the thing granted.

grantee, *n* a person or entity to which something is granted, especially an interest in real property

grantor, *n.* **1.** a person or entity that grants something, particularly an interest in real property **2.** The SETTLOR of a trust. See also *grantor trust* (under TRUST)

gratuitous, *adj.* **1.** given, said, or done without an obligation to do so and without receiving or expecting anything in return; without CONSIDERATION See, for example, *gratuitous* BAILMENT, PROMISE under these words **2.** describing a party to a gratuitous transaction; for example, a *gratuitous bailee* (see under BAILMENT)

gravamen, *n.* the fundamental or material part of an accusation; the essence of a complaint or charge. Lawyers who do not understand the full meaning of this word sometimes use it to mean the essence or gist of anything (the gravamen of my argument; the gravamen of the expert's report), thereby using the wrong word in the wrong place in an effort to sound professional

Great Charter, the MAGNA CARTA.

Great Writ, the writ of HABEAS CORPUS. Also called the **great writ of liberty.**

green card, *Informal.* an identification card—formerly colored green—issued to foreign nationals who have been granted permanent resident status in the United States and thus have full employment rights in the country. See also *resident alien* (under ALIEN)

grievance, *n.* **1.** in a unionized workplace, a formal complaint by an employee, the union, or the employer, alleging a violation of the *collective bargaining agreement* (see under COLLECTIVE BARGAINING) or complaining about working conditions. **2.** a similar internal complaint concerning some condition in a nonunionized workplace, school, prison, or other institution with formal procedures for dealing with such complaints. **3. grievance committee,** a committee provided for by union contract or otherwise established to evaluate and attempt to remedy grievances. **4. grievance procedure,** a formal procedure for dealing with grievances.

gross, *adj.* **1.** (of a sum of money) total before taking account of deductions or adjustments: *gross income* (see under INCOME). See also *gross lease* (under LEASE). **2.** flagrant or extreme (as distinguished from SIMPLE or ORDINARY) *gross negligence* (see under NEGLIGENCE).

ground lease. See under LEASE

group boycott. See under BOYCOTT

group insurance. See under INSURANCE

guarantee, *v.* **1.** to give a GUARANTY or become a SURETY; to act as a surety or GUARANTOR of someone else's obligation: *The bank would give me a loan only if my parents guaranteed it.* **2.** to assure: *The purpose of the program is to guarantee access to medical care.* **3.** *Informal.* to issue or stand behind a WARRANTY on a product. —*n.* **4.** a guaranty or suretyship agreement. **5.** any assurance· *The Fifth Amendment guarantee of due process.* **6.** *Informal.* a non-lawyer's term for a warranty on a product

guaranteed security. See under SECURITY[2]

guarantor, *n.* a person or entity that issues or is obligated under a GUARANTY.

guaranty, *n.* **1.** in the strictest sense, a promise or contract to make someone whole if a third person fails to fulfill an obligation; that is, a promise by A to B that if C fails to pay a debt or perform some other obligation owed to B, then A will pay the debt or otherwise compensate B. **2.** any promise to answer for the debt, default, or miscarriage of another. In this broader sense, guaranty includes SURETYSHIP. Under the STATUTE OF FRAUDS, any such promise must be in writing and signed to be enforceable. **3.** in the broadest sense, any GUARANTEE. —*v.* **4.** to GUARANTEE anything.

guardian, *n.* **1.** a person, especially one appointed by a court, with responsibility for the care of a child or an incompetent adult (the WARD) and legal control of the ward's affairs. Sometimes one person, such as a relative, is designated to take personal care of the ward, and another individual or a financial institution is designated to manage the ward's money and property; the former is then referred to as the **guardian of the person** and the latter as the **guardian of the property**. See also COMMITTEE; CONSERVATOR. **2. guardian ad litem,** a person, usually a lawyer, appointed by the court to represent the interests of an infant or incompetent person or a class of such people in a case. Of course, in some cases opinions might vary as to what those interests really are. See also AD LITEM. **3. testamentary guardian,** a guardian for a minor child, designated in the parent's will. —**guardianship,** *n.*

guest statute. See AUTOMOBILE GUEST STATUTE.

guilty, *adj.* **1.** (of a criminal defendant) adjudged by a court to have committed an offense, either on the basis of a finding or verdict at trial, or because the defendant admitted or did not contest the charge. See also ADJUDGE; JUDGMENT. Cf. NOT GUILTY; INNOCENT **2.** designating a PLEA entered by a criminal defendant, admitting the charge. This is usually the result of a PLEA BARGAIN. Cf NOLO CONTENDERE; NOT GUILTY **3.** having committed a tort, a breach of contract, or an act damaging to one's position in a civil case: *guilty of breach of contract; guilty of contributory negligence.*

gun control, legal restrictions on the manufacture, importation, distribution, or possession of guns. Despite arguments that gun control laws violate the Second Amendment (see Appendix), no gun control law has ever been struck down under the Second Amendment. See also RIGHT TO BEAR ARMS.

H

habeas corpus, *Latin.* (lit "have the body") **1.** an ancient English writ commanding an official holding someone in custody to have the "body" (that is, the person) of the prisoner brought before the court so that the lawfulness of the imprisonment can be inquired into and the prisoner set free if not being held legally. **2.** a modern procedure or writ for testing the legality of custody, usually of a criminal defendant or suspect, but sometimes of a child or civil detainee, such as a person committed to a mental hospital. **3.** particularly, the constitutionally guaranteed procedure by which the constitutionality of a state conviction and imprisonment can be tested in federal court **(federal habeas corpus).** Habeas corpus is sometimes referred to as the **great writ of liberty,** or simply the **Great Writ.**

habitable, *adj.* **1.** fit to live in; in compliance with building codes and free of dangers to health and safety. See also TENANTABLE. **2. warranty of habitability,** a landlord's WARRANTY, regarded by law in most states as inherent in every residential lease, that the premises are habitable and will be kept that way.

habitual criminal or **habitual offender,** a person previously convicted of several crimes, and thus subject to a more severe sentence for any subsequent crime. See also REPEAT OFFENDER, THREE STRIKES LAW

haec verba. See IN HAEC VERBA.

halfway house, a residence for individuals who have been in prison, providing a supervised and structured environment to help them adjust to outside life. Cf WORK RELEASE.

hand, *n.* **1.** Same as SIGNATURE. **2. hand and seal,** one's signature and seal (see SEAL¹) placed together on a document —*v* **3. hand down,** to render a judicial opinion, ruling, sentence, etc. This phrase is used whether the decision is rendered orally or in writing, and whether rendered from the bench or from chambers See also ISSUE⁴. **4. hand up,** to pass a document or exhibit up to the judge in court. This phrase is used whether the object is handed directly to the judge or simply given to a bailiff or clerk to hand up.

handicap, *n.* Same as DISABILITY, which is generally the preferred term today. —**handicapped,** *adj.*

hang *v.* **1.** (of a jury) to be unable to agree upon a decision; to be deadlocked Past tense: **hung.** **2.** (of a condemned person) to be suspended by the neck until dead. Past tense: **hanged.**

harassment, *n.* **1.** the crime of deliberately and repeatedly annoying or interfering with a person, as by telephoning repeatedly, sending anonymous messages, following, taunting, etc. See also INTENTIONAL INFLICTION OF MENTAL DISTRESS; STALKING. **2.** annoying or offensive conduct in the workplace, directed toward an employee or group of employees because of their race, color, religion, sex, or national origin. Such harassment, when engaged in or tolerated by an employer, constitutes unlawful employment discrimination. See also HOSTILE WORKING ENVIRONMENT; SEXUAL HARASSMENT.

hardships, balancing of. See BALANCING OF THE EQUITIES

harmless, *adj.* **1.** not harmful or prejudicial; inconsequential. **2.** unharmed; safe from harm or prejudice. **3. harmless error.** See under ERROR **4. hold** (or **save**) **harmless, a.** to release from liability or responsibility for loss or damage; to abandon any claim that one might have against someone **b.** to indemnify; to promise to compensate someone for any loss that might be incurred by reason of claims asserted later by others.

hate crime, a crime motivated by bias against a group identified by race, religion, sexual orientation, or other group characteristic, or a crime in which the victim is chosen because of perceived membership in such a group States may impose extra penalties for such crimes. Also called **bias crime.**

hate speech. See under SPEECH.

head of household, an unmarried person (or married person living separately from his or her spouse and filing a separate tax return) who lives with and maintains a household for an unmarried child or a dependent relative. Under the Internal Revenue Code, such a person qualifies for special income tax rates.

headnote, *n.* a capsule summary, usually in one sentence, of a legal point in a judicial opinion, inserted by an editor at the head of the published version of the opinion as an aid to legal research. Most published opinions are preceded by several headnotes. Cf DIGEST; SYLLABUS

health care proxy, a document, provided for by statute in some states, authorizing another person to make medical decisions for the signer if the signer is unable to do so Also called DURABLE POWER OF ATTORNEY FOR HEALTH CARE See also *durable power of attorney* (under POWER OF ATTORNEY); LIVING WILL; RIGHT TO DIE

hear, *v* **1.** (of a court or judge) **a.** to handle a case **b.** to receive evidence and argument, usually orally and without a jury: *to hear a motion; to hear an appeal; to hear a case without a jury.* Cf. TRY (def. I); *take on submission* (under SUBMIT). See also OPPORTUNITY TO BE HEARD **2. hear and determine,** to hear and reach a decision on. **3. hear and report,** to hear and make a recommendation on In the federal courts, certain matters may be referred by a judge to a magistrate to hear and determine or hear and report

hear ye, a phrase often called out (usually two or three times) at the opening of court proceedings, to get the undivided attention of everyone present and impress upon them the seriousness and importance of the proceedings about to commence. Means the same thing as the Law French OYEZ, which is still used in many courts Cf. KNOW ALL MEN BY THESE PRESENTS

hearing, *n.* **1.** any factfinding proceeding at which testimony is taken, except a full-scale court trial; for example, a hearing by a court on a motion for a preliminary injunction, a trial before an administrative tribunal or arbitration panel, or a hearing before a legislative committee **2.** loosely, any proceeding at which legal matters are presented for consideration or decision, including full-scale court trials, appellate arguments, and even matters submitted entirely on papers. **3. hearing examiner** (or **officer**). Same as ADMINISTRATIVE LAW JUDGE **4. preliminary hearing,** an early stage in a felony prosecution, in which the prosecutor must show a court that there is sufficient evidence to justify a trial Also called **probable cause hearing, bindover hearing. 5. public hearing,** a hearing held by an administrative agency at which the general public is invited to comment on proposed rules or actions of the agency.

hearsay, *n.* **1.** (in a courtroom proceeding) any assertion, other than one made on the witness stand in that very proceeding, that is offered as evidence of the matter asserted; often loosely summarized as "an out-of-court declaration offered for its truth." For example, the statement "I saw my husband shoot Smith," made by a suspect's wife to police shortly after an incident, is hearsay if offered by the prosecution at the husband's trial to help prove that he is the person who shot Smith; but a testator's statement "I am Napoleon," if offered at the trial of a challenge to the will to show that the testator was of unsound mind, is *nonhearsay*, because it is not offered as evidence that the declarant truly was Napoleon. A hearsay assertion may be either oral or written, or even nonverbal (such as a nod of the head). **2. hearsay evidence,** any testimony or document offered in court that contains hearsay; for example, a police officer's testimony, "She told me she saw her husband shoot Smith," or a letter written by the defendant's wife containing the sentence, "I saw my husband shoot Smith." **3. hearsay exception,** any of the numerous exceptions to the *hearsay rule* under which hearsay evidence is deemed admissible, usually because the circumstances under which the hearsay assertion was made are thought to provide reasonable assurance of its reliability. See, for example, PRESENT SENSE IMPRESSION; EXCITED UTTERANCE; *dying declaration* and *declaration against interest* (under DECLARATION); *business record* and *public record* (under RECORD); *unavailable witness* (under WITNESS) **4. hearsay rule,** the American rule of evidence under which hearsay is generally deemed inadmissible because the assertion presented as "truth" is usually not made under oath and is not subject to cross examination under the scrutiny of the judge and jury

heat of passion, extreme anger or other emotional disturbance provoked by circumstances that the law regards as sufficient to make a reasonable person lose control. The classic example is the man who discovers his wife in bed with another man, goes and gets his gun, and deliberately shoots them to death "in the heat of passion." (His, not theirs.) It is still the law in nearly all American jurisdictions that this is not murder, but merely *voluntary manslaughter* (see under MANSLAUGHTER)

heightened scrutiny, a test of constitutionality applied by the Supreme Court to laws that are alleged to violate EQUAL PROTECTION because they treat people differently on the basis of a QUASI-SUSPECT CLASSIFICATION, usually sex. This test is stricter than the RATIONAL BASIS TEST but less demanding than STRICT SCRUTINY. Under heightened scrutiny, a law will be upheld only if it is found to serve an "important governmental objective" and to be "substantially related" to the achievement of that objective. Also called **intermediate scrutiny.** See also SCRUTINY.

heir, *n.* **1.** the person, or one of the people, to whom one's property passes by operation of law if one dies without leaving a will. Also called **legal heir, heir at law.** See also *direct heir* (under DIRECT[1]); *collateral heir* (under COLLATERAL[2]); PRETERMITTED HEIR; INTESTATE SUCCESSION. Cf LEGATEE; DEVISEE. **2. and his heirs,** at common law, words that had to be included in any grant of real property to someone if the intent was to convey the property permanently—that is, to convey a *fee simple* (see under FEE[1]), so that the new owner could pass it on to his heirs or otherwise dispose of it. If the property was conveyed only to "John Smith," rather than to "John Smith and his heirs," Smith received only a *life estate* (see under ESTATE[1]), and upon his death the property reverted to the original owner (or his successors). Although this rule has been abolished nearly everywhere, these traditional words are still found in many deeds **3. heirs and assigns,** everyone to whom one might leave, give, or sell property; a standard phrase covering anyone who might succeed to one's interest in a piece of property or rights in a matter. For example, a defendant who gives a plaintiff money to settle a case will normally receive in return a RELEASE against any further claims in the matter, executed by the plaintiff "for herself and her heirs and assigns"; this precludes anyone else from coming along and asserting a new claim as her successor. See also ASSIGN.

high crimes and misdemeanors, the phrase used in the Constitution to denote misconduct by the President or another federal officer of sufficient gravity to warrant impeachment and removal from office. Whenever impeachment is considered, arguments arise over just what kind of crime meets this test, or whether conduct within the scope of this phrase necessarily must be punishable as a crime at all The Supreme Court has never had occasion to construe the phrase

high treason. See under TREASON.

higher court. See under COURT

highest and best use. See under USE.

highest degree of care. See under CARE.

hindering. See under ACCESSORY.

His (or **Her**) **Honor.** See under HONOR.

hold, *v.* **1.** (of a judge, court, or judicial opinion) to state the court's conclusion in a case, or on a particular issue in a case, especially an issue of law (as distinguished from fact). See also HOLDING. **2. hold harmless.** See under HARMLESS. **3. hold out,** to act in such a way as to create the impression—especially a false impression—that something or someone (often oneself) has certain qualities or status: *He held himself out as a qualified lawyer.* Depending upon the circumstances, this may lead to criminal penalties, civil liability for FRAUD, or an application of the doctrine of ESTOPPEL. **4. hold over,** to continue to occupy rented premises after the lease expires or the tenancy is legally terminated. The tenant who does this is commonly called a **holdover tenant.** See also *tenancy at sufferance* (under TENANCY).

holder, *n.* **1.** a person in possession of a *bearer instrument* (see under BEARER), or a person in possession of an instrument issued or indorsed to him or to his order. **2. holder in due course,** a holder who gives value for an instrument and takes it in an honest transaction in the normal course of the transferor's business, without knowledge of any facts that might make it unenforceable. The right of a holder in due course to receive payment on an instrument is often stronger than that of an ordinary holder.

holding, *n.* **1.** the ruling of a court in a case, or upon a particular issue in a case, especially an issue of law (as distinguished from fact). Cf. DICTUM. **2. holding company.** See under COMPANY. **3. holding period, a.** the period of time that a taxpayer keeps a piece of property before selling it. **b.** the length of time that a taxpayer must keep a piece of property before selling it in order to qualify for special reduced tax rates on the gain realized on the sale. See also *capital gains tax* (under CAPITAL¹).

holdover tenancy. Same as *tenancy at sufferance* (see under TENANCY).

holdover tenant. See under HOLD.

holographic will. See under WILL.

home owner's warranty. Same as *construction warranty* (see under WARRANTY).

home rule, the right of a city, town, or other local government to make its own laws on matters of local concern to the extent permitted by the state constitution or statutes.

homestead, *n.* **1.** a dwelling and surrounding land occupied by the owner as a home. **2. homestead exemption,** the principle that property designated as one's homestead in accordance with a state statute (generally called the **homestead law, homestead exemption statute,** or the like) may not be seized by creditors to satisfy one's debts. The scope of such laws varies from state to state; under the most generous, a debtor can sometimes live quite luxuriously while leaving his creditors unpaid.

homicide, *n.* **1.** an act or omission resulting in the death of another person. **2.** Also called **criminal homicide.** The crime of causing of another's death through conduct that was intentional, knowing, reckless, or extremely negligent, without JUSTIFICATION. All states recognize several degrees of the crime depending on the circumstances and the actor's STATE OF MIND. The major categories of homicide are usually called MURDER, MANSLAUGHTER, and *negligent homicide.* **3. justifiable homicide,** homicide committed under circumstances regarded by the law as justification for such an extreme act, the most common of which is SELF-DEFENSE. Justifiable homicide is not a crime **4. negligent homicide,** the crime of causing another's death through *criminal negligence* (see under NEGLIGENCE); the lowest degree of criminal homicide Called **criminally negligent homicide** in some states; in others, included in *involuntary manslaughter* (see under MANSLAUGHTER). **5. vehicular homicide,** a special category of homicide recognized in some states for dealing with homicides by careless and drunk drivers. Also called **homicide by automobile.**

honor, *v.* **1.** to pay, or to ACCEPT and pay, a check, note, or other instrument for the payment of money. —*n.* **2. Your** (or **His** or **Her**) **Honor,** a respectful form of address or reference for a judge.

Honorable, *adj.* the title accorded to judges; used with either the full name or an additional title, or both. *the Honorable Samuel S Smith; the Honorable Samuel S Smith, Judge; the Honorable Judge Smith.*

horizontal price fixing. See under PRICE FIXING.

horizontal union. See under UNION.

hornbook, *n.* **1.** a one-volume text or treatise organizing and summarizing a significant area of law, such as torts or corporation law. Cf. CASEBOOK; TREATISE. **2. hornbook law,** a legal principle regarded as so basic and well established as to require no citation to case authority: *"It is hornbook law that a principal is bound by the act of an agent within the scope of the agent's authority."* Also called **black letter law.**

hostile environment harassment. See under SEXUAL HARASSMENT.

hostile witness. See under WITNESS.

hostile working environment, working conditions in which an employee is subjected to HARASSMENT because of the employee's race, color, religion, sex, or national origin. The maintenance of such an environment constitutes unlawful employment discrimination. See also SEXUAL HARASSMENT.

hot blood. Colloquial expression for HEAT OF PASSION.

hot pursuit. Same as FRESH PURSUIT.

house counsel. See under COUNSEL.

HR-10 plan. See under PENSION PLAN.

hung jury. See under JURY See also HANG.

hypnotically refreshed recollection. See under RECOLLECTION; see also RECOVERED MEMORY.

hypothecate, *v.* to pledge property (either tangible or intangible) as collateral to secure a debt, especially without giving up possession of the property.

hypothetical, *adj.* **1.** assumed for purposes of discussion: *hypothetical facts; hypothetical case.* **2.** based upon or relating to facts assumed for purposes of discussion *hypothetical question* (see under QUESTION¹) —*n.* **3.** *Informal.* (used especially in law schools) short for hypothetical case or *hypothetical question* (see under QUESTION¹).

I

id., *Latin.* abbreviation for *idem* (lit. "the same one") (in citations) the case or other writing just mentioned. A term used for all but the first of a series of citations to the same source. For example, three successive references to an appellant's brief (the first two to page 25 and the third to page 27) might read· "Appellant's Brief at 25," "id.," "id. at 27."

illegal, *adj.* contrary to law; a term usually applied to conduct that is criminal or directly contrary to a specific statute or court order, or to a person engaged in such conduct. See *illegal* ALIEN, DISCRIMINATION under those words. Cf. the more general term UNLAWFUL.

illusory promise. See under PROMISE.

immaterial, *adj.* not MATERIAL See, for example, *immaterial breach* (under BREACH).

immigrant, *n.* a person who enters a country intending to reside there permanently.

immigration, *n.* the entry of people into a country for the purpose of establishing permanent residence. The Supreme Court has interpreted the Constitution as conferring upon Congress virtually unlimited power to regulate immigration into the United States

immunity, *n.* **1.** exemption from civil suit or criminal prosecution for allegedly wrongful acts, granted by law to certain classes of persons or by prosecutorial discretion to certain individuals, either by constitutional mandate or for reasons of public policy. In most cases the exemption is unqualified **(absolute immunity),** but sometimes it applies only if the wrongful acts were done in the good-faith (albeit erroneous) belief that they were legally justified **(qualified immunity). 2. diplomatic immunity,** immunity from civil and criminal liability granted to foreign diplomats by the United States and most or all other countries. **3. judicial immunity,** immunity from tort liability for any official act of a judge within the scope of judicial functions. **4. legislative immunity,** constitutionally granted immunity from tort liability, and to a limited extent from criminal liability, for acts by members of Congress and their aides in carrying out legislative functions, including particularly the absolute right to speak freely in House and Senate debates without fear of liability for defamation. State legislators generally enjoy similar immunity. **5. official immunity,** a general term for immunity of governmental officials of all sorts from liability for acts within the scope of their duties. Such immunity may be absolute or qualified, depending upon the official and the nature of the alleged wrong. **6. sovereign immunity,** the traditional immunity of the government itself from any suit at all—derived from the notion that "the King can do no wrong." The federal government and most states now have statutes permitting the assertion of most tort and contract claims against them. In addition, in certain kinds of cases sovereign immunity can be circumvented by seeking an injunction against a specific state officer rather than against the state itself. **7. transactional immunity,** immunity granted by a prosecutor to a witness, guaranteeing that the witness will not be prosecuted in connection with any event ("transaction") testified about. A witness who has been granted such immunity cannot refuse to testify on the basis of the Fifth Amendment privilege against SELF-INCRIMINATION. Cf. *use immunity.* **8. use immunity,** immunity granted by a prosecutor to a witness, guaranteeing that neither the witness's testimony nor any information derived from it will be used in any future prosecution against the witness. Although this does not preclude prosecution of the witness for involvement in the events testified about, any such case must be based entirely upon independently derived evidence. Therefore, like *transactional immunity,* use immunity makes it impossible for a witness to claim a Fifth Amendment privilege not to testify.

impanel, *v.* to select and seat the jury for a case.

impeachment, *n.* **1.** the instituting of formal misconduct charges against a government officer as a basis for removal from office. Under the Constitution, the House of Representatives has exclusive power to impeach federal officers, including the President, which it does by voting for ARTICLES OF IMPEACHMENT. A trial is then held in the Senate, and if convicted of an impeachable offense by the Senate, the officer may be removed from office See also HIGH CRIMES AND MISDEMEANORS. **2.** the introduction of evidence calling into question the credibility of a witness; for example, a *prior inconsistent statement* (see under STATEMENT), evidence of interest (see INTEREST²) or bias; evidence that the witness has been convicted of crimes involving dishonesty; or simply evidence contradicting the witness's testimony. This is referred to as "impeaching the credibility of the witness," or simply "impeaching the witness." See also *hostile witness* and *interested witness* (both under WITNESS). Cf. REHABILITATION. —**impeach,** *v.*

impediment, *n.* a legal bar; especially a circumstance rendering one legally incapable of making a contract or entering into a legal relationship; for example, being underage is an impediment to marriage.

impertinent, *adj.* not pertinent to the case at hand. A court may order impertinent matter stricken from a pleading so that a party will not have to respond to allegations that have no place in the case.

implead, *v.* to serve a complaint on a third party alleging that the third party should be held liable for all or part of any damages one is required to pay in a lawsuit; that is, to initiate a *third-party action* (see under THIRD PARTY): *The injured pedestrian sued the driver of the car, and the driver impleaded the auto mechanic, claiming that the accident was caused by the mechanic's poor work on the car's brakes.*

impleader, *n.* the act of impleading and the procedures for third-party actions.

implied, *adj.* **1.** suggested by conduct or circumstances rather than explicitly stated; describing a right, interest, obligation, authority, or status recognized by law even though not put into words—and perhaps not even intended—by the parties involved; opposite of EXPRESS. See *implied* CONTRACT, REPEAL, RIGHT OF ACTION under those words. **2.** Also called **implied in fact.** inferred from what a person has said or done; recognized by law because evidently reflecting a party's actual intent, even though nothing was specifically said about it. See *implied* AUTHORITY[1], WAIVER under those words, and *contract implied in fact* (under CONTRACT). **3.** Also called **implied in law.** imposed by law without regard to the intent of the parties; CONSTRUCTIVE. In essence, this means that in the eyes of the law, if the parties did not intend a certain result, they should have. See *implied warranty* (under WARRANTY); *contract implied in law* (under CONTRACT).

imply, *v.* to impose an obligation or status, or declare it to exist, by operation of law: *The law implies duty of good faith in all contracts. The judge implied a contract to pay for life-saving medical treatment given while the defendant was unconscious, even though the defendant's intent was to commit suicide.*

impossibility, *n.* the occurrence of an unforeseen circumstance rendering performance of a contract impossible. For example, a building to be rented might burn down, or a transaction to be completed might be made illegal, of the person whose services were contracted for might die. Under modern principles of contract law, further performance of the contract is usually excused in such cases (that is, the party whose performance became impossible will not have to pay damages for breach of contract), so long as this would not be unfair to the other party. Cf. IMPRACTICABILITY.

impost, *n.* a tax; especially a duty on goods imported from another country.

impound, *v.* to take property into custody of a court or law enforcement agency for such purposes as testing, use as evidence, possible forfeiture, or holding pending a decision as to its proper disposition. —**impoundment,** *n.*

impracticability, *n.* an unforeseen circumstance that renders performance of a contract far more difficult and expensive than either party had reason to expect when the contract was entered into. Except in limited circumstances (notably contracts for the sale of goods), the law has not yet recognized impracticability as providing an excuse for nonperformance of a contract in most situations. Cf. IMPOSSIBILITY.

impress, *v* to impose a *constructive trust* (see under TRUST) upon property; that is, to deem or declare property in the hands of one person to be held, as a matter of equity, in trust for another: *The judge impressed a trust on the property obtained by fraud. Equity deems misdelivered* *property to be impressed with a trust for the benefit of the intended recipient.* —**impressment,** *n.*

impression. See FIRST IMPRESSION.

imprisonment, *n.* the placing or keeping of a person in jail or prison as punishment for a crime. Cf. DETAIN; FALSE IMPRISONMENT.

improvement, *n.* a permanent change in real property that increases its value, prolongs its useful life, or adapts it to a new use, and is more than a repair or maintenance.

improvident, *adj.* unwise, ill-considered, or based upon inadequate information. A term often used by courts in explaining a change of mind: *The injunction is vacated as improvidently granted.*

improvident exercise of discretion. Same as ABUSE OF DISCRETION.

imputed, *adj.* describing an act, fact, or state of mind attributed to a person by operation of law, often because of that person's relationship to a person more directly involved, as in the case of negligence of a driver imputed under the law of many states to the owner of the vehicle, or knowledge of an employee imputed to the employer. See also *imputed knowledge* (under KNOWLEDGE).

in bar. See under BAR.

in blank, describing an indorsement that does not specify a particular *indorsee* (see under INDORSE). See also *blank indorsement* (under INDORSEMENT).

in camera, *Latin.* (lit. "in the chamber") (of judicial business or proceedings) in private; not in open court. Usually referring to something that takes place in CHAMBERS, in the ROBING ROOM, or in a courtroom from which spectators have been excluded: *The judge met with the lawyers in camera. The judge ordered that the disputed documents be submitted to her for in camera inspection.*

in common, signifying ownership of an interest in property by two or more people or entities with *undivided interests* (see under INTEREST[1]) in the whole, responsibility for expenses and a right to profits from the property in proportion to their interests, and no RIGHT OF SURVIVORSHIP. For example, one co-owner might own a one-half undivided interest in an apartment building while two others each own a one-fourth interest; upon the death of one, that owner's interest would pass to her heirs or to a taker designated in her will, instead of vesting in the surviving co-owners as in the case of joint ownership or ownership by the entirety: *estate in common; ownership in common; tenancy in common; tenant in common.* Cf. JOINT; BY THE ENTIRETY; IN SEVERALTY. See also COMMUNITY PROPERTY.

in esse, *Latin.* in being; existing at the time under consideration. See example under IN POSSE.

in evidence, 1. describing an EXHIBIT that the judge has admitted into evidence: *Exhibits 1 and 3 are in evidence; Exhibit 2 is not.* **2.** describing a fact for which testimony or other evidence has been introduced that, if believed, establishes the fact· *That the defendant owned a gun is already in evidence.*

in forma pauperis, *Latin.* (lit "in the character of a poor person") a method of proceeding in court under which filing fees and certain other requirements, such as the filing of multiple copies of printed briefs, are waived for indigent litigants. In certain situations indigent parties have a constitutional right to proceed in forma pauperis, but in most civil cases (including, ironically, petitions for bankruptcy) they do not.

in futuro, *Latin.* in the future; taking effect at a future date. Cf. IN PRAESENTI.

in haec verba, *Latin.* (lit. "in these words") using exactly the same words; verbatim: *The court's opinion sets forth the allegedly indecent material in haec verba.*

in house, 1. (of a company's legal work) handled by lawyers and paralegals who are salaried employees of the company, rather than by an outside lawyer or law firm: *We saved money by drafting the brief in house.* **2. in-house,** designating such work or the lawyers who do it: *an in-house project; the in-house staff.* See also *in-house counsel* (under COUNSEL).

in kind, 1. referring to a payment made in goods or services rather than money. See also BARTER. **2.** not the same, but of the same kind. For example, a neighbor who borrows a cup of sugar for baking will return it in kind—that is, will return a similar cup of sugar but not the same sugar that was borrowed.

in limine, *Latin.* (lit. "at the threshold") at the outset; before beginning a trial or other proceeding. A "motion in limine" is one filed before a trial begins in order to get an issue that is bound to arise resolved in advance.

in loco parentis, *Latin.* (lit. "in the position of a parent") describing a person or institution that has assumed, at least for some purposes, the rights and responsibilities of a parent toward a child: *For purposes of consenting to emergency treatment when the parents could not be located, the school acted in loco parentis.*

in pari delicto, *Latin.* (lit. "in equal fault") **1.** a defense sometimes available in a civil case, in which it is argued that the plaintiff should not be permitted to complain of wrongful conduct by the defendant because the plaintiff's conduct in the matter was equally wrongful; it applies particularly to situations in which the plaintiff and defendant were involved together in some unlawful activity. **2.** describing participants in a crime whose roles make them guilty in the same degree: *The person who robbed the bank and the person who stood watch during the robbery are in pari delicto.*

in pari materia, *Latin.* (lit. "in regard to the same matter") referring to statutes, passages of a contract, clauses of an instrument, or the like that deal with the same matter. In general, writings that are in pari materia are to be construed to the extent possible as consistent with each other, each being interpreted in light of the other.

in personam *Latin.* (lit. "directed at the person") describing the fundamental nature of a legal proceeding as focused on a person or entity rather than a piece of property. For details, see under JURISDICTION[1], ACTION, and JUDGMENT. Cf. IN REM; QUASI IN REM.

in point. Same as ON POINT. See also *case in point* (under CASE[1])

in posse, *Latin.* (lit. "in potentiality") potential; not yet existing at the time under discussion. *The term "grandchildren" in the will was interpreted as meaning grandchildren in esse and in posse* (i.e., not only grandchildren existing at the time of the testator's death but also any future grandchildren). Cf. IN ESSE.

in praesenti, *Latin* in the present; effective immediately, Cf IN FUTURO.

in propria persona, *Latin* (lit. "in one's own person") personally; in person; especially, not represented by an attorney; PRO SE. Abbreviated **in pro. per.**

in re, *Latin.* in the matter of. This introductory phrase appears in certain case names; it is also used in citations as a concise substitute for such introductory phrases as "petition of" and "application of " Thus a case captioned "Petition of John J. Smith for a Writ of Habeas Corpus" would most likely be cited as "In re Smith " See also IN THE MATTER OF.

in rem *Latin.* (lit "directed at the thing") describing the fundamental character of a legal proceeding as focused on a piece of property (real or personal, tangible or intangible) or occasionally on a legal relationship (e.g , a marriage), rather than on a particular person or entity. For details, see under JURISDICTION[1], ACTION, and JUDGMENT. See also ALL THE WORLD. Cf. IN PERSONAM; QUASI IN REM

in severalty, signifying ownership of an interest in property by one person or entity only, with no co-owners: *estate in severalty; ownership in severalty; tenancy in severalty; tenant in severalty.* Cf. JOINT; BY THE ENTIRETY; IN COMMON. See also COMMUNITY PROPERTY.

in specie, *Latin.* (lit "in kind") **1.** in original form: *Some of the decedent's property was distributed to the heirs in specie; the rest was sold and the proceeds distributed.* **2.** of the kind or in the manner specified: *performance of the contract in specie.*

in terrorem, *Latin.* (lit "for the purpose of fear") describing anything intended as a threat; especially a clause in a will ("in terrorem clause"), permitted in some states, that nullifies any bequest to a beneficiary who unsuccessfully contests the will.

in the matter of, an introductory phrase in certain case names, often shortened to **matter of** or IN RE in citations

in toto, *Latin.* (lit. "in the entirety") completely; in its entirety; as a whole: *The statute was repealed in toto.*

in trust. See under TRUST.

inadmissible, *adj.* (of evidence) not ADMISSIBLE.

inapposite, *adj.* describing a PRECEDENT that is regarded as not sufficiently similar to the present case to provide much guidance; *distinguishable* (see under DISTINGUISH)

incapacity, *n.* the absence of legal CAPACITY to perform an act; for example, if a party to a marriage is underage or already married, the marriage will be void on the ground of incapacity.

incest, *n.* the crime of having sexual intercourse, or living as husband and wife, with a close relative, such as an ancestor, descendant, or sibling. The exact list of prohibited relationships varies from state to state.

inchoate, *adj.* incipient; commenced but not yet completed or matured. For example, an "inchoate lien" is one agreed to by a debtor and creditor but not yet recorded in accordance with laws requiring filing of liens in a public office; the crimes of ATTEMPT, SOLICITATION, and CONSPIRACY are sometimes classified as "inchoate crimes."

included offense. See LESSER INCLUDED OFFENSE.

inclusionary zoning. See under ZONING

income, *n.* **1.** money received, or the value of property or services received. **2. earned income,** income derived from working for another **(wages)** or in one's own business **(self-employment income).** Cf. *unearned income.* **3. gross income,** total income potentially subject to income tax and required to be reported on an income tax return, before subtraction of any deductions. **4. net income,** in a business, the excess of total income over expenses; profit **5. ordinary income,** income subject to taxation at ordinary rates; that is, all income reportable on income tax returns except *capital gain* (see under CAPITAL[1]), which is subject to special lower tax rates **6. taxable income, a.** any type of income subject to income tax; e.g., wages or alimony, but not gifts (usually) or child support **b.** the portion of a taxpayer's income upon which income tax is based, consisting of *gross income* minus DEDUCTIONS **7. unearned income,** income derived from investments and other sources other than employment or self-employment. Cf. *earned income.*

income tax, a federal, state, or local tax on the annual INCOME of an individual or married couple **(personal income tax),** a corporation **(corporate income tax),** or a trust or estate. See also *capital gains tax* (under CAPITAL[1]); *flat tax* and *progressive tax* (under TAX); *marginal tax rate* and *effective tax rate* (under TAX RATE).

incompetent, *adj.* **1.** not competent (see COMPETENT[1] and COMPETENT[2]). —*n.* **2.** an individual who is not mentally competent (see COMPETENT[1]): *a law protecting infants and incompetents.*

inconsistent statement. See *prior inconsistent statement* (under STATEMENT).

inconsistent verdict. See under VERDICT

incorporate, *v.* **1.** to organize as a corporation; to attain the status of a corporation by going through the formalities required by state law. **2.** to include as a part of: *Please incorporate these changes and additions into a revised draft of the legislation.* **3. incorporate by reference,** to make one document a part of another, not by physically reproducing the first in the second (although it typically would be attached for ease of reference), but by means of a statement in the second document simply declaring the first to be part of it. —**incorporation,** *n*

incorporated, *adj.* formed as a corporation. This word (or its abbreviation, **inc.**) in an entity's name indicates that the entity is a corporation; not all corporate names include this word, however.

incorporation doctrine, the principle by which most of the BILL OF RIGHTS, which originally operated only as a limitation on the power of the federal government, has been made binding upon state governments as well. The key to the process is the Fourteenth Amendment to the Constitution, which was adopted after the Civil War and provided, for the first time, that no *state* may deprive any person of life, liberty, or property without DUE PROCESS of law Over time, the Supreme Court decided that most of the protections in the Bill of Rights—including both procedural protections (such as the right to a jury trial in criminal cases) and substantive rights (such as the right to speak one's mind or practice one's religion)—are inherent in the concept of due process, and hence protected from state governmental interference by the due process clause of the Fourteenth Amendment. Thus almost the entire Bill of Rights was ultimately "incorporated" or "absorbed" into the Fourteenth Amendment.

indecent, *adj.* **1.** offensive to generally accepted standards of propriety in matters relating to sex, bodily functions, and display of the human body. **2. indecent exposure,** the crime of exposing one's genitals under circumstances likely to cause alarm or offense See also *indecent* ASSAULT, SPEECH under those words. —**indecency,** *n.*

indefinite, *adj.* (of a contract) not sufficiently certain to be enforceable. If the material terms of a purported contract are so indefinite that a court cannot reasonably ascertain who is to do what, the contract "fails for indefiniteness "

indefinite failure of issue. See under ISSUE²

indemnify, *v.* to compensate or reimburse a person for loss or liability, or agree to do so if a loss or liability arises in the future.

indemnity, *n.* **1.** a right to receive compensation for a loss from someone other than a wrongdoer who caused the loss, or to receive reimbursement for a payment that one has had to make to someone else to compensate that other person for a loss A right of indemnity can arise in two ways: (a) by contract. An insurance policy is a contract by which the insurance company agrees (for consideration in the form of payment of premiums) to indemnify the insured against losses or liabilities specified in the policy. (b) by operation of law. In certain situations a person held liable for a tort is entitled to indemnity from another tortfeasor regarded as more directly at fault. For example, if the owner of a car is held liable under state law for injury caused by negligence of the driver, or an employer is held liable for the tort of an employee under the doctrine of RE- SPONDEAT SUPERIOR, the owner or employer is entitled to reimbursement from the driver or employee whose tortious conduct actually caused the injury. **2.** the compensation or reimbursement received pursuant to a right of indemnity.

indemnity insurance, insurance that protects the insured against injury or loss suffered by the insured directly, as distinguished from losses to others for which the insured might be held liable. For example, automobile collision insurance is a form of indemnity insurance that compensates the insured for damage to his own automobile in an accident. Cf. LIABILITY INSURANCE.

indenture, *n.* **1.** an old term for a deed or written contract, especially one under seal (see SEAL[1]). **2.** Also called **trust indenture.** an instrument stating the terms and conditions governing an issue of bonds, setting forth the rights of bondholders and providing various measures for the protection of those rights, including appointment of a trustee to handle necessary transfers of money and to look out for the interests of bondholders.

independent, *adj* free, or at least relatively free, from control by others; autonomous. See *independent* CONTRAC- TOR, COUNSEL, PROSECUTOR, UNION under those words.

indeterminate sentence. See under SENTENCE

indicium, *n., pl.* **indicia.** an indicator; a clue which by itself might not justify a conclusion, but may be persuasive when viewed together with other indicia pointing to the same conclusion. Often used in the plural, since it is only when several indicia are present that they are of much significance: *indicia of reliability; indicia of apparent authority.*

indict, *v.* to issue an INDICTMENT against a person.

indictment, *n.* the act of a *grand jury* (see under JURY) in formally charging a person with a crime, or the written instrument setting forth the charge. The written indictment is typically drawn up by the prosecutor, voted on by the grand jury after hearing evidence, endorsed with the words "a *true bill* " if approved by the jury (see under BILL), and then filed with the court, where it becomes the instrument upon which the rest of the case is based Cf INFORMATION.

indispensable party. See under PARTY.

individual, *n.* **1.** a human being as distinguished from an entity such as a corporation; a *natural person* (see under PERSON). —*adj.* **2.** involving only one individual or entity; not JOINT: *individual account* (see under ACCOUNT); *individual return* (see under RETURN) See also SEVERAL.

individual retirement account (or **arrangement**) **(IRA),** an arrangement under which an individual can save or invest a certain amount of each year's earned income for retirement and not be taxed on it until then.

indorse, *v.* to sign one's name, sometimes with additional instructions or conditions, on the back of a NEGOTIABLE IN- STRUMENT for the purpose of assigning the rights under it to someone else. The person whose name is signed is the

indorser; the person (if any) named in the indorsement to receive the rights is the **indorsee.** Ordinarily the indorser will be liable to the indorsee or any subsequent holder of the instrument if the instrument is ultimately dishonored See also NEGOTIATE; RECOURSE; and see discussion under ENDORSE (def. 3).

indorsement, *n.* **1.** the act of indorsing an instrument, or the signature and accompanying writing indorsed on the instrument. Also called *endorsement* (see ENDORSE). **2. blank indorsement,** an indorsement that does not name a specific person to receive rights under the instrument, usually consisting of a signature alone; for example, John Smith's signature (without more) on the back of a check made out to the order of John Smith. This turns the instrument into a *bearer instrument* (see under BEARER). Also called **indorsement in blank.** Cf. *special indorsement.* **3. qualified indorsement,** an indorsement that includes the words "without recourse." See RECOURSE for discussion. **4. restrictive indorsement,** an indorsement that limits or purports to limit the instrument in some way; for example, a signature with the phrase "for deposit," which forbids further negotiation except through banking channels. **5. special indorsement,** an indorsement that specifies the person to whose order it makes the instrument payable. This turns the instrument into an *order instrument* (see under ORDER²). Cf. *blank indorsement.*

inducement. See *fraud in the inducement* (under FRAUD).

industrial performance zoning. See under ZONING

industrial union. See under UNION.

inevitable discovery exception, an exception to the EXCLUSIONARY RULE under which evidence obtained through an illegal search may be used against a defendant in a criminal case if the prosecution can show that it would have found the evidence sooner or later even without the illegal search.

infancy, *n.* the state or period of being an INFANT; MINORITY· *Since the actress was 17 when she signed the $3.5 million movie contract, the contract was voidable on the ground of infancy.*

infant, *n.* a person under the *age of majority* (see under AGE); a MINOR.

inferior court, a court from which appeals may be taken to a higher court within the same judicial system. Especially, a court of *limited jurisdiction* (see under JURISDICTION¹) such as a probate court, family court, justice of the peace court, or municipal court, from which appeals are taken to the lowest court of *general jurisdiction* (see under JURISDICTION¹).

infliction of mental distress. See INTENTIONAL INFLICTION OF MENTAL DISTRESS.

information, *n.* a formal instrument charging a person with a crime, filed by a prosecutor instead of an INDICTMENT in cases where the law does not require involvement of a *grand jury* (see under JURY) In the federal courts this is possible only for misdemeanors.

information and belief, a basis for including facts in a pleading or in an affidavit, verification, or other sworn statement, even though one cannot claim personal knowledge of them. If one has received what one reasonably regards as reliable information, on the basis of which one believes a certain fact to be true, one can include that fact in the pleading or other writing, introduced by the phrase "On information and belief." Cf *personal knowledge* (under KNOWLEDGE).

informed consent. See under CONSENT.

infra, *adv. Latin.* (lit "below") later in the same document. Opposite of SUPRA.

infraction, *n.* **1.** the violation of a rule or law; especially a minor violation. **2.** the name given in some states to an offense below the level of MISDEMEANOR, punishable only by a fine or forfeiture and not classified as a crime: *a traffic infraction.*

infringe, *v.* to violate another's COPYRIGHT, PATENT, or TRADEMARK by copying or using the protected work, invention, or mark without permission from the owner. —**infringement,** *n.*

inherit, *v.* **1.** strictly, to receive property by INTESTATE SUCCESSION; to take as an HEIR. **2.** broadly, to receive property from the estate of a decedent either by intestate succession or by will.

inheritance, *n.* **1.** the act or fact of inheriting. **2.** property that one has inherited: *an inheritance worth $150,000.*

inheritance tax, a tax upon the recipient of money or property under a will or by intestate succession, based upon the value received. Cf. ESTATE TAX

initiative, *n.* a lawmaking procedure, available in some states, that bypasses the state legislature Under this procedure, if a certain number of citizens sign a petition calling for it, a proposed statute must be put to a vote at a general election, and becomes law if a majority of the voters vote for it. Cf. REFERENDUM.

injunction, *n* **1.** a court order directing a person to do or refrain from doing some act. **2. mandatory injunction,** an injunction requiring a person to do some affirmative act. **3. permanent injunction,** an injunction granted as part of the judgment at the end of a case, directing a party forever to refrain from certain conduct. **4. preliminary injunction,** an injunction granted shortly after the beginning of a case, to maintain the status quo while the case proceeds A preliminary injunction will be issued only after a hearing If, for example, the plaintiff initiates an action to prevent an owner from tearing down a landmark building, the typical sequence of events would be (1) a *temporary restraining order* (see under RESTRAINING ORDER) preventing the owner from tearing down the building until a hearing can be held; (2) if the hearing convinces the judge that the plaintiff may be right, a *preliminary injunction* prohibiting the owner from tearing down the building until a trial can be held; and (3) if the trial persuades the judge that it would be illegal for the owner to tear down the building, a *permanent injunction* against tearing down the building. **5. prohibitory injunction,** an injunction prohibiting a person from taking certain action This is the most common kind of injunction Also called a RESTRAINING ORDER.

injurious falsehood. Same as DISPARAGEMENT.

injury, *n.* **1.** any harm to an individual or entity through conduct regarded by the law as wrongful, including bodily injury, mental suffering, harm to reputation, property damage, financial loss, or deprivation of a legal right. **2. irreparable injury,** injury of a sort that cannot be suitably remedied by an award of damages, and for which a superior remedy exists in the form of equitable relief such as an INJUNCTION or SPECIFIC PERFORMANCE. In general, a party must show irreparable injury, or the prospect of irreparable injury, in order to obtain equitable relief **3. personal injury, a.** narrowly, physical harm to an individual, as through disease, bodily injury, or death **b.** broadly, any harm or loss suffered by an individual as a result of a tort.

innocent, *adj.* **1.** acting without knowledge of circumstances making an act or transaction legally defective or wrongful, and without reason to have such knowledge, acting in good faith For example, a purchaser of property who has no reason to know that the seller had no right to sell it is an innocent purchaser; a person who wanders onto another's land while lost in the dark is an innocent trespasser **2.** done in good faith. *an innocent trespass.* **3.** (in criminal cases) genuinely free from guilt, even if convicted of a crime and thus guilty in the eyes of the law: *Newly discovered evidence indicates that the prisoner is innocent of the crime for which he was convicted* "Innocent" is not used in law as a synonym for NOT GUILTY, a defendant cannot "plead innocent" or be "found innocent."

inquest, *n.* a name given to certain kinds of factfinding proceedings, including a proceeding in which the plaintiff in an action in which the defendant has failed to appear presents evidence to the court to establish the damages to be awarded in a default judgment. The traditional "coroner's inquest"—a hearing conducted by a coroner to inquire into the cause and circumstances of a suspicious death—has largely been supplanted by a combination of autopsy to determine the cause and police investigation to determine the circumstances.

inquire, *v.* to ask questions, largely restricted to the formal phrase "You may inquire," sometimes said by a judge to a lawyer to grant permission for the lawyer to begin questioning a witness.

inquiry notice. See under NOTICE.

inquisitorial system, a method of adjudication in which judges play a prominent role in investigating facts and questioning witnesses; used in CIVIL LAW countries. Cf ADVERSARY SYSTEM; ACCUSATORIAL SYSTEM

insanity defense, an *affirmative defense* (see under DEFENSE) to a criminal charge, under which a defendant who proves that he was insane at the time of the crime is held not to be responsible for the crime The verdict then is NOT

GUILTY BY REASON OF INSANITY, and the usual consequence is incarceration in a mental institution Most states (but not all) recognize some type of insanity defense, applying a variety of rules or tests as to what constitutes insanity, usually some form of the M'NAGHTEN RULE, the IRRESISTIBLE IMPULSE TEST, or the SUBSTANTIAL CAPACITY TEST.

insider trading, buying or selling stock in a publicly held corporation on the basis of "inside information"—that is, information that is known only to people inside the company (or outsiders who have been told privately) and has not yet been disclosed to the general public. Insider trading is illegal

insolvent, *adj* **1.** usually, unable to pay one's debts in the ordinary course of business as they become due. **2.** for some purposes, having liabilities exceeding assets. Opposite of SOLVENT —**insolvency,** *n.*

installment, *n* **1.** one of a series of payments, deliveries, or other steps required of a party by a contract, all of which together constitute the complete performance called for. —*adj.* **2.** describing a contract calling for performance in installments, or referring to some aspect of such a transaction: *installment note* (see under NOTE[1]); *installment contract; installment loan*

instant, *adj.* referring to that which is currently under consideration; at hand; current: *the instant case; the instant decision; the instant crime.*

instanter, *adv.* immediately; forthwith; usually used in connection with a court order, and often suggesting that the limits of the judge's patience have been reached. *The Court will brook no further delay; the documents are to be produced instanter. So ordered.*

instruct, *v.* **1.** Same as DIRECT[2] **2.** to issue an INSTRUCTION or set of instructions to the jury. *The judge will instruct the jury tomorrow afternoon.*

instruction, *n.* **1.** a judge's explanation and direction to a jury concerning a particular legal principle or duty of the jury *The plaintiff objected to the court's instruction as to the inference that may be drawn from the plaintiff's failure to call his wife as a witness.* **2. instructions,** the comprehensive explanation of the applicable law and duties of the jury given by the judge to the jury at the end of a trial, just before the jury begins to deliberate. Also called the CHARGE to the jury **3. cautionary instruction,** any warning, reminder, or admonishment to the jury; for example, not to commence deliberations until after all the evidence is in, or not to consider anything that a lawyer says as evidence **4. curative instruction,** an instruction directing the jury to disregard certain inadmissible testimony, statements of counsel, or other potentially prejudicial events that occurred in their presence

instrument, *n.* **1.** a formal legal document, especially one that embodies legal rights or a legal interest (such as a stock certificate), or one that operates to cause legal consequences (such as a deed or will). See also *sealed in-*

strument (under SEAL[1]); ACCUSATORY INSTRUMENT. **2.** a NEGO-
TIABLE INSTRUMENT or NONNNEGOTIABLE INSTRUMENT.

insufficient cause, a legally insufficient reason for taking
a particular action or seeking a particular court order. Cf
GOOD CAUSE.

insurable interest, an interest in person or property justifying one in obtaining insurance on that person or that
property. For example, since a company might suffer fi-
nancially if its chief executive dies, the company has an
"insurable interest" that it may protect by purchasing a life
insurance policy under which the company will be compensated if the executive dies The law prohibits people
from taking out insurance on lives or property in which
they have no insurable interest, since that amounts to
nothing more than a gambling contract, and moreover
would put the policyholder in the unseemly position of
hoping that harm will befall someone else so that the policyholder can obtain a windfall.

insurable title. See under TITLE.

insurance, *n.* **1.** a contractual arrangement whereby a
company (the **insurer**), in consideration for a payment or
periodic payments of money (the PREMIUM), agrees to compensate its customer (the **insured**) in the event that the insured suffers some loss or injury (in the case of INDEMNITY
INSURANCE) or liability (in the case of LIABILITY INSURANCE) of
a kind specified in the written contract (the POLICY). **2.**
group insurance, insurance covering an identified group
of people, such as employees of a company or members
of an association, upon terms agreed to between the insurance company and the employer, association, or the
like. **3. mutual insurance,** insurance provided by a company that is owned solely by its policyholders in proportion
to the amount of insurance they have purchased from the
company, rather than by stockholders. Since a mutual insurance company is not in business to make profits for
stockholders, it can offer insurance at cost. See also COIN-
SURANCE; *employers' liability insurance* (under WORKERS'
COMPENSATION); EXCESS INSURANCE; FIDELITY INSURANCE; NO-
FAULT INSURANCE; LIFE INSURANCE; REINSURANCE; *term insurance* (under LIFE INSURANCE); TITLE INSURANCE; *unemployment insurance* (under UNEMPLOYMENT COMPENSATION); *workers' compensation insurance* (under WORKERS' COMPEN-
SATION). Cf. SELF-INSURANCE.

insurance broker. See under BROKER.

intangible property. See under PROPERTY.

intellectual property. See under PROPERTY.

intent, *n.* **1.** broadly, a STATE OF MIND in which one either
desires to achieve a certain result by one's conduct (even if
that result is unlikely to occur) or knows that such a result
is practically certain to occur (even if that is not what is desired). This is the usual meaning of "intent" in tort law and
the traditional meaning in criminal law. See, for example,
intentional tort (under TORT); *intent to kill* (under MURDER).
2. narrowly, a conscious objective of causing a certain result. This is the usual meaning of the term under modern

criminal codes, which classify KNOWLEDGE of likely results without an actual intent to achieve them as a separate state of mind. See also PURPOSELY **3.** Also called **intention.** the purpose or design underlying a statute, contract, will, or other instrument: LEGISLATIVE INTENT; *intent of the parties; the testator's intent.* —**intentional,** *adj.* —**intentionally,** *adv.*

intentional infliction of mental distress, the tort of intentionally causing serious emotional distress to a person by means of conduct of an extremely outrageous nature.

inter alia, *Latin.* among other things: *The contract provides, inter alia, that the parties will submit any dispute to binding arbitration*

inter se, *Latin.* among themselves; between themselves.

inter vivos, *Latin.* (lit. "among the living") describing a transaction completed during one's lifetime, as distinguished from one occurring at death or effected by will or intestacy: *inter vivos gift* (see under GIFT); *inter vivos trust* (see under TRUST). Cf TESTAMENTARY.

interest¹, 1. a legally enforceable right with respect to real or personal property. An interest may be designated as either a **legal interest** or a **beneficial** (or **equitable**) **interest,** depending upon whether it is viewed from the perspective of the *legal owner* or, in the case of property held in trust, the *beneficial owner* (see both phrases under OWNER). See also ESTATE¹; TENANCY. **2. contingent interest,** an interest which may give the holder a right of possession, use, or enjoyment of the property at some time in the future, but only upon the occurrence of specific circumstances which are possible but not certain to arise; for example, a *contingent estate* (see under ESTATE¹). Cf. *vested interest.* **3. executory interest,** a *future estate* (see under ESTATE¹) which will become possessory only upon termination of a fee simple, and which is held by someone other than the person (or the successors of the person) who transferred the fee to its present owner. See also *fee simple determinable* (under FEE¹). Cf. POSSIBILITY OF REVERTER. **4. future interest,** an interest which does not confer a present right of possession, use, or enjoyment of property, but may do so in the future; for example, a REMAINDER or a POSSIBILITY OF REVERTER. Cf. *present interest.* **5. possessory interest,** a present right to possession of property, particularly real property. **6. present interest, a.** (in personal property) a present right to possession, use, or enjoyment of property. For example, the current beneficiary of a trust fund has a present interest in the fund. **b.** (in real property) Same as *possessory interest.* Present interests in real property may be classified as either a **freehold interest** (same as FREEHOLD) or a **leasehold interest** (same as LEASEHOLD). **7. security interest,** an interest in the property of another consisting of the right to sell that property in order to satisfy some obligation of the owner if the owner defaults; for example, the right of an automobile dealer or financer to take back your car and sell it to someone else if you do not keep up the payments. See also LIEN; MORTGAGE. **8. undivided interest,** the rights of each of two or more co-owners of a single interest in property when, instead of dividing the property up physically, they all share the right to use the whole property Also called **undivided fractional interest. 9. vested interest,** a legally enforceable right to possession, use, or enjoyment of property which either exists at present or is certain to arise in the future; a present interest or a future interest that is not subject to any contingency Cf *contingent interest.* See also INSURABLE INTEREST, *successor in interest* (under SUCCESSOR)

interest², *n* **1.** a financial or other direct legal stake in a matter, such that one's pocketbook or legal rights are directly affected For example, a shareholder has an interest in a suit by or against the corporation; a child has an interest in a custody dispute between the parents. See also *real party in interest* (under PARTY) **2.** broadly, any close personal stake in a matter; for example, one's interest in a suit against a friend, a relative, or a personal enemy. See also CONFLICT OF INTEREST.

interest³, *n.* **1.** a sum paid or charged for the use of money or for the privilege of deferring a payment, expressed either as a dollar amount or as a percentage of the principal amount involved in the transaction **2. legal interest, a.** the rate of interest set by law for certain kinds of debts, such as an unpaid judgment. **b.** the maximum rate of interest that can be charged without violating laws against USURY.

interested, *adj.* having an *interest* (see INTEREST²) in a matter: *interested person* (see under PERSON); *interested witness* (see under WITNESS) Cf. DISINTERESTED

interlocutory, *adj.* interim; describing an order or other step occurring in the course of a case but not ending the case: *interlocutory order* (see under ORDER¹); *interlocutory appeal* (see under APPEAL)

intermeddler. See OFFICIOUS INTERMEDDLER

intermediate appellate court. See under COURT

intermediate scrutiny. Same as HEIGHTENED SCRUTINY.

Internal Revenue Code (I.R.C.), the portion of the UNITED STATES CODE that contains all federal tax laws

Internal Revenue Service (I.R.S.), the federal agency that administers most federal tax laws.

International Court of Justice, the chief judicial agency of the United Nations, based in the Hague, Netherlands. It is authorized to render advisory opinions to the United Nations and to decide disputes between nations voluntarily submitted to it by the nations involved.

international law, 1. Also called **public international law** or the **law of nations.** a body of principles that are generally accepted among the nations of the world as governing their dealings with each other and each other's citizens or subjects. It is a combination of long-established custom and specific treaty obligations, depending for its vitality largely upon each nation's good will or desire for international acceptance See also FEDERAL LAW   **2. private international law,** the branch of CONFLICT OF LAWS that deals with the application of potentially conflicting national laws to transactions, events, or litigation concerning two or more countries.

interpleader, *n* a type of action that may be commenced by a STAKEHOLDER in possession of property or funds known to belong to someone else but claimed by more than one other person, so that a court can determine which claimant should get the property This procedure permits the stakeholder to deposit the property with the court and leave it to the competing claimants to plead their claims against each other (to **interplead**), freeing the stakeholder both of the burden of litigating over the property and of the risk of turning it over to the wrong claimant.

interpretation. See under CONSTRUCTION

interrogation, *n.* **1.** the questioning of a criminal suspect by law enforcement authorities **2. custodial interrogation,** the questioning of a suspect who has been arrested or otherwise deprived of his freedom of action in any significant way. This is the situation to which the MIRANDA RULE applies. —**interrogate,** *v.*

interrogatory, *n.* one of a set of written questions about the facts and contentions in a case (**interrogatories**) submitted to an adversary as part of the DISCOVERY process Interrogatories are required to be answered in writing under oath See also *special interrogatories* (under VERDICT).

interstate commerce. See under COMMERCE

interstate compact. See under COMPACT.

intervene, *v.* to insert oneself as a party in a lawsuit that is already pending between other parties, in order to assert or protect some interest that one has in the subject matter of the case Depending upon the extent of an intervenor's need to be involved and the extent to which intervention would contribute to or detract from efficient dispute resolution, intervention might or might not be allowed. See also *proper party* (under PARTY) —**intervenor,** *n.* —**intervention,** *n*

intestacy, *n.* the fact or state of being INTESTATE at death

intestate, *adj.* **1.** lacking a valid will, especially at the time of one's death. *to die intestate.* —*n.* **2.** a person who dies without leaving a valid will.

intestate succession, taking as an HEIR; succeeding to property of a decedent by operation of law, either because the decedent left no valid will or because the will did not effectively dispose of all of the decedent's property Each state has laws dictating how such property is to be distributed among surviving relatives, generally referred to as laws of intestate succession or laws of DESCENT AND DISTRIBUTION.

invalid. See *invalid as applied* and *invalid on its face* (both under UNCONSTITUTIONAL)

invasion of privacy, the tort of unreasonable and highly offensive publicity about an individual or intrusion into an individual's private life and personal affairs. The contours of the tort vary from state to state, but in general it includes improper intrusions by such means as wiretapping, peeping, searching an individual's property and effects, or persistent telephoning; public disclosure of personal information about a private person without a legitimate news purpose; placing a person in a false public light (as by associating her with ideas or events with which she has no connection); and use of a person's name or image without consent for advertising or other commercial purposes.

investigative privilege. See under PRIVILEGE.

invidious discrimination. See under DISCRIMINATION.

invitee, *n.* a person invited to enter real property to conduct business with the occupier or as a member of the general public invited for a public function. In tort law, the property owner owes a higher degree of care to an invitee than to a mere LICENSEE. But in most states an invited social guest is usually deemed to be a licensee rather than an invitee, on the theory that such a guest is like "one of the family" and thus is owed no special duty of care.

involuntary, *adj.* **1.** compelled by law, by duress, by necessity, or otherwise. See *involuntary* BANKRUPTCY, CONFESSION, DISMISSAL, SERVITUDE under those words. **2.** unintentional; accidental. For example, *involuntary manslaughter* (see under MANSLAUGHTER). Cf. VOLUNTARY.

irrebuttable presumption. See under PRESUMPTION.

irrelevant, *adj.* not RELEVANT.

irreparable injury. See under INJURY.

irresistible impulse test, the principle that an INSANITY DEFENSE may be established by evidence that the crime was committed under the influence of a mental disease that made it impossible for the defendant to control her behavior, even if she knew that what she was doing was wrong This test, also called **uncontrollable impulse test,** is recognized in a few states as a supplement to the M'NAGHTEN RULE.

issue¹, *n.* **1.** a disputed proposition presented in a case; any material fact or legal principle upon which the two sides disagree. Same as QUESTION², although many standard legal phrases customarily employ only one or the other of the two words. **2. constitutional issue.** See under CONSTITUTIONAL. **3. issue of fact** or **factual issue.** See under QUESTION². **4. issue of law** or **legal issue.** See under QUESTION². **5. issue preclusion.** Same as *collateral estoppel* (under ESTOPPEL). **6. join issue,** to file papers denying or contradicting an allegation in a case, thereby creating an issue for judicial determination The point in a case where this occurs is called **joinder of issue.**

issue², *n.* **1.** descendants (children, grandchildren, etc), normally construed to include generations yet unborn, not just those descendants existing at a particular time **2. failure of issue,** the absence of surviving issue. **a. definite failure of issue,** the absence of surviving issue at the moment when property would have passed to them under the terms of a deed or will. This is the modern interpretation of the phrase *failure of issue*. **b. indefinite failure of issue,** the ultimate dying out of a person's line of descendants, which may (or may not) occur at an unknown time in the future. This older interpretation of the phrase *failure of issue* has been largely abandoned.

issue³, *v.* **1.** (of a corporation or other entity) to sell or put on the market a block of one's stock or other securities. —*n.* **2.** an entire class or block of securities sold or offered for sale at the same time. See also ISSUER.

issue⁴, *v.* **1.** to formally announce an order, rule, decision, etc., either orally or in writing. **2.** (of such an order, rule, etc.) to come forth; be announced: *The writ of mandamus issued from the Court of Appeals at 4:30 p.m.*

issuer, *n.* the corporation or other entity that issued a particular security; the entity in which one is investing if one purchases a security.

itemized deduction. See under DEDUCTION

J

J., *pl.* **JJ.** abbreviation for Judge or Justice, always placed after the name. *The majority opinion was by White, J.; Brennan and Marshall, JJ., filed dissents.*

jail, *n.* an institution, usually run by a county or municipality, for locking up offenders serving short sentences and accused people awaiting trial. Cf PRISON.

Jane Doe. See under JOHN DOE.

J.D., *Latin.* abbreviation for *Juris Doctor* (lit "doctor of law," "teacher of law"), the lowest law degree; the degree granted to everyone who graduates from law school. The degree was formerly called LL.B., for Bachelor of Laws, but the name was changed in the 1960's because lawyers felt that "J.D " made them sound more important. Cf. LL.M.

jeopardy, *n.* risk of punishment for an offense. A criminal defendant is put in jeopardy when the jury is sworn in or, in a nonjury trial, when the first witness is sworn in. See also DOUBLE JEOPARDY

JJ., See J.

j.n.o.v., See under JUDGMENT.

John (or **Jane**) **Doe,** a fictitious name used, sometimes with slight variations, in case names and in legal documents such as warrants and summonses, either to conceal a person's identity, or because the person's real name is not known, or because it is not yet known whether the person exists

join, *v* to bring an additional claim or party into a case. See also *join issue* (under ISSUE¹). Cf SEVER.

joinder, *n.* **1.** the joining together in one action of more than one plaintiff or defendant **(party joinder** or **joinder of parties)** or more than one claim or charge **(claim joinder** or **joinder of claims).** Modern practice generally encourages joinder in the interest of resolving all aspects of a complex dispute in a single trial. **2. compulsory joinder,** joinder of a *necessary party* or *indispensable party* (see under PARTY). Such a party must be joined in the action if possible; and if a party found by the judge to be indispensable cannot be joined, the action will be dismissed. **3. permissive joinder,** joinder of a *proper party* (see under PARTY) The court will allow, but not require, the joinder of such a party. See also MISJOINDER; NONJOINDER Cf CONSOLIDATION; *joinder of issue* (under ISSUE¹); SEVER

joint, *adj.* **1.** collective; involving two or more people or entities acting or being dealt with together. See, for example, joint ACCOUNT, CUSTODY, LIABILITY, OBLIGATION, OWNER, TORTFEASOR, WILL under those words. Cf. SEVERAL; JOINT AND SEVERAL **2.** referring to concurrent ownership of an interest in property by two or more people with equal *undivided interests* (see under INTEREST¹) in the whole, equal rights to possession and use of the property, and RIGHT OF SURVIVORSHIP: *joint estate; joint owner; joint ownership; joint ten-*

ancy; joint tenant. Cf. BY THE ENTIRETY; IN COMMON; IN SEVER-
ALTY. See also COMMUNITY PROPERTY. —**jointly,** *adv.*

joint and several, susceptible of being treated legally either as JOINT or as SEVERAL—that is, as either collective or
individual—at the option of the person initiating an action·
joint and several liability (see under LIABILITY); *joint and
several obligation* (see under OBLIGATION). Cf. JOINT; SEV-
ERAL. —**jointly and severally.**

joint stock company (or **association**) See under COM-
PANY.

joint venture, an arrangement between two or more
people or entities to work together on a specific project.
Joint ventures are usually entered into because each participant (**venturer** or **joint venturer**) possesses some
necessary skill or resource that the other lacks. Also called
joint adventure.

journalists' shield law. See under SHIELD LAW.

judge, *n.* **1.** a public official whose function is to hear and
decide legal disputes, preside over trials, and generally
monitor the conduct of cases presented to a court or administrative body and move the cases toward a final settlement or decision. **2.** (*cap*) the title accorded to judges in
many courts, including the United States District Courts
and United States Courts of Appeals. See also ADMINISTRA-
TIVE LAW JUDGE Cf. MAGISTRATE; JUSTICE.

judge trial. Same as *bench trial* (see under TRIAL).

judgment, *n.* **1.** a court's final decision in a case, or occasionally on a particular aspect of a case. **2.** the formal
document embodying such a judgment, usually written in
very formal and turgid prose. Cf OPINION. **3. declaratory
judgment,** a judgment resolving a dispute about legal
rights or status but not awarding any relief For example,
two parties with conflicting claims to the same land might
ask a court simply to declare which claim is valid. **4. default judgment,** a judgment against a party for failing to
appear or to proceed with a case. Also called **judgment
by default. 5. deficiency judgment,** in a case in which
property of a debtor was sold at a court-supervised auction
to satisfy a debt but failed to bring in enough money, a
judgment against the debtor for the balance still owed. **6.
in personam judgment** or **judgment in personam,** a
judgment against a specific person or entity. If a money
judgment against a party goes unpaid, any available property of that party may be seized to satisfy the judgment.
Also called **personal judgment.** See also IN PERSONAM. **7.
in rem judgment** or **judgment in rem,** a judgment determining the status or disposition of an item of property
or a legal relationship. See also IN REM. **8. judgment notwithstanding the verdict,** a judgment contrary to the
jury's findings in a case, entered by the judge on the
ground that the jury's verdict lacked evidentiary support or
was contrary to law. Also called **judgment n.o.v.** or, informally, **j.n.o.v.,** from the Latin *non obstante veredicto* (lit.
"notwithstanding the verdict"). **9. judgment on the
pleadings,** judgment granted to one side or the other

even before the parties have commenced pretrial discovery, because the pleadings themselves contain admissions that, as a matter of law, permit only one possible outcome. **10. judgment on the verdict,** judgment in accordance with the jury's findings. Cf. *judgment notwithstanding the verdict.* See also *verdict against the weight of the evidence* (under VERDICT). **11. summary judgment,** judgment entered without a full trial because the evidence (or lack of evidence) brought out in pretrial discovery makes it clear which side must prevail as a matter of law. See also *judgment* CREDITOR, DEBTOR, LIEN under those words.

judgment proof, describing a person or entity without assets that could be seized to satisfy a money judgment, making such a judgment worthless

judicial, *adj.* **1.** relating to a court or the courts **2.** relating to a judge or judges: *judicial convention; judicial ethics.* **3. judicial economy,** efficiency in the management of judicial business; conservation of court resources: *The court consolidated the two related cases for trial in the interest of judicial economy.* **4. judicial notice,** acceptance of a fact by the judge in a case without requiring it to be proved. This is permitted when a fact is beyond reasonable dispute—either because it is generally known (the White House is located in Washington, D.C.) or because it is ascertainable from standard sources (on the night of the crime, the moon was 93% full) See also judicial DISCRETION, GLOSS, IMMUNITY, LEGISLATION, REVIEW, SALE, under those words.

judiciary, *n.* **1.** the judicial branch of government; the system of courts. **2.** judges collectively

jump bail. See under BAIL[1]

junior. Same as **subordinate.**

juridical, *adj.* pertaining to law or legal proceedings See also *juridical person* (under PERSON).

Juris Doctor. See J.D

jurisdiction[1], *n.* **1.** the power and authority of a court or administrative tribunal to decide legal issues and disputes. The scope of a particular court's jurisdiction is determined by a combination of constitutional and statutory provisions **2. ancillary jurisdiction, a.** broadly, the power of a court to decide issues incidental to a case properly within its jurisdiction, when those issues standing alone would have been beyond its jurisdiction. **b.** specifically, in a case that is properly before a federal court because the plaintiffs and defendants are from different states, the power to dispose at the same time of a related claim between two parties from the same state. See also *diversity jurisdiction; supplemental jurisdiction.* **3. appellate jurisdiction,** jurisdiction to review orders and judgments of a lower tribunal Cf *original jurisdiction.* **4. concurrent jurisdiction,** jurisdiction of more than one court or agency with respect to the same type of case. For example, the state and federal courts have concurrent jurisdiction to enforce many federal laws. Cf. *exclusive jurisdiction.* **5. continuing jurisdiction,**

jurisdiction over a case retained by the court even after final judgment has been rendered, for the purpose of dealing with any problems that arise in implementing the judgment. **6. diversity jurisdiction,** the jurisdiction of federal courts to entertain controversies between citizens of different states. See also CITIZEN; JURISDICTIONAL AMOUNT. **7. exclusive jurisdiction,** jurisdiction with respect to a type of case that may not be brought in any other tribunal. Specialized tribunals such as probate court or traffic court often have exclusive jurisdiction over cases within their specialty, and the federal courts have exclusive jurisdiction over cases in certain areas of federal law. Cf. *concurrent jurisdiction.* **8. federal question jurisdiction,** the jurisdiction of federal courts to decide cases arising under FEDERAL LAW. **9. general jurisdiction,** jurisdiction to hear any kind of case except one restricted to some specialized court. Cf *limited jurisdiction.* **10. in personam jurisdiction** or **jurisdiction in personam,** jurisdiction to render a judgment that will be binding upon a particular person or entity. In a civil case, in personam jurisdiction exists over a party if that party either has appeared voluntarily in the case or has been properly served with a summons within the state or (in cases where *long-arm jurisdiction* applies) elsewhere. Also called **jurisdiction of** (or **over**) **the person.** See also *personal jurisdiction;* IN PERSONAM. **11. in rem jurisdiction** or **jurisdiction in rem,** jurisdiction to render a judgment with respect to property or a relationship located within the state in an action concerning the property or relationship itself, such as an action to QUIET TITLE to land or to condemn contraband goods intercepted by federal agents at the border. See also *personal jurisdiction;* IN REM **12. jurisdiction of** (or **over**) **the case,** jurisdiction to entertain a particular case; a court has jurisdiction over a case if it has both *subject matter jurisdiction* and *personal jurisdiction.* **13. limited jurisdiction,** jurisdiction to deal only with a particular category of cases; for example, the jurisdiction of a family court or a small claims court. Unlike some state courts, all federal courts are courts of limited jurisdiction, because they may hear only certain categories of cases specified in the Constitution and authorized by Congress. Also called **special jurisdiction.** Cf. *general jurisdiction.* See also *subject matter jurisdiction.* **14. long-arm jurisdiction,** jurisdiction to render a judgment binding upon a person or entity outside the state in a case arising out of conduct by that person or entity, either in person or through an agent, that either occurred within the state or occurred elsewhere and had an impact within the state. **15. original jurisdiction,** jurisdiction to give a case its first hearing and issue a judgment. Every new case must be filed in a court or agency that has original jurisdiction with respect to such cases. Cf *appellate jurisdiction.* **16. pendent jurisdiction,** in a case that is properly before a federal court because it arises under federal law, the power to dispose at the same time of related state-law claims. See also *federal question jurisdiction; supplemen-*

tal jurisdiction. **17. personal jurisdiction,** jurisdiction to render a binding decision with respect to a particular person or thing. Traditional analysis divides personal jurisdiction in civil cases into three categories. *in personam jurisdiction, in rem jurisdiction,* and *quasi in rem jurisdiction.* Cf. *subject matter jurisdiction.* **18. quasi in rem jurisdiction** or **jurisdiction quasi in rem,** jurisdiction to render judgment upon a claim against a person who has property within the state to the extent of the value of that property, even when the dispute in the case has nothing to do with the property. Traditionally this has been used as a device for initiating actions against people over whom *in personam jurisdiction* could not be obtained, but this would now generally be considered unconstitutional. See also *personal jurisdiction;* QUASI IN REM. **19. subject matter jurisdiction,** jurisdiction to hear and decide cases of a particular type. The two major categories of subject matter jurisdiction in the federal courts are *diversity jurisdiction* and *federal question jurisdiction.* Cf. *personal jurisdiction.* **20. supplemental jurisdiction,** the name now used in the federal courts for *ancillary jurisdiction* (def a) The principal categories of supplemental jurisdiction are *ancillary jurisdiction* (def. b) and *pendent jurisdiction* —**jurisdictional,** *adj.* —**jurisdictionally,** *adv.*

jurisdiction², *n.* the geographic area throughout which the authority of a court, legislative body, law enforcement agency, or other governmental unit extends. "Jurisdiction" is a convenient shorthand for "a state, the District of Columbia, or the federal government": *Most jurisdictions today have the death penalty for at least some crimes.*

jurisdictional amount, the amount of money or the value of property that must be at stake in order for a case to be within the jurisdiction of a particular court. For example, Congress has decided that the federal courts should not be available to hear cases founded upon *diversity jurisdiction* (see under JURISDICTION¹) unless there is a lot of money at stake—currently more than $50,000 Diversity cases involving less than this jurisdictional amount must be brought in state court.

jurisprudence, *n* **1.** the philosophy of law; the consideration of broad questions relating to such matters as the sources, functions, and meaning of law. **2.** a body of judicial opinions: *the civil rights jurisprudence of the Supreme Court from 1954 to 1969.*

juristic person. See under PERSON.

juror, *n.* **1.** a member of a jury. **2.** loosely, a member of a jury array; a person who has appeared in response to a summons for jury duty.

jury, *n.* **1.** Also called **petit** (or **petty**) **jury.** a group of citizens called upon to hear the evidence at a trial, decide the facts, and render a verdict in accordance with the judge's instructions on the law. Traditionally this was a group of twelve men, often all white, required to reach a unanimous verdict. Under current interpretations of the Sixth and Seventh Amendments (see Appendix), people may not be excluded from a jury solely on the basis of race or sex; states may provide for six-member juries or nonunanimous verdicts in state criminal cases; and six-member juries may be used in civil cases in the federal courts. See also *jury trial* (under TRIAL); PETIT; PETTY. Cf *grand jury.* **2. grand jury,** a group of citizens summoned to hear evidence presented by a prosecutor and issue an INDICTMENT if they find sufficient evidence to warrant trying a particular person for a particular crime. The Fifth Amendment (see Appendix) requires such screening of accusations by a grand jury before anyone can be prosecuted on a serious federal criminal charge. Federal grand juries are made up of 16 to 23 people, and it takes a vote of twelve to authorize an indictment. The constitutional requirement of indictment by grand jury has never been extended to state prosecutions; and since in practice grand juries seldom amount to more than a rubber stamp for prosecutors, they have been abolished, reduced in size, or given a reduced role in most states. **3. hung jury,** a jury unable to reach a verdict. This usually results, first, in an *Allen charge* (see under CHARGE), and if that fails, then a MISTRIAL. **4. jury array.** Same as VENIRE. **5. jury duty,** service as a JUROR. **6. jury nullification,** the power, and occasional practice, of a jury in a criminal case to ignore the judge's instructions on the law and acquit a defendant despite overwhelming evidence of guilt and absence of reasonable doubt. Because of the constitutional protection against DOUBLE JEOPARDY, the jury's acquittal must stand Depending upon one's view of a particular case, jury nullification is either a gross injustice or the final safeguard against callous and overzealous prosecution. **7. jury panel.** Also called **panel. a.** the jury in a particular case. **b.** sometimes, the entire VENIRE from which a jury is to be chosen See also IMPANEL. **8. jury trial.** See under TRIAL.

just compensation, the compensation that the Fifth Amendment (see Appendix) requires the state or federal government to pay to a property owner whose property is taken for *public use* (see under USE) In general, it is the MARKET VALUE of the property at the time of the taking, taking into account the *best and highest use* (see under USE) to which a private buyer could have put the property See also TAKING; EMINENT DOMAIN.

justice, *n.* **1.** the ideal of fair and beneficent treatment of all people by each other and by their governments, which law in a democratic society attempts to serve. **2.** the system of law and administration of law. *administration of justice;* OBSTRUCTION OF JUSTICE. **3.** (*cap.*) the title given to judges in certain courts, particularly those designated "supreme" courts (most notably the Supreme Court of the United States) and inferior courts at the very lowest level of the judicial system (such as justice of the peace courts and police courts) Cf. JUDGE; MAGISTRATE

justiciable, *adj.* appropriate for adjudication; suitable for resolution by a court. In general, to be justiciable a case must involve a genuine dispute over legal rights or interests, resolution of which will have some real effect beyond satisfying the litigants' curiosity. In addition, the issue involved must not be one that, under the Constitution, lies within the exclusive province of the legislative or executive branch of government. Cases that might be dismissed as nonjusticiable include a case seeking an ADVISORY OPINION, a *collusive suit* (see under SUIT), a case that is MOOT, and a case raising a *political question* (see under QUESTION²) —**justiciability,** *n.*

justifiable homicide. See under HOMICIDE.

justification, *n.* a legally sufficient excuse for having done something that otherwise would constitute a tort or a crime; for example, ENTRAPMENT, DURESS, or NECESSITY.

juvenile, *n.* **1.** a person not yet old enough to be treated as an adult by the criminal justice system. The ages and circumstances under which a young person in trouble with the law will be treated as a juvenile vary from state to state; typically, state statutes set one age below which a youngster must be treated as a juvenile and a higher age above which a person must be treated as an adult, with treatment between those ages depending upon the circumstances of the case. **2. juvenile court,** a special court established in some states to handle criminal matters in which the accused is treated as a juvenile, and sometimes also child protection proceedings. As compared with criminal courts for adult offenders, the emphasis in juvenile courts is upon rehabilitation of youthful offenders rather than punishment. **3. juvenile offender,** a young person who violates a criminal law but is dealt with as a juvenile rather than as an adult. Also called **youthful offender** and sometimes **delinquent** or **juvenile delinquent,** although the latter two terms are often used more broadly to include young people who engage in troublesome or antisocial conduct that falls short of criminality.

K

kangaroo court, *Slang.* **1.** a mock court set up by criminals or vigilantes to reach a predetermined verdict of guilty. **2.** a highly derogatory term for an actual judicial proceeding regarded as outrageously improper or manifestly unfair. See also STAR CHAMBER.

Keogh plan. See under PENSION PLAN.

kickback, *n.* **1.** a form of BRIBERY in which a company that is awarded a contract, or from which a purchase is made, turns over a portion of the money received to an official or employee of the other party to the transaction, as a reward for helping to bring about the transaction or as an incentive to exercise sucn influence in the future. **2.** a form of EXTORTION in which an employer, supervisor, or union official demands a portion of a worker's rightful wages as a condition of continued employment.

kidnapping, *n.* the crime of carrying off or isolating a person for the purpose of demanding money (**ransom**) for his release, using him as a hostage, harming or terrorizing him or others, or the like. Despite the allusion to "kids," the victim may be either a child or an adult. See also ABDUCTION; PARENTAL KIDNAPPING. —**kidnap,** *v.*

kind. See IN KIND.

King's Bench, an English court of general jurisdiction for both civil and criminal cases. The court goes back centuries and is the source of much of the common law still in effect in America today. When a queen is on the throne, the court is called **Queen's Bench.**

kite, *v.* to write a check knowing that there are not yet sufficient funds in the account to cover it. Depending upon the circumstances, check kiting may be a crime, especially where such a check is deposited in another bank account to create a false balance which is then withdrawn.

knock and announce rule, the general rule that police officers must knock and announce themselves before breaking into a place to make an arrest or execute a search warrant.

knock off, to make unlicensed copies of someone else's trademark or copyrighted design (for example, of clothing, fabric, watches, or furniture), usually for sale at a substantially lower price than the original. The copy is called a **knockoff.**

know all men by these presents, an ancient but still quite common formulaic expression that may be placed at the beginning of a legal instrument, meaning essentially, "Let the world be put on notice by this instrument." The purpose is to impress upon both the person who signs the document and anyone who reads it the seriousness and legally binding nature of the instrument Thus it serves for legal writings much the same function that HEAR YE or OYEZ does for courtroom proceedings

knowledge, *n.* **1.** Also called **actual knowledge.** awareness of a fact "Knowledge" that a certain result will follow from certain action means awareness that the result is practically certain to occur. Knowledge is a crucial element in many tort cases and criminal cases, since assessment of culpability often depends upon what the people involved knew; for example, in a homicide case, the degree of guilt might depend in part on whether the defendant knew the gun was loaded. See also STATE OF MIND. Cf *constructive knowledge; imputed knowledge.* **2.** Also called **personal knowledge.** awareness of a fact gained from direct observation or experience, as distinguished from a belief based upon what others have said or upon a less-than-certain chain of reasoning from other information. In general, witnesses are allowed to testify only to matters within their personal knowledge, and statements in affidavits and pleadings, unless expressly made upon INFORMATION AND BELIEF, should be based upon personal knowledge. Cf. HEARSAY; OPINION; *opinion evidence* (under EVIDENCE). **3. constructive knowledge,** knowledge that the law attributes to a person regardless of whether that person has actual knowledge of the matter, usually because the circumstances are such that a failure to know a fact is regarded as inexcusable. For example, an individual who was personally served with a court order but failed to read it would be said to have constructive knowledge of its contents despite the lack of actual knowledge **4. imputed knowledge,** in a relationship of principal and agent, employer and employee, or the like, the superior's constructive knowledge of facts of which the subordinate was made aware in the course of the subordinate's duties. See also CARNAL KNOWLEDGE. **—know,** *v.* **—knowing,** *adj.* **—knowingly,** *adv.*

L

labor organization, the term used in the National Labor Relations Act for a UNION. It is defined very broadly to include any group of employees whose purposes include dealing with employers with regard to grievances or terms and conditions of employment

labor union. Same as UNION

laches, *n* unreasonable delay in pursuing a known right against someone Laches is an *equitable defense* (see under DEFENSE) that may be raised in a case in which the defendant's position has been prejudiced by the plaintiff's delay in taking legal action. In cases at law, a plaintiff ordinarily may wait until the last day before expiration of the STATUTE OF LIMITATIONS to sue; but if an injunction or other equitable relief is sought, the court may take laches into account For example, a landowner may not sit back and watch a building being built knowing that it encroaches on his land, and then expect a sympathetic hearing in a suit to have the building torn down, although he might still be entitled to compensatory damages for the loss of a little piece of his land.

lading. See BILL OF LADING.

land. Same as *real property* (see under PROPERTY) Although the term is sometimes used in the narrow sense of earth or soil, in law it is usually used as a shorthand for real property in general.

landlord, *n* the person who grants a LEASEHOLD interest in real property to a TENANT See also LEASE

landmark case. See under CASE¹

lapse, *v.* **1.** to expire because of the passage of time or be extinguished by the happening of some event For example, an OFFER of a contract will lapse if not accepted within the time specified in the offer (or within a reasonable time, if no time is specified); a BEQUEST or DEVISE will lapse if the taker named in the will dies before the testator (unless the bequest is saved by an ANTILAPSE STATUTE); a statute enacted with an expiration date will lapse if not renewed —*n* **2.** such expiration or extinguishment.

larceny, *n.* the crime of wrongfully taking possession of personal property from another with intent to convert it to one's own use Often designated as **grand larceny** if the value of the property exceeds a certain amount, and **petit** (or **petty**) **larceny** otherwise The term has been abandoned in many modern criminal codes in favor of the broader concept of THEFT. See also GRAND; PETIT; PETTY.

last clear chance, a doctrine under which, as between two people whose negligence contributed to an accident, the one who clearly had the last opportunity to avoid the accident may be held liable for injuries to the other Thus a person who negligently placed himself in a dangerous situation might nevertheless be able to recover in full from another who should have realized the danger and avoided the accident. In most states this principle has been abandoned in favor of the more flexible doctrine of *comparative negligence* (see under NEGLIGENCE)

last will and testament, a WILL. Sometimes called **last will.** The word "testament" adds nothing. In fact, the word "last" adds nothing; you can make a new "last will" every day.

latent, *adj.* not obvious; present but not such as would be discovered in an inspection made with reasonable care· *latent ambiguity; latent defect.* Allocation of liability for defects in products or property sometimes depends upon whether the problem was latent or PATENT

law, *n.* **1.** the body of rules and principles for human behavior and the conduct of government in an organized community, state, or nation, created or recognized by custom or by government institutions and implemented or enforced by the government. **2.** a body of law relating to a subject: *constitutional law; the law of evidence* **3.** a STATUTE. **4.** one of the two systems of justice—to some extent competing and to some extent complementary—that existed side by side in England prior to the MERGER OF LAW AND EQUITY The law courts enforced criminal laws and granted awards of money damages for torts and breaches of contract. See also COMMON LAW (def 3). Cf. EQUITY **5.** the profession that deals with law and legal procedures: *the practice of law.* See also ADMINISTRATIVE LAW; AS A MATTER OF LAW; BAD LAW; BY OPERATION OF LAW; CASE LAW; CIVIL LAW; CONCLUSION OF LAW; CONFLICT OF LAWS; *corporate law* (under LAW); federal law; good law; *implied in law* (under IMPLIED); INTERNATIONAL LAW; *maritime law* (under MARITIME); POSITIVE LAW; PROCEDURE; PUBLIC INTEREST LAW; *question of law* and *mixed question of fact and law* (both under QUESTION²); SUBSTANCE. Cf. CANON LAW; NATURAL LAW; PARLIAMENTARY LAW

law clerk. See under CLERK.

law of nations. Same as *public international law* (see under INTERNATIONAL LAW).

law of the case, the principle that once an issue has been decided by one judge or panel of judges in a case, it will not be reconsidered if the case comes before a new judge or panel at the same level; except in special circumstances, the subsequent judges will adhere to the prior decision as the "law of the case" even if they disagree with it.

law review, a journal for scholarly writing on legal topics. Most law schools publish one or more such periodicals, usually with the word "Review" or "Journal" in the title.

lawful, *adj.* **1.** authorized or permitted by law; in harmony with law: *lawful conduct; a lawful enterprise.* **2.** recognized or sanctioned by law. *lawful marriage; lawful money* Cf. LEGAL.

lawsuit, *n.* a SUIT.

lawyer, *n.* a person whose profession is to advise or act for clients in legal matters; a person licensed by a state to practice law.

leading case. See under CASE¹

leading question. See under QUESTION[1].

lease, *n.* **1.** the grant of a LEASEHOLD interest in real property, usually in the form of a contract under which the person receiving possession of the property (the TENANT or **lessee**) agrees to pay rent to the grantor (the LANDLORD or **lessor**). **2.** a contract temporarily conveying the right to exclusive possession and use of tangible personal property from one person (the **lessor**) to another (the **lessee**). **3.** the instrument embodying such a grant or contract. **4. gross lease,** a lease at a fixed rate of rent. Cf. *net lease; percentage lease.* **5. ground lease,** a long-term lease (typically for 99 years) on the ground upon which a large commercial building sits or is to be built. **6. net lease,** a lease under which the rent consists of a fixed minimum amount plus a variable sum to cover specified expenses of the landlord, such as taxes and maintenance. **7. percentage lease,** a lease of real property for commercial use in which the rent is based at least in part upon a percentage of the lessee's sales. —*v* **8.** to convey property rights by lease. **9.** to take or hold by lease.

leaseback. See *sale and leaseback* (under SALE).

leasehold, *n.* a right to temporary possession of real property by agreement with the owner of the FREEHOLD or of a superior leasehold on the same property Also called **leasehold estate; leasehold interest.** For types of leasehold, see TENANCY. See also ESTATE[1]; LANDLORD; TENANT; LEASE.

leave, *n.* permission from a court to take some action. Also called **leave of court.** See also *dismissal with leave to replead* (under DISMISSAL).

legacy, *n.* Same as BEQUEST. See also LEGATEE.

legal, *adj.* **1.** not against the law; not a crime: *Although it was legal to publish the defamatory statement, the publisher was ordered to pay damages for libel.* **2.** satisfying requirements or formalities of the law; sufficient under the law: *legal consideration; legal demand.* **3.** created, recognized, or imposed by law: LEGAL TENDER; *legal separation* (see under SEPARATION); *legal duty.* **4.** pertaining generally to law or the practice of law: *legal theory; legal ethics.* **5.** pertaining to law as distinguished from fact: *legal question.* **6.** pertaining to, enforceable under, or derived from principles of LAW (def 4) as distinguished from EQUITY: *legal title* (see under TITLE); *legal remedy* (see under REMEDY) **7.** CONSTRUCTIVE· *legal fraud* (see under FRAUD). See also *legal* ACTION, AGE, CAPACITY, DISABILITY, ESTATE[1], FORM, HEIR, INTEREST[1], INTEREST[3], OWNER, PERSON, RIGHT under those words, and *legal relief* (under REMEDY).

legal assistant. Same as PARALEGAL.

legal fiction, a court's assumption of a fact known to be untrue in order to fit a case into a category recognized by the law, so that relief can be granted and justice done. Legal fictions have been an important mechanism in the evolution of common law For example, "larceny" is traditionally defined as wrongfully taking property from another's possession; to cover situations in which a wrongdoer steals property that someone has accidentally left behind, the courts adopted the fiction that lost property is still in the "possession" of the person who lost it. See also CONSTRUCTIVE.

legal tender, currency that may lawfully be used in payment of debts and may not be deemed inadequate by a creditor to whom it is tendered in the proper amount; the ordinary money of a country

legalize, v. to adopt legislation making conduct that formerly was unlawful lawful. See discussion under DECRIMINALIZE.

legatee, n. **1.** a recipient of a BEQUEST. Cf DEVISEE **2. residuary legatee,** a person designated by will to receive or share in the *residuary estate* (see under ESTATE²)

legislation, n. **1.** the enactment of statutes by a LEGISLATURE. **2.** a statute or body of statutes enacted or proposed. **3. judicial legislation,** a disparaging term for a court decision that interprets or applies the law in a way that the speaker disagrees with, suggesting that the court has usurped the function of the legislature It is usually used in situations where the court has extended some right to a class of people. But if a court seriously misreads the will of the legislature and the people, the legislature can always pass a law overruling the court—even amending the Constitution if necessary.

legislative, adj. **1.** pertaining to the making of law or having the function of making law: *legislative power; legislative proceedings.* **2.** pertaining to a LEGISLATURE· *legislative hearings; legislative salaries.*

legislative history, the process that a bill went through to become a law, often looked to by the courts as an aid in CONSTRUCTION of the statute that finally emerged. For example, if at some point a particular provision was removed from the bill, that may indicate the legislature's desire to limit the scope of the statute. Of course, it could also indicate the legislature's belief that other parts of the statute already cover that provision, so drawing conclusions from legislative history requires caution

legislative immunity. See under IMMUNITY

legislative intent, the purpose of a legislature in enacting a particular statute. In the case of federal legislation, also called **congressional intent.** Legislative intent is looked to by the courts for assistance in such matters as CONSTRUCTION of a statute, determination of whether a federal statute preempts local legislation (see PREEMPTION), and determination of whether a superficially neutral statute was enacted for a discriminatory purpose. Sometimes courts attempt to glean intent solely from the words of the statute (see PLAIN MEANING); often they resort to LEGISLATIVE HISTORY.

legislature, n. a deliberative body elected and authorized to write laws; the lawmaking branch of government· *state legislature; county legislature.* Congress is the national legislature. See also SEPARATION OF POWERS.

lemon law, a statute that entitles the purchaser of a car that turns out to have substantial defects to return it for a refund or replacement.

lessee. See under LEASE (defs. 1 and 2).

lesser included offense, an offense whose definition is included within the definition of a more serious crime, so that one cannot commit the more serious offense without also committing the lesser; for example, LARCENY is a lesser included offense of ROBBERY, and ATTEMPT to commit a crime is always a lesser included offense of the crime attempted. It is proper to charge a jury that if it fails to find that all the elements of the crime charged have been proved, it may nevertheless convict on a lesser included offense.

lessor. See under LEASE (defs. 1 and 2)

let, v. **1.** to LEASE real property to someone. **2.** to award a contract for the performance of certain work, especially to one of several bidders for it.

lethal weapon. See under WEAPON.

letter of credit, a letter in which a bank or other person, at the request of a customer, promises a third person (the beneficiary) that it will honor demands by the beneficiary for payment of drafts drawn or sums owed by the customer upon satisfaction of specified conditions, such as presentation of documents proving that goods shipped to the customer have arrived and payment is due The letter of credit facilitates long-distance commercial transactions by assuring the seller that payment will be made when the goods arrive while assuring the buyer that payment will not be made if the goods do not arrive.

letter of intent, a letter confirming an *agreement to agree* (see under AGREEMENT). See also *memorandum of understanding* (under MEMORANDUM).

letters, *n.pl.* **1.** a formal document granting a right, privilege, or authorization, or conveying an official request. **2. letters of administration,** a document issued by a court appointing someone as ADMINISTRATOR of an estate. **3. letters patent,** a document issued by the government granting some right; in particular, letters granting a PATENT (a term derived from the phrase "letters patent") to an inventor. **4. letters rogatory,** a formal request by a court in one country to a court in another, asking the second court to take the testimony of a certain witness and transmit it to the first court for use in a case. **5. letters testamentary,** a document issued by a court formally authorizing someone to act as EXECUTOR under a will.

levy, v. **1.** to impose a tax or fine: *The court levied a $500 fine for contempt.* **2.** to collect or seize property in accordance with legal authority; especially, to attach or seize property of a judgment debtor in order to satisfy a judgment **(levy execution):** *The plaintiff levied on the defendant's car and bank account.* —n **3.** the act of levying.

lex, *n. Latin.* law; a term that shows up in countless Latin legal maxims and phrases, especially in older writing. (See, for example, **de minimis non curat lex,** under DE MINIMIS.) The following three phrases are still seen in discussions of

CONFLICT OF LAWS: **lex fori,** the law of the forum; that is, the law of the state in which a case is pending; **lex loci contractus,** the law of the place of the contract; that is, the law of the state or country where the agreement at issue in a contract case was entered into; and **lex loci delicti,** the law of the place of the wrong; that is, the law of the state or country where the conduct complained of in a tort case took place.

liability, *n.* **1.** legal responsibility for a crime (**criminal liability**) or, more commonly, for a tort or breach of contract (**civil liability**). **2.** the sum that one might be or has been ordered to pay in damages or fines because of such responsibility. **3.** any debt or other financial obligation of a person or entity. Cf. ASSET. **4. contingent liability,** a specific financial obligation that may or may not arise or become payable, depending upon future events. **5. joint and several liability,** liability for damages caused by the combined action of two or more persons, or for an obligation undertaken by two or more persons, under circumstances in which the law permits the plaintiff to proceed either against the whole group or against any member individually. Cf. *joint liability; several liability.* **6. joint liability,** liability of two or more persons as a group, as for a tort in which they all participated or for repayment of a loan made to them collectively. Cf. *several liability; joint and several liability.* **7. primary liability,** liability of a person directly responsible for an obligation, in a situation where another person has *secondary liability.* **8. secondary liability,** liability that arises only if another person (the one with *primary liability*) defaults in an obligation. In a GUARANTY arrangement, the principal debtor is primarily liable and the guarantor is secondarily liable. **9. several liability,** **a.** liability of each individual member of a group for damages caused, or an obligation owed, by all of them together. **b.** liability of a member of a group for damages caused or an obligation undertaken by that member separately from the others Cf. *joint liability; joint and several liability.* **10. strict liability,** civil or criminal liability imposed upon a person without regard to whether the person intentionally or knowingly did anything wrong or was in any way reckless or negligent. In tort law, also called **liability without fault.** Typical examples in tort law include PRODUCTS LIABILITY and liability for ABNORMALLY DANGEROUS ACTIVITY; in criminal law, *statutory rape* (see under RAPE) and speeding. **11. vicarious liability,** liability imposed by law upon one person for acts of another; for example, the liability of an employer, under the doctrine of RESPONDEAT SUPERIOR, for acts committed by an employee, or the liability of all partners in a law firm for malpractice committed by one of them. See also LIMITED LIABILITY; PRODUCTS LIABILITY.

liability insurance, insurance that protects the insured against liability to third persons. For example, automobile liability insurance covers (up to the maximum amounts specified in the policy) damages assessed against the insured for personal injuries or property damage suffered by others in an automobile accident for which the insured is held responsible. Cf. INDEMNITY INSURANCE.

liable, *adj.* legally responsible; subject to liability. One is said to be "strictly liable," "jointly and severally liable," "vicariously liable," etc., according to the nature of the LIABILITY.

libel¹, *n.* **1.** the form of DEFAMATION in which the defamatory statement is communicated in writing or another medium having a degree of permanence, such as film. In some states, libel also includes defamatory statements broadcast on radio or television Cf. SLANDER. —*v.* **2.** to publish a libel against a person. —**libelous,** adj.

libel², *n.* the former name for the complaint in an ADMIRALTY case. The plaintiff was called the **libelant;** the defendant was called the **libelee.** This terminology, still encountered in legal research, has nothing to do with defamation.

liberal construction. See under CONSTRUCTION.

liberty, *n.* freedom of action. As used in the constitutional provisions protecting people from deprivation of "liberty" without DUE PROCESS, the term is interpreted as including not only freedom from physical restraint (as by being put in jail or deported), but also, at least in a few basic areas, the broader freedom to control one's own life and engage in pursuits of one's choosing (as by traveling, pursuing an education, or deciding for oneself whether to bear a child). See also ENTITLEMENT; FUNDAMENTAL RIGHT; RIGHT OF PRIVACY; RIGHT TO TRAVEL; *substantive due process* (under DUE PROCESS).

license, *n.* **1.** government permission for a person to do something otherwise forbidden, such as practice medicine, drive a car, or sell liquor. **2.** a certificate evidencing such permission. **3.** permission given by the owner of a patent, copyright, or trademark for another to exploit it. Such licenses are usually embodied in detailed licensing agreements. **4.** consent of the owner or tenant of real property for another's entry upon the property, especially when the person entering is doing so solely for her own purposes (e.g., to take a shortcut or solicit for charity) or as a social guest. See also discussion under INVITEE. —*v.* **5.** to grant a license.

licensee, *n.* a person to whom a LICENSE has been granted. Cf. INVITEE.

licensor, *n.* a person who grants a LICENSE.

lie, *v.* (of a cause of action or procedural right) to exist; to be sustainable: *The action lies in tort. Since the order was nonfinal, an appeal will not lie.*

lie detector. Same as POLYGRAPH.

lien, *n.* **1.** a *security interest* (see under INTEREST¹) in property of a debtor or other obligor. Liens may arise either by agreement between the parties or, very often, by operation of law—especially in various commercial situations where they serve to ensure payment of a supplier of goods or services, as in the case of an *attorney's lien, mechanic's* *lien,* or *warehouser's lien.* **2. attorney's lien,** a lien on money, papers, and property of a client in the hands of an attorney, or a lien that an attorney may request from a court on a fund or judgment obtained for the client by the attorney's efforts, to secure payment of attorney's fees **3. judgment lien,** a lien that a judgment creditor may obtain on property of the judgment debtor, so that the property may be seized if the debtor fails to pay the judgment. **4. mechanic's lien,** the lien of one who works on, or supplies materials for use in, construction or repair of property (e.g., a house or automobile), imposed upon the property to secure payment for the work and materials. **5. tax lien,** a lien placed by the government on specific property to secure payment of back taxes on that property, or upon a taxpayer's property in general to secure payment of back income taxes. **6. warehouser's** (or **warehouseman's**) **lien,** the right of a warehouser to refuse to return a customer's goods until the storage bill is paid, and if necessary to sell them for payment.

life estate (or **tenancy**). See under ESTATE[1].

life in being. See under PERPETUITY

life insurance, 1. insurance under which the insurance company's undertaking is to pay out a specified sum of money upon the death of the insured person, either to the estate of the insured or to a beneficiary designated in the policy. **2. straight life insurance,** life insurance for which the annual premium never increases, and which remains in effect as long as the insured individual lives, provided that the premiums are paid. Also called **whole life insurance. 3. term life insurance,** life insurance that remains in effect only for a specified period of time, after which the policy usually may be renewed for another term, but at a higher premium. Also called **term insurance.**

limine. See IN LIMINE.

limitation (or **limitations**) **period.** See under STATUTE OF LIMITATIONS.

limitations. See STATUTE OF LIMITATIONS.

Limited (Ltd.), *adj.* at the end of a company name, indicates that the company is a corporation. (Short for "limited company"—a reference to the LIMITED LIABILITY of the shareholders.)

limited appearance. See under APPEARANCE.

limited jurisdiction. See under JURISDICTION[1]

limited liability, 1. the characteristic of corporations and certain other forms of organization that insulates investors from liability for debts or other obligations of the company, so that the most a shareholder can lose is the value of her shares. **2.** a contractual arrangement by which one party agrees to a ceiling on the other's liability in case something goes wrong; for example, a commercial film processor usually accepts film only upon the customer's agreement that if the film is lost or destroyed, the processor's liability will be limited to the cost of a new roll of film.

limited liability partnership. See under PARTNERSHIP.

limited partner. See under PARTNER.

limited partnership. See under PARTNERSHIP.

limited warranty. See under WARRANTY.

lineup, *n.* a police procedure in which a number of individuals, including a criminal suspect, are displayed to a witness to see if the witness identifies the suspect as the perpetrator. Unduly suggestive lineups, as when the suspect is the only individual resembling the witness's description, violate due process. Cf. SHOWUP

liquid asset. See under ASSET.

liquidate, *v.* **1.** to fix with certainty the amount of a debt or other liability, either because the obligation is certain by nature (e.g., a promissory note), or by agreement between the debtor and creditor or by judgment of a court. See also *liquidated damages* (under DAMAGES) **2.** to eliminate a debt or claim by paying or settling it. **3.** to sell assets for cash, especially other than in the ordinary course of business. **4.** to WIND UP an enterprise. —**liquidation,** *n.*

lis pendens, *Latin.* (lit. "a pending suit") the name of a notice that must be recorded in some jurisdictions to warn that certain real estate is the subject of pending litigation. A buyer of such property would be subject to the court's ultimate decision about the property.

litigant, *n.* a party to a lawsuit.

litigate, *v* **1.** to make something the subject of a lawsuit or to contest an issue in a judicial proceeding: *My client will not hesitate to litigate her claim. Since the legality of the search and seizure was fully litigated in the pretrial hearing, the issue will not be reopened at the trial.* **2.** to perform all the tasks entailed in the pursuit of a court case—filing papers, taking discovery, making motions, questioning witnesses, arguing appeals, etc.· *The suit was litigated in the federal courts.*

litigation, *n.* **1.** the process of litigating. **2.** a case or a set of cases discussed collectively. See also VEXATIOUS LITIGATION.

litigator, *n.* a lawyer who specializes in litigation.

litigious, *adj.* readily or excessively inclined to litigate *America is a litigious society.*

living trust. Same as *inter vivos trust* (see under TRUST).

living will, a formal instrument in which an individual states what medical measures he wants taken or withheld in the event of terminal illness or permanent unconsciousness. It will theoretically be followed if it is executed in conformity with state law, if those into whose hands the maker falls know about it and are sympathetic, and if the requests made are not contrary to public policy (see *physician-assisted suicide,* under SUICIDE); but the maker should also execute a HEALTH CARE PROXY so that somebody will have clear authority to insist that the living will be obeyed.

LL.B., See J.D.

LL.M., abbreviation for Master of Laws, a degree typically requiring one year of study beyond law school. Such degrees are most often sought by lawyers who plan to concentrate their practice in a specialized field, such as taxation. Cf. J.D

local, *adj.* **1.** referring to a jurisdiction smaller than a state, such as a city, county, town, or village: *a local ordinance; federal, state, and local taxes.* **2.** sometimes, referring to a state and its subdivisions, as distinguished from the federal government: *In deciding the case, the federal court looked to local law.* **3.** any small region: *local custom; the local economy.* —*n.* **4.** Short for *local union* (see under UNION).

local counsel. See under COUNSEL

local rules. See under RULE.

lockout, *n.* the temporary closing of a business or refusal of an employer to allow employees to come to work, in order to pressure workers into accepting the employer's conditions. Cf. STRIKE[1].

loco parentis. See IN LOCO PARENTIS.

long-arm jurisdiction. See under JURISDICTION[1]

loss, *n.* **1.** in a sale or exchange of property, the amount by which the value received for the property falls short of the owner's BASIS in the property. See also *capital loss* (under CAPITAL[1]). Cf. GAIN. **2.** any injury to person or property for which damages might be awarded in a civil action or payment obtained under an insurance contract.

loss causation. See under CAUSATION.

loss of consortium. See under CONSORTIUM.

lower court. See under COURT.

L.S., See under SEAL[1].

magistrate, *n.* **1.** broadly, any JUDGE **2.** specifically, a judge of an inferior court such as a police court, town court, or justice of the peace court, with limited jurisdiction to deal with minor offenses and sometimes some minor civil matters. **3.** in federal district courts, an officer authorized to carry out a wide range of judicial functions that otherwise would have to be performed by judges. **4.** (*cap*) the title accorded to some magistrates, though others have titles such as Justice of the Peace or Town Justice Cf. JUDGE; JUSTICE.

Magna Carta, *Latin.* (lit. "great charter") a document executed by King John of England in 1215, recognizing certain rights of English subjects and establishing the principle that came to be known as DUE PROCESS, under which even the sovereign is required to follow the law in taking action against a subject. The Magna Carta, often referred to as the **Great Charter,** is the source for many concepts embodied in the United States Constitution, and is still referred to in judicial opinions. Sometimes spelled "Magna Charta," but always pronounced "magna karta"

mail fraud. See under FRAUD.

main brief. See under BRIEF.

maintenance, *n.* **1.** money for basic living expenses paid to a spouse from which one is separated or divorced See also ALIMONY. **2.** giving financial or other assistance to a litigant in a case in which one has no interest Instead of praising this as charity toward poor people who otherwise would be unable to obtain justice, English and American law have traditionally frowned upon it, and even today there is a strong current of opinion against support for legal services for the poor. See also BARRATRY; CHAMPERTY

majority. See under AGE

majority opinion. See under OPINION.

make, *v.* to execute an instrument *make a contract; make a will; make a promissory note* Although the term can be applied to any instrument for the payment of money (e.g., *to make a check*), in strict usage one "draws" a check or other draft but "makes" a note. The person who promises payment in a promissory note is thus the **maker** of the note, not the "drawer" Cf DRAW

make a record. See under RECORD

make bail. See under BAIL¹

make law, (of a court) to decide a significant issue on which the courts have not previously spoken, or announce a significant new principle of law.

make whole, to compensate a person fully for injury or loss; to award or pay *compensatory damages* (see under DAMAGES).

malfeasance, *n.* the doing of an unlawful act; especially, misconduct by a public official, corporate officer, or other person in a position of trust. Cf MISFEASANCE; NONFEASANCE.

malice, *n.* **1.** (in criminal law) **a.** any of the mental states required for the different kinds of MURDER intent to kill or knowledge that one's conduct is substantially certain to cause death, intent to do serious bodily injury, extreme indifference to human life, or willing participation in a felony **b.** generally, criminal intent; a purpose to perform an act that is a crime. **2.** (in tort law) improper purpose or lack of legally recognized justification. Such "malice" is often said to be an element of such torts as ABUSE OF PROCESS, DEFAMATION, DISPARAGEMENT, and MALICIOUS PROSECUTION **3.** spite or ill will. Occasionally courts or lawyers use "malice" in this ordinary (nonlegal) meaning Since the legal and nonlegal meanings of the word tend to get mixed up, the modern trend in law is to avoid the word altogether in defining torts and crimes. See STATE OF MIND **4. actual malice,** (in defamation cases) knowledge that a statement one is publishing is false, or reckless disregard of its truth or falsity. The Supreme Court has held that a PUBLIC FIGURE cannot recover damages for defamation unless the person who uttered the defamatory words (usually a newspaper or other news medium) knew that they were false, or did not know one way or the other and recklessly plunged ahead with the comments anyway. Although the Court designates this as "actual malice," no actual spite or ill will is required; the publisher's feelings toward the subject of the comments are completely irrelevant. **5. malice aforethought, a.** strictly, an intent to kill formulated in advance. See also PREMEDITATION. **b.** broadly, a term applied to any form of murder, whether premeditated or not and with or without intent to kill (see def. 1a above) —**malicious,** *adj* —**maliciously,** *adv.*

malicious prosecution, the tort of initiating or continuing a criminal prosecution or civil case without probable cause and for an improper purpose. Cf. ABUSE OF PROCESS

malpractice, negligence or other failure by a professional, such as a lawyer, doctor, or accountant, to live up to reasonable professional standards in the peformance of services for a client. The client may sue in tort to recover resulting damages.

mandamus, *n. Latin.* (lit. "we command") a writ by which a court directs a public or corporate body or officer, or a lower court or judge, to perform an official duty. This is a discretionary writ issued only in rare cases to remedy an injustice that otherwise might not be curable Cf. PROHIBITION.

mandate, *n.* **1.** an order from an appellate court to the lower court from which a case was appealed, communicating the higher court's decision as to how the case should be dealt with. **2.** loosely, any court order or legal requirement.

mandatory injunction. See under INJUNCTION.

mandatory presumption. See under PRESUMPTION

manipulation. See STOCK MANIPULATION

manslaughter, *n.* **1.** the crime of causing the death of another person under circumstances falling short of MUR-

DER. Some states recognize different grades of manslaughter. **2. involuntary manslaughter,** causing death through RECKLESSNESS or, in some states, *criminal negligence* (see under NEGLIGENCE). In addition, some states include the unintentional causing of another's death while performing an unlawful act other than a felony, such as speeding or trespassing. (Cf. FELONY MURDER.) The most common occasion for involuntary manslaughter is reckless driving. See also *vehicular homicide* (under HOMICIDE). **3. voluntary manslaughter,** conduct that would be regarded as murder but for the fact that the killing, though not legally justified, occurred under extenuating circumstances. The most common example is killing in the HEAT OF PASSION.

marginal tax rate. See under TAX RATE.

marital rape. See under RAPE.

maritime, *adj.* **1.** pertaining to navigation and commerce by water, both at sea and on inland waters. **2.** Also, **admiralty.** pertaining to *maritime law* or its administration: a *maritime* (or *admiralty*) *case; maritime* (or *admiralty*) *jurisdiction.* **3. maritime law,** the body of law governing maritime matters, including contracts relating to shipping by water, torts occurring at sea, property rights in vessels and freight, and the labor of ship and harbor workers. Maritime law is made and administered primarily by the federal government and the federal courts. Also called **admiralty law.**

mark, *n.* **1.** a distinctive word, phrase, logo, or design, or even a sound or musical motif, used to identify products or services made, provided, or certified by a particular company or organization. See also ® and TRADEMARK. **2.** a design—usually an X—used as a signature by someone who does not know how to write. See also X. —*v.* **3.** to place a letter or number on a document or other article used at a trial, hearing, or deposition, so that it can be referred to unambiguously in testimony and colloquy. See also EXHIBIT.

market, *n.* **1.** a place where people come together to buy and sell things, or a mechanism (such as a computer network or informal network of buyers, sellers, and agents) that puts people in touch with each other for that purpose. *stock market; real estate market.* **2.** a geographic area where goods or services are sold: *the domestic market; the Los Angeles market.* **3.** demand for goods or services, or a body of existing or potential buyers: *the market for personal computers.* **4.** the level of prices prevailing in a market: *a rising market for shoes.* —*v* **5.** to sell or offer for sale in a market.

market manipulation. Same as STOCK MANIPULATION.

market value, the price that a willing purchaser would pay and a willing seller would accept for a particular item in an ARM'S-LENGTH transaction in an open market, where both are acting with full information and neither is under particular pressure to buy or sell. Also called **fair market value.**

marketable, *adj.* suitable for sale; readily salable.

marketable security. See under SECURITY[2]

marketable title. See under TITLE

marriage, *n.* **1.** the legal relationship of husband and wife, entered into in conformity with state law and carrying various rights and duties imposed by law. **2.** a formal ceremony in which a marriage relationship is entered into. **3. common law marriage,** a marriage entered into without the usual ceremony; it is effected by an agreement to be married, followed by living together as husband and wife The common law recognized such do-it-yourself marriages if the parties had the legal capacity to marry, but this method of marrying is no longer permitted in most states. Simply cohabiting has never been sufficient to create a marriage.

marshal, *n.* **1.** a federal officer who serves summonses, executes writs, escorts criminal defendants between court and jail, and otherwise assists in the functioning of a federal court. **2.** the name given to certain state or local law enforcement or other officials in various localities. —*v.* **3.** to gather up the assets of a trust, estate, corporation, or the like and put them in order for distribution.

martial law, government by the military, using military law and institutions in place of civilian. The Supreme Court has interpreted the Constitution as permitting martial law in the United States only in wartime and only if civilian courts are no longer able to function.

Massachusetts trust or **Massachusetts business trust.** Same as *business trust* (see under TRUST).

master, *n.* **1.** the traditional common law term for an employer (the employee being referred to as a SERVANT) **2.** Also called **special master.** an individual appointed by a court to assist it in handling particular aspects of a case. See also REFEREE.

master and servant, the traditional phrase for the area of common law concerned with the employment relationship and the rights and duties of employer and employee. This terminology is still in common use.

material, *n.* **1.** important; of consequence; potentially dispositive; such as a reasonably prudent person would take into account in making a decision. To say that something is "material" usually simply means that it matters: *material fact, issue, mistake, variance, representation, misrepresentation, omission,* etc. **2.** essential; describing a component without which the whole will fail: *material allegation in a complaint; material element of a tort or crime; material term of a contract.* **3.** logically related to a material fact or issue: *material evidence.* —**materiality,** *n.*

material breach. See under BREACH.

material witness. See under WITNESS.

matter of. See under IN THE MATTER OF.

matter of law. See AS A MATTER OF LAW.

mature, *adj.* **1.** due; presently payable or enforceable. Said of any right, claim, or obligation, but especially of bonds, notes, or other financial instruments. —*v.* **2.** to become mature.

maturity, *n.* **1.** the state of being mature. **2.** the date upon which, or the time within which, a bond or negotiable instrument becomes due: *bonds with a maturity of 30 days.*

maxim, *n.* a saying that expresses a general principle of law. See examples under DE MINIMIS and UNCLEAN HANDS.

mayhem, *n.* the crime of maiming—that is, disabling, dismembering, or disfiguring—a person, either intentionally or, in some states, by any conduct intended to cause serious injury. This was a special offense at common law because it deprived the victim of the ability to fight; the modern trend is to include it in the general crime of assault and battery.

means test, a requirement that people receiving a particular public benefit show that their income and assets are below a certain level.

measuring life, 1. the lifetime, or one of the lifetimes, determining the duration of a *life estate* (see under ESTATE[1]). **2.** the lifetime of the person, or of the longest survivor of the group of persons, identified for purposes of applying the *rule against perpetuities* (see under PERPETUITY).

mechanic's lien. See under LIEN.

mediation, *n.* a procedure in which a neutral outsider (a **mediator**) assists the parties to a dispute in reaching a settlement. Mediation differs from ARBITRATION in that the purpose of mediation is to facilitate an agreement rather than to impose a decision on the parties.

meeting of the minds, a misleading phrase sometimes used to signify the making of a contract, derived from an earlier view that there is no contract unless the parties share the same understanding of the deal. The contemporary view is that people are entitled to rely upon the normal and reasonable meaning of each other's words and actions; thus a party can generally enforce a contract on certain terms if a reasonable person in her position would have understood it that way, even if the other party can show that he had something different in mind, or did not intend to enter into a contract at all.

Megan's Law, a New Jersey statute requiring registration by prior sex offenders whenever they take up residence in the state and prior to any subsequent change of address, and providing for official notification regarding their past records to the police, and sometimes to community groups and the general public, in the areas where they reside or intend to reside. The name has also been applied to similar legislation in other states providing various mechanisms by which law enforcement officials or private persons can monitor the whereabouts of such prior offenders.

memorandum, *n., pl.* **memoranda. 1.** a brief written record or communication. **2.** a *memorandum of law* or *memorandum of points and authorities* (see under BRIEF) **3.** Also called **memorandum decision, memorandum or-**

der, or **memorandum opinion.** a brief judicial decision, usually ranging in length from two words (e.g., "Motion denied.") to a long paragraph. When cited, such decisions are usually indicated by the abbreviation "mem." **4. memorandum of understanding,** a writing memorializing an *agreement to agree* (see under AGREEMENT). See also LETTER OF INTENT.

memorialize, *v.* to make a written record of; confirm in writing: *Their telephone agreement was memorialized in an exchange of letters.* —**memorial,** *n.*

memory. See RECOLLECTION; RECOVERED MEMORY.

mens rea, *Latin.* (lit. "guilty mind") the STATE OF MIND that makes the performance of a particular act a crime, or a crime of a particular degree; the element of fault that makes an otherwise innocent act or omission punishable. For example, a careful driver who hits a child who darts out from between parked cars may be guilty of no crime, whereas a driver who had time to avoid the child but carelessly failed to do so may be guilty of homicide. See also ACTUS REUS.

mental state. Same as STATE OF MIND.

merchantable, *adj.* **1.** (of goods) fit for the ordinary purposes for which such goods are used, and of a quality that would be acceptable to merchants who regularly deal in goods of that kind. **2. warranty of merchantability,** in a sale of goods by a merchant who regularly deals in goods of that kind, an implied WARRANTY that the goods are merchantable. —**merchantability,** *n.*

merchantable title. Same as *marketable title* (see under TITLE).

meretricious, *adj.* describing a relationship or contract having a sexual component unblessed by law, such as a living-together arrangement. Because "meretricious" contracts are contrary to PUBLIC POLICY, plaintiffs seeking PALIMONY upon the breakup of a relationship must be careful not to allege that sex was any part of the consideration for the relationship.

merger, *n.* the absorption of one entity, right, interest, claim, agreement, or other thing into another, so that the first ceases to have independent existence and is superseded by the second. For example, one corporation may merge into another; a debt upon which a plaintiff sued and won is merged into the judgment, so that the debt no longer exists as an obligation distinct from the debtor's obligation to pay the judgment; and a **merger clause** in a contract provides that all prior negotiations and agreements between the parties are merged into the new contract, so that neither party can claim that the other has any obligation other than those expressed in the current contract. —**merge,** *v.*

merger of law and equity, the blending of the two systems of justice that evolved side by side in England—LAW and EQUITY—into a single legal system. For centuries these systems dispensed different kinds of remedies in different kinds of cases from separate courts, using different procedures and even different basic vocabularies. It was not until 1937 that the federal courts in the United States adopted a unified procedure for law and equity cases, and provided that both legal and equitable relief can be sought in a single action. Although the formal separation of law and equity is now largely a thing of the past, substantive and procedural distinctions between "legal" and "equitable" principles still pervade American law.

merits, *n.pl.* the substance of a case, claim, controversy, or the like, as distinguished from procedural or technical aspects; the heart of a matter. A decision, judgment, opinion, trial, or the like is said to be **on the merits** if it disposes of or is based upon the actual claim or charge presented in a case.

military law, the rules and procedures governing conduct in the armed forces. The Constitution gives Congress the power to enact such law for the American military, and it has done so in the UNIFORM CODE OF MILITARY JUSTICE.

militia, *n.* a military body with officers appointed by a state and members trained by the state. The Constitution gives Congress the power to organize, arm, and discipline the militia, making it primarily an arm of the federal government. The principle unit of the militia is the National Guard. See also RIGHT TO BEAR ARMS.

ministerial, *adj.* done in accordance with specific instructions or requirements; carrying out a delegated task; nondiscretionary: *ministerial act; ministerial function.*

minor, *n.* a person who has not yet reached the *age of majority* (see under AGE). See also *emancipated minor* (under EMANCIPATION).

minority, *n.* **1.** the state or period of being a MINOR. **2.** Also called **minority group. a.** a group of people sharing a characteristic that distinguishes them from the majority; e.g., a racial or religious minority. **b.** a group identified for protection by civil rights laws or the Constitution. In this sense the term includes women even though they are a numerical majority.

minority opinion. See under OPINION.

Miranda rule, the rule that criminal suspects must be informed of certain basic constitutional rights before being questioned. In the 1966 case of Miranda v Arizona, the Supreme Court held that police who detain a person for questioning must inform him of his right to remain silent, his right to have a lawyer present, his right to have a lawyer appointed if he cannot afford one, and the fact that anything he says may be used against him. This information is referred to as the **Miranda warning.** See also *custodial interrogation* (under INTERROGATION).

misbranding, *n.* placing a false or misleading label on a product.

misdemeanant, *n.* a person who commits a MISDEMEANOR.

misdemeanor, *n* a crime less serious than a FELONY, usually one punishable by incarceration for up to one year. In some states misdemeanors include some offenses punishable only by a fine. See also HIGH CRIMES AND MISDEMEAN-ORS; INFRACTION; OFFENSE; VIOLATION.

misfeasance, *n.* **1.** the negligent or otherwise improper performance of an otherwise permissible act. Cf. MALFEA-SANCE, NONFEASANCE. **2.** broadly, any wrongful affirmative act.

misjoinder, *n.* inappropriate JOINDER into a single action of unrelated parties, claims, or charges.

misprision of felony, failure to report a known felony, in the absence of any agreement with or assistance to the felon. This was a misdemeanor under English common law, but absent some affirmative act to conceal the felony it is not a crime in the United States. Cf. *accessory after the fact* (under ACCESSORY); COMPOUNDING A CRIME.

misrepresentation, *n.* **1.** a false or misleading REPRE-SENTATION, or words or conduct having the effect of pre-venting another's discovery of material facts In this usual sense, misrepresentation is an element of the tort of FRAUD. **2.** sometimes, another name for FRAUD.

mistake, *n.* an erroneous belief about a material fact **(mistake of fact)** or about the legal effect or significance of known facts **(mistake of law).** When a contract is en-tered into on the basis of mistake, it may be a misconcep-tion of one party only **(unilateral mistake)** or one shared and relied upon by both parties **(mutual mistake).** The le-gal effect or status of an act or transaction (e.g., a con-tract, a marriage, an alleged crime) may be altered if the parties were acting under the influence of mistake, de-pending upon such factors as the nature of the mistake, the reasonableness of the mistake, the mutuality of the mistake, and whether one party knew that the other was acting under a mistaken impression.

mistrial, *n.* a trial that ends without a verdict, decision, or settlement. The most common cause of a mistrial is a *hung jury* (see under JURY), but sometimes a mistrial is precipitated by an error so serious that no instruction to the jury can cure it (such as seriously prejudicial remarks by a lawyer) or by circumstances such as the death of a ju-ror or a natural disaster. The usual result is a new trial. See also DOUBLE JEOPARDY.

mitigate, *v.* **1.** to ameliorate; make less serious or se-vere. **2. mitigating circumstances,** circumstances reduc-ing or limiting (but not eliminating) the liability of a person for a crime or tort; e.g., DIMINISHED CAPACITY. **3. mitigation of damages,** the use of reasonable efforts by the victim of another's breach of contract to limit the adverse conse-quences of the breach. As a general rule, the plaintiff in an action for breach of contract may not recover for any por-tion of the damages that could have been avoided by rea-sonable effort; this is often referred to as the "duty to miti-gate damages" or just "duty to mitigate " —**mitigation,** *n*

mixed nuisance. See under NUISANCE

mixed question of fact and law. See under QUESTION².

M'Naghten rule (or **test**), the traditional test used in determining whether an INSANITY DEFENSE has been established, under which a defendant is not responsible for a crime if, because of a disease of the mind, he did not know the nature of his act or did not know that it was wrong. This is the test used in most American jurisdictions, augmented in a few jurisdictions by the IRRESISTIBLE IMPULSE TEST.

model law (or **act** or **statute**), any proposed statute drafted by anyone and promoted for adoption by state legislatures. Two of the most successful such proposals, upon which statutes in a great many states have been based, are the American Bar Association's Model Business Corporation Act, which provides a general framework for regulating corporations, and the MODEL PENAL CODE See also UNIFORM LAWS.

Model Penal Code, a comprehensive model statute organizing, rationalizing, and unifying the basic areas of state criminal law. The Model Penal Code was drafted over a number of years by the American Law Institute and finally promulgated in 1962; it provides the underlying theoretical framework, the overall approach, and a great deal of the exact language for the modern criminal codes that have been enacted in most states since then.

moiety, *n.* half; a one-half interest. Sometimes used to mean any portion or fractional interest.

money had and received, an action to compel payment of money received by another that should have gone to the plaintiff.

money order, an instrument similar to a check, which is purchased from a bank, post office, or other institution by a person wishing to make a payment or transfer money to another, naming the other as payee and entitling the payee to payment, by the issuer, of the sum specified in the instrument.

monopolization, *n.* the intentional acquisition or maintenance by a company or group of cooperating companies of a monopoly in the market for a product or service—that is, of such dominance of the market that it can fix prices and exclude competition. See also ANTITRUST; SHERMAN ANTITRUST ACT.

month-to-month tenancy. See under TENANCY.

moot, *adj.* **1.** (of a claim, issue, case, etc.) dead; no longer a real controversy with practical consequences for the parties. For example, a constitutional challenge to a law would become moot if the law is repealed while the case is pending. Cases that become moot are usually dismissed as no longer presenting a JUSTICIABLE controversy; but exceptions can be made for cases that are "capable of repetition, yet evading review" because they become moot too quickly, such as a case brought by a pregnant woman with regard to rights of pregnant women. —*v.* **2.** to make moot: *The parties' stipulation mooted the motion for a protective order.*

moot court, a mock court proceeding in which law students or lawyers practice argument or trial techniques in hypothetical cases

moral turpitude, dishonesty or immorality. Statutes providing special penalties or disadvantages (e.g., deportation or ineligibility for a professional license) for people convicted of a "crime involving moral turpitude," though notoriously vague, generally refer to more serious, intentional crimes as distinguished from less serious, technical crimes.

mortgage, *n.* **1.** a *security interest* (see under INTEREST¹) in real property, usually to secure repayment of a substantial debt—often the debt incurred in borrowing the money to buy the property. The debtor whose land is subject to the mortgage is called the **mortgagor;** the creditor who holds the mortgage is the **mortgagee. 2.** the instrument evidencing a mortgage. **3. chattel mortgage,** a similar security interest in personal property, **4. second mortgage,** an additional mortgage on property that is already subject to a mortgage (the **first mortgage**). If the debtor defaults and the property is sold in a FORECLOSURE proceeding, the debt to the first mortgagee is paid off first, and the second mortgagee is entitled to repayment only to the extent that there are proceeds left over

motion, *n.* an application to a court for an order, made while a case is pending. Motions may be made orally or in writing, and ON NOTICE or EX PARTE, depending upon the circumstances. See also *motion papers* (under PAPERS); *on its own motion* (under SUA SPONTE)

movant, *n.* the party or lawyer who makes a motion.

move, *v.* to make a motion. *The attorney moved to strike the witness's answer. The defendant moved for judgment notwithstanding the verdict.*

municipal, *adj.* relating to a MUNICIPALITY or to local governments in general.

municipal corporation, a city, town, village, or other local governmental unit that operates under a corporate charter granted by the state legislature

municipal security. See under SECURITY²

municipality, *n.* a MUNICIPAL CORPORATION or other local governmental unit.

murder, *n.* **1.** the most serious form of *criminal homicide* (see under HOMICIDE). The exact scope of the crime varies from state to state, but always includes unjustified conduct resulting in a person's death and undertaken with **intent to kill**—that is, either a conscious purpose to kill or knowledge that death is substantially certain to result; depending upon the state, murder may also include one or more of the following: (1) causing death by unjustified conduct intended to cause serious bodily injury, (2) causing death by extremely negligent or reckless conduct that creates a very high risk of death or serious bodily injury to others or manifests extreme indifference to human life, or (3) FELONY MURDER. Murder is usually divided into two or more degrees depending upon factors that vary from state to state See also MALICE; PREMEDITATION. —*v.* **2.** to commit murder; to kill by an act constituting murder.

mutiny, *n.* **1.** a concerted refusal by two or more members of the military or of the crew of a ship to obey officers or perform duties. —*v* **2.** to engage in mutiny.

mutual fund, a company whose sole business is to invest in securities and return the profit to its own shareholders

mutual insurance. See under INSURANCE.

mutual mistake. See under MISTAKE.

mutual releases. See under RELEASE

N

nail and mail, a form of *substituted service* of process (see under **SERVICE**) consisting of affixing the process to the door of the person to be‑served and sending a follow-up copy by mail.

naked, *adj.* mere; simple; unsupported; and nothing more. Thus "naked possession" is possession without ownership or authority; a "naked promise" is one unsupported by consideration; a "naked licensee" is a person permitted, but not invited, to be on another's land (see **LICENSE**, def. 4). Used interchangeably with **bare.**

narrow construction. See under **CONSTRUCTION**

national, *n.* **1.** a person who owes allegiance to a government and is entitled to its protection, but not necessarily to full citizenship status. All United States citizens are also nationals of the United States; however, persons born in American Samoa are United States nationals but not citizens. See also **CITIZEN.** —*adj.* **2.** pertaining or belonging to the nation as a whole. *national affairs; a national park.*

natural law, a hypothetical body of fundamental principles of ethics and government supposedly inherent in nature Natural law is a philosophical and religious concept rather than a scientific or legal one Cf. **POSITIVE LAW.**

natural person. See under **PERSON.**

naturalize, *v.* to confer citizenship upon an individual who was not a citizen Congress has virtually unlimited power to establish the criteria and procedures for naturalization; once naturalized, however, such a citizen has the same status and rights as a natural born citizen in almost all respects, a notable exception being that, under the Constitution, only a natural born citizen may become President. See also **CITIZEN.** —**naturalization,** *n.*

necessaries, *n.pl.* basic goods and services needed by a child, dependent person, or family Most or all states make both spouses liable for debts incurred by either one for necessaries for the children or family, though the range of goods and services covered usually depends upon the financial circumstances of the particular family; what is "necessary" for a rich family might be a luxury for a poor family.

Necessary and Proper Clause, the clause of the Constitution that authorizes Congress to enact all laws "necessary and proper" to carry out the powers of the federal government under the Constitution It is not limited to laws that are essential or indispensable; rather, it gives Congress discretion to adopt any convenient or appropriate means for accomplishing any constitutionally permissible objective

necessary party. See under **PARTY**

necessity, *n.* a circumstance leaving a person no reasonable choice but to do something that normally would be a tort or crime in order to avoid a greater evil. Where a person's conduct is reasonable under the circumstances, necessity (also called **choice of evils**) generally affords a defense to a tort action or criminal prosecution, especially if the harm avoided would have affected the public at large (**public necessity**) rather than only the individual interests of the person sued (**private necessity**).

negative act. See under ACT.

negative easement. See under EASEMENT

negative pregnant, a denial that leaves open the possibility that the proposition being denied may be partly or even substantially true, for example, "Defendant denies that he recklessly drove the car onto the sidewalk, striking the plaintiff and injuring her." Such a denial is said to be "pregnant with an admission" (In the example, the defendant may be denying only that he was reckless, or only that the plaintiff was injured, or only that she was on the sidewalk when his car struck and injured her.) Under flexible modern pleading rules this might not have serious adverse consequences, but it is still bad form.

neglect, n. **1.** failure to perform some act or fulfill some duty specifically required by law **2. child neglect,** failure of a parent to support a child or to safeguard a child's health and well-being. Also called **parental neglect. 3. excusable neglect,** a failure to perform some procedural step or court-ordered act in a case, for which there is an excuse that the law will recognize and the judge deems adequate **4. neglect of duty,** failure of a public official or a member of the military to carry out official or military duties. **5. willful neglect,** intentional, knowing, or reckless failure to fulfill a legal duty, especially with respect to the care of a child.

negligence, n. **1.** (in tort law) conduct involving an unreasonable risk of injury or loss to others; conduct that falls short of the degree of care that a *reasonable person* (see under REASONABLE) would have exercised in the same circumstances. Negligence is determined by an OBJECTIVE TEST: a person who considered a situation thoroughly and took what he genuinely regarded as a reasonable risk would nevertheless properly be found negligent if the jury concludes that a person of ordinary intelligence and prudence in that situation would not have done what the defendant did. Negligence is a tort; the wrongdoer is generally liable for any injury to person or property directly resulting from it. See also PROXIMATE CAUSE Cf. *intentional tort* (under TORT); RECKLESSNESS **2.** Also called **criminal negligence.** (in criminal law) a gross deviation from the standard of care that a reasonable person would observe, under circumstances posing a substantial and unjustifiable risk of which the actor should have been aware Except for relatively rare STRICT LIABILITY offenses, this is usually the minimum level of fault that will subject a person to criminal liability; *ordinary negligence* is normally insufficient See also *negligent homicide* (under HOMICIDE); STATE OF MIND. **3. comparative negligence,** the modern doctrine that as between a plaintiff and a defendant in a tort case, and sometimes as among several defendants, fault (and liability for damages) should be allocated in proportion to each party's contribution to the injury or loss complained of. Cf. *contributory negligence.* **4. contributory negligence, a.** negligence by a plaintiff contributing to the injury or loss that is the subject of a tort case, as when a plaintiff sues over an automobile accident that was primarily caused by the defendant but was also partly caused or made worse by inattentiveness on the part of the plaintiff. **b.** the traditional doctrine that any contributory negligence by a plaintiff, however slight, bars the plaintiff from recovering in a negligence case In most states this harsh common law doctrine has been superseded by some form of *comparative negligence.* **5. gross negligence,** highly unreasonable conduct; a term used primarily in civil contexts, sometimes interpreted as RECKLESSNESS but more often representing essentially the same degree of fault as *criminal negligence.* In most civil contexts it does not matter whether negligence is "gross" or "slight"; often the phrase "gross negligence" is used just for rhetorical effect. **6. ordinary** (or **simple**) **negligence,** conduct falling short of the standard of *ordinary care* (see under CARE); negligence as described in def. I above. **7. willful** (or **wanton**) **negligence,** in theory, RECKLESSNESS. In practice, these concepts tend to shade into *gross negligence.* —**negligent,** *adj.* —**negligently,** *adv.*

negligent homicide. See under HOMICIDE.

negotiable, *adj.* (of an instrument evidencing certain rights) transferable by INDORSEMENT and delivery. The concept of negotiability applies particularly to three kinds of instruments: a DOCUMENT OF TITLE; a security evidenced by a certificate, such as a STOCK CERTIFICATE (see SECURITY² and BOND¹); and a check or other "negotiable instrument" in the narrow sense of that phrase (see NEGOTIABLE INSTRUMENT, def 2). In each case, if the instrument satisfies certain requirements specified in the UNIFORM COMMERCIAL CODE, then ownership of the instrument and the rights it represents may be transferred simply by indorsing it and delivering it to the transferee—and sometimes even the indorsement is unnecessary (see NEGOTIATE). See also *negotiable document of title* (under DOCUMENT OF TITLE). —**negotiability,** *n.*

negotiable instrument, 1. broadly, any document that is NEGOTIABLE, including a negotiable document of title or a security. **2.** specifically and usually, a financial instrument that (1) contains an unconditional promise or order to pay a specific sum of money, but (with certain exceptions) no other promise, order, power, or obligation; (2) is payable on demand or at a definite time; (3) is payable to order or to bearer; and (4) is signed by the issuer. If it is a promise it is usually called a note (see NOTE¹); if it is an order it is a DRAFT, the most common example of which is an ordinary CHECK. See also BEARER; DEMAND; ORDER²; TIME.

negotiate, *v.* **1.** to transfer a check or other negotiable instrument or document in such a way that the transferee becomes a HOLDER. In the case of a *bearer instrument* (see under BEARER), this can be done simply by handing over the instrument. In the case of an *order instrument* (see under ORDER²), it is done by indorsing the instrument and then delivering it For example, a check may be negotiated by cashing it, depositing it, or signing it over to someone else. Negotiation transfers ownership of the instrument and the rights it represents to the person to whom the instrument is delivered. **2.** to bargain or haggle: *to negotiate a contract.* —**negotiation,** *n.*

net assets. See under ASSET

net income. See under INCOME.

net lease. See under LEASE.

next friend, a person who files a lawsuit on behalf of a minor or incompetent who lacks legal capacity to sue or be sued, and stands in for that person as a party in the case.

no bill. See under BILL

no contest. Same as NOLO CONTENDERE.

no-fault divorce. See under DIVORCE.

no-fault insurance, a type of automobile insurance required in some states, under which compensation for minor personal injuries incurred in an accident is made by the insurance company covering the car in which the injured person was riding (or, in the case of pedestrian injuries, the car that struck the pedestrian), regardless of which driver involved in the accident was more at fault. The purpose of no-fault insurance laws is to spare everyone involved the time and expense of lawsuits to apportion blame for relatively minor accidents.

no-par stock. Same as *stock without par value* (see under STOCK).

nolle prosequi, *Latin.* (lit. "to be unwilling to pursue") the formal abandonment of a criminal charge by the prosecuting attorney. If the trial has not begun and the statute of limitations has not expired, the defendant can be reindicted on the same charge. Often shortened informally to **nolle** or **nol pros** and used as a verb: *Counts 12 and 13 of the indictment were nollied* (or *nol prossed*).

nolo contendere, *Latin.* (lit "I will not contest") a PLEA to a criminal charge, permitted in the federal courts and in many states (subject to the judge's consent), whereby the defendant states that he will not contest the charge. The result of such a plea is a conviction on the charge, and for sentencing purposes it is the same as a guilty plea. Unlike a guilty plea, however, it may not be used in a subsequent civil case as proof of guilt. Also called **non vult contendere** or **no contest.**

nominal, *adj.* **1.** in name only; in form rather than in substance. For example, a nominal party is one (such as a NEXT FRIEND) named as a plaintiff or defendant only to satisfy technical requirements. **2.** symbolic, token: *nominal consideration* (see under CONSIDERATION); *nominal damages* (see under DAMAGES).

nominate, *v.* to select or appoint as one's agent, representative, or designee: *The powers granted to my executor by this will are to be exercised by her or by such other person as she may nominate.* A person so selected is called a **nominee.**

non compos mentis, *Latin.* (lit. "not in possession of the mental faculties") insane or incompetent.

non obstante veredicto (n.o.v.), *Latin.* (lit "notwithstanding the verdict") See *judgment notwithstanding the verdict* (under JUDGMENT).

non prosequitur, *Latin.* (lit. "he/she does not pursue") an older term for a judgment against a plaintiff who stops pursuing a case at some point after filing it. Shortened informally to **non pros.** Today this would usually take the form of a dismissal for FAILURE TO PROSECUTE or a *default judgment* (see under JUDGMENT).

non vult contendere, *Latin.* (lit. "he/she will not contest") Same as NOLO CONTENDERE

nonage, *n.* the state of being under the *age of majority* or *legal age* (see both under AGE).

nonassessable stock. Opposite of *assessable stock* (see under STOCK).

nonconforming use. See under USE.

nonfeasance, *n.* unjustified failure to perform a required act or carry out an official duty. Cf. MALFEASANCE; MISFEASANCE.

nonjoinder, *n.* the failure of a party asserting a claim in a case to JOIN a *necessary* or *indispensable party* (see under PARTY). See also JOINDER.

nonjury trial. Same as *bench trial* (see under TRIAL).

nonnegotiable document of title. See under DOCUMENT OF TITLE.

nonnegotiable instrument, an instrument that is substantially in the form of a NEGOTIABLE INSTRUMENT, but fails in some particular respect to meet the exact requirements for negotiability; for example, an unsigned check, or a note that says "I promise to pay to Mary Jones" instead of "I promise to pay *to the order of* Mary Jones" (see under ORDER[2]).

nonpar stock. Same as *stock without par value* (see under STOCK).

nonprofit, describing an organization or institution organized for purposes other than to make a profit, such as an educational, charitable, or cooperative organization; for example, a *nonprofit corporation* (see under CORPORATION).

nonrecourse, *adj.* lacking the right to proceed against a particular obligor personally in the event of nonpayment or default. See examples under RECOURSE.

nonresident alien. See under ALIEN.

nonresponsive, *adj.* (of a witness's answer to a lawyer's question) avoiding the question, answering some other question, or including commentary beyond what was asked for. Depending upon strategic considerations, a lawyer might "move to strike" the answer or the nonresponsive portion of the answer (see STRIKE²), request the judge to instruct the witness to answer, repeat the question, or simply move on. If the judge strikes an answer or part of an answer, she will usually specifically instruct the jury to disregard it, although just saying "it is stricken" amounts to such an instruction.

nonstock corporation. See under CORPORATION

nonsuit, *n.* **1.** an older term for DISMISSAL of a civil case —*v.* **2.** to issue a nonsuit against· *The judge nonsuited the plaintiff.*

nonsupport, *n.* the crime of failing to provide needed financial support that one has the resources to provide to one's child, spouse, or other dependent where there is a duty to provide such support.

not found. Same as *no bill* (see under BILL).

not guilty, 1. acquitted of a criminal charge; tried and not proved guilty. Cf. INNOCENT. **2.** a PLEA by which a criminal defendant preserves the right to a trial to determine guilt Cf GUILTY; NOLO CONTENDERE

not guilty by reason of insanity, deemed not legally responsible for a criminal act on the ground that the actor was insane at the time See also INSANITY DEFENSE and specific tests listed there.

not-for-profit corporation. See under CORPORATION.

notarial, *adj.* pertaining to or done by a NOTARY PUBLIC.

notarize, *v.* to authenticate a document or attest to the performance of some other notarial act by affixing the signature and seal of a notary public

notary public, a person authorized by the government to administer oaths and affirmations, take acknowledgments, authenticate signatures, and tend to various other formalities relating to legal documents and transactions. Often shortened to **notary.**

note¹, *n.* **1.** an instrument representing a promise to pay a sum of money, and often interest, to (or to the order of) the bearer or a named PAYEE. A note is a NEGOTIABLE INSTRUMENT if it meets the requirements listed under that entry Also called **promissory note.** See also MAKE; *to the order of* (under ORDER²) **2. cognovit note,** a note in which the maker's promise to pay is coupled with a confession of judgment, so that the payee can automatically obtain a judgment against the maker if a payment is missed. See discussion under CONFESSION OF JUDGMENT. See also COGNOVIT. **3. installment note,** a note promising payments at fixed intervals over a period of time, or one of a set of notes each of which provides for one such payment

note², *n.* an article on a legal topic, typically written by a law student and published in a law review, and usually quite comprehensive. Cf. *case note* (under ANNOTATION); COMMENT.

notice, *n.* **1.** the act of conveying information of legal significance to a person, or, when such information is conveyed in writing, the document itself· *notice of deposition; notice of increase in rent.* See also ON NOTICE; SERVICE **2.**

information of legal significance to a person that is known to, or at least available to, that person. **3.** for purposes of satisfying DUE PROCESS, **a.** the publication of laws and regulations, so that no one will be charged with a crime for conduct that they had no way of knowing was illegal **b.** formal warning of proposed action to be taken against a person (such as a criminal charge, a civil suit, or termination of welfare benefits), so as to advise the person of the nature of the charges, allegations, or proposed action and provide an OPPORTUNITY TO BE HEARD In civil cases this is normally accomplished by service of a SUMMONS and COMPLAINT; in criminal cases, by ARRAIGNMENT **4. actual notice,** notice actually received by, or information actually known to, a person. **5. constructive notice,** information that a person could have or should have known, or information conveyed in a way that was reasonably calculated to give actual notice **6. inquiry notice,** notice of facts sufficient to cause a reasonably prudent person to make further inquiry with regard to a matter if she wishes to safeguard her rights or avoid liability. **7. judicial notice.** See under JUDICIAL. **8. notice by publication,** publication of a notice in a newspaper in the hope of reaching persons affected by a matter who cannot otherwise be identified or located. Such notice is allowed or required in certain legal situations, but only as a last resort. **9. notice pleading.** See under PLEADING. —v **10.** to give formal legal notice of or to: *The judge noticed the hearing for Wednesday. Each of the defendants has been noticed for a deposition*

notorious, *adj* open; well known; not concealed *notorious possession; notorious cohabitation.*

n.o.v., See *judgment notwithstanding the verdict* (under JUDGMENT)

novation, *n.* the substitution of a new contract for an old one, extinguishing all rights and obligations under the old one, by agreement of all parties to both contracts. For example, the new contract might substitute new terms for the terms of the original contract, or substitute a new party for one of the original parties

NSF check. See under CHECK.

nuisance, *n.* **1.** Also called **private nuisance.** the tort of engaging in conduct, or maintaining a condition on one's property, that substantially and unreasonably interferes with another's use and enjoyment of her own property; for example, activities that create unreasonable noise, vibrations, foul odors, or a health or fire hazard. **2.** Also called **public nuisance.** conduct, especially in the use of one's own land, that unreasonably interferes with the health, safety, welfare, comfort, or rights of the public at large, or of a large number of people. Examples include extending a building so that it encroaches on a public sidewalk; maintenance of an illegal establishment, such as a brothel or gambling house; violating zoning restrictions; or any kind of conduct that might constitute a private nuisance but is severe enough to interfere with more than a few immediate neighbors. Conduct amounting to a public

nuisance is usually a crime, and may independently constitute a private nuisance with respect to certain individuals
particularly affected, in which case it may be called a
mixed nuisance. Cf ATTRACTIVE NUISANCE.

null or **null and void.** Same as VOID

nullification. See *jury nullification* (under JURY)

nunc pro tunc, *Latin* now for then; a phrase making an
order retroactive to a certain date For example, an order
correcting an error in a previous order would normally be
made "nunc pro tunc" to make it clear that the first order
should be regarded as having said what was originally intended all along.

nuncupative will. See under WILL

O

oath, *n.* **1.** a solemn declaration that certain facts are true or that one will speak the truth, faithfully carry out one's official duties, uphold the law, or the like. The taking of an oath to tell the truth renders any dishonest statement punishable as FALSE SWEARING or PERJURY In its traditional and strict sense, an oath is an invocation of God, as distinguished from an AFFIRMATION (def 1), which lacks religious content. Broadly, an oath may take any suitably solemn form and need not refer to God; in this sense "oath" includes affirmations. See also OATH OR AFFIRMATION; SWEAR **2.** the words recited in giving or taking an oath **3. oath of office,** the oath or affirmation of a person elected or appointed to public office, undertaking to support the Constitution and to perform the duties of the office faithfully

oath or affirmation, a phrase used to avoid the religious issues raised by the use of OATH alone *The application must be accompanied by a statement made upon oath or affirmation.* The Constitution states that all state and federal officeholders must "be bound by Oath or Affirmation, to support this Constitution." See also SWEAR OR AFFIRM

obiter dictum, *pl* **obiter dicta.** *Latin* (lit "a thing said in passing") Same as DICTUM (see discussion there) Occasionally shortened instead to **obiter** (lit. "in passing," "by the way") *Although the court's remark was obiter in the context of that case, we believe that it correctly states the rule applicable here*

objection, *n.* **1.** a formal statement or notice that one regards a claim or procedural step as impermissible or invalid; a request that a particular course of action not be permitted or pursued **2.** especially, such a statement or request in regard to a question asked, evidence sought to be admitted, or other conduct at a trial or hearing It is made by saying "Objection" or "I object" and, if necessary, adding just enough explanation to make clear what is being objected to and the legal grounds for the objection. If testimony and other evidence is not objected to at the time it is sought to be introduced, it cannot be complained about on appeal. For some types of questions likely to be objected to, see QUESTION[1] (defs. 3–6). The court's response to an objection is to SUSTAIN or OVERRULE it **3. continuing objection,** a single objection applicable to all questions in a line of questioning If an attorney regards an entire area of questioning as improper but the judge disagrees, then instead of requiring the attorney to object to each question in turn in order to preserve the issue for appeal, the judge may grant the attorney a "continuing objection" to the entire line of inquiry. **4. speaking objection,** an objection in a jury trial that contains more than the minimum necessary information for the judge to rule, often in an attempt to sway the jury. Many judges forbid lawyers to give any grounds for their objection unless specifically requested to do so, and some require lawyers to give their reasons by citing sections of a state evidence code or the federal rules of evidence by number, so that the jury will not understand what they are talking about. —**object,** *v.*

objective test, a legal test that does not depend upon what is in someone's mind, but on external criteria. For example, any legal principle that depends upon whether someone's conduct was REASONABLE involves an objective test, because what matters is not how the person involved viewed the situation, but how a reasonable person in that situation would have viewed it. Cf. SUBJECTIVE TEST.

obligation, *n.* **1.** a legal requirement that one perform or refrain from performing some act, or the act that one is required to perform. **2. joint and several obligation,** a contractual obligation undertaken by two or more persons with the understanding that performance may be sought in court either from all of them collectively or from any one of them individually. **3. joint obligation,** a contractual obligation for which two or more persons have agreed to be liable as a group but not individually.

obligee, *n.* a person or entity owed an obligation under a contract or negotiable instrument, especially an obligation to pay money.

obligor, *n.* **1.** a person or entity owing an obligation under a contract or negotiable instrument, especially an obligation to pay money. **2. principal obligor.** See under PRINCIPAL.

obscenity, *n.* any form of expression, such as a book, painting, photograph, movie, or play, that deals with sex in a way that is regarded as so offensive as to be beyond the protection of the constitutional guarantee of FREEDOM OF SPEECH. Under the most recent of the Supreme Court's efforts to define obscenity, the term applies to material that appeals to PRURIENT INTEREST, depicts or describes sexual conduct in a way that is PATENTLY OFFENSIVE, and lacks "serious literary, artistic, political, or scientific value." See also PORNOGRAPHY; PRIOR RESTRAINT; SPEECH. —**obscene,** *adj.*

obstruction of justice, the crime of attempting to impede or pervert the administration of justice, as by concealing or falsifying evidence, or by bribing, threatening, or otherwise attempting to influence witnesses, jurors, or court officials improperly. The term is sometimes extended to acts that impede police or other law enforcement activities as well. The exact terminology and classification scheme for such offenses varies from state to state.

occupancy, *n. actual possession* (see under POSSESSION), or the act of taking actual possession, of real property. This does not require physical presence on the property at all times, but at the very least diligence in keeping others out except with one's own permission. Also called **occupation.** —**occupy,** *v.*

occupy the field. See under PREEMPTION.

of age, having reached the *age of majority*, or *legal age* for a particular activity (see both under AGE) Cf UNDERAGE

of counsel, 1. referring to a lawyer who assists the *attorney of record* (see under ATTORNEY) in a trial or appeal; a member of a legal team other than the leader. **2.** a lawyer associated in some way with a law firm, but not as a member or employee; for example, one retained to assist in a particular matter, or a retired member of the firm who consults with it on specific matters when called upon

of record. See under RECORD.

of the essence, 1. essential; said of contract terms whose exact performance is so central to the purposes of the contract that any failure by a party to adhere to them would be deemed a *material breach* (see under BREACH), justifying cancellation of the contract by the other party. **2. time is of the essence,** a phrase signifying that any failure to perform within the time specified in the contract will constitute a material breach, even if the delay is slight

off the record. See under RECORD.

offender, *n.* a person who commits an OFFENSE

offense, *n.* **1.** any CRIME or other violation of law for which a penalty is prescribed. **2. petty offense,** a very minor offense, defined in some jurisdictions to include any misdemeanor for which the possible sentence does not exceed six months, in others as an offense below the level of misdemeanor, for which no jail sentence can be imposed. See also BAILABLE OFFENSE; LESSER INCLUDED OFFENSE.

offer, *n.* **1.** a proposal to enter into a CONTRACT upon specified terms. A proposal is an offer if it is made in such a way that the person to whom it is made has only to ACCEPT it to bring the contract into existence. See also TENDER OFFER **2.** any PROFFER. **3. firm offer,** an offer to buy or sell goods, made by a merchant in a signed writing that includes an assurance that the offer will be held open Contrary to the usual rule that an offer may be withdrawn at any time before acceptance, an offer meeting these requirements is irrevocable for the period of time stated in the offer, or for a reasonable time if no specific time is stated —*v* **4.** to make an offer **5.** to request admission of an exhibit into evidence *"I offer this as Plaintiff's Exhibit 57."*

offer of proof, a brief statement by a lawyer to a judge, out of the hearing of the jury, of the testimony that a particular witness is expected to give in response to a particular question or line of questioning A lawyer may request permission to make an offer of proof, also called a **proffer,** in response to a judge's initial ruling sustaining an objection to a question, both to try to persuade the judge that the testimony is admissible and to make a record for arguing on appeal that the judge was wrong to exclude it

offeree, *n.* a person to whom an offer is made

offeror, *n.* a person who makes an offer

officer, *n.* **1.** a person appointed or elected to a position of responsibility or authority in government or a private organization **2.** in a corporation, **a.** strictly, one of the handful of individuals selected by the board of directors to have overall responsibility for day-to-day management of the corporation's business **b.** loosely, anyone in a management position to which an impressive title has been assigned, partly for their own satisfaction and partly to give them credibility in dealing with the public A corporation may have thousands of such officers

officer of the court, any employee of a court or any lawyer involved in a matter before the court. The phrase is used to emphasize the responsibility of all such individuals to conduct themselves with utmost honesty and good faith in all matters involving the court

official immunity. See under IMMUNITY

officious intermeddler, a person who intrudes into the business of others without an invitation or a reasonable basis for believing that his involvement is needed Even if the officious intermeddler's motives are good, he generally receives little sympathy from the law if, for example, he subsequently seeks payment for his services or compensation for an injury sustained.

offset. Same as *setoff* (see under SET OFF)

omission, *n.* a failure to do something that one should have done. An omission may be viewed as a type of act (see *act of omission*, under ACT), or as a failure to act (often appearing in the phrase "act or omission").

on all fours, a perfect fit A phrase describing a PRECEDENT that is claimed to be so similar in its facts to the case at hand as to be legally indistinguishable

on bail. See under BAIL[1]

on consent. See under CONSENT

on demand. See under DEMAND

on its (his, her, their) own motion. Same as SUA SPONTE

on its face. See under FACE

on notice, 1. with advance notice, describing a procedural step taken after all concerned parties have been given sufficient notice, usually in writing, to allow them an opportunity to argue against the step *The plaintiff moved on notice for summary judgment The injunction was issued on notice. The judge ordered the defendant to submit a proposed order on three days' notice to the plaintiff.* Procedural rules dictate how many days' notice must normally be given for most steps in a case. **2.** having received sufficient information so that one should be aware of a certain fact: *The owner was on notice of the dog's dangerous disposition, because the dog had already bitten the letter carrier.*

on or about, on approximately the date specified; a phrase often used to qualify a date when the exact date is not important, to avoid petty and irrelevant disputes over the accuracy of the date specified and allow for the possibility of a slight error

on papers. See under PAPERS.

on point, referring to a precedent or authority regarded as particularly relevant or instructive with respect to an issue under discussion: *The remarks of Smythe, J., dissenting in Cox v. Swaine, are on point* Also called **in point.** See also *case in point* (under CASE¹)

on the merits. See under MERITS.

on the record. See under RECORD

on the relation of. Same as EX REL

open, *v.* **1.** to reconsider a matter that once was regarded as closed· *open a judgment* **2.** to deliver an OPENING STATEMENT· *Ms. Smith will open for the prosecution.* —*adj.* **3.** accessible to public view or knowledge; not private or concealed· *After the plea bargain was worked out in chambers, the judge took the guilty plea in open court*

open the door, to raise an issue at a trial or hearing by asking questions or submitting evidence about it, or sometimes just by commenting on the subject to the jury, thereby entitling the other side to introduce additional or contrary evidence or make adverse comment that otherwise would not have been allowed

opening statement, a lawyer's address to the judge or jury in advance of presenting evidence, to outline the case Often described informally as a "road map of the case." Also called **opening.** Cf. SUMMATION.

operation of law. See BY OPERATION OF LAW

opinion, *n.* **1.** the beliefs, conclusions, and inferences one draws from observation of an incident or from scientific or other specialized knowledge and experience, as distinguished from a mere description of what one has observed. See also *opinion evidence* (under EVIDENCE); *expert witness* (under WITNESS). Cf. FACT **2.** Also called **opinion of counsel.** a formal document (sometimes in the form of a letter called an **opinion letter**) setting forth an attorney's conclusions about the legality of a transaction or the legal aspects of a situation **3.** a court's explanation of how it reached a particular decision in a matter; its analysis and resolution of the legal issues involved in a motion or appeal. If the case was heard by a panel of judges (for example, the nine justices of the Supreme Court), there may be several opinions: Usually a majority of judges will agree upon both the result and most of the reasoning, which they give in a **majority opinion,** sometimes referred to as the **opinion for the court.** Judges who wish to add something to the majority opinion or express some disagreement with it may issue a **separate opinion,** which is also referred to as a **concurring opinion** or **concurrence** if it reaches the same result as the majority opinion, and as a **minority opinion** or **dissenting opinion** or **dissent** if it advocates a different result If no reasoning commands a majority of the court, the largest group that agrees upon the result reached may issue a **plurality opinion.** If all judges are in accord, they may issue a **unanimous opinion** or **opinion for a unanimous court.** Each of the foregoing opinions would normally be issued under the name of the judge who principally authored it, with a listing of other judges who have added their names to it In cases not regarded as meriting elaborate discussion, a court may issue a short, unsigned opinion called a **per curiam opinion** or **opinion by the court,** or issue a decision with no opinion at all. See also ADVISORY OPINION; *concurring in the result* (or *judgment*) (under CONCUR); FINDINGS OF FACT AND CONCLUSIONS OF LAW; *memorandum opinion* (under MEMO-RANDUM); PER CURIAM; *reported opinion* (under REPORT); SLIP OPINION.

opportunity to be heard, 1. the DUE PROCESS right to present evidence and argument to a neutral decision maker in a fair proceeding when the government or a private person takes judicial or administrative action intended to affect one's legal rights. **2.** an opportunity often granted by a legislature or administrative agency, but not constitutionally required, for members of the public at large to comment formally on proposed legislation or administrative action at a public hearing or in writing.

option, *n.* **1.** a contractual right, good for a specified length of time, to go through with a certain transaction on specified terms or to cancel it. **2.** Also called **option contract.** a contract that gives one such a right; for example, a contract under which A, in exchange for a certain payment to B, is given the right for 60 days to purchase ten tons of wheat from B at a specified price. The decision whether to go ahead with the purchase during that time is entirely A's, because A has paid for the privilege of keeping the choice open. See also STOCK OPTION.

oral, *adj.* spoken rather than written; see *oral* ARGUMENT, CONTRACT, WILL under those words Cf. VERBAL

order[1], *n.* **1.** a ruling or direction of a court, administrative tribunal, or legislative or executive body or official. Willful violation of a court order directing a person to do or not to do something is punishable as CONTEMPT **2. appealable order, a.** a court order from which an immediate appeal can be taken. As a general rule in most jurisdictions, only a *final order,* such as an order granting a motion to dismiss the case, is immediately appealable. **b.** a court order that can be challenged in connection with an ultimate appeal of the entire case, but must be complied with in the meantime. For example, an order denying a motion to dismiss a case ordinarily cannot be appealed at once, but can be challenged on appeal if the case eventually goes to judgment and the judgment is appealed See also *interlocutory appeal* (under APPEAL). **3. consent order,** an order entered with the consent of all parties to a case. **4. final order,** a JUDGMENT or other order disposing of a case; one that leaves nothing for the litigants to do except comply with the order or take an appeal **5. interlocutory order,** an order that concerns some matter connected with a case but does not end the case, such as an order granting or denying temporary alimony in a divorce case. **6. order to show cause,** a court order directing a party to appear and present reasons why a certain order, such as an injunction or an order of contempt, should not be issued If the party to whom the order to show cause is directed fails to appear or appears but fails to make a sufficient showing, the threatened order will be issued. An order to show cause is usually an emergency measure, issued because there is reason to believe that a party is doing something or about to do something that routine court procedures would be too slow to deal with adequately. It is often issued EX PARTE, usually accompanied by a *temporary restraining order* (see under RESTRAINING ORDER), and almost always RETURNABLE on very short notice See also *confidentiality order* (under CONFIDENTIALITY STIPULATION); EXECUTIVE ORDER; INJUNCTION; PROTECTION ORDER; PROTECTIVE ORDER; *stipulation and order* (under STIPULATION). —*v.* **7.** to issue an order; to direct that something be done or not done See also SO ORDERED.

order², *n.* **1.** a written direction to pay money For example, a check is an order addressed to one's bank, directing it to pay out a certain sum of money from one's account See also NEGOTIABLE INSTRUMENT; MONEY ORDER **2. to the order of,** to the person named or a subsequent HOLDER The use of these words is one way of signifying that a document or instrument is intended to be NEGOTIABLE. For example, an instrument that just says "pay to John Jones" may normally be enforced only by Jones, but if it says "pay to the order of John Jones," then Jones may sign it over to anyone else, making it payable to that person instead. Such an instrument is said to be **payable to order** and referred to as an **order instrument.** See also *order bill of lading* (under BILL OF LADING). Cf **bearer instrument** (under BEARER).

ordinance, *n.* a municipal law, a law adopted by a city, town, county, or other local government with respect to a matter permitted by the state to be regulated at the local level.

ordinary, *adj.* describing the normal, usual, or common, as against the unusual or exceptional For example, compare *ordinary care* with *utmost care* (under CARE); *ordinary negligence* with *gross negligence* (under NEGLIGENCE); *ordinary income* (under INCOME) with *capital gain* (under CAPITAL¹).

ordinary course of business, the routine activities of one's business as distinguished from extraordinary events. For example, maintaining routine records as distinguished from writing a special report on a unique occurrence, or selling inventory piece by piece to different customers over time as distinguished from suddenly selling one's entire remaining stock of goods to a single purchaser at a discount.

original intent, a theory of constitutional interpretation under which it has been suggested that the meaning and proper application of constitutional provisions should be determined from the intent of the Constitution's framers But there were at least a hundred people involved in the Constitutional Convention of 1787 and the first United States Congress (which put forth the Bill of Rights), and just about the only thing that can be said with certainty about how they would want their broad language to be applied today is that they would disagree among themselves as much as constitutional scholars and Supreme Court Justices do today.

original jurisdiction. See under JURISDICTION[1]

out on bail. See under BAIL[1].

outside, *prep.* not covered by; not governed by: *outside the statute.* Cf. WITHIN.

outside counsel. See under COUNSEL.

overbreadth, *n.* a constitutional doctrine applicable to laws that are intended to forbid certain impermissible conduct but are drafted so broadly that they also forbid a good deal of constitutionally protected conduct; for example, a law that attempts to deal with violent picketing by prohibiting all picketing, even if it is peaceful. Under the overbreadth doctrine, the Supreme Court will usually strike down such a law in its entirety and leave it to the legislature to draft a narrower law.

overreaching, *n.* taking advantage of trickery or superior knowledge or bargaining power to obtain a contract that is grossly unfair to the other party, especially in a consumer transaction. A contract resulting from such overreaching may be voided by a court on the ground of UNCONSCIONABILITY.

overrule, *v.* **1.** (of a trial court) to rule unfavorably upon a motion or, especially, an objection raised at trial; to refuse to sustain an objection. **2.** (of an appellate court) to nullify a legal principle announced or relied upon in a previous case by reaching a result inconsistent with it in a subsequent case; for example, a state supreme court, by issuing an opinion adopting the principle of comparative negligence, might overrule its prior cases holding that contributory negligence is a complete bar to recovery by the plaintiff in a negligence case. Sometimes courts overrule a prior case expressly; on other occasions they do so SUB SILENTIO Direct overruling of precedents is rather unusual, because it violates the principle of STARE DECISIS

overt act, an act in furtherance of a criminal purpose As an element in a prosecution for CONSPIRACY, the overt act need not itself be illegal, but it must constitute a step toward attainment of the unlawful objective To convict a person of TREASON the Constitution requires "Testimony of two Witnesses to the same overt Act," and this has been construed as meaning an actual act of treason. Thus in the United States merely speaking out against government policy, without an intent to aid the enemy, is not treason

owner, *n.* **1.** a person or entity with a right to control and dispose of an interest in real or personal property, or for whose benefit such a right must be exercised **2. beneficial owner,** a person for whose benefit another (the *legal owner*) holds property Also called **equitable owner. 3. joint owner, a.** one of the owners of equal undivided interests in property with right of survivorship, as described under JOINT (def 2) **b.** informally, any co-owner, a person who shares ownership of something with another person upon any legally feasible terms. **4. legal owner,** a person with the actual legal right to control or dispose of an interest in property, either for his own benefit or as a trustee or constructive trustee for the benefit of another (the *beneficial* or *equitable owner*). **5. record owner,** the person whose name appears in a public record as the owner of land and thus as the person liable for property taxes, or in the records of a corporation as the owner of stock and thus as the person entitled to receive dividends and vote on corporate matters. Also called **owner of record.**

ownership, *n.* the status or rights of an owner regarding an interest in property. In addition to the types of ownership described under OWNER (*beneficial* or *equitable, joint,* etc.), ownership may be characterized as BY THE ENTIRETY, IN COMMON, or IN SEVERALTY, as appropriate.

oyez, *interj. Law French.* hear ye. In many courts, this is called out (usually two or three times) at the opening of each session to impress upon those present the solemnity of the proceedings. See also HEAR YE; KNOW ALL MEN BY THESE PRESENTS. **—Pronunciation.** Pronounced "oh yes" or "oh yez." The pronunciation "oh yay," which is sometimes heard, is inauthentic—an effort to pronounce this as if it were a modern French word.

P

paid-up stock. See under STOCK.

pain and suffering, physical and mental suffering caused by another's tortious conduct, as when one has suffered a personal injury or emotional loss. The compensatory damages awarded in a tort case may include a sum of money for the plaintiff's pain and suffering.

palimony, *n.* an ALIMONY-like financial provision upon the breakup of an unmarried couple who lived together. The courts in some states have expressed a willingness to make such awards in limited circumstances, but few if any separated lovers have actually received such an award. See also MERETRICIOUS.

palming off. Same as PASSING OFF.

pandering. Same as PROMOTING PROSTITUTION.

panel, *n.* **1.** the set of judges hearing a case. For example, appeals in the United States Courts of Appeals are normally heard by a panel of three judges selected at random from among the several judges assigned to the court. Cf. EN BANC. **2.** Same as *jury panel* (see under JURY).

paper. See COMMERCIAL PAPER; PAPERS.

papers, *n.pl.* **1.** the lawyer-generated documents in a case; for example, pleadings, affidavits, briefs. Occasionally a single such document is referred to as a **paper. 2. motion papers,** the set of papers submitted to a court in support of or in opposition to a motion. **3. on papers,** the manner of submission of a matter to a court when no oral argument or testimony is offered or is allowed.

par value, 1. the face value of a share of STOCK or of a bond (see BOND¹). In the case of a bond or preferred stock, the par value is the basis upon which dividends and interest are calculated. In the case of common stock, par value used to represent the original selling price of the stock, but now is an arbitrary and largely meaningless figure, typically $1.00. Many states have eliminated the requirement that corporations assign a par value to stock. **2. par value stock.** Same as *stock with par value* (see under STOCK).

paralegal, *n.* a nonlawyer employed to assist a lawyer or lawyers by performing, subject to supervision by the lawyers, a variety of legal tasks requiring less than a full legal education. Also called **legal assistant.**

paramount title. See under TITLE

pardon, *n.* **1.** the release of a person from penalties for a past offense or alleged offense. For federal offenses a pardon can be issued only by the President; for state offenses, usually only by the governor. A pardon may be granted before or after an arrest or conviction, and even after death It bars any further prosecution or punishment, but it does not remove a conviction from one's record. **2.** the document in which a pardon is declared. —*v.* **3.** to grant a pardon to someone: *President Ford pardoned ex-President*

Nixon for all crimes that he may have committed as President. Cf. AMNESTY, COMMUTE, REPRIEVE See also CLEMENCY.

parens patriae, *Latin* (lit. "parent of the country," originally a reference to the King or Queen) a state government in its role as protector of the people, and especially of children and the mentally infirm. In this role, the state may initiate certain civil actions to protect the interests of the state on behalf of all its people, or to protect people who lack the legal capacity to protect their own interests, as by taking children away from abusive parents or institutionalizing incompetents who pose a danger to themselves or others.

parent company, *n.* a corporation that owns more than 50% of the voting stock of another corporation. Also called **parent corporation** or simply **parent.** Cf. SUBSIDIARY.

parental kidnapping, the taking or secreting of a child by one parent in violation of the custody or visitation rights of the other parent.

parental liability, liability of parents for damages caused by tortious conduct of their children, imposed to varying extents by statutes in some states. Extensions of this concept to the criminal law, so that parents can be fined for offenses committed by their children, have been tried, but are of uncertain constitutionality.

parental neglect. See under NEGLECT.

pari delicto. See IN PARI DELICTO.

pari materia. See IN PARI MATERIA.

parliamentary law, rules of procedure for meetings of organizations. Parliamentary "law" is not part of federal or state law except in the peripheral sense that Congress and state legislatures necessarily adopt certain rules for the orderly conduct of their own debates and business.

parol, *adj.* **1.** oral: *parol promise; parol statement.* Cf. PAROL EVIDENCE. —*n.* **2.** an oral declaration or communication.

parol evidence, **1.** literally, either evidence of oral communications or evidence given orally. **2.** in its customary use, any oral or written information about a written contract, or a transaction involving a written contract, apart from the language of the instrument itself; for example, prior correspondence in which the contract was negotiated **3. parol evidence rule,** the rule of contract law that generally prohibits the use of extrinsic evidence, whether written or oral, to contradict contract terms that have been reduced to writing; in addition, if the writing was intended by the parties to embody their entire agreement, extrinsic evidence may not be used to add terms to it.

parole, *n.* **1.** release of a convicted criminal from jail or prison after serving part of a sentence, on the condition that he stay out of trouble with the law and comply with other requirements, such as meeting regularly with a parole officer. If parole conditions are violated, parole can be revoked and the parolee returned to confinement. Cf. PROBATION. —*v.* **2.** to release on parole

partial breach. See under BREACH

particulars. See BILL OF PARTICULARS.

partition, *v.* **1.** to divide property up among its co-owners, either physically or, more often, by selling it and dividing the proceeds. —*n.* **2.** such a division, or a civil action seeking such a division by court order

partner, *n.* **1.** a member of a PARTNERSHIP. **2. general** (or **full**) **partner, a.** a partner in a *general partnership* (see under PARTNERSHIP) **b.** one of the partners in a *limited partnership* (see under PARTNERSHIP) having responsibility for operation of the business and unlimited liability for its debts; a partner other than a *limited partner* Unless otherwise specified, "partner" normally means general partner **3. limited partner,** a partner in a limited partnership who merely invests money in the enterprise; one who does not participate in its management or operation and whose liability is limited to the amount invested **4. silent partner,** a partner whose involvement in the partnership is kept secret, or at least is not generally known Referred to in England as a **sleeping partner** —a term that might be misunderstood in America

partnership, *n.* **1.** an association of two or more people or entities to carry on a business for profit Profits and losses are shared by the partners and taxed to them directly; the partnership as an entity does not pay income taxes. See also DOMESTIC PARTNERSHIP. **2. general partnership,** an ordinary partnership, in which each partner is personally liable for the acts of every other partner in the conduct of the business and has unlimited personal liability for the debts of the partnership, and usually all partners participate in the management and conduct of the business. Unless otherwise specified, "partnership" means general partnership. **3. limited liability partnership (L.L.P.),** a form of partnership in which individual partners are not subject to personal liability for claims against the partnership. **4. limited partnership (L.P.),** a partnership consisting of one or more *general partners* and one or more *limited partners* (see under PARTNER).

party, *n.* **1.** a person or entity directly and officially involved in a transaction; especially, one of those bound by a contract **2.** a person or entity by or against whom a claim or charge is asserted in a case, especially one who has appeared or been served in the action. **3. indispensable party,** a person or entity whose rights are so bound up in a matter in suit that the case will not be allowed to proceed unless that person or entity is joined as a party. See also *compulsory joinder* (under JOINDER). Cf. *necessary party; proper party.* **4. necessary party,** a person or entity whose rights are sufficiently involved in an action to require joinder as a party if that is possible; but if it is not possible, the action will be allowed to proceed without that additional party. See also *compulsory joinder* (under JOINDER). Cf. *indispensable party; proper party.* **5. party of the first part,** in old drafting syle, the first party named in a contract or other instrument, often the maker or drafter;

subsequently named parties were identified as "party of the second part," "party of the third part," and so on. This terminology is no longer used, but shows up in old legal instruments, old judicial opinions, old movies, and old and new works of all kinds satirizing lawyers. **6. proper party,** a person or entity with a sufficient interest in a matter in suit to justify inclusion in the case, but whose absence would not hinder a just adjudication. A person bringing a case need not join every proper party in the action, although a proper party who is left out normally has a right to INTERVENE. See also *permissive joinder* (under JOINDER). Cf. *indispensable party; necessary party.* **7. real party in interest,** the person or entity possessing the legal right sued upon, or having a direct *interest* in the outcome of a case (see INTEREST[2], def. 1). Under old procedural rules, actions sometimes had to be brought in the name of someone other than the real party in interest; modern rules eliminate such technicalities. See also THIRD PARTY; *charter party* (under CHARTER[1]).

party joinder. See under JOINDER.

passing off, marketing one thing as if it were another; for example, a counterfeit as an original, another's product as one's own, or, particularly, one's own inferior product as if it were the superior product of a better-known company. Also called **palming off.**

passport, *n.* a document issued by a national government to one of its citizens, subjects, or nationals, authorizing travel out of the country and requesting other countries to permit entry and grant legal protection to the person

past consideration. See under CONSIDERATION.

past recollection recorded. See under RECOLLECTION.

patent, *n.* **1.** the exclusive right to exploit an invention for a number of years, granted by the federal government to the inventor if the inventor applies for it and the invention qualifies (is **patentable**). —*v.* **2.** to apply for and receive a patent on one's invention. —*adj.* **3.** open to public inspection; intended for public view. *letters patent* (see under LETTERS). **4.** obvious; apparent at a glance or upon reasonable inspection: *patent defect; patent ambiguity.* Cf. LATENT. —**patently,** *adv* —**Pronunciation.** For the noun and the verb, the first syllable rhymes with *hat.* For the adjective and the adverb, the first syllable rhymes with *hate.*

patently offensive, obviously offensive. For purposes of an OBSCENITY prosecution, a depiction of sexual conduct is patently offensive if the jury regards it as patently offensive, unless the highest court to which the case is appealed subsequently decides that it is clearly not patently offensive.

paternity suit (or **action** or **proceeding**), an action to establish that a particular man is the father of a child born out of wedlock The action may be brought, for example, by the mother, in order to obtain child support payments; by the state, in order to compel such payments; or by the putative father himself, in order to obtain parental rights.

pawn, *n.* **1.** the deposit of goods as security for a loan or other obligation, especially an individual's deposit of personal possessions to secure a personal loan. **2.** an item so deposited; the collateral for the loan. **3.** the state of being deposited or held as security. *His television set is in pawn.* —*v.* **4.** to make such a deposit: *She pawned her wedding ring.*

pawnbroker, *n.* a person in the business of making loans secured by pawns of personal property.

payable, *adj.* supposed to be paid; now due or to become due: *accounts payable; a check payable to the order of Jane Smith.* See also *payable on demand* (under DEMAND); *payable to bearer* (under BEARER); *payable to order* (under ORDER²).

payee, *n.* a person to whom, or to whose order, money is paid or is supposed to be paid; especially, the person so named in an instrument, such as the person or entity to which a check is made out.

payment bond. See under BOND²

payor, *n.* the person who makes, or is supposed to make, a payment; especially, the person or entity so designated in a negotiable instrument, such as the bank upon which a check or other draft is drawn (**payor bank**).

payroll tax, any of several kinds of tax collected from employers on the basis of employee count or employee salaries. Some such taxes are paid by the employer in addition to the employees' salaries; others are paid by the employees through withholding from their salaries. See SOCIAL SECURITY TAX for an example.

penal, *adj.* **1.** pertaining to a penalty or to penalties generally. **2.** pertaining to crime and punishment

penalty, *n.* **1.** a punishment for a crime; e.g., the *death penalty* (see under CAPITAL PUNISHMENT). **2.** a sum specified in a contract to be paid, beyond or instead of payment of damages, in the event of a breach, or agreed to as the price of being excused from an obligation. **3. civil penalty,** a fine or forfeiture provided for by statute or regulation, not for commission of a crime but for failure to fulfill a legal obligation or adhere to regulations. Civil penalties are often imposed by administrative agencies. Examples: a percentage added to one's income tax bill as a penalty for failure to pay on time; removal of one's license to conduct a food business for persistent failure to maintain health standards. **4. penalty clause,** a contract clause requiring payment of a specific sum of money, unrelated to and usually greater than anticipated damages, as a penalty in the event of breach. As a general rule, such clauses are unenforceable Cf *liquidated damages* (under DAMAGES) **5. prepayment penalty,** in connection with a mortgage or other loan agreement, a penalty that the debtor must pay if the debt is repaid early. Prepayment penalties are often enforceable because they compensate the lender for loss of interest.

pendent jurisdiction. See under JURISDICTION¹.

pendente lite, *Latin.* (lit. "with a lawsuit pending") during litigation; while a case is in progress: *injunction pendente lite.*

penitentiary. Same as PRISON.

pension, *n.* **1.** regular payments to a retired employee from a fund (**pension fund**) created by the employer or by a combination of employer and employee contributions, or the right to receive such payments **2. vested pension,** a pension to which an employee will become entitled upon retirement even if she quits or loses her job before then Ordinarily an employee must stay with a particular employer for five to seven years for a pension associated with that position to become fully vested

pension plan, 1. a program established by an employer for the provision of pensions to employees. The standards for such plans are set by the **Employee Retirement Income Security Act of 1974 (ERISA). 2. defined-benefit plan,** a pension plan that guarantees a certain level of pension payments after retirement, based upon the employee's length of employment, salary, and age at retirement. **3. defined-contribution plan,** a pension plan under which the level of employer and employee contributions is fixed, and the level of benefits ultimately received may be higher or lower depending upon how successful the pension fund's investments have been. **4. qualified pension plan,** a pension plan conforming to certain provisions of the Internal Revenue Code, making the employer's contributions tax deductible and deferring income tax for the employee until benefits are actually received, after retirement. A qualified pension plan set up by a self-employed individual, a sole proprietor, or a partnership is called a **Keogh plan** or **HR-10 plan. 5. simplified employee pension (SEP),** a pension plan affording most of the tax advantages of other qualified plans, under which the employer simply makes contributions to each employee's INDIVIDUAL RETIREMENT ACCOUNT. See also RETIREMENT PLAN.

people, *n.pl.* **1.** human beings; especially, the inhabitants of a state or nation collectively. **2.** *cap.* in many states, the name by which the state government and the prosecution are identified in criminal cases under state law See also STATE. Cf. GOVERNMENT.

per capita, *Latin.* (lit. "by the heads") **1.** per person; divided equally among all the people in a defined group. **2.** a principle for distributing a decedent's estate under which all takers of a particular portion of the estate, or at least all takers at the same generational level, receive equal shares without regard to what branch of the family they belong to. Cf. PER STIRPES.

per curiam, *Latin.* by the court. See also *per curiam opinion* (under OPINION)

per se, *Latin.* (lit "by itself") intrinsically; without more. Said of acts that constitute such strong evidence of wrongdoing that no further evidence is needed. For example, under the law forbidding UNREASONABLE RESTRAINT OF TRADE, price fixing is regarded as "unreasonable per se," and certain kinds of insult are regarded as so inherently defamatory as to constitute "slander per se "

per stirpes, *Latin.* (lit. "by the stems"; "by the branches") describing a principle for distributing a decedent's estate under which the descendants of any person who would have received a share of the estate if he had still been alive at the time of the decedent's death divide up that person's share. Thus the portion left to each branch of the family is divided and subdivided only within that branch. Cf. PER CAPITA

percentage lease. See under LEASE.

peremptory challenge. See under CHALLENGE.

perfect, *v.* to take all legal steps necessary to secure or put on record a claim, right, or interest: *perfect a security interest; perfect title to land; perfect an appeal.*

perform, *v.* to carry out a legal duty; to fulfill one's obligations, especially under a contract. See also SPECIFIC PERFORMANCE; SUBSTANTIAL PERFORMANCE. —**performance,** *n.*

performance bond. See under BOND².

periodic tenancy (or **estate**). See under TENANCY.

perjury, *n.* the crime of making a false statement under oath or affirmation on a material issue in a judicial or administrative proceeding, other than in the belief that what is being said is true. Cf. FALSE SWEARING.

permanent injunction. See under INJUNCTION

permissive, *adj.* permitted but not required; opposite of compulsory or mandatory. See *permissive* COUNTERCLAIM, JOINDER, PRESUMPTION under those words.

perpetuate, *v.* to obtain and preserve testimony in a form suitable for later use at a trial, in case the witness is unavailable. See also DEPOSITION.

perpetuity, *n.* a *contingent interest* in real property (see under INTEREST¹) that might remain contingent for a length of time regarded by the law as excessive; that is, the contingency that would cause the interest to VEST might remain unresolved—not having occurred, but still possible—for a longer time than permitted by law. At common law, the maximum time limit was the lifetime of someone alive (or at least conceived) at the time the interest was created and identified in the instrument creating the interest (a **life in being**), plus 21 years. This allowed, for example, a testator to leave his estate to his children for as long as they live, then finally "to such of my grandchildren as reach the age of 21 " Under the **rule against perpetuities,** any interest that might remain contingent longer than lives in being plus 21 years was just too uncertain, and was declared void. Some version of the rule against perpetuities exists in all or virtually all states, but the details vary from state to state. See also RESTRAINT ON ALIENATION.

person, *n., pl.* **persons. 1.** a human being (**natural person**) or an organization or entity (**juridical person, juristic person, artifical person,** or **legal person**) such as a corporation, recognized by the law as capable of performing legal acts (such as entering into a contract) and having legal rights and responsibilities (such as the right to due process and liability for torts) The exact scope of the term depends upon the context. In this dictionary, the phrase "person or entity" is often used to emphasize that a definition applies to juridical as well as natural persons, and the nonlegalistic plural "people" is sometimes used to indicate that a concept applies exclusively or primarily to natural persons rather than juridical persons. See also INDIVIDUAL. **2.** the human body: *injury to person and property.* **3. interested person,** a person with an interest (see INTEREST[2]) in a matter; particularly a person whose legal and financial rights will be directly affected by the outcome of a case or the disposition of a decedent's estate. Persons having such an interest will normally be allowed to INTERVENE in a case or otherwise assert their claims and rights in a matter if their interest is not already adequately represented. **4. protected person,** an individual, especially an incompetent person, for whom a court has appointed a GUARDIAN or made some other order of protection. **5. reasonable person.** See under REASONABLE.

personal. See *personal* BOND[2], INCOME TAX, INJURY, JUDGMENT, JURISDICTION[1], KNOWLEDGE, PROPERTY, SERVICE under those words, and *release on personal recognizance* (under RELEASE ON OWN RECOGNIZANCE).

personalty. Same as *personal property* (see under PROPERTY).

personam. See IN PERSONAM.

persuasion. See *burden of persuasion* (under BURDEN[1]).

persuasive authority. See under AUTHORITY[2].

petit, *adj. Law French.* (lit. "small") small, minor, lesser. Used in certain legal phrases of ancient origin, usually in contrast to GRAND; e.g., *petit jury* (see under JURY), *petit larceny* (see under LARCENY). Pronounced, and often written, "petty."

petition, *n.* **1.** a formal request, addressed to a person or body in a position of authority, soliciting some benevolent exercise of power. The right to present such petitions to the government is one of the rights guaranteed by the First Amendment (see Appendix). **2.** the name given to the initial pleading in certain kinds of judicial or administrative proceedings, and to certain requests for special permission or relief from appellate courts: *petition for a writ of habeas corpus; petition in bankruptcy; petition for leave to appeal.* —*v.* **3.** to present or file a petition: *to petition the governor for a pardon; to petition the legislature for a change in the law; to petition for a writ of mandamus.* —**petitioner,** *n.*

petty, *adj.* small, minor, lesser. See *petty* JURY, LARCENY, OFFENSE under those words. In certain phrases, often rendered in the original French form: PETIT. Cf. GRAND.

physician-assisted suicide. See under SUICIDE.

physician-patient privilege. See under PRIVILEGE.

picket, *v.* **1.** to stand or parade in front of a place of employment carrying signs, in order to publicize a labor grievance and discourage customers and other employees from entering or patronizing the establishment until the dispute is resolved. **2.** to engage in any similar demonstration in front of a government or private building or site for the purpose of publicizing a cause, protesting conduct, or petitioning for action. Since picketing is *speech plus* (see under SPEECH), it is subject to greater regulation than pure speech. —*n.* **3.** an individual engaged in picketing.

pierce the corporate veil. See under CORPORATE.

piracy, *n.* **1.** plundering, violence, or other criminal acts on a ship or airplane, or the stealing or highjacking of such a vessel. **2.** the unauthorized reproduction, imitation, or use of a copyrighted work, patented invention, or trademarked product; especially, unauthorized reproduction of copyrighted books, records, tapes, videotapes, and software on a large scale for commercial purposes. —**pirate,** *v., n.*

plagiarize, *v.* to present another's ideas, words, or other form of expression as if they were one's own. This may or may not be unlawful, depending upon whether it involves unauthorized use of copyrighted work and other factors, but in academic and scholarly contexts it is always unethical and may lead to disciplinary proceedings. —**plagiarism,** *n.*

plain error. See under ERROR.

plain meaning, the apparent meaning of a statutory or constitutional provision as gleaned solely from the words of the provision itself, without consideration of other factors, such as the context in which the words were written and the objective the writers were trying to achieve. The **plain meaning rule** is a theory of statutory and constitutional CONSTRUCTION that regards the "plain meaning" of a provision as dispositive. This theory disregards the fact that writing is an inherently inexact activity, that reasonable people can reach very different conclusions as to what a particular provision "plainly means," and that the "plain meaning" found by a judge is often as much a reflection of what the judge wants to find in the provision as of what the drafter put there. Cf. LEGISLATIVE INTENT.

plain view doctrine, the principle that police who are lawfully in a place do not need a search warrant to seize evidence of crime that is in plain view; similarly, an officer may seize evidence obvious to the touch in the conduct of a lawful patdown for weapons.

plaintiff, *n.* the person who starts a lawsuit by serving or filing a complaint.

plaintiff in error, the APPELLANT in a case in which the appeal is commenced by *writ of error* (see under WRIT)

plan of reorganization. See under BANKRUPTCY.

plea, *n.* **1.** a criminal defendant's formal response to the charges: GUILTY, NOT GUILTY, or NOLO CONTENDERE. At ARRAIGNMENT, the usual plea is "not guilty," but this is often changed later, usually as the result of a PLEA BARGAIN. **2.** any of a considerable number of specific pleadings and motions that were used in civil cases prior to the adoption of modern rules of procedure, seldom referred to in modern cases.

plea bargain, a negotiated agreement between the prosecution and a criminal defendant whereby the prosecution grants some concessions in exchange for the defendant's plea of guilty to at least one charge Typical concessions include dropping certain charges, especially the most serious ones, and agreeing to make a particular sentencing recommendation Most criminal cases end in a plea bargain.

plead, *v.* to enter a PLEA or file a PLEADING, or to assert in a pleading. *He pleaded the defense of statute of limitations.* "Pleaded" is the conventional past tense; "pled," though increasingly common in the United States, still carries for traditionalists an overtone of uneducated speech.

pleading, *n.* **1.** the formal document in which a party to a civil case sets out or responds to a claim or defense Under modern rules, the principal pleadings are the COMPLAINT, the ANSWER, and if the answer contains counterclaims, a REPLY. **2.** the act of asserting or filing a claim, defense, or plea **3. alternative pleading,** the inclusion in a pleading of allegations or defenses based upon varying—or even conflicting—interpretations of the facts or the law. For example, "Defendant either negligently failed to see a red light or, in the alternative, saw the red light and deliberately ignored it";"Defendant's conduct constitutes a fraud, or alternatively a breach of contract." Such pleading was formerly disfavored, but under modern procedure is freely allowed. **4. notice pleading,** the modern philosophy that the function of pleadings is simply to give reasonable notice of the nature of one's claims or defenses, the details of which can be developed through DISCOVERY. This is in contrast to earlier practice, in which pleading was a highly technical exercise and cases could easily be lost because of minor pleading defects even if the facts supported the pleader. See also *burden of pleading* (under BURDEN[1]), *judgment on the pleadings* (under JUDGMENT)

pledge, *n.* **1.** a deposit of personal property, or of documents (such as stock certificates) representing intangible property, with a lender or other person as security for a loan or other obligation —*v.* **2.** to make such a pledge.

plenary, *adj.* **1.** full, complete, sufficient, unqualified: *plenary jurisdiction over a case; plenary trial.* **2.** involving all members of a body *a plenary session of the legislature.*

plurality opinion. See under OPINION

pocket part, a common form of supplement to a book of statutes or a treatise or other legal reference work, in which updated portions are tucked into a pocket in the back of the book.

point, *n* **1.** a proposition of fact or law **2.** a section of a brief devoted to argument in support of a particular point of significance in the case See also *case in point* (under CASE[1]); *memorandum of points and authorities* (under BRIEF); ON POINT

poisonous tree. See FRUIT OF THE POISONOUS TREE.

police power, state legislative power; the inherent power of state governments, and of local governments to the extent delegated by the state, to enact laws safeguarding the health, safety, morals, convenience, and general welfare of people in the state, subject only to the constraints of the Constitution and the supremacy of federal law in matters within its purview

policy, *n* **1.** Also called **insurance policy.** the written instrument embodying a contract of INSURANCE **2.** See PUBLIC POLICY

political asylum. See under ASYLUM

political question. See under QUESTION²

poll tax, a "head tax", a fixed tax imposed on everyone regardless of income. After the Civil War, poll taxes were enacted in many states as a condition of being allowed to vote, making it difficult for the poor, and in particular the black populace, to vote In 1964 this requirement was eliminated in elections for national office by the Twenty-fourth Amendment (see Appendix); two years later the Supreme Court abolished it for state and local elections, on the ground that it denied impoverished voters equal protection of the laws

poll the jury, to require the jurors in a case in which a verdict has just been announced to declare in open court, usually one by one, whether that is, in fact, their verdict. This is done by the judge or a court officer if requested by a party.

polygraph, *n.* a device for measuring certain involuntary bodily responses, such as blood pressure and perspiration, from which an opinion is drawn as to whether or not the person being tested is telling the truth. Also called, somewhat optimistically, a **lie detector.** The problem with it is that while it may yield accurate opinions in many cases, it can make nervous or confused truth-tellers look like liars and amoral or self-deluding liars look like truth-tellers, and there is no way to know which results are accurate and which are not Accordingly, polygraph results are excluded from evidence under most circumstances in most jurisdictions, and federal law prohibits employers, except in very limited circumstances, from using the device on employees and applicants for employment

pornography, *n.* **1.** broadly, any sexually explicit material intended primarily to provide sexual entertainment and arousal to those who read or view it for that purpose. **2.** narrowly, sexual material satisfying the constitutional test for OBSCENITY. In general, any commercial, and sometimes noncommercial, involvement with such pornography is a crime. **3. child pornography,** any sexually explicit visual depiction of an individual under the age of 18 Courts have held that such material may be banned even if it is not obscene and does not involve nudity

positive law, human-made law as distinguished from so-called NATURAL LAW; the actual rules of behavior and government enforced by a society.

posse. See IN POSSE; POSSE COMITATUS

posse comitatus, *Latin.* (lit. "force of the county") a group of people who may be called upon to assist law enforcement authorities in preserving the peace, making an arrest, or the like; or a group actually called upon and assembled for such a purpose Also called a **posse.** It is in the tradition of the posse comitatus that the National Guard may be called out for such purposes as enforcing school integration, quelling riots, or maintaining order after a natural disaster

possession, *n* **1.** occupation or control of real property to the exclusion of others (save with permission of the possessor), or knowing dominion and control over personal property. **2. actual possession,** direct or immediate physical occupation or control of property See also AD-VERSE POSSESSION; OCCUPANCY. **3. constructive possession,** the power and intention of exercising control over property that is in the hands of someone else For example, the owner of a house currently occupied by a lessee, or of furniture stored in a warehouse, has constructive possession of the house or furniture, while the tenant or the warehouser has actual possession To sustain a charge of "criminal possession" of contraband, such as illegal drugs or stolen property, it is usually sufficient to show constructive possession

possession is nine-tenths of the law, a somewhat overstated adage reflecting two realities. (1) that in disputes over real property, a person in possession can only be ousted by one with a superior right; a person with no right or a lesser right has no standing to complain, even if the present occupant's possession is wrongful, and (2) that because of the expense, uncertainty, and difficulty of obtaining and enforcing legal judgments, a person in possession of disputed property or a disputed sum of money has a strategic advantage over an adverse claimant. Sometimes, especially in England, the idiom is **possession is nine points of the law.** See also *paramount title* (under TITLE).

possessory action, an action to recover or maintain possession of real or personal property, such as an action to evict a holdover tenant or for REPLEVIN

possessory estate. See under ESTATE[1]

possessory interest. See under INTEREST[1]

possibility of reverter, the *future estate* (see under ES-TATE[1]) retained by the owner of a fee (see FEE[1]) in real property (or her heirs) when she transfers the entire fee to someone else but imposes a condition on its continued existence so that, upon violation of the condition, the fee will revert to the original owner or her heirs See also *fee simple determinable* (under FEE[1]). Cf. *executory interest* (under INTEREST[1])

post bail. See under BAIL[1]

power, *n.* **1.** legal authority to perform acts affecting legal rights and relationships, especially the authority of a legislative body to make laws on certain subjects (e.g , *commerce power,* under COMMERCE; POLICE POWER), the authority of other governmental bodies or officers to perform their respective duties (*e g., executive power; judicial power*), or specific authority granted to a private person to take actions having legal consequences (e.g , POWER OF APPOINT-MENT; POWER OF ATTORNEY) See also SEPARATION OF POWERS. **2. delegated power, a.** power granted by one person or body to another, to do something that the first could have done; especially, regulatory power conferred upon an administrative agency by Congress. **b.** Another name for *enumerated power*. **3. enumerated power,** a power conferred upon the federal government by the Constitution, such as the commerce power. The United States government is a "government of enumerated powers," having only those powers provided for in the Constitution. **4. reserved power,** a governmental power left to the states by the Constitution—that is, any governmental power that the Constitution neither grants to the federal government nor denies to state governments.

power of appointment, the authority, granted by the owner of property (the DONOR of the power) to a person (the DONEE), to designate (APPOINT) the person or persons who are to receive the property upon the death of the donor, the death of the donee, or the termination of some intervening interest in the property

power of attorney, 1. an instrument by which one individual (the PRINCIPAL) confers upon another (the *attorney in fact*; see under ATTORNEY) the power to perform specified acts or kinds of acts on behalf of the principal. **2.** the power possessed by an attorney in fact by reason of such an instrument **3. durable power of attorney,** a form of power of attorney allowed by statute, which remains effective if the principal becomes incompetent to perform or consent to the acts delegated. At common law, the power of attorney was automatically revoked upon incapacity of the principal **4. durable power of attorney for health care.** Same as HEALTH CARE PROXY **5. general power of attorney,** a power of attorney granting wide power to perform any act of a specified kind or of a range of kinds, such as handling all business and financial matters for the principal. **6. special power of attorney,** a power of attorney to perform a certain act, such as signing a particular document or purchasing a particular parcel of land.

practice, *n.* **1.** the procedural aspects of law; the presentation of matters to courts and the manner in which cases are handled *civil practice; rules of practice; Supreme Court practice.* **2.** the pursuit of a profession: *the practice of law; the practice of architecture* **3.** one's usual way of dealing with a particular kind of situation *Her practice is to have her secretary open her mail The practice in our industry is to ship by truck unless another method is specified.* —*v.* **4.** to engage in a profession

praesenti. See IN PRAESENTI

prayer for relief, the portion at the end of a COMPLAINT in which the plaintiff states the damages or other remedy being sought in the action Also called **demand for relief.**

preamble, *n.* an introduction to a constitution, statute, contract, or other instrument, stating the reasons for enacting or writing it. It is usually not regarded as a part of the instrument, but is sometimes looked to for help in construing the instrument.

precatory, *adj.* expressing or reflecting a hope, desire, or preference, but not a direction or command

precatory language, language in a trust instrument or will that indicates the maker's desire but is not legally binding; for example, "It is my hope that these funds will be used for educational purposes." Also called **precatory words.** Often it is difficult to know whether such language was intended to be mandatory or merely precatory See also WISH.

precedent, *n.* **1.** a judicial decision cited as authority by an attorney or court in a subsequent case involving similar or analogous facts and issues. Virtually all judicial decisions are based upon precedent, which is central to the doctrine of STARE DECISIS. —*adj.* **2. condition precedent.** See under CONDITION. —**Pronunciation.** The noun is PRESSedent; the adjective is more appropriately preSEEdent

preclusion, *n.* being prevented from making certain arguments or contesting certain issues in a case, either because one has already litigated them in an earlier case and lost, or because one has failed to provide information on the issue to the other side in compliance with discovery requirements, as a result of which the judge has issued a **preclusion order.** See also *issue preclusion* (under ESTOPPEL)

predator. See SEXUAL PREDATOR

predatory pricing, selling goods or services at an unreasonably low price in the hope of driving competitors out of business and then raising the price This is a violation of ANTITRUST laws

predecessor, *n.* one who previously possessed a right, interest, or duty now belonging to another (a SUCCESSOR) Also called **predecessor in interest.**

preemption, *n.* **1.** the doctrine that a comprehensive federal regulatory scheme in a field of federal interest may be held to preclude any state regulation whatever in that field. In such a situation federal law is said to **occupy the field** and to **preempt** state law **2.** the enactment of a federal law that preempts state law, or the preemptive effect of a federal law. See also SUPREMACY

preference, *n.* **1.** a payment or transfer of property or of an interest in property by an insolvent debtor to a creditor in such a way that the creditor gets more than its share of the debtor's property as compared with other creditors. **2. voidable preference,** a preference shortly before the debtor formally goes into bankruptcy, under circumstances permitting the bankruptcy court to recover whatever was given from the creditor who received it, so that it can be distributed fairly among all creditors.

preferred stock. See under STOCK.

pregnancy discrimination, discrimination in employment on the basis of pregnancy, childbirth, or related medical conditions After the Supreme Court held that this does not constitute discrimination against women, Congress in 1978 adopted a statute making it clear that pregnancy discrimination is to be regarded as a form of illegal sex discrimination

prejudice, *n* **1.** bias or prejudgment in a case; a tendency to favor one side over the other See also INTEREST[2] **2.** adverse effect on, or loss of, a legal right, particularly a procedural right in a lawsuit or criminal case. **3. with prejudice,** having the effect of precluding a party from asserting a particular claim or right or contesting a particular issue in the future **4. without prejudice,** preserving a party's right to assert a particular claim or right or contest a particular issue in the future. See also *dismissal with prejudice* and *dismissal without prejudice* (under DISMISSAL) —*v* **5.** to cause prejudice to a party or to a specified right of a party

prejudicial effect, the tendency of a piece of evidence to inflame the jury unduly or to divert its attention to irrelevant matters Relevant evidence in a case may be excluded if the judge concludes that its PROBATIVE VALUE IS outweighed by its prejudicial effect

prejudicial error. See under ERROR.

preliminary hearing. See under HEARING.

preliminary injunction. See under INJUNCTION

premarital agreement. Same as PRENUPTIAL AGREEMENT

premeditation, *n* contemplating something with a cool mind before doing it, if only briefly and on the spot. Premeditation is an element of the highest degree of MURDER in some states —**premeditated,** *adj*

premium, *n.* **1.** money paid to an insurance company for insurance coverage or for an annuity **2.** an extra amount paid or received for something; especially the amount by which the market value of a bond exceeds its face value if the bond carries interest at a higher rate than the current rate for newly issued bonds

prenuptial agreement, a contract between two people who are about to marry regarding their respective property and support rights upon termination of the marriage by divorce or death, and sometimes regarding property rights during the marriage as well. Such agreements are generally enforceable, and supersede otherwise applicable rules Also called **antenuptial agreement** or **premarital agreement.**

prepayment penalty. See under PENALTY

preponderance of the evidence, the lowest STANDARD OF PROOF; the degree of persuasion necessary to find for the plaintiff in most civil cases. It requires just enough evidence to persuade the jury that a fact is more likely to be true than not true. If the evidence is equally balanced, then the party with the *burden of persuasion* (see under BURDEN[1]) loses Sometimes called **preponderance of the credible evidence** or **fair preponderance of the evidence.**

prerogative writ. Same as *extraordinary writ* (see under WRIT).

prescription, *n.* a method of obtaining an EASEMENT over real property belonging to someone else, such as the right to use a path across it, consisting of openly and consistently using it for a period of time set by statute, usually ten to twenty years. Acquisition of an easement by prescription is analogous to acquisition of title by ADVERSE POSSESSION.

present estate or **present possessory estate.** Same as *possessory estate* (see under ESTATE¹).

present interest. See under INTEREST¹.

present recollection refreshed. See under RECOLLECTION.

present sense impression, a statement describing an event or situation, or the declarant's own physical condition or state of mind, made by a person while actually observing or experiencing the thing being described or immediately thereafter. Statements of present sense impression are commonly admitted into evidence as an exception to the rule against HEARSAY.

presentence report, a background report on a convicted defendant, prepared by a probation department to assist the judge in deciding upon a sentence.

presentment, *n.* **1.** the act of presenting an instrument for the payment of money, such as a check or promissory note, to the payor for acceptance or payment. **2.** a written statement of an offense prepared by a grand jury on its own initiative, as distinguished from an INDICTMENT requested by the prosecutor. **3.** the formal act of presenting a matter to a body or official for legal action.

presents, *n.pl.* the present writings; the contents of this legal instrument. Now limited almost exclusively to the phrase KNOW ALL MEN BY THESE PRESENTS or some minor variation of it.

press. See FREEDOM OF THE PRESS.

presumption, *n.* **1.** a legal assumption that if one fact or group of facts exists, then another fact must also exist, so that the second can sometimes be proved in a court case simply by introducing evidence of the first **2. conclusive presumption,** a rule of law under which once one set of facts is established, the facts that normally follow from it must be found to be true, and no evidence to the contrary will be permitted; for example, the presumption that if a driver's blood alcohol content was above a certain level, then the driver was drunk Also called **irrebuttable presumption. 3. mandatory presumption,** a presumption that the factfinder in a criminal case must accept unless the defendant produces some evidence to rebut it. **4. permissive presumption,** a presumption that the factfinder in a criminal case may, but need not, accept in the absence of evidence to rebut it **5. rebuttable presumption,** a presumption that can be defeated by introduction of sufficiently persuasive contrary evidence.

presumption of innocence, the principle that a criminal defendant need not introduce evidence of innocence to be found not guilty; rather, the prosecution must prove each element of the crime in order to convict.

pretermitted heir, a child or other heir omitted from mention in a will, usually because the will was made before the heir was born A pretermitted heir—at least one who is a child of the testator—is entitled to a share of the estate by statute in most states

pretrial conference, a conference among the judge and the lawyers for all parties in a case, convened by the judge at any time after the pleadings have been filed and before the trial, to discuss discovery issues, scheduling, and the general status of the case, and usually to discuss the possibility of settlement.

pretrial discovery. See under DISCOVERY.

pretrial order, an order issued by a judge just before a trial, usually reflecting things discussed or agreed upon at a final PRETRIAL CONFERENCE, setting forth ground rules for the trial.

preventive detention, keeping a criminal defendant in jail before trial; not allowing release on bail. This is permitted in serious felony cases upon a finding that it is necessary to protect individuals or the community at large.

price discrimination, selling goods or services at different prices to different customers. This can be a violation of ANTITRUST laws if done in such a way as to harm competitors and reduce competition.

price fixing, the setting of prices at which goods or services are to be sold, by means of an agreement or understanding between competing sellers (**horizontal price fixing**) or an agreement or arrangement between the seller and the producer or wholesaler who provided the product in question (**vertical price fixing**). Price fixing is a violation of the SHERMAN ANTITRUST ACT.

prima facie, *Latin.* (lit. "at first appearance") **1.** so far as it appears; subject to further evidence, unless the contrary is shown: *The deed is in proper form, and so is prima facie valid.* **2. prima facie case** (or **evidence** or **proof**), evidence sufficient to justify submitting a party's claim or affirmative defense to a jury, and to support a verdict in favor of that party on that issue, if the jury so finds; that is, evidence sufficient to satisfy a party's *burden of producing evidence* (see under BURDEN[1])

primary boycott. See under BOYCOTT.

primary liability. See under LIABILITY.

prime contractor. Same as *general contractor* (see under CONTRACTOR).

principal, *n.* **1.** a person who authorizes another to act as her AGENT. If the agent does not disclose to those he deals with that he is acting on behalf of someone else, the principal is called an **undisclosed principal.** See also AGENCY. **2.** Also called **principal debtor** or **principal obligor.** the person whose debt or other obligation is the subject of a SURETYSHIP contract or a GUARANTY If the SURETY or GUARANTOR is required to pay or perform, that person normally has a right of reimbursement from the principal. **3.** a direct participant in a crime; either an actual perpetrator or an aider and abettor who is present (personally or through an innocent agent) when the crime is committed **4.** a basic sum of money upon which interest or profit is calculated; e.g., the face amount of a bond (see BOND¹). **5.** the CORPUS of a trust, especially if the trust property consists almost entirely of money or securities. —*adj.* **6.** primary, most important.

prior inconsistent statement. See under STATEMENT

prior restraint, a ban on publishing something. The First Amendment (see Appendix) has been construed as prohibiting most prior restraints, allowing publishers to publish even wrongful or potentially wrongful material (e.g., LIBEL¹) if they are willing to take the risk of resulting liability or punishment. The primary exception to this rule is OBSCENITY, which may be censored in advance

priority, *n.* **1.** the right to satisfaction of one's claim against some property, such as the estate of a decedent or a bankrupt, ahead of someone else. **2.** the order in which the law ranks claims to property.

prison, *n.* a state or federal facility in which people convicted of serious crimes and given long sentences are incarcerated. Also called **penitentiary.** Cf. JAIL.

privacy, *n.* freedom from unwarranted intrusion into one's personal life and unwanted publicity about oneself Various types of privacy interest are protected from private interference by tort law (see INVASION OF PRIVACY) and from governmental interference by statutes and by the Constitution (see RIGHT OF PRIVACY).

private, *adj.* **1.** pertaining or belonging to one person or a limited group of persons rather than to the government or the public at large· *private property.* Cf. PUBLIC. **2.** pertaining to a person acting other than as a government official: *private attorney general* (see under ATTORNEY GENERAL); *private discrimination.* **3.** kept away from the public at large: *private information; private conduct.* See also *private* CORPORATION, INTERNATIONAL LAW, NECESSITY, NUISANCE, RIGHT OF ACTION, WRONG under those words

privately held corporation. See under CORPORATION

privilege, *n.* **1.** in general, a special right or exemption that the law allows to a person or class of persons, or to people under certain circumstances, for reasons of public policy Some privileges cannot be taken away under any circumstances **(absolute privilege);** others may be relied upon only if certain conditions are met, or may be defeated under certain circumstances **(qualified privilege** or **conditional privilege). 2.** in tort law, the right to take actions that are necessary and reasonable under the circumstances even if they injure the person, property, or reputation of another; for example, the right to use reasonable force in SELF-DEFENSE (constituting a defense to a claim of BATTERY), or the absolute privilege of legislators to speak freely in legislative debate or of persons involved in court cases to speak freely in court (rendering them immune from any claim of DEFAMATION) **3.** Also called **testimonial privilege.** an absolute or qualified right to withhold certain evidence in judicial proceedings. The public policy reason for such privileges is usually to protect confidential relationships. The number, scope, and even names of such privileges vary from state to state; among the most common are the following: **a. attorney-client privilege,** the privilege of a client to prevent disclosure of confidential communications to her lawyer. **b. clergy-communicant privilege,** the privilege protecting confidential communications to one's spiritual advisor. **c. investigative privilege,** the privilege of law enforcement agencies to keep information gathered for law enforcement purposes secret. **d. physician-patient privilege,** the privilege of a patient to prevent her doctor from disclosing medical records and information obtained from her in connection with medical services. **e. spousal privilege,** the privilege to prevent disclosure of confidential communications to one's spouse. See also EXECUTIVE PRIVILEGE; SHIELD LAW.

privileged communication, a communication that may be withheld from evidence because of a *testimonial privilege* (see under PRIVILEGE).

privileges and immunities, fundamental rights associated with state citizenship The Constitution requires each state in the United States to accord citizens of other states the same privileges and immunities as its own citizens.

privity, *n.* the relationship between two or more persons participating in, or having related interests in, a transaction, proceeding, or piece of property. For example, there is **privity of contract** between the parties to a contract; and the grantor and grantee, lessor and lessee, or co-owners of an estate in land are in **privity of estate.** Persons in privity with each other are called **privies;** each one is the other's **privy.**

pro bono publico, *Latin.* for the public good. A phrase (usually shortened to **pro bono**) signifying that legal services are being provided without charge: *The firm is handling the matter pro bono.*

pro hac vice, *Latin.* (lit. "for this turn") for a single case or occasion only; a phrase used in reference to a lawyer—usually from out of state—who is given special permission to represent a client in a court to which the lawyer has not been admitted. The attorney is said to "appear pro hac vice " When this is permitted, the court invariably requires that *local counsel* (see under COUNSEL) also be retained, so that there will be an attorney involved who is close by and familiar with the court's rules. See also *admission pro hac vice* (under ADMISSION)

pro se, *Latin.* for himself or herself; relating to a party who acts as his or her own lawyer in a case: *The plaintiff is appearing pro se. This is a pro se case.*

pro tanto, *Latin.* (lit "for so much") to that extent; proportionable.

probable cause. 1. reasonable grounds, based on substantial evidence, for believing a fact to be true Under the Fourth Amendment (see Appendix), a person cannot be arrested for a crime unless there is probable cause to believe she committed it, and one's person and property cannot be searched unless there is probable cause to believe that evidence of a crime will be found. **2. probable cause hearing.** See under HEARING.

probate, *n.* a judicial proceeding in which a will is proved to be genuine and distribution of the estate is monitored.

probation, *n.* a sentence allowing a convicted criminal to remain free instead of going to jail or prison, or to go free after serving a brief period of confinement, provided that certain conditions are met, including staying out of trouble with the law and reporting regularly to a probation officer If the conditions of probation are violated, probation can be revoked and the probationer sent to prison.

probative value, usefulness and persuasiveness of a piece of evidence in establishing a relevant fact Cf PREJUDICIAL EFFECT. See also WEIGHT.

procedural due process. See under DUE PROCESS.

procedure, *n.* **1.** the methods used in investigating, presenting, managing, and deciding legal cases. **2.** Also called **procedural law** or **adjective law.** The body of law that determines which of these methods will be allowed and governs how they will be used: *appellate procedure; California procedure.* Cf. SUBSTANCE (def. 2) **3. administrative procedure,** the body of law applicable to the procedures used by adminstrative agencies in carrying out all of their rulemaking, regulatory, and adjudicative functions **4. civil procedure,** the procedural aspects of a *civil action* (see under ACTION), including principles of jurisdiction, pleading, discovery, conduct of trials, and enforcement of judgments. **5. criminal procedure,** the body of law—much of it based directly on the Constitution—governing all aspects of criminal law enforcement, including not only judicial proceedings but also police procedures and post-sentencing procedures such as probation, imprisonment, and parole.

proceed, *v.* to take action in court; to file or pursue a case: *The tenants voted to proceed against the landlord.*

proceeding, *n.* any matter handled by or filed with a court or administrative tribunal; a case or some aspect of a case.

process, *n.* **1.** a formal document through which a court obtains jurisdiction over a person or property, or compels a person to appear in court or participate in a proceeding; e.g., a SUMMONS, a writ of ATTACHMENT, or a SUBPOENA. See also *service of process* (under SERVICE); ABUSE OF PROCESS **2.** Same as PROCEDURE. The term "process" in this sense is used almost exclusively in connection with the concept of DUE PROCESS.

production of documents, a DISCOVERY procedure in which a party is required, upon request from the other side, to produce potentially relevant DOCUMENTS for inspection and copying.

products liability, **1.** the liability—usually strict liability—of manufacturers for damage caused by defects in their products. In cases dealing with a particular product, sometimes referred to as "product liability." **2.** the area of tort law dealing with such liability. See also *strict liability* (under LIABILITY)

professional corporation (or **association**) See under CORPORATION

proffer, *v.* **1.** to present or put forth for acceptance; to offer. Said especially of evidence, explanation, or argument. *The court excluded the proffered testimony as cumulative. The jury apparently accepted the explanation proffered by the defendant* —*n* **2.** the act of proffering, or the thing proffered. **3.** an OFFER OF PROOF

profit, *n.* **1.** financial gain from an investment, enterprise, or transaction. **2.** Short for **profit à prendre,** *Law French* (lit. "benefit for the taking") **a.** an interest in land owned by another, consisting of a right to take something of value from it; e.g., mining rights, fishing rights, or timber rights **b.** the thing taken pursuant to such a right. Cf EASEMENT

progressive tax. See under TAX.

prohibition, *n.* **1.** a writ by which a court directs a lower court or public agency to cease all proceedings with respect to a particular matter over which it has no jurisdiction. Cf. MANDAMUS. **2.** a ban on manufacture, distribution, and consumption of alcoholic beverages **3.** **Prohibition Amendment,** the Eighteenth Amendment to the United States Constitution, ratified in 1919 and repealed by the Twenty-First Amendment in 1933 (see Appendix)

prohibitory injunction. See under INJUNCTION.

promise, *n.* **1.** a commitment to perform, or refrain from performing, some act in the future. The person who makes a promise is the **promisor;** the person to whom it is made is the **promisee. 2. gratuitous promise,** a promise for which nothing is given or promised in return; e g , "When I die I will leave you my fortune." As many have learned the hard way, most such promises are unenforceable. See also CONSIDERATION **3. illusory promise,** a statement that sounds like a promise but actually promises nothing; e.g., "For $25,000, I will give such assistance to your project as I deem appropriate for one year." Traditionally such promises, and "contracts" based upon them, were unenforceable; the modern trend is to read into them a duty to act in GOOD FAITH and enforce them. —*v* **4.** to make a promise

promissory estoppel. See under ESTOPPEL

promissory note. Same as NOTE[1]

promissory warranty. See under WARRANTY

promoter, *n.* **1.** a person involved in arranging a business transaction or launching a business venture **2.** a person who sets up a corporation.

promoting prostitution, the crime of inducing someone to become a prostitute, soliciting customers for a prostitute, or otherwise assisting in or benefiting from another's prostitution. Also called **pandering.**

proof, *n.* **1.** the persuasive effect of evidence in the mind of a factfinder. **2.** the evidence submitted to establish a fact or support a position. **3.** the presentation of evidence See also *burden of proof* (under BURDEN¹), *prima facie proof* (under PRIMA FACIE;) STANDARD OF PROOF.

proper party. See under PARTY

property, *n.* **1.** a thing, interest, or right that is capable of being owned and, usually, transferred See also ENTITLE-MENT. **2. intangible property,** a property right in something that does not have physical existence, such as a copyright or trademark, a contract right or CHOSE IN ACTION, or an insurance policy or an ownership interest in a corporation (although the documents representing such interests are tangible property) **3. intellectual property,** copyrights, patents, and other rights in creations of the mind; also, the creations themselves, such as a literary work, painting, or computer program **4. personal property,** all property other than *real property;* movable things (including animals in captivity, trees that have been cut down, coal that has been mined) and all intangible property. For historical reasons, a LEASEHOLD interest is often classified as personal property as well, even though it is an interest in land. Also called **personalty.** See also CHATTEL. **5. real property,** an interest in land or things attached to it, including buildings or other structures and substantial vegetation. Also called **realty** or **real estate,** and very often referred to simply as LAND See also FIXTURE. **6. tangible property,** physical property; property you can touch.

property tax, a state or local tax imposed annually on owners of real or personal property within the state or municipality, based upon the value of the property. See also *assessed value* (under ASSESS).

proponent, *n.* one who offers or proposes something, in particular, one who offers or presents evidence in a case, or offers a will for PROBATE

propria persona. See IN PROPRIA PERSONA.

proprietary, *adj.* **1.** pertaining to ownership. *proprietary rights; proprietary interest* **2.** owned by someone; describing something with respect to which a particular person or entity has the right to control use or access· *proprietary drug; proprietary information.*

proprietorship. See SOLE PROPRIETORSHIP.

prosecute, *v.* to pursue a civil or criminal action against someone: *The plaintiff prosecuted her case with vigor. The state prosecuted the young defendant as an adult.*

prosecution, *n* **1.** the act of prosecuting a case. *The prosecution went smoothly.* **2.** the attorney or group of attorneys involved in prosecuting a criminal case, or the party they represent (e g , the STATE or the PEOPLE): *The prosecution moved for a restraining order* **3.** Also called **criminal prosecution.** A criminal case. **4. civil prosecution,** the bringing of a civil case by a private party, particularly under the RACKETEER INFLUENCED AND CORRUPT ORGANIzations Act, to remedy what the party (often a business entity) believes to be illegal conduct (often by a competitor) that has resulted in damage to the plaintiff

prosecutor, *n* **1.** a public official whose job it is to oversee the prosecution of criminal cases in a particular jurisdiction; for example, a county attorney, district attorney, or United States Attorney. **2.** an attorney prosecuting a particular criminal case **3. independent** (or **special**) **prosecutor,** an outside person appointed to investigate and, if necessary, prosecute a case in which there has been an allegation of criminal conduct, when the prosecutor who would normally handle it has a conflict of interest This occurs most commonly in cases of wrongdoing in high state or federal office.

prosecutorial discretion. See under discretion

prospectus, *n* a document prepared by the issuer of a security giving detailed information about the security and the issuer, including information bearing upon the riskiness of the security as an investment Federal regulations determine what information must be included in a prospectus, require it to be accurate, and require the prospectus to be provided to each prospective purchaser of a new security being offered to the public.

prostitution, *n.* the crime of engaging in sexual intercourse or other sexual activity for hire. See also promoting prostitution.

protected person. See under person

protected speech. See under speech

protection order, a court order that one person keep away from another, to protect the other from harassment and threatened harm—a difficult kind of order to enforce, as attested by repeated reports of women murdered by present or former husbands or lovers who had been ordered to stay away. Also called **order of protection.**

protective order, a court order prohibiting a party to a case from engaging in procedures that unnecessarily annoy, burden, or embarrass the adversary. Such orders are usually granted to limit discovery that exceeds the needs of a case

protest, *n.* a formal written statement objecting to some action of another, made to preserve one's rights, lay the groundwork for a suit, and avoid any contention that by not speaking up one in effect consented to the action. See also under protest.

provisional remedy (or **relief**). See under remedy.

proximate cause, in tort cases, wrongful conduct by a defendant leading to the injury complained of in a sufficiently direct way to justify holding the defendant liable for the plaintiff's damages. To recover for a tort, it is not enough to show that the defendant did something wrong and that the plaintiff suffered some injury; it must also be shown that the wrong was a proximate cause of the injury.

proxy, *n.* **1.** an instrument authorizing one person to act on behalf of another, especially by voting or otherwise participating in a meeting **2.** the authority given by such an instrument. **3.** Also called **proxy holder.** The person to whom the instrument and the authority are given

prurient interest, an unacceptable interest in sex. The Supreme Court has said that, for purposes of its current test of OBSCENITY, material appeals to prurient interest if it has "a tendency to excite lustful thoughts," that is, "sexual responses over and beyond those that would be characterized as normal."

public, *adj.* **1.** pertaining, belonging, or available generally to the people of a municipality, a state, or the United States, or to the government on their behalf, rather than to a specific and limited group of persons: *public record* (see under RECORD); *public property; public office.* Cf PRIVATE **2.** occurring in a place open to the public or to public view: *public intoxication; public lewdness* —*n* **3.** the people of a community, state, or nation, collectively

public accommodation, a place offering services to the general public, such as a hotel, restaurant, gas station, or theater. Federal civil rights laws prohibit discrimination on the basis of race, color, religion, or national origin in places of public accommodation

public corporation. See under CORPORATION

public defender, a lawyer whose job is to represent indigent defendants in criminal cases. See also RIGHT TO COUNSEL

public domain, 1. the status of a work or invention upon which the copyright or patent has expired, or which never was protected by a copyright or patent; such a work is said to be "in the public domain" and may be copied or used by anyone. **2.** land owned by the government.

public easement. See under EASEMENT

public figure, a public official or any other individual who has intentionally assumed a prominent role in matters of public importance or interest. In part because such individuals have intentionally subjected themselves to public attention, and in part because of the importance of the First Amendment right to publish facts and opinions on matters of public interest, the law makes it more difficult for public figures than for ordinary people to recover for INVASION OF PRIVACY or DEFAMATION. See also *actual malice* (under MALICE).

public forum, a public place of a sort where people traditionally gather to express views and exchange ideas, such as a park, street, or sidewalk, or which the government has opened to such uses, such as a school that is open after hours for community activities. The Supreme Court has held that the First Amendment (see Appendix) precludes the government from banning speech or assembly in such areas, although the time, place, and manner of such activities can be regulated so long as the regulations do not restrict the content of the speech

public hearing. See under HEARING.

public interest law, an area of legal practice that emphasizes the handling of cases of importance to the public at large rather than just to the individual litigants, such as cases concerning civil rights, the environment, or the political process. A commonly used procedure in such a practice is the *class action* (see under ACTION).

public international law. See under INTERNATIONAL LAW

public necessity. See under NECESSITY.

public nuisance. See under NUISANCE.

public policy, a general concept of public good that colors judicial decisions in every field; in interpreting statutes, extending the common law, and enforcing (or refusing to enforce) private instruments, courts strive to do so in ways that conform to "public policy" as they perceive it. The concept arises particularly in contract law, because for most purposes a contract that violates "public policy" is void. This includes contracts whose performance would be criminal or tortious, and occasionally other contracts that the courts regard as immoral, unconscionable, or otherwise unworthy of enforcement.

public trial. See under TRIAL.

public use. See under USE.

public wrong. See under WRONG

publicly held corporation. See under CORPORATION.

publicly traded stock. See under STOCK.

publish, *v.* **1.** generally, and of a copyrightable work, to make public; to offer or distribute to the general public. See also *service by publication* (under SERVICE). **2.** to communicate a defamatory statement to a person other than the subject of the statement. There is no cause of action for libel or slander if the defamatory statement has not been "published" to a third person. **3.** to declare formally to witnesses that a document one is signing is one's will. "Publishing" one's will to the witnesses who sign it is one of the formalities that the law usually requires in an effort to eliminate disputes after a person is dead over whether a document is in fact her will **4.** to pass an instrument, especially a forged instrument, or present it for payment; to UTTER —**publication,** *n.*

puffing, *n.* conventional sales talk expressing a high opinion of a product but not intended to be taken too literally; for example, "It's a great little car. You won't find a better one. You can't beat the price. I'm sure you'll be completely satisfied." The law does not regard such talk as legally binding. Cf WARRANTY.

punishment. See SENTENCE; CAPITAL PUNISHMENT.

punitive damages. See under DAMAGES

pur autre vie. See *estate* (or *tenancy*) *pur autre vie* (under ESTATE[1]).

purchase, *n* **1.** in the most common usage, to acquire rights or property of any kind, or an interest in property, by promising or giving something in exchange See also GOOD FAITH PURCHASER. **2.** as used in the UNIFORM COMMERCIAL CODE, the term also includes receipt of a negotiable instrument or a gift **3.** in its most general and traditional legal sense, "purchase" means any acquisition of an interest in property other than by INTESTATE SUCCESSION, and thus includes acquisition by gift or by will as well as by giving value

purge, *v.* to remedy a CONTEMPT. For example, after a person has been jailed for refusing to testify in a case despite a court order to do so, she can change her mind and obey the order to testify; this is said to "purge the contempt" or "purge her of the contempt," and secures her release from jail.

purposely, *adv.* with INTENT (def 2)

pursuit of happiness, a phrase from the Declaration of Independence, often erroneously thought to appear in the Constitution. The phrase is often used for rhetorical effect in legal arguments and occasionally appears in judicial opinions, but it has no specific or generally agreed-upon legal meaning.

putative, *adj.* alleged; supposed; seeming: *putative father; putative marriage*

quaere, *Latin.* (lit "You should ask," "you should question") a word used to cast doubt on, or raise a question about, a stated or suggested proposition of law. Pronounced, and now often spelled, the same as the English word **query,** which is derived from this Latin word: *Quaere (or query) the court's statement that a husband can never be guilty of raping his wife. Quaere (or query) whether the decision would have been the same if the husband and wife were separated.*

qualification[1], *n.* **1.** the act of taking those steps required by law to acquire some legally recognized power or status. **2.** a quality required by law for a person or organization to hold a certain status or power. See also BONA FIDE OCCUPATIONAL QUALIFICATION; VOTER QUALIFICATION.

qualification[2], *n.* **1.** a limitation or condition **2.** the process of limiting or imposing a condition.

qualified[1], *adj.* officially recognized as having a certain legal status as a result of possessing the legal qualifications and taking the legally required actions: *qualified pension plan* (see under PENSION PLAN).

qualified[2], *adj* limited, conditional. See *qualified* IMMUNITY, INDORSEMENT, PRIVILEGE under those words.

qualify[1], *v.* **1.** to take the steps required by law to acquire some legally recognized power or status. **2. qualify as an executor,** to post a bond or take such other steps as a state requires before a person designated in a will as an executor may begin managing and distributing the decedent's property. **3. qualify as an expert** (or **expert witness**), to demonstrate to the satisfaction of the court that one has sufficient training and experience to be permitted to express expert opinions on a particular issue in a trial. See also VOIR DIRE (def. 2) **4. qualify for tax-exempt status,** to file necessary documents and obtain certification from the Internal Revenue Service showing that a nonprofit organization is not subject to taxation under the Internal Revenue Code. **5. qualify to do business,** (of a corporation) to register with the Secretary of State of a state other than the state of incorporation, so as to be authorized to do business in the new state

qualify[2], *v.* to limit; place conditions on.

quantum meruit, *Latin.* (lit. "so much as he deserved") **1.** a cause of action for the reasonable value of services rendered, or occasionally of goods or materials provided, under circumstances in which there was no enforceable contract to pay for them but it would be unfair to leave the plaintiff uncompensated. **2.** the measure of recovery in such an action; that is, the reasonable value of the services or goods provided as found by the court. See also QUASI CONTRACT; RESTITUTION; UNJUST ENRICHMENT.

quash, *v.* to nullify a previously issued legal process or order, such as a summons, warrant, or injunction See also SET ASIDE; VACATE

quasi, *Latin* (lit "as if," "a sort of") a word or prefix placed in front of a legal term to mean "resembling, but different from in some legally insignificant respect "

quasi contract, 1. a *contract implied in law* (see under CONTRACT). **2.** a name for any claim for RESTITUTION, particularly a claim in QUANTUM MERUIT

quasi in rem, *Latin* (lit. "as if directed at the thing") describing the fundamental character of a legal proceeding as being, in form, directed at a piece of property, but in substance, directed at the owner of the property For details, see under JURISDICTION[1] and ACTION Cf IN PERSONAM; IN REM

quasi-suspect classification, a law's CLASSIFICATION of people into categories regarded by the Supreme Court as requiring HEIGHTENED SCRUTINY, but not STRICT SCRUTINY, under the EQUAL PROTECTION clause of the Fourteenth Amendment (see Appendix) So far, the only classifications deemed to call for this level of SCRUTINY are those that discriminate on the basis of sex or illegitimacy Cf SUSPECT CLASSIFICATION.

Queen's Bench. See under KING'S BENCH

query, *n* **1.** a question —*v* **2.** to raise a question **3.** to call into question See also QUAERE

question[1], *n* **1.** something asked at a trial, hearing, or deposition, or in investigating an incident or crime Cf INTERROGATORY. **2. argumentative question,** a question that asks a fact witness to agree with an inference or conclusion favorable to the lawyer's case rather than merely eliciting facts This is improper **3. compound question,** a combination of two or more questions into one; for example, "Did she speed through a red light?" instead of "Did she go through a red light? Was she speeding?" Compound questions can be confusing and misleading, and are therefore objectionable. **4. hypothetical question, a.** a question in which a witness is asked to assume certain facts and express an opinion based upon that assumption This is permitted with expert witnesses if the assumed facts are related to the evidence in the case and the opinion sought is within the scope of the witness's expertise, but it is generally not allowed with fact witnesses **b.** such a question as posed by a law professor to law students, to make them think about how slight changes in the facts of a case can alter the legal principles that apply and the legal conclusions that follow; referred to informally as "a **hypothetical.** " See also SOCRATIC METHOD **5. leading question,** a question phrased so as to suggest the desired answer Except for routine preliminary questions intended to introduce a topic, this is generally forbidden in direct examination but allowed in cross examination and in examining a *hostile witness* (see under WITNESS) Examples "What color was the light?" is nonleading; "The light was red, wasn't it?" is leading. "Was the light red?" might be either, depending on the context **6. special questions.** See under VERDICT. —*v.* **7.** to ask questions of anyone *to question a witness; to question a suspect.* Cf. the more specialized terms EXAMINE; INQUIRE; *interrogate* (under INTERROGATION).

question², *n* **1.** Same as ISSUE¹ (see discussion under that word) **2. mixed question of fact and law,** an issue in which facts and law are intertwined; for example, whether the defendant's conduct, as to which witnesses gave varying accounts, was "negligent" as that term is defined in law. In a jury case, such questions are typically submitted to the jury, but with careful instructions from the judge as to the law **3. political question,** an issue that the courts will refuse to decide on the ground that it is of a type committed by the Constitution to the legislative or executive branch of government, rather than the judicial branch **4. question** (or **issue**) **of fact,** a dispute over what circumstances and events have actually occurred or are likely to occur In a jury trial, such questions are submitted to the jury for decision **5. question** (or **issue**) **of law,** an issue concerning interpretation of law These questions are decided by the judge rather than the jury **6. questions presented,** a formal section in an appellate brief or petition, stating the precise issues that the appellate court is being asked to consider See also *constitutional question* (under CONSTITUTIONAL); FEDERAL QUESTION.

qui tam, *Latin* (lit "who both") a civil action brought by a private citizen pursuant to a statute that defines certain conduct as illegal and authorizes private suits against violators to collect a penalty, which is to be divided between the plaintiff (also called the RELATOR) and for the state Thus the relator brings the action both for herself and for the state.

quid pro quo, *Latin.* (lit "What for what?") **1.** an informal expression, used more by nonlawyers than by lawyers, for CONSIDERATION in a contract **2.** something demanded or expected, legally or illegally, in exchange for a favor, concession, or performance; for example, ransom demanded by a kidnapper in exchange for release of the victim, or a favorable vote expected from a corrupt legislator in exchange for a bribe See also *quid pro quo harassment* (under SEXUAL HARASSMENT)

quiet enjoyment, 1. the use and possession of real property free from interference or dispossession by someone with a superior right to the property **2. covenant** (or **warranty**) **of quiet enjoyment,** the express or implied promise of a landlord or grantor of real property that no one with superior title will come along and put the lessee or grantee out of possession Also called **covenant of warranty.**

quiet title, to remove uncertainties about one's title to real property by bringing an action (called an "action to quiet title") against others who may have some claim to the property, challenging them to prove any claim they have or be forever barred from asserting any claim to the property. See also CLOUD ON TITLE.

quit, *v.* to remove oneself from real property; vacate the premises. Cf DISPOSSESS.

quitclaim, *n.* **1.** abandonment of a claim (for example, to land, or against another person), or a document given as evidence of such abandonment. —*v.* **2.** to abandon a claim. See also *quitclaim deed* (under DEED).

quo warranto, *Latin.* (lit. "by what authority") **1.** a judicial proceeding brought by the state to determine whether a person or entity purporting to act in a public capacity has the legal authority to do so. **2.** a writ by which such a proceeding traditionally was commenced, directing the defendant to appear and produce evidence of his authority

quotient verdict. See under VERDICT.

R

®, a symbol used to identify a name or design as a *registered trademark* (see under TRADEMARK) or other MARK registered with the United States Patent and Trademark Office This serves both as an assurance to consumers that the product or service with which the mark is associated is made or provided or approved by the company or organization identified with the mark, and as a warning to other companies that they may not use that mark Cf. TM.

race, *n.* as used in the Constitution and civil rights laws, a term generally applicable to any grouping on the basis of race, ancestry, or ethnicity. As used in the Fifteenth Amendment (see Appendix), the term also includes national origin.

racial discrimination, discrimination on the basis of racial or ethnic identification or ancestry. See also SEPARATE BUT EQUAL; STRICT SCRUTINY.

racially restrictive covenant. See under COVENANT.

Racketeer Influenced and Corrupt Organizations Act (RICO), a federal statute enacted in 1970 and subsequently copied in many state statutes (informally called "Little Rico" statutes), designed to attack organized crime by providing special criminal penalties and civil liabilities for persons who engage in, or derive money from, repeated instances of certain types of crime. The statute permits persons who are injured by such conduct to sue the wrongdoers for *treble damages* (see under DAMAGES); this has provided an opportunity for many plaintiffs, with a little artful pleading, to turn what used to be routine tort claims for fraud into treble damage actions for "racketeering," much to the dismay of mainstream corporate defendants who chafe at being labled as "racketeers."

raise, *v.* **1.** to invoke or bring into being: *to raise a defense; to raise the bar of statute of limitations; circumstances sufficient to raise a presumption of knowledge.* **2.** to increase fraudulently the face amount of a financial instrument: *a raised check.*

ransom, *n.* **1.** money paid to secure the release of a kidnapped person —*v.* **2.** to secure the release of a kidnapped person by paying ransom. See also KIDNAPPING.

rape, *n.* **1.** generally, the crime of forcing or causing a person to submit to sexual intercourse (whether vaginal, oral, or anal) against his or her will, or when consent is obtained by unfair and unlawful means (as by putting a drug in a drink), or under circumstances in which the person is incapable of giving legally valid consent (as with a person who is unconscious or UNDERAGE). The terminology for such offenses, and the exact range of conduct covered by each term used (such as "rape," "sexual imposition," or "sexual assault") varies from state to state. **2. acquaintance rape,** rape by someone known to the victim, such as a friend of the family or a former lover. **3. date rape,** rape by a person with whom the victim is on a date Like *acquaintance rape*, this term was coined to draw attention to the fact that such rapes are more frequent than previously recognized, and traditionally prosecuted less consistently and with less vigor than rapes by strangers **4. marital rape,** rape by one's spouse. Rape has traditionally been regarded as a crime committed by a man against a woman other than his wife. In recent years, many states have eliminated the exception for forced sex with one's wife and made marital rape a crime; the modern view, though not yet universally adopted, is that if one spouse finds the other's refusal to have sex intolerable, the remedy is not force, but divorce. Also called **spousal rape. 5. statutory rape,** the crime of having sexual intercourse, even with consent, with a person (or at least with a female) below the AGE OF CONSENT. In 1981 the Supreme Court held that statutory rape laws may constitutionally discriminate on the basis of sex, upholding the conviction of a 17½-year-old male for having sex with a 16½-year-old female under a statutory rape law that made sexual intercourse by an unmarried couple under the age of 18 a crime for the male but not for the female. See also *strict liability* (under LIABILITY). —*v.* **6.** to commit a rape upon someone.

rape shield law. See under SHIELD LAW.

ratify, *v.* to manifest approval of a previous action by oneself or another so as to make it legally binding. Treaties negotiated by the President must be ratified by the Senate; constitutional amendments adopted by Congress must be ratified by three-quarters of the states; a contract entered into by a party under legal age may be ratified by that party after reaching legal age; a contract entered into on behalf of a principal by an agent who lacked authority to do so may be ratified by the principal. In the contract situations, ratification may be either express (by announcing one's intent to adhere to the contract) or implied (by continuing to perform under the contract or by accepting benefits under it). Cf. AVOID‡. —**ratification,** *n*

rational basis test, the level of SCRUTINY applied to a law whose constitutionality is challenged as a violation of due process when no FUNDAMENTAL RIGHT is at stake, or as a violation of EQUAL PROTECTION when the challenged CLASSIFICATION is not one that the Supreme Court has recognized as meriting HEIGHTENED SCRUTINY or STRICT SCRUTINY Under this test, the Supreme Court has said, "A statutory discrimination will not be set aside if any state of facts reasonably may be conceived to justify it " Findings of unconstitutionality under this test are extremely rare

re, *prep.* regarding; concerning. *Memo to Mr. Smith re year-end inventory.* See also IN RE.

real estate. Same as *real property* (under PROPERTY)

real estate broker. See under BROKER.

real evidence. See under EVIDENCE.

real party in interest. See under PARTY

real property. See under PROPERTY.

realize, *n.* to receive something of value from a transaction, especially from a sale or exchange of property. For income tax purposes, the amount realized includes the money received plus the market value of any property or services received The amount by which this exceeds or falls short of the taxpayer's BASIS in the property transferred is the realized gain or loss. See also RECOGNIZE

realty. Same as *real property* (under PROPERTY)

reargument, *n.* **1.** a second round of argument, or sometimes of briefing and argument, held by a court on a matter previously argued and submitted. Occasionally this is requested by the court because it wants further discussion of certain points before deciding a motion or appeal; more often (but still rarely) it is permitted at the request of the losing party after the matter has been decided, upon a showing that the court may have misunderstood or overlooked an important point Also called **rehearing** or, in cases where the court rendered a decision after its first argument, **reconsideration. 2. reargument** (or **rehearing** or **reconsideration**) **en banc,** reargument before all the judges of a court, of a matter previously heard and decided by a panel of some of them. This is occasionally permitted in matters of particular importance. See also EN BANC.

reasonable, *adj.* **1.** appropriate in view of the circumstances; legally sufficient. *reasonable care* (see under CARE); *reasonable notice; reasonable reliance* (see under RELIANCE). **2.** having a basis in fact or evidence; sensible; not arbitrary and capricious or purely speculative. *reasonable belief; reasonable exercise of discretion.* See also BEYOND A REASONABLE DOUBT **3. reasonable person,** a person of ordinary intelligence and prudence. Traditionally referred to as a **reasonable man,** this is an imaginary person who sets the standard by which the defendant's conduct is evaluated in a negligence case: If a reasonable person would have done the same thing the defendant did in the same situation, then the defendant was not negligent. See also OBJECTIVE TEST

reasonable doubt. See BEYOND A REASONABLE DOUBT.

rebut, *v.* **1.** to present evidence or argument to overcome or weaken the evidence or argument previously presented by an adversary. **2.** to present evidence to overcome a *rebuttable presumption* (see under PRESUMPTION). **—rebuttable,** *adj.*

rebuttal, *n.* **1.** broadly, the presentation of any evidence or argument in response to that of an adversary, or to overcome a PRESUMPTION **2.** specifically, a *rebuttal case* (see under CASE²). **—***adj.* **3.** presented for purposes of rebuttal: *rebuttal case; rebuttal evidence; rebuttal witness.*

recall, *v.* **1.** to vacate a previous order or judgment of the same court, especially because of a factual error. **2.** to call a witness who previously testified in a case back to the stand for further testimony **3.** to remove an elected official from office before expiration of her term, by a special vote of the people.

receive, *v.* to admit into evidence, especially in a nonjury case: *Exhibit 12 will be received.*

receiver, *n.* a person appointed by a court to take over and manage property that is the subject of judicial proceedings—often the property or business of an insolvent debtor—and ultimately to dispose of it in accordance with the court's judgment.

receivership, *n.* a proceeding in which a RECEIVER is appointed to preserve and distribute assets of an insolvent debtor.

receiving stolen property, the crime of receiving, retaining, or disposing of property that one knows was stolen. It includes purchase, fencing, and receipt by gift.

recess, *n.* **1.** a brief break in a trial or hearing: *a 15-minute recess.* **2.** a lengthy period during which a court holds no sessions: *The Supreme Court is in recess from July through September.* —*v.* **3.** to take a recess: *We will recess for the weekend.*

recidivist, *n.* a person who, after being convicted of a crime and serving a sentence or being released, commits the same kind of crime again —**recidivism,** *n.*

reciprocity, *n.* a relationship between two entities, especially two states of the United States, in which each grants certain rights to the other, or to people from the other, in exchange for equivalent rights for itself and its own people. For example, two states might agree to share certain kinds of information with each other, or to allow each other's lawyers to be admitted to their own bar without having to take a second bar examination.

recital, *n.* a formal statement of fact or of a reason or purpose for taking certain action, typically appearing at the beginning of a contract or other instrument and introduced by the word "Whereas." An instrument may have many recitals or none; they are not an operative part of an instrument, but may help in understanding and interpreting it.

recklessness, *n.* conscious disregard of the safety or the rights of others. Sometimes the term is used as just another word for NEGLIGENCE, but usually it signifies a higher degree of culpability. To be negligent, it is enough that one fail to perceive a risk that a reasonably careful person would have perceived; to be reckless is to be aware of a significant risk to others and proceed anyway. But recklessness is a less culpable mental state than KNOWLEDGE, which requires not just awareness of a risk that something bad might happen, but awareness of the near certainty of such an outcome. See also *actual malice* (under MALICE); STATE OF MIND. —**reckless,** *adj.* —**recklessly,** *adv.*

recognizance, *n.* See RELEASE ON OWN RECOGNIZANCE.

recognize, *v.* to include, or be required to include, a gain or loss in one's income tax calculations. Usually a gain or loss is recognized in the year in which it is received (see REALIZE), but in special circumstances a gain may be realized in one year but not recognized until a later year, or perhaps never recognized at all.

recollection, *n* **1.** memory; ability to remember; remembered facts. **2. hypnotically refreshed recollection,** facts supposedly brought forth from a witness's repressed or forgotten memory through hypnosis Since hypnosis is as likely to create a memory as to refresh it, testimony based upon such a procedure is normally inadmissible. But see RECOVERED MEMORY. **3. past recollection recorded,** a written record of an event, prepared or reviewed by a witness while the event was fresh in her mind If the witness can no longer recall the details of the event by the time of the trial, but can recall writing or reviewing that record and for that reason can swear that it is true, then the contents of the writing may be admitted into evidence and read to the jury. Also called **recorded recollection. 4. present recollection refreshed,** facts about an event that a witness at the trial cannot recall when first asked, but can recall when shown something that jogs her memory. Anything at all can be used to refresh a witness's memory, but the most common item is a writing containing the details she could not remember. If after seeing the item as a refresher the witness recalls the details, she can then testify to her recollection. The material used to jog her memory does not come into evidence. Also called **refreshed recollection.**

reconsideration. See under REARGUMENT.

reconsideration en banc. See under REARGUMENT.

record, *n.* **1.** generally, any writing or set of writings setting forth the facts of an event or series of events, made as the events happen or shortly thereafter and intended to be preserved as a reliable account for future reference. **2.** in a judicial or administrative action, **a.** the transcript of a deposition, trial, hearing, or argument. **b.** a full set of the papers, orders, and judgments filed, transcripts made, and evidence offered in a case. **c.** Also called **record on appeal.** those portions of the full record of a case that may be considered by the reviewing court in connection with an appeal. See also DEHORS. **3. business record,** a record made and kept in accordance with the normal practice of a business or organization, from information provided by an individual with personal knowledge of the event recorded. Such records are normally admissible into evidence under a *hearsay exception* (see under HEARSAY). **4. for the record,** describes something said or done, especially in a case, not in the expectation that it will produce any immediate benefit, but in order to preserve a right or argument for the future. **5. make a record,** to say or do something *for the record.* Failure to make a record on an issue may constitute an *implied waiver* (see under WAIVER). **6. of record,** recorded; contained in a record: *attorney of record* (see under ATTORNEY); *owner of record* (see under OWNER). See also *court of record* (under COURT). **7. off the record,** describing informal discussion that the court reporter in a proceeding is requested not to take down. **8. on the record,** describing anything said in a proceeding that is taken down by the court reporter. **9. public record,** any record, investigative report, or compilation of information or data created by a public office or agency pursuant to its legal authority or duties. Such records are usually admitted into evidence under a *hearsay exception* (see under HEARSAY). **10. spread upon the record,** to include something in the record of a case; to make sure something is clear from the record. —*v.* **11.** to make a record of; especially, to file a deed, security agreement, or other instrument creating or transferring an interest in property with a county clerk or other designated public official so as to put the general public on notice of it See also TITLE RECORDING SYSTEM.

record owner. See under OWNER

recorded recollection. Same as *past recollection recorded* (see under RECOLLECTION).

recourse, *n.* **1.** resort or access to a person or thing for help, or the person or thing resorted to. **2.** the right to receive payment on a negotiable instrument from the drawer or any previous indorser if the instrument is dishonored. For example, if A draws a check payable to the order of B, who indorses it to the order of C, and the check bounces when C deposits it, C ordinarily has a right of recourse against A and B. A negotiable instrument confers no such liability upon a drawer or indorser who adds the words "without recourse" to her signature; the instrument is then a NONRECOURSE instrument and subsequent holders are said to take it **without recourse. 3.** the right to repayment of a loan from the borrower personally, out of any available assets she has. If a secured loan is made with the understanding that in the event of default the lender will look only to the collateral (see COLLATERAL¹) or to the GUARANTOR or SURETY for compensation, it is a NONRECOURSE loan.

recover, *v.* to obtain through litigation—usually by way of judgment, but sometimes through settlement; usually money or property, but sometimes other relief; usually compensation for what has been lost, but sometimes punitive damages: *Plaintiff A recovered $1,000 in a settlement; plaintiff B went to trial and recovered a judgment for $1,000 actual damages, $10,000 punitive damages, and injunctive relief.* —**recoverable,** *adj.* —**recovery,** *n.*

recovered memory, the theory that a victim's entire memory of systematic, long-term physical and sexual abuse during childhood can be repressed for many years and then "recovered" in adulthood. Although there is as yet no scientific evidence that this can happen, and the techniques by which such material is recovered often have much in common with hypnosis (see *hypnotically refreshed recollection,* under RECOLLECTION), in recent years recovered memory has been a popular basis for legal actions and has been admitted into evidence in some courts.

recross or **redirect examination.** See under EXAMINATION.

recuse, *v.* to remove oneself from participation in a matter because of an actual or apparent CONFLICT OF INTEREST. Said especially of judges. —**recusal,** *n.*

redact, *v* to cover up or white out portions of a document; for example, to delete nondiscoverable information from a document being produced in DISCOVERY

redeem, *v.* **1.** to buy back or reacquire; especially, to re-acquire property pledged as security for a loan by repaying the loan, or to extinguish a bond or other debt instrument by payment in accordance with its terms See also *redeemable security* (under SECURITY²) **2.** to turn in a bond or other certificate for cash or property in accordance with its terms. —**redeemable,** *adj.* —**redemption,** *n.*

redirect or **redirect examination.** See under EXAMINATION.

redlining, *n.* refusal by a financial institution to make mortgage loans on property in certain neighborhoods. Redlining is an illegal discriminatory practice.

reentry, *n.* taking back possession of real property pursuant to a right reserved when possession was transferred to someone else, as in a lease

referee, *n.* a MASTER to whom a court refers a case for certain purposes, especially for the taking of testimony and reporting of proposed findings of fact

referendum, *n.* a procedure existing in most states by which certain proposed statutes or constitutional amendments may or must be put to a vote of the people before becoming effective In some states, a statute adopted by the legislature must also be put to such a vote if a certain number of citizens sign a petition requesting it.

reform, *n.* **1.** a change or proposed change in the law regarded by its proponents as an improvement Since people never propose changes that they regard as detrimental, all proposed change is called "reform " Unfortunately, calling something an improvement does not always mean that it *is* an improvement —*v* **2.** to bring about a reform of: *The bill reforms the rules of civil procedure* **3.** to effect a REFORMATION of. *Plaintiff asks the court to reform the contract.*

reformation, *n.* **1.** judicially ordered interpretation or rewriting of a written instrument, usually a contract, which through fraud, mistake, or other circumstances failed to reflect the actual intent or agreement of the parties, so as to make it reflect what was originally intended or agreed upon. **2.** a proceeding or decree by which reformation is accomplished.

refresh, *v.* to jog memory See also *refreshed recollection* or *present recollection refreshed* (under RECOLLECTION)

register, *n.* **1.** an official list, file, or record, such as a corporation's list of stockholders or a municipality's list of eligible voters. **2.** the official who maintains such records —*v.* **3.** to cause to be listed in such a record

registered trademark. See under TRADEMARK.

registration statement, a statement containing detailed information about the issuer of a security and the security itself, which in most cases must be filed with the federal Securities and Exchange Commission before a security can be issued to the public

regressive tax. See under TAX

regular, *adj.* **1.** normal, usual, customary **2.** in conformity, or apparently in conformity, with law, particularly with legal requirements as to form; not such as would arouse suspicion *The check was regular on its face.*

regular course of business. Same as ORDINARY COURSE OF BUSINESS.

regulation, *n.* **1.** a directive adopted by an administrative agency, either for its own internal procedures or to govern public behavior in matters over which it has authority, and having the force of law *income tax regulations, regulations of the city Department of Buildings.* See also RULE; rule-making. **2.** broadly, any rule or statute, or the act of controlling or attempting to control conduct by rules and laws.

regulatory agency, an ADMINISTRATIVE AGENCY to which Congress or a legislature has delegated the power to adopt regulations governing public conduct; e.g., the federal Food and Drug Administration, a state Department of Motor Vehicles.

regulatory taking. See under TAKING

rehabilitation, *n* **1.** questioning of a witness or introduction of evidence designed to restore the credibility of a witness whose credibility has been attacked. Cf IMPEACHMENT **2.** resolving an insolvent debtor's financial situation in bankruptcy court, especially through a *Chapter 13 bankruptcy* proceeding (see under BANKRUPTCY). —**rehabilitate,** *v.*

rehearing or **rehearing en banc.** See under REARGUMENT.

reinsurance, *n.* insurance purchased by one insurance company from another, under which the second company agrees to cover all or part of a risk insured by the first company.

relation, *n.* See *on the relation of* (under EX REL.).

relation back, the principle applied in various situations under which an act is deemed effective as of a date earlier than when it actually took place For example, a new claim added in an amended complaint but arising from the same events that are the subject of the original complaint "relates back" to the date of the original complaint, so that expiration of the statute of limitations during the period between the two pleadings does not operate to bar the claim.

relator, *n.* person at whose request, or for whose benefit, certain kinds of actions are brought. See also EX REL.; QUI TAM.

release, *n.* **1.** the relieving of another person from an obligation or liability, or alleged obligation or liability, to oneself; the formal, permanent abandonment of a claim. **2.** a formal document embodying such a release, given to the person being released. When a case is settled, it is usual for the parties to exchange **mutual releases** whereby each assures the other that no further claim will be asserted with respect to the matter being settled Often a release given in connection with a settlement is a **general release,** which bars any claim by the releasor against the releasee in connection with anything that has happened "from the beginning of time to the date of this release." —*v.* **3.** to give someone a release.

release on own recognizance (ROR), pretrial release of a criminal defendant upon his promise to appear in court as needed, without any requirement of bail. Also called **release on personal recognizance.**

relevant, *adj.* tending to make the existence of a fact that is of consequence in a case more probable or less probable. Relevant evidence includes evidence bearing on the credibility of a witness. Evidence must be relevant to be admissible at a trial, but even relevant evidence may be excluded by the rules of evidence (see, for example, HEARSAY; *testimonial privilege,* under PRIVILEGE) or as a matter of judicial discretion (see, for example, *cumulative evidence,* under EVIDENCE; PREJUDICIAL EFFECT). —**relevance,** *n.*

reliance, *n.* **1.** the taking of or failure to take some action because of trust in what someone else has said or done. Reliance is an element of certain causes of action, such as FRAUD and PROMISSORY ESTOPPEL. **2. detrimental reliance,** reliance that results in a loss; an expenditure of time, effort, or money; or a change for the worse in one's legal position. **3. reasonable reliance,** conduct such as a reasonable person might have undertaken under the circumstances in light of another's words or actions. To support a claim for fraud or promissory estoppel, reliance must have been reasonable and detrimental.

relief, *n.* **1.** the remedy or totality of remedies sought or awarded in a proceeding. See discussion and additional entries under REMEDY. **2. affirmative relief, a.** relief awarded to a plaintiff beyond payment of damages, especially relief that requires the defendant to perform some specific action. **b.** any relief granted to a defendant against a plaintiff beyond simple dismissal of the plaintiff's case. **3. specific relief,** any type of *equitable remedy* (see under REMEDY) that requires a party to take specified steps or that affects interests in specified property; for example, a judgment ordering *specific restitution* (see under RESTITUTION) or SPECIFIC PERFORMANCE.

religion. See FREEDOM OF RELIGION.

rem. See IN REM.

remainder, *n.* **1.** the *future estate* (see under ESTATE[1]) created by a GIFT OVER of the balance of an estate in connection with a transfer of an estate of shorter duration, as when the owner of a fee grants a life estate in the property to A and the remainder to B. Cf. REVERSION. **2.** a right to receive trust property upon expiration of the trust, as when a will specifies that certain assets are to be held in trust with the income to be used for the benefit of the testator's children until they reach the age of 21, then given to a particular charity. The charity has a remainder interest in the trust assets.

remand, *v.* **1.** to send a case back from an appellate court to the lower court from which it was appealed, for further proceedings in accordance with the appellate court's instructions. **2.** to send a criminal defendant back into custody. —*n.* **3.** the act of remanding or the state of being remanded. A case in a lower court after remand is said to be "on remand."

remedy, *n.* **1.** redress sought from or awarded by a court; any type of judgment that can be issued by a court in a civil action. Before the MERGER OF LAW AND EQUITY, the conventional terminology was "a remedy at law" or "relief in equity." Now the terms "remedy" and "relief" are largely interchangeable, although the former is more often used in reference to damages and the latter in reference to other kinds of relief. In addition, one uses "a" or "the" with "remedy," but not with "relief." See also RELIEF. **2.** a right of action or a procedure for obtaining satisfaction of a claim or grievance: *If the car payments are not kept up, the lender has a remedy either in court or through repossessing the car.* **3. adequate remedy at law,** a *legal remedy* (almost always damages) that the law deems sufficient to compensate a plaintiff, making an *equitable remedy* (such as specific performance) unnecessary **4. equitable remedy** (or **relief**), relief of a type traditionally available only in courts of EQUITY, such as SPECIFIC PERFORMANCE, an INJUNCTION, or REFORMATION or a contract. Also called **relief in equity.** Cf. *legal remedy.* **5. extraordinary remedy** (or **relief**), relief of a sort traditionally available only by *extraordinary writ* (see under WRIT). **6. legal remedy** (or **relief**), a remedy of a type traditionally available in the law courts (rather than the equity courts), the most common of which is DAMAGES. Also called **remedy at law.** See LAW (def. 4). Cf. *equitable remedy.* **7. provisional** (or **temporary**) **remedy** (or **relief**), an order issued during the course of an action to protect the interests of a party while the action proceeds; e.g., a *preliminary injunction* (see under INJUNCTION), temporary alimony, or appointment of a RECEIVER.

remittitur, *Latin.* (lit. "it is given back") an order reducing the amount of damages awarded by a jury. If the plaintiff does not accept the reduced amount, the defendant will be granted a new trial. Cf. ADDITUR.

remove, *v.* **1.** to move or transfer a person or thing; to change the location of: *to remove a person from office; to remove property from the state.* **2.** to take away; to eliminate. *to remove a cloud on title* **3.** to transfer a case from one court to another; especially, to transfer a case, upon motion of the defendant, from a state court to a federal court of appropriate jurisdiction. —**removal,** *n.*

render, *v.* **1.** to issue or announce: *render a judgment; render a verdict.* **2.** to give or perform: *render payment; render the performance called for by the contract.* —**rendition,** *n.*

renew, *v.* **1.** to begin again: *renew a lease; renew a contract.* **2.** to repeat or revive a request previously denied, in light of subsequent developments: *renew a motion; renew an objection.* —**renewal,** *n.*

renounce, *v.* **1.** to give up a right, interest, or claim **2.** to abandon a criminal enterprise voluntarily and absolutely, before the crime is committed. In some jurisdictions renunciation is an affirmative defense to a criminal charge of ATTEMPT, SOLICITATION, or the like —**renunciation,** *n.*

reorganization, *n.* **1.** Also called **corporate reorganization.** Any substantial restructuring of a corporation's financial structure. **2.** Also called **bankruptcy reorganization.** The restructuring, and usually reduction, of a corporation's debt in a *Chapter 11 bankruptcy* proceeding (see under BANKRUPTCY).

reorganization plan. See under BANKRUPTCY.

repeal, *n.* the nullification of a statute, constitutional provision, or regulation by subsequent enactment. Usually the subsequent enactment explicitly states that the earlier is repealed (**express repeal**), but sometimes the earlier provision is regarded as null simply because the later enactment is inconsistent with it (**implied repeal**).

repeat offender, **1.** a person convicted more than once of the same kind of offense. Many laws and regulations provide more severe penalties for a second or third violation. **2.** a person convicted more than once of different crimes. See also HABITUAL CRIMINAL; THREE STRIKES LAW.

replevin, *n.* **1.** an action to recover possession of tangible personal property wrongfully withheld by another. **2.** to return goods to a prior possessor who seeks them in an action for replevin.

replevy, *v.* to recover goods by means of an action of REPLEVIN.

reply, *n.* **1.** a plaintiff's PLEADING in response to a COUNTERCLAIM asserted by the defendant. A reply to a counterclaim is exactly like an ANSWER to a complaint. **2.** generally, any response to an adversary's submission in opposition to one's own motion, argument, or appeal in a case. See, for example, *reply brief* (under BRIEF). —*v.* **3.** to make or serve a reply.

report, *n.* **1.** a written account of something based upon the writer's observation, investigation, or analysis: *a master's report; a police report.* **2. reports,** a published compilation of opinions of a particular court, agency, or set of courts, usually in an unending succession of volumes Sometimes called a **reporter.** A **reported opinion** (**case, decision,** etc.) is one that has thus been published. Cf. SLIP OPINION. —*v.* **3.** to issue a report. See also *hear and report* (under HEAR).

reporter, *n.* **1.** a person, sometimes a court official, who compiles and supervises publication of the decisions of a court or set of courts. **2.** the *reports* (see under REPORT) so published. **3.** a COURT REPORTER.

repossess, *v.* to take back property in which one has retained a security interest upon failure of the buyer to keep up with the payments. —**repossession,** *n.*

represent, *v.* **1.** to act on behalf of another or take over the position of another in a matter: *The lawyer represents the client. The executor represents the decedent.* **2.** to assert as a fact, particularly in a context in which others may rely upon the assertion: *Counsel represented to the court that her client was on his way. The seller represented that the paint contained no lead.*

representation, *n.* **1.** the act of representing or state of being represented. **2.** words or conduct amounting to an assertion of fact, particularly one that others may rely upon. See also FRAUD.

reprieve, *n.* **1.** the postponement of execution of a criminal sentence by executive order The classic situation for a reprieve occurs when a person is about to be put to death for a capital crime; a reprieve does not necessarily mean that the prisoner will not be executed, but it does give her some extra time to make arguments. See also *stay of execution* (under STAY). **2.** the document in which a reprieve is granted. —*v.* **3.** to grant a reprieve to someone. Cf. COMMUTE; PARDON. See also CLEMENCY

republican form of government. See under GOVERNMENT.

repudiation, *n.* **1.** refusal to carry out a duty, or denial that a duty exists. Repudiation may be rightful or wrongful, depending upon the circumstances. **2.** especially, refusal to perform, or to continue performing, a contract. If a party repudiates a contract before any performance is due, that may be called *anticipatory repudiation* (see under BREACH).

request for admissions. See under ADMISSION.

requests for instructions, a party's list of proposed instructions for the jury, with citations to authority, usually submitted to the judge shortly before the end of the case. Also called **requests to charge.** See also INSTRUCTION.

res, *n., pl.* **res.** *Latin.* (lit. "thing," "matter," "property," "case") **1.** generally, a matter under discussion: *Whether property can be taxed by a state or seized by a sheriff depends upon the location of the res.* **2.** the tangible or intangible property or relationship that is the subject of an IN REM or QUASI IN REM action. **3.** the CORPUS of a trust; the property of a trust or estate.

res gestae, *Latin.* (lit. "things done," "deeds," "exploits") an entire occurrence that is the subject of a legal action, including particularly the words spoken by participants and bystanders. The concept of res gestae is a traditional exception to the *hearsay rule* (see under HEARSAY), on the theory that the jury is entitled to learn about the entire event in dispute, including words as well as actions. Modern rules of evidence shun the term as vague, and substitute such concepts as PRESENT SENSE IMPRESSION and EXCITED UTTERANCE

res ipsa loquitur, *Latin* (lit. "the thing itself speaks," "the situation speaks for itself") the doctrine that the plaintiff in a negligence case need not show exactly how the defendant caused an accident if the accident was of a type that normally could not have occurred but for some negligence by the defendant. For example, if a sponge was left in the plaintiff's body after surgery, the plaintiff can prevail in a malpractice case against the surgeon even though the plaintiff cannot describe how the incident happened, because "the thing speaks for itself." Such a case is said to be a res ipsa loquitur case, or "res ipsa case" for short.

res judicata, *Latin.* (lit "an adjudicated matter," "a decided case") the doctrine that prevents relitigation of a claim that has been fully considered and finally decided in the courts.

rescission, *n.* the cancellation of a contract and restoration of the parties to the positions they held before the contract was made. Rescission may be agreed to by the parties or sought in a judicial action as an equitable remedy when a contract was entered into as a result of fraud, mutual mistake, or the like —**rescind,** *v*

reserve, *v.* **1.** to retain specified rights or interests in a transaction otherwise disposing of property or rights **2.** to set aside funds for a particular purpose or contingency. **3.** to withhold for the time being; specifically, a judge or panel that does not rule from the bench upon a matter that has been argued is said to "reserve decision" or "reserve judgment." —*n.* **4.** a fund set aside for a particular purpose or for future contingencies

reserved power. See under POWER.

residence, *n.* **1.** in some contexts, same as DOMICILE. **2.** usually, any place where one has a home, even if one's domicile is elsewhere.

residency, *n.* **1.** the state of being a RESIDENT—that is, of having a residence or domicile within a jurisdiction **2. residency requirement, a.** any legal requirement that a person have a residence or domicile within a particular state or local jurisdiction in order to vote, hold office, hold public employment, or receive public benefits in that jurisdiction. **b.** a state or municipal regulation that denies certain benefits or status, such as welfare or voting rights, to newcomers until they have resided within the jurisdiction for a specified length of time. Many such waiting periods have been struck down as unconstitutional infringements on the RIGHT TO TRAVEL. Also called **waiting period.**

resident, *n.* one who has a RESIDENCE, or sometimes his DOMICILE, in a specified place: *a noted resident of Newport, Palm Beach, Aspen, and Monte Carlo, domiciled in Monaco.* See also *resident alien* (under ALIEN)

residuary bequest (or **legacy**). See under BEQUEST

residuary estate. See under ESTATE*¹*

residuary legatee. See under LEGATEE.

residue, *n.* Same as *residuary estate* (see under ESTATE*¹*)

resolution, *n.* an expression of sentiment or opinion adopted by vote of a legislative body, not having the force of law.

respondeat superior, *Latin.* (lit "let the superior answer") the doctrine that an employer is liable for the torts of an employee acting within the SCOPE OF EMPLOYMENT, and in many situations a principal of any kind is liable for the torts of an agent arising from conduct within the agent's SCOPE OF AUTHORITY See also *vicarious liability* (under LIABILITY)

respondent, *n.* the name given in certain situations to the party who must respond to a procedural step in a case, such as a petition, motion, or appeal. In the case of an appeal, some courts use the term "respondent" and others APPELLEE.

responsive, *adj* **1.** describing papers, evidence, or argument offered in answer or opposition to something submitted by an adversary *responsive pleading; responsive brief.* **2.** describing a witness's answer to a lawyer's question that gives the information requested rather than avoiding the question or adding unsolicited information See discussion under NONRESPONSIVE

restitution, *n* **1.** any remedy or order for the prevention of UNJUST ENRICHMENT, usually involving the defendant's giving up some benefit that in justice should have gone to the plaintiff or paying for some benefit received from the plaintiff. It may also involve giving back some piece of property (**specific restitution**), or other forms of relief tailored to the case at hand **2.** in criminal law, giving back ill-gotten gains or paying for property damage as part of one's sentence, as a condition of probation, or as part of a plea bargain

restraining order, 1. an INJUNCTION that prohibits someone from taking some action **2. temporary restraining order (TRO),** an injunction granted for a very short time, just to keep things as they are until a hearing can be held to determine whether it would be appropriate to issue a *preliminary injunction* (see under INJUNCTION) A TRO may be granted EX PARTE to avoid tipping off the person to whom it is directed and thus giving that person a chance to hurry up and do the act in question before being ordered not to.

restraint of trade. See UNREASONABLE RESTRAINT OF TRADE

restraint on alienation, 1. a provision in an instrument transferring land which forbids the taker from subsequently transferring the land to anyone else Such provisions are usually unenforceable **2.** the practical effect of a transfer creating interests in land that may or may not vest for many years to come, making the future status of the land so uncertain that the property is unlikely to be marketable. A primary purpose of the *rule against perpetuities* (see under PERPETUITY) is to limit such de facto restraints on alienation.

restricted stock. See under STOCK

restrictive covenant. See under COVENANT.

restrictive indorsement. See under INDORSEMENT

resulting trust. See under TRUST

retainer, *n.* **1.** the act of contracting for someone's services—especially a lawyer's—or the fact of being so retained. **2.** an initial fee paid to a lawyer upon being re-

balance, as when the owner of a fee simple absolute conveys a life estate or a one-year tenant conveys the property to another for one week. Cf. REMAINDER.

reverter, *n.* See POSSIBILITY OF REVERTER.

review, *n.* **1.** Also called **appellate review.** examination of the proceedings and decision in a court case by a higher court or, in an administrative matter, by a court or a higher authority or tribunal within the same agency, to determine if the result should be affirmed. **2. administrative review,** review of an administrative decision, especially by a higher authority or tribunal within the agency itself. **3. de novo review,** review in which the reviewing court or authority may completely disregard the findings of the original factfinder and draw its own conclusions from the evidence See also DE NOVO. **4. judicial review, a.** the power of the courts to declare laws unconstitutional. **b.** review by a court of an administrative decision. See also SCOPE OF REVIEW; STANDARD OF REVIEW. Cf LAW REVIEW.

revoke, *v.* **1.** to nullify something one has done: *revoke a will; revoke an offer of contract.* **2.** to take away a previously granted right or privilege by judicial or administrative action: *revoke a driver's license; revoke parole.* —**revocable,** *adj.* —**revocation,** *n.*

RICO. See RACKETEER INFLUENCED AND CORRUPT ORGANIZATIONS ACT.

rider, *n.* a separate sheet of paper or set of pages containing one or more additions or amendments to a legal document such as a contract or an insurance policy, attached to and intended to be read as if integrated with the main document. See also CODICIL.

right, *n.* **1.** a freedom, interest, power, protection, or immunity to which a person is entitled by reason of law, and for which one ordinarily may look to the government, and particularly the courts, for protection, enforcement, or, if a violation has already occurred, compensation or other remedy. **2.** a term used by advocates to describe something that they believe should be a legally protected right, or that they claim as a right even if the law is otherwise. **3. constitutional right,** a right protected by a constitution; unless the context clearly indicates otherwise, the constitution referred to is that of the United States. See also FREEDOM; LIBERTY; FUNDAMENTAL RIGHT. **4. equitable right,** a right or interest of a *beneficial owner* of property (see under OWNER), or a right for the violation of which one would be entitled to *equitable relief* (see under REMEDY). **5. legal right, a.** broadly, any right protected by law; same as def 1 above. **b.** in a narrow sense, a right or interest of a *legal owner* of property (see under OWNER), or a right for the violation of which one would be entitled to a *legal remedy* (see under REMEDY). **6. vested right, a.** a VESTED property interest. **b.** in constitutional law, a contract right that cannot be interfered with by a state, a property right that cannot be taken away by the government without just compensation, or an ENTITLEMENT. See also BILL OF RIGHTS; CIVIL RIGHTS; VICTIMS' RIGHTS.

right of action, 1. a right to sue; a CAUSE OF ACTION or *claim for relief* (see under CLAIM). **2. private right of action,** a right to sue for damages caused by another's violation of a criminal or regulatory law. A statute outlawing certain conduct may expressly provide that persons injured by such conduct may sue the violator for damages. In the absence of language expressly creating such a right, under traditional principles of tort law an **implied right of action** nevertheless exists under a statute or regulation that was designed to protect people in certain situations from a certain kind of harm, if the defendant's violation in fact caused such harm

right of (or **to**) **privacy, 1.** in tort law, the complex of interests protected by the tort of INVASION OF PRIVACY. **2.** under the federal Privacy Act and similar state statutes, the right to have personal information that is on file with the government kept confidential and used only for authorized purposes. **3.** in constitutional law, **a.** the Fourth Amendment right to be free from unreasonable searches and seizures by the government, which the Supreme Court has held applicable in any area or situation in which the target would have a reasonable "expectation of privacy." **b.** the limited right to make decisions about marriage and procreation, including contraception and abortion, free from government interference, which the Supreme Court has found to be included in the concept of LIBERTY protected by the Fourteenth Amendment. The Court has been reluctant to expand this right to other areas of personal decision making and conduct; for example, under recent rulings the government still has the right to specify what sexual acts consenting adults may legally engage in in private. See also *substantive due process* (under DUE PROCESS); SODOMY.

right of survivorship, the characteristic of JOINT ownership of property (as distinguished from ownership IN COMMON) whereby, upon the death of any co-owner, that owner's interest passes automatically to the surviving owners, until finally the last survivor owns the entire property alone.

right to bear arms, a popular phrase taken from the Second Amendment, which states· "A well regulated Militia, being necessary to the security of a free State, the right of the people to keep and bear Arms, shall not be infringed." This amendment applies only to the federal government, and so is not a hindrance to state or local GUN CONTROL legislation. Since Congress has never enacted significant restrictions on gun ownership, the potential effect of the Second Amendment at the federal level remains a matter of debate. The Supreme Court's few comments on the amendment, however, suggest that the right to bear arms may extend only so far as necessary to enable the government to maintain a well regulated MILITIA.

right to counsel, the right of a criminal defendant to have a lawyer, guaranteed by the Sixth Amendment (see Appendix). It includes the right to have a lawyer present at any significant step of a criminal prosecution, including custodial questioning, plea bargaining, and lineups; the right to a lawyer at government expense if the defendant cannot afford one; and the right of a mentally competent defendant to represent himself. It also includes the right to a lawyer with some minimal level of professional competence, for which reason it is also called the **right to effective assistance of counsel.** The right does not extend to civil cases.

right to die, a phrase of varying scope, referring at a minimum to the right of a competent adult to refuse medical care that would prolong life, which is generally recognized by law, and at a maximum to a purported right to *physician-assisted suicide* (see under SUICIDE), which is generally not recognized in the United States. The Supreme Court has yet to find any such right in the Constitution. See also HEALTH CARE PROXY; LIVING WILL.

right to travel, the constitutional right of Americans to travel freely from state to state and somewhat less freely to foreign countries. The right of interstate travel includes not only the right to go to another state, but also the right of a newcomer to a state to be treated equally with those already there. The right of foreign travel can be restricted to some extent on national security or foreign policy grounds. See also FUNDAMENTAL RIGHT; *residency requirement* (under RESIDENCY).

right to work laws, anti-union legislation enacted in many states, protecting the right of workers to gain and keep employment without joining or contributing to a union.

ripe, *adj.* (of a case) ready for the next procedural step: *ripe for decision; ripe for review.* Under the doctrine of **ripeness,** a court may decline to entertain a case that it feels is still speculative and has not "matured" into a real controversy, as when a plaintiff seeks to challenge the constitutionality of a law on the ground that it might be used against her when it has not yet been used in that way.

risk, *n.* **1.** the potential injury or loss covered by an insurance policy. **2.** any possibility of harm or loss. See also ASSUMPTION OF RISK.

risk of nonpersuasion. Same as *burden of persuasion* (see under BURDEN[1]).

robbery, *n.* the crime of taking someone's money or other personal property from the victim's person or in the victim's presence by force or threat of imminent harm. Robbery is essentially LARCENY with the added factor of personal danger. In general, the kinds of threat that suffice as an element of robbery are threat of imminent bodily harm to the victim or to another, or threat to destroy the victim's home (but not other property).

robing room, a room just off a courtroom, where the judge can put on and take off the robe worn on the bench, meet with clerks or study papers during breaks in the proceedings, or meet with the lawyers out of public hearing and without the formality of a courtroom.

royalty, *n.* **1.** a sum paid to the creator of a copyrighted work or the inventor of a patented invention, or to the holder of a copyright or patent, for the right to exploit the creation. Such royalties are usually based on the number of units sold, such as copies of a book or units of machinery **2.** a sum paid to the owner of land for the privilege of extracting oil, gas, or minerals, based on the number of barrels, tons, or other units extracted

rule, *n.* **1.** any of a set of principles and directives formally adopted by or imposed upon a body for its own administration, the governance of its members, or the guidance of those dealing with it. **2.** especially, a regulation governing procedures in the courts: *rules of civil procedure; rules of criminal procedure; rules of appellate procedure; rules of evidence.* In addition to such generally applicable bodies of law, every court has a set of its own rules (**court rules, rules of court,** or, especially in the federal district courts, **local rules**) detailing how matters in that court are to be presented and handled **3.** an administrative REGULATION. **4.** a legal principle, especially one of common law; e.g., the *rule against perpetuities* (see under PERPETUITY). **5.** an old word for a court order. —*v.* **6.** to decide an issue in a case; to issue a RULING: *The court will rule on our motion after lunch.*

rule against perpetuities. See under PERPETUITY

rulemaking, *n.* the enactment by an administrative agency of REGULATIONS governing conduct in those industries or areas of activity over which it has authority; the LEGISLATIVE function of an administrative agency.

ruling, *n.* a judicial or administrative decision or order

running covenant. See under COVENANT

S

/s/ or **s/,** signed; a symbol sometimes placed before the name of the signer of a document on a copy of the document, or put on the copy in place of the signer's name, to make it clear that the original (but not the copy) was actually signed by that person. For example, this symbol typically appears before the judge's name on the signature line of a CONFORMED COPY of an order signed by the judge.

S corporation. See under CORPORATION

safe harbor, in a statute or regulation governing some activity (usually a business activity) in broad terms, a provision setting forth specific steps that, if taken, will guarantee that one is in compliance with the law The safe harbor is not the only way to comply, but if followed it eliminates all doubt about whether one is in compliance.

said, *adj.* previously referred to; mentioned above; aforesaid: *Said defendant there and then took said gun and shot said victim.* Though still common in formal documents such as wills and indictments, this classic mark of the lawyer is now generally recognized as completely unnecessary: *The defendant then shot the victim with the gun.*

sale, *n.* **1.** a transfer of title to property for money or its equivalent, or a contract for such a transfer See also BILL OF SALE; BOILER ROOM SALES. Cf. BARTER. **2. sales,** income received from the sale of goods: *The company had sales of $350,000 last year.* **3. judicial sale,** a sale of property ordered by a court, either to satisfy a debt of the owner or to effect a PARTITION of the property. **4. sale and lease-back,** a contract in which one party buys property from the other and simultaneously agrees to rent it back to the seller for a period of time; in effect, the buyer is lending money to the seller and holding title to the property as security for repayment, which is made in the form of "rent." **5. tax sale,** a *judicial sale* of property to satisfy back taxes. **6. wash sale,** a sale, especially of stocks or bonds, entered into at about the same time as a purchase of the same thing, leaving the seller in the same position as if the transactions had never occurred. Tax law prohibits the taking of tax benefits from such a transaction, and the securities laws prohibit such transactions as a means of creating a false impression of market activity.

sales tax, a tax imposed by many states and municipalities on purchasers of goods and services, consisting of a fixed percentage added to the selling price in each retail transaction. It is a *regressive tax* (see under TAX), since people with modest incomes must spend proportionately more of their income on taxable goods and services, and have proportionately less left over for investments that are not subject to sales tax, than people with high incomes

sanction, *v* **1.** occasionally, to manifest approval of something, either in advance or after the fact: *The court* *sanctioned the defendant's conduct* (i.e , approved of it). **2.** usually, to punish someone or impose a punishment for something: *The court sanctioned the defendant's conduct* (i e., imposed a penalty for it); *the court sanctioned the defendant* (i.e , punished her). —*n.* **3.** permission or approval. **4.** penalty or punishment. **5.** Often, **sanctions.** punitive measures taken by one or more countries toward another to force it to comply with international law.

satisfaction, *n.* **1.** full performance of an obligation; especially, payment of a debt in full: *satisfaction of a mortgage; satisfaction of a judgment.* **2.** discharge of an obligation or undertaking by a performance or payment accepted in lieu of what was originally contemplated or agreed to· *satisfaction of a legacy by transfer of the property to the legatee prior to the testator's death.* **3.** a document or notation by an obligee that an obligation, especially a judgment, has been satisfied. **4.** fulfillment of a description, requirement, or set of requirements. See also *accord and satisfaction* (under ACCORD). —**satisfy,** *v.*

save harmless. See under HARMLESS.

saving clause, 1. in a legislative enactment that repeals a previous statute, a clause that continues the previous law's effectiveness for certain purposes, such as for purposes of any lawsuit initiated prior to the effective date of the repeal. **2.** Also called **separability clause** or **severability clause.** a clause in a statute or contract providing that if any part of the statute or contract is found to be void or unenforceable, that part will be carved out and the balance enforced to the extent possible.

scienter, *Latin.* (lit. "knowingly") guilty knowledge; in a fraud case, the element of intent to defraud, or knowledge of the falsity of one's representations. The term is used particularly in connection with SECURITIES FRAUD.

scope of authority, the range of an agent's duties or permitted activities on behalf of a principal The principal is normally bound by and liable for the acts of an agent within the scope of the agent's *actual* or *apparent authority* (see under AUTHORITY¹). Also called **scope of agency.** See also RESPONDEAT SUPERIOR.

scope of employment, any job-related activity by an employee. The employer is normally liable for torts committed by an employee acting within the scope of employment, as when a company driver causes an accident while making a delivery. See also RESPONDEAT SUPERIOR. Cf. FROLIC OF ONE'S OWN.

scope of examination, the range of subjects inquired into in the questioning of a witness at a hearing or trial. See also EXAMINATION; BEYOND THE SCOPE.

scope of expertise, the area of an expert witness's specialized knowledge An expert witness may not testify to opinions on matters beyond the scope of her expertise See also *expert witness* (under WITNESS).

scope of review, the extent of a court's power to review a decision of a lower court or of an administrative agency. Such power is usually limited by a combination of constitutional provisions, statutory provisions, judicial policy, and the court's own discretion. See also STANDARD OF REVIEW

scrutiny, *n.* judicial consideration of the purposes and effects of an administrative regulation or a state or federal law or policy in order to determine whether it is valid, especially under the DUE PROCESS and EQUAL PROTECTION clauses of the Constitution. In constitutional challenges under those clauses, the Supreme Court has defined three levels of scrutiny, the choice of which depends upon the nature of the rights at stake or the CLASSIFICATION involved RATIONAL BASIS TEST; HEIGHTENED SCRUTINY; STRICT SCRUTINY

seal[1], *n.* **1.** originally, an impression made in melted wax on a document such as a contract, deed, or will, containing the unique mark of the maker of the document and signifying the maker's intent to be bound by it. **2.** today, any mark on the paper intended to represent such a seal, most commonly the word "seal" or the letters **L.S.** (for the Latin "locus sigilli," lit "the place of the seal") placed next to the maker's signature **3. corporate seal,** an identifying design adopted by a corporation, embossed on legal documents executed by the corporation to authenticate them and to act as a seal. **4. sealed instrument** or **instrument under seal,** an INSTRUMENT to which the SIGNATURE and seal of the maker have been affixed. At common law, such an instrument became legally effective upon delivery to the person benefited by it (hence the phrase "signed, sealed, and delivered") The legal significance of the seal has been modified by statutes which vary from state to state, and in some states it no longer has any significance at all See also *hand and seal* (under HAND); *contract under seal* (under CONTRACT). —*v.* **5.** to affix a seal to; to execute with a seal

seal[2], *v* to place or keep items or records relating to a case in a sealed envelope, or otherwise shield them from public access. See also *file under seal* (under FILE); CONFIDENTIALITY STIPULATION.

search, *n.* **1.** inspection by law enforcement officials of a person's body, home, or any area that the person would reasonably be expected to regard as private, for weapons, contraband, or evidence of criminal activity. Under the Fourth Amendment (see Appendix), a search ordinarily may not be conducted without PROBABLE CAUSE. Cf. STOP AND FRISK. **2. border search,** a search of a person or property coming into the country If not unduly intrusive, this is permitted without any reason to suspect wrongdoing; strip searches and body cavity searches require an objective basis for suspicion of smuggling, but less than probable cause. **3. consent search,** a search conducted with the consent of the subject, or of a person with control over the area searched. This is legal even in the absence of probable cause, and even if the consent was given only because the subject did not know and was not told that she had any choice in the matter, so long as the consent was not the product of duress. **4. unreasonable search,** a search conducted without probable cause and in the absence of other considerations making it constitutionally permissible, such as consent or protection of the nation's borders See also EXCLUSIONARY RULE **5. warrantless search,** a search conducted without a warrant (see WARRANT[1]). This is permissible under EXIGENT CIRCUMSTANCES requiring prompt action. —v **6.** to conduct a search.

search and seizure, 1. a SEARCH leading to a SEIZURE of property Because searches and seizures are often linked in practice and are governed by the same body of law, they are often discussed jointly by use of this phrase. **2. unreasonable search and seizure,** an *unreasonable search* (see under SEARCH) leading to a seizure of property

search warrant. See under WARRANT[1].

seasonable, *adj.* timely; within the time agreed upon; within a reasonable time

second mortgage. See under MORTGAGE.

secondary boycott. See under BOYCOTT

secondary liability. See under LIABILITY

section, *n.* a subdivision of a statute or document, represented by the symbol § (or §§ for "sections"). Most statutes and codes are divided into sections.

secure, *v.* **1.** to provide assurance that a debt will be paid or that funds will be available to pay damages if an obligation is not performed, particularly by giving the obligee a lien, mortgage, or other *security interest* (see under INTEREST[1]) in property. Lawyers speak interchangeably of securing the obligee (who is then a **secured creditor**) or securing the obligation (which is then a **secured debt**). **2. secured transaction,** any transaction which has as one of its elements the creation of a security interest in favor of one of the parties —**secured,** *adj*

securities acts, statutes regulating the issuance and marketing of stocks, bonds, and other securities (see SECURITY[2]) to the public. They seek to avoid the conditions that led to the stock market crash of 1929 by assuring that investors will have access to full and accurate information and will be treated fairly The principal federal securities acts are the **Securities Act of 1933,** which regulates the initial distribution of a new security to the public, and the **Securities Exchange Act of 1934,** which regulates all subsequent trading of a security. See also BLUE SKY LAW.

securities broker. See under BROKER

securities fraud, the tort and crime of knowingly making any materially misleading statement, or failing to disclose a material fact, in connection with the purchase or sale of a security.

security[1], *n.* **1.** something given or deposited to provide assurance of payment of a debt or fulfillment of an obligation; especially, a *security interest* (see under INTEREST[1]) in property. **2. security deposit,** money set aside and held as security; particularly, money paid by a tenant at the beginning of a lease and held by the landlord in case the tenant damages the property or leaves without paying rent.

security[2], *n.* **1.** an ownership interest in an enterprise (the ISSUER) or a right to share in profits from it or a debt owed by it, deriving from an investment in the enterprise rather than from participation in it Most commonly, a bond (see BOND[1]) or shares of STOCK **2.** a certificate evidencing such an interest or right. **3. convertible security,** a security that can be exchanged for another kind of security from the same issuer upon specified conditions; e.g., a bond convertible into stock, or preferred stock convertible into common stock. **4. corporate security,** a security issued by a corporation. **5. debt security,** a bond or other security representing a right to receive a share of each payment of interest or principal made by an enterprise in connection with a particular debt owed by it **6. equity security,** stock or another security representing an ownership interest in an enterprise, or carrying a right to acquire such an interest; e.g , a warrant (see WARRANT[2]) **7. government security,** a security issued by the federal government or a federal agency; sometimes, a security guaranteed by the federal government **8. guaranteed security,** a security in which the issuer's obligation to make payments is guaranteed by an entity other than the issuer **9. marketable security,** a security that can easily be sold if the present owner needs cash or no longer wants the security. **10. municipal security,** a security issued by, or sometimes guaranteed by, a state or local government or governmental agency. **11. redeemable security,** a security that the issuer has a right to buy back (or, in the case of a *debt security,* to pay off prior to maturity) upon specified conditions. Also called **callable security.**

security interest. See under INTEREST[1].

seduction, *n.* inducing a person, especially an unmarried woman, to engage in sexual intercourse. The term includes both honest and dishonest means of persuasion, but usually not force. Depending upon various factors such as the age of the person seduced, her previous chastity, the means used, and the state where the conduct occurred, seduction may be a crime, a tort for which the seduced person may sue, or a tort for which her father or mother may sue.

seizure, *n* **1.** (of a person) an ARREST **2.** (of property in criminal matters) the taking of possession, by law enforcement officials, of a weapon, contraband, or evidence of a crime, usually pursuant to a SEARCH. The government's right to make such seizures is limited by the Fourth Amendment (see Appendix); a seizure resulting from an *unreasonable search* (see under SEARCH) is unlawful See also SEARCH AND SEIZURE; EXCLUSIONARY RULE. **3.** (of property in civil cases) an ATTACHMENT or other procedure by which property is brought under the control of the court —**seize,** *v.*

selective conscientious objector. See under CONSCIENTIOUS OBJECTOR.

self-authenticating. See under AUTHENTICATE

self-dealing, *n.* transactions by a trustee or other FIDUCIARY in which the fiduciary has a personal interest that might conflict with the interest of the party to whom she owes a fiduciary duty. Self-dealing usually constitutes a *breach of fiduciary duty* (see under BREACH).

self-defense, *n* the use of reasonable force against an aggressor by one who reasonably believes it necessary to avoid imminent bodily harm. Self-defense is a justification for conduct that would otherwise be a crime or tort See also RETREAT

self-employment income. See under INCOME.

self-employment tax, a tax on self-employed individuals requiring them to make a double contribution to the SOCIAL SECURITY system, paying both the employer's share and the employee's share. See also SOCIAL SECURITY TAX.

self-help, *n.* the taking of action to remedy a wrong without calling upon the police or initiating legal proceedings Some kinds of self-help are permitted by law, such as (usually) the repossession of an automobile whose buyer has fallen behind in installment payments.

self-incrimination, *n.* the making of a statement that may expose the speaker to criminal penalties Under the Fifth Amendment (see Appendix), the government may not require people to make such statements or penalize them for refusing to do so. See also *transactional immunity* and *use immunity* (under IMMUNITY).

self-insurance, *n.* the setting aside of funds to cover certain potential risks or losses instead of purchasing insurance for those particular risks.

senior, *adj.* having priority among potential recipients of payment or benefits in the event that resources run short and a conflict arises among claimants with similar interests· *senior creditor; senior lien; senior security.* Opposite: JUNIOR; SUBORDINATE; SUBORDINATED — **seniority,** *n.*

seniority system, an employment policy, often required by union contract, under which workers who have worked for the same employer for longer periods are entitled to better benefits and more protection against firing than workers who have been there a shorter time. Although such policies perpetuate racial and other imbalances due to past discrimination in hiring, they are expressly permitted by most civil rights laws.

sentence, *n* **1.** a court's JUDGMENT imposing a penalty upon a person convicted of an offense, or the penalty imposed, such as imprisonment, a fine, community service, or death. See also CAPITAL PUNISHMENT **2. concurrent sentences,** sentences on different charges to be served simultaneously. Concurrent sentences are often imposed so that if the defendant obtains a reversal of conviction on one or more counts, but less than all, it will not affect the length of time spent in prison. **3. consecutive sentences,** sentences on different charges to be served one after the other. Consecutive sentences may be imposed when a defendant's conduct constituted several distinct crimes, in order to maximize the total time of imprisonment. Also called **cumulative sentences. 4. determinate sentence,** a sentence setting a definite term of incarceration

5. indeterminate sentence, a sentence specifying minimum and maximum terms of imprisonment, with exact date of release between those limits to be determined by the parole board. **6. suspended sentence,** a sentence that the defendant will not be required to serve unless she commits another crime or violates some other condition imposed by the court. —**sentence,** v.

separability clause. See under SAVING CLAUSE

separate but equal, the doctrine, formally adopted by the Supreme Court in 1896 in the infamous case of Plesssy v. Ferguson, holding that legally mandated racial segregation does not violate the constitutional requirement of EQUAL PROTECTION, so long as the law contemplates the provision of "separate but equal" facilities for people of color. In the 1954 case of Brown v. Board of Education, the Supreme Court finally recognized that separate facilities are "inherently unequal" as well as demeaning, and took the first step away from this doctrine by declaring racially segregated public schools unconstitutional. But the doctrine may still be alive in slightly altered form: In 1977 the Court affirmed a decision permitting a city to maintain two separate high schools for academically gifted students—"Central High" for boys and "Girls High" for girls—upon a finding that "the academic facilities are comparable, with the exception of those in the scientific field where Central's are superior."

separate opinion. See under OPINION

separate return. See under RETURN.

separation, n. **1.** the termination of cohabitation of a husband and wife, or the status of a husband and wife who are living apart, either preliminary to a divorce or instead of divorcing. **2. legal separation,** separation of spouses pursuant to a court order or, sometimes, a *separation agreement*. **3. separation agreement,** a formal agreement between spouses stating that they will live apart and setting forth the terms of their separation.

separation of church and state, a phrase commonly used to summarize the purpose of the First Amendment's guarantee of FREEDOM OF RELIGION. The phrase has been in use at least since 1802, when President Thomas Jefferson described the First Amendment as creating "a wall of separation between church and state."

separation of powers, the theory that government should have three separate branches: a legislative branch to make laws, an executive branch to administer them, and a judicial branch to interpret them and resolve disputes arising under them. For the national government of the United States, the first three articles of the Constitution define the powers of each of these three branches in turn. In practice there is much overlap and interplay among the three branches.

sequester, v. to segregate, isolate, or set apart, especially by court order. To sequester property is to hold it aside pending a decision on its disposition; to sequester witnesses is to keep them from talking to each other or listening to testimony during a trial; to sequester a jury is to shield it from outside influence. —**sequestration,** *n.*

servant, *n.* an employee; a person hired to perform services for another (the MASTER) and subject to the other's control both as to what work is done and how it is done (in contrast to an INDEPENDENT CONTRACTOR, who has more autonomy). See also MASTER AND SERVANT.

serve, *v.* to effect SERVICE of papers or process. One can speak of serving either the person or the papers: *The marshal served the defendant with the summons. The marshal served the summons on* (or *upon*) *the defendant.*

service, *n.* **1.** Also called **service of process.** the giving of formal notice of judicial proceedings or a judicial act to a person involved, by delivering a copy of the PROCESS to the person or following some other procedure prescribed by law. **2.** the act of providing a copy of any paper filed with the court, such as a motion or affidavit, to the other parties or attorneys in the case. Normally a court will reject the paper if this has not been done. Cf. EX PARTE. **3. personal service,** hand delivery of a copy of the process directly to the intended recipient or to an agent authorized to accept process. **4. service by publication,** the printing of notice of an action in a newspaper in the hope that the person affected by it will see it. This is the least effective method of service, allowed only in certain situations and only as a last resort. **5. substituted service,** any of several methods of service permitted in place of personal service under certain circumstances, such as service by mail. Also called **constructive service.** See also NAIL AND MAIL.

services, *n.pl.* originally, the labor of a wife or child contributing to the economic welfare of a man's household. The common law recognized a man's right to recover damages for the loss of such services from anyone who injured or enticed away his wife or child. Since the husband owed no services to his wife, she had no such right of action. To the extent that loss of economic services of a family member is recognized as giving rise to a tort claim today, it applies without regard to the sex of the spouse or the parent. See also CONSORTIUM.

servitude, *n.* **1.** Also called **involuntary servitude.** forced labor; working for another against one's will, whether for pay or not. This includes not only SLAVERY but also such schemes as requiring a person to work for one to whom he is indebted in order to work off the debt. It is outlawed by the Thirteenth Amendment (see Appendix), except as punishment for a crime. Public responsibilities such as jury duty and military service for draftees are not barred by the Thirteenth Amendment. **2.** a right to use another's land for a particular purpose, and the corresponding burden upon the land (see BURDEN²); for example, an EASEMENT or PROFIT.

set aside, to nullify a judgment, verdict, or court order. See also QUASH; VACATE.

set off, to balance two opposing claims against each

other, eliminating the smaller and reducing the larger by that amount The reduction is called a **setoff** or **offset:** *The landlord's claim against the tenant for $1000 in property damage was set off against the tenant's claim for refund of the $3000 security deposit, and the landlord was ordered to refund the remaining $2000.*

settle, *v* **1.** to reach agreement resolving a dispute· *settle a case.* **2.** to pay in full: *settle a bill.* **3.** to complete all the tasks of administration and distribution of a decedent's property: *settle an estate* **4.** to transfer title to property; especially, to create a TRUST by placing money or property in the hands of a TRUSTEE for administration: *settle a trust.* **5.** to submit to a court for approval· *settle an order* —**settlement,** *n.*

settlor, *n.* the person who creates a TRUST by transferring money or property to a TRUSTEE for administration. Also called the DONOR or GRANTOR of the trust.

sever, *v.* to split off a part of a case and make it a separate case, in order to avoid prejudice or for administrative convenience: *to sever a claim; to sever a party; to sever the case.* Cf. CONSOLIDATE; JOIN —**severance,** *n.*

severability clause. See under SAVING CLAUSE

several, *adj.* separate; individual, independent of others in a group: *several liability* (see under LIABILITY) Cf. JOINT; JOINT AND SEVERAL. —**severally,** *adv.*

severalty, *n.* the condition of being under individual ownership. See also IN SEVERALTY

sex discrimination, discrimination against women for not being men, or occasionally against men for not being women. Sex discrimination permeated American law at every level until the 1960's, when statutes and constitutional decisions limiting such discrimination began to appear See also BONA FIDE OCCUPATIONAL QUALIFICATION; HEIGHTENED SCRUTINY; PREGNANCY DISCRIMINATION; SEPARATE BUT EQUAL; SEXUAL HARASSMENT; STATUTORY RAPE.

sex-plus discrimination, discrimination based upon a combination of sex and other factors; for example, refusing to hire married women while hiring men without regard to marital status, or harassing young female employees but not older ones. For purposes of laws against employment discrimination, such conduct constitutes sex discrimination.

sexual assault. See under ASSAULT.

sexual harassment, a form of unlawful employment discrimination consisting of HARASSMENT of an employee or group of employees, usually women, because of their sex. This may take the form of requiring or seeking sexual favors as a condition of employment (**quid pro quo harassment**) or otherwise subjecting an employee to intimidation, ridicule, or insult because of her sex, whether or not the harassing conduct is sexual in nature (**hostile environment harassment**). See also HOSTILE WORKING ENVIRONMENT.

sexual predator, a person with a history of sexual offenses against others, who is regarded as unlikely to be able to control the impulse to commit more such crimes in the future. Also called **sexually dangerous person.**

share, *n.* a partial right or interest allotted to one of several people who together have the whole right or interest; in particular, a unit of ownership of a CORPORATION or *joint stock company* (see under COMPANY) —that is, one of the equal fractional parts into which a class of STOCK of such an entity is divided. See also ELECTIVE SHARE.

shareholder. Same as STOCKHOLDER

shareholder derivative action. See under ACTION

shell corporation. See under CORPORATION

Sherman Antitrust Act, the first federal ANTITRUST law. It prohibits MONOPOLIZATION, attempted monopolization, and any concerted action in UNREASONABLE RESTRAINT OF TRADE Also called **Sherman Act.**

shield law, a statute creating a *testimonial privilege* (see under PRIVILEGE) This phrase is most commonly used to describe laws protecting reporters from having to disclose news sources **(journalists' shield law)** or victims in rape cases from unnecesssary inquiry into the sexual history of the victim **(rape shield law).**

shift. See *burden shifting* (under BURDEN¹).

shop, *n.* **1.** a business or place of employment, especially one in which the workers have a UNION **2. agency shop,** a shop in which workers are required to pay union dues whether they join the union or not **3. closed shop,** a shop in which one must be a union member to get a job, and must remain a member to keep it. Although federal labor law forbids closed shops, as a practical matter one cannot get work in some fields except through a union. **4. open shop,** a shop in which union and nonunion workers are treated equally. **5. preferential shop,** a shop in which union members are given preferential treatment over non-members. **6. union shop,** a shop in which nonunion workers may be hired but must then join and remain a member of a union. See also RIGHT TO WORK LAWS.

shoplifting, *n.* the crime of taking possession of merchandise in a store with the intention of keeping or using it without paying for it. Shoplifting is a form of LARCENY.

show, *v.* **1.** to convince or try to convince a court of something by evidence and legal argument: *The plaintiff failed to show a need for an injunction; an injunction will issue only upon a showing that without it the applicant will suffer irreparable harm.* **2. show cause,** to present reasons why a court should issue, or refuse to issue, a particular order. See also *order to show cause* (under ORDER¹) —**showing,** *n.*

showup, *n.* the displaying of a criminal suspect singly to a witness for the purpose of identification, usually within a few hours after the crime; an inherently suggestive procedure that is nevertheless common. Cf LINEUP.

sidebar, *n.* in a jury trial, a brief courtroom conference among the judge and the lawyers, either on or off the record, conducted at or to the side of the bench so that the jury cannot hear it. Also called **bench conference.**

sight draft. See under DRAFT

sign, v. to affix a SIGNATURE to a document. See also SEAL¹

signatory, n. **1.** a person or entity whose SIGNATURE appears on a document. **2.** a nation that has agreed to a treaty.

signature, n. the name or mark of a person or entity placed on a document to authenticate it. It need not be written by hand, and it need not be placed there by the person named so long as it is authorized or adopted by that person. See also HAND; seal¹; X

silent partner. See under PARTNER

simple, adj. **1.** describing the basic form of something; lacking special or complicating features See *fee simple* (under FEE¹). **2.** (of a tort or crime) unaggravated; often used to describe the lowest grade of an offense *simple negligence* (see under NEGLIGENCE), *simple assault.*

simplified employee pension. See under PENSION PLAN

sinking fund, money or other assets set aside and accumulated to meet a future need, particularly the paying of a debt.

sister corporations. See under CORPORATION

sit, v. **1.** (of a court or other official body) to hold a formal session for the conduct of business. *The Supreme Court normally sits from October to June.* **2.** to preside over a particular case: *The appeal was decided by the Court of Appeals sitting en banc*

situate, adj. situated; located. A term found in descriptions of real property

situs, n. Latin. (lit. "site") the place where a thing (tangible or intangible) is deemed to be located for legal purposes For example, the situs of personal property for tax purposes is usually the domicile of the owner; the situs of a debt is generally deemed to be wherever the debtor is at the moment.

slander, n **1.** the form of DEFAMATION in which the defamatory statement is communicated orally Cf LIBEL¹. —v. **2.** to utter a slander against a person; to defame orally —**slanderous,** adj.

slavery, n. the ownership of one person by another, outlawed by the Thirteenth Amendment (see Appendix) See also SERVITUDE.

sleeping partner. See under PARTNER

slip opinion, a judicial OPINION in the form in which it is first issued, typed or printed on slips of paper; cited as "slip op." Cf *reported opinion* (under REPORT)

small claims court, a state or municipal court established to handle certain civil cases involving very small sums of money, using informal, streamlined procedures and often dispensing with lawyers

smuggling, n. the crime of importing or exporting prohibited matter, or importing or exporting permitted matter without paying required DUTY —**smuggle,** v.

so ordered, a formal expression often used by judges, both orally and in writing, to make it clear that a pronouncement is an official order of the court See the example under INSTANTER.

social security, a federal program designed to provide some continuing income to most workers after they retire or become disabled, and under some circumstances to their surviving spouse or children when they die The program was established by the **Federal Insurance Contributions Act (FICA)** in 1935

social security tax, a payroll tax, paid one-half by the employee and one-half by the employer, to help fund the social security and Medicare programs; usually identified on pay stubs as "FICA" (see under SOCIAL SECURITY). It is a *regressive tax* (see under TAX), because it is paid only on *earned income* (see under INCOME) and not on income from investments, and also because most of it applies only to wages up to a certain maximum amount each year, so that employees with very high salaries (usually executives) pay the full tax only on a portion of their salary, whereas most ordinary workers pay it on their entire salary. Moreover, individuals without a regular employer to pay the employer's share must pay double on whatever they earn, in the form of SELF-EMPLOYMENT TAX.

Socratic method, a teaching method heavily used in law schools today, based upon the technique used by Socrates in ancient Greece, in which students are led to analyze legal issues and principles through a series of *hypothetical questions* (see under QUESTION[1]) from the teacher See also CASE METHOD.

sodomy, *n.* a term varying in meaning from state to state, but generally referring to any type of sex act disapproved by the legislature. At a minimum it includes oral and anal sexual intercourse between men, but it may extend to those or other acts between men and women (sometimes exempting married couples, sometimes not), or women and women, or people and animals. Sodomy is still a crime in many states, and as recently as 1986 the Supreme Court upheld a law providing for 20 years' imprisonment for either heterosexual or homosexual sodomy, as applied to a man who was found in bed with another man in his own home by police who entered to serve an arrest warrant for public drinking. Cf. RIGHT TO PRIVACY.

sole custody. See under CUSTODY

sole proprietorship, ownership of an unincorporated business by one individual, or the business so owned. For income tax purposes, the profits of such a business are taxed directly to the individual.

solicitation, *n* **1.** the crime of asking, advising, encouraging, or ordering another person to commit a crime, whether or not the offense solicited is then committed This is usually punishable as a crime one degree lower in severity than the offense solicited **2.** the offense of offering to engage in sexual activity with a person for money or of attempting to entice a person to patronize a prostitute

solicitor, *n.* **1.** in England, a lawyer who gives legal advice and performs general legal services outside the courtroom, including preparing cases for a BARRISTER to present in court, but who normally does not appear in court personally except in certain lower courts **2.** in America, a title sometimes given to the chief legal officer of a municipality or governmental department: *county solicitor; town solicitor.* **3. Solicitor General,** the officer who oversees all legal representation of the United States government before the Supreme Court

solvent, *adj.* **1.** usually, able to pay one's debts in the ordinary course of business as they become due. **2.** for some purposes, having assets greater than liabilities. Opposite of INSOLVENT. —**solvency,** *n.*

sound, *adj* **1.** (of body or mind) healthy, fit, normal. **2. sound mind** or **sound and disposing mind and memory,** the mental CAPACITY necessary to make a valid will; having a reasonable understanding of what property one has, what options for it one has, and what one is doing with it.

sound in, (of a civil action) to have its basis in; to have as its fundamental nature: *To determine which statute of limitations applies, the court must decide whether the action sounds in tort or in contract.*

sovereign immunity. See under IMMUNITY.

speaking objection. See under OBJECTION.

special, *adj.* describing a form of something that is distinctive, particularized, limited, expanded, or otherwise worthy of separate consideration, often calling into play particular legal rules. Sometimes contrasted with GENERAL. See *special* APPEARANCE, COUNSEL, DAMAGES, INDORSEMENT, JURISDICTION[1], master, power of attorney, prosecutor, verdict under those words, and *special questions* (or *interrogatories*) (under VERDICT).

special circumstances, aggravating or mitigating circumstances affecting the degree of a crime or the severity of punishment; especially, aggravating circumstances that justify a prosecutor in seeking or a jury in imposing the death penalty for a murder, such as a defendant's infliction of torture on the victim or commission of multiple murders.

specie. See IN SPECIE.

specific, *adj.* **1.** particular or special; not vague or general: *specific bequest* (or *legacy*) (see under BEQUEST). **2.** as specified; in the manner or of the kind agreed to: SPECIFIC PERFORMANCE. **3.** referring to a particular thing: *specific restitution* (see under RESTITUTION). See also *specific relief* (under RELIEF).

specific performance, an *equitable remedy* (see under REMEDY) in which a party is ordered to perform a contract according to its terms. The usual remedy for breach of contract is damages (a legal remedy), but in cases where money is not a satisfactory substitute for the thing contracted for, as in a contract for the sale of land or of a unique article such as a painting, the breaching party may be ordered to "perform specifically."

specification, *n.* a detailed listing or description, such as a litigant's listing of errors in appellate papers, the prosecution's listing of charges in a court martial, or an inventor's detailing of an invention in a patent application.

speculate, *v.* **1.** to guess; to reach conclusions not based on knowledge or evidence Testimony based on speculation is ordinarily not admissible. See also *speculative damages* (under DAMAGES). **2.** to make risky investments. The purpose of the SECURITIES ACTS is to make it possible for investors to know to what extent they are speculating. —**speculation,** *n.* —**speculative,** *adj.*

speech, *n.* **1.** within the meaning of the First Amendment (see Appendix), any form of expression, including words (whether written or spoken), pictures or other visual devices, and expressive conduct **2. commercial speech,** advertising or other speech promoting economic interests. Formerly regarded as constitutionally unprotected, commercial speech that is not false or misleading and does not promote illegal goods, services, or conduct is now given considerable protection under the First Amendment, though still not to the extent of noncommercial speech. **3. hate speech,** speech that grossly insults or demeans people because of a group characteristic such as race or religion. Such speech may not be censored or penalized by the government because of its group-related content, although FIGHTING WORDS may be outlawed. **4. indecent speech,** speech that does not amount to OBSCENITY, but uses vulgar words or deals with sex or bodily functions in a way that is regarded as PATENTLY OFFENSIVE. Unlike obscenity, speech that is merely indecent has been given considerable constitutional protection (for example, "dial-a-porn" services cannot be completely banned); at the same time, some restrictions that would not be allowed for "decent" speech have been upheld, particularly in regard to broadcasting. **5. protected speech,** speech held by the courts to be within the scope of the First Amendment's guarantee of FREEDOM OF SPEECH **6. speech plus,** speech accompanied by conduct deemed nonexpressive. Conduct is not immune from reasonable regulation merely because it is accompanied by speech **7. symbolic speech,** expression other than through words The expression may be political (waving a flag or burning a flag), artistic (painting or dance), or anything else In general, symbolic speech is constitutionally protected to the same extent as verbal speech. See also FREEDOM OF SPEECH

speedy trial. See under TRIAL.

spendthrift trust. See under TRUST.

spontaneous declaration (or **statement** or **exclamation**) Same as EXCITED UTTERANCE.

spot zoning. See under ZONING.

spousal abuse, physical or psychological ABUSE of one spouse by the other, more often of the wife by the husband (**wife abuse**). Traditionally viewed more as a ground for divorce than as a crime; now taken seriously as a crime. See also BATTERED PERSON SYNDROME; CRUELTY.

spousal privilege. See under PRIVILEGE.

spousal rape. Same as *marital rape* (see under RAPE).

spousal support. Same as ALIMONY.

spouse's election. See under ELECTION.

spouse's elective (or **statutory**) **share.** Same as ELECTIVE SHARE.

spread upon the record. See under RECORD.

squeeze-out, *n.* any of a number of techniques permitted by law to force minority shareholders out of a corporation ("squeeze them out"). See also GO PRIVATE.

ss., an abbreviation of uncertain origin and no particular meaning, customarily placed at the top of an affidavit or affirmation beside the statement of VENUE and followed by a colon, thus serving as a kind of introduction to the instrument.

stakeholder, *n.* a person in possession of money or property to which she herself has no claim, but to which two or more others may have competing claims, so that the stakeholder cannot turn over the property to any claimant without the risk of being sued by one or more of the others. For the way out of this dilemma, see INTERPLEADER.

stale, *adj.* rendered ineffective or unenforceable by the passage of time: *stale check; stale claim; stale offer.*

stalking, *n.* **1.** the crime of following a person about in such a way as to instill fear of bodily harm. This is typically dealt with as a form of criminal HARASSMENT. It may also give rise to a tort action for ASSAULT or INTENTIONAL INFLICTION OF MENTAL DISTRESS. **2.** secretly following a person about or lying in wait for the purpose of committing a crime. In most states this is punishable as an ATTEMPT to commit a crime. —**stalk,** *v.* —**stalker,** *n.*

stamp tax, a tax imposed upon a product (e.g., liquor or cigarettes) or a transaction (e.g., a transfer of land) by requiring someone to purchase a stamp and affix it to the product or instrument.

stand, *n.* **1.** in a trial, the place where a witness sits while testifying; short for **witness stand. 2. take the stand,** to go to the stand to testify.

stand bail. See under BAIL[1].

standard deduction. See under DEDUCTION.

standard of care, the level or nature of conduct necessary to avoid liability for MALPRACTICE, NEGLIGENCE, or *breach of fiduciary duty* (see under BREACH). Also called **degree of care.** See details under CARE

standard of proof, the degree to which the TRIER OF FACT must be persuaded of a fact in order to find in favor of a party in a trial or hearing. Also called **degree of proof.** Depending upon the nature of the case or the issue, the standard may be proof by a PREPONDERANCE OF THE EVIDENCE, proof by CLEAR AND CONVINCING EVIDENCE, or proof BEYOND A REASONABLE DOUBT.

standard of review, the test by which a court or administrative tribunal determines whether to uphold or reverse an administrative or judicial decision submitted to it for RE-VIEW. The applicable standard depends upon many factors, including whether the issue being reviewed is one of fact or of law, and whether it was decided by a judge or by a jury. The usual test for upholding a jury verdict is whether there was evidence in the case on the basis of which a reasonable jury, applying the proper STANDARD OF PROOF, could have arrived at that verdict. For other standards of review, SEE ABUSE OF DISCRETION; CLEARLY ERRONEOUS; *de novo review* (under REVIEW); SUBSTANTIAL EVIDENCE; and *harmless error, plain error,* and *reversible error* (all under ERROR).

standby counsel. See under COUNSEL.

standing, *n.* the right to have a court adjudicate a matter in which one is interested. To have standing to bring an action or otherwise raise an issue in court, one must have a legally cognizable interest in the matter (see INTEREST¹, def. 1).

Star Chamber, 1. an English court, finally abolished in 1641, whose unfettered powers, lack of procedural safeguards, and arbitrary punishments made it a symbol of much that our constitutional protections and rules of criminal procedure seek to guard against **2. star chamber proceeding,** a phrase used to characterize a legal proceeding as grossly unfair to the defendant. See also KANGAROO COURT.

stare decisis, *Latin.* (lit. "to stand by the things decided") the doctrine that legal principles established in previous judicial decisions will normally be followed in subsequent cases. This doctrine lends stability and fairness to the law; without it, each judge could make up a new rule for each case. But it also makes the law slow to react to social and scientific change. The evolution of common law depends upon judicious application of this doctrine

state, *n.* **1.** a nation or national government. See also ACT OF STATE. **2.** one of the fifty states making up the United States, or the government of such a state. In many contexts, the word is used a little more broadly to include the District of Columbia. **3.** *(cap.)* the government of a particular state. In many states, this is how the government and the prosecution are identified in criminal cases under state law. See also PEOPLE. Cf. GOVERNMENT.

state action, action taken by the government (especially a state government) or in which the government is intimately involved, as distinguished from purely private action. The constitutional guarantees of DUE PROCESS and EQUAL PROTECTION apply only to state action, not private action.

state of mind, 1. generally, the condition of mind or the element or degree of fault or blameworthiness that accompanies an act or omission. **2.** particularly, the additional condition that is required in most crimes, beyond the mere fact that the defendant committed a certain act causing certain results, to make the act a particular crime; MENS

REA. The common law used many overlapping and poorly defined terms to describe different states of mind; e g., MALICE, WANTON, WILLFUL Most states now have criminal codes that define most crimes in terms of four distinctly defined states of mind signifying successively greater levels of culpability· NEGLIGENCE, RECKLESSNESS, KNOWLEDGE, INTENT. See also STRICT LIABILITY.

state statute. See under STATUTE

statement, *n.* **1.** an oral or written assertion, or nonverbal conduct intended as an assertion Often interchangeable with DECLARATION, though in most contexts one word is more common than the other. **2.** Also called **financial statement.** a concise and systematic presentation of the financial status of a person or entity. **3.** Also called **statement of account.** a summary of the status of an ACCOUNT, showing the balance due and usually listing recent transactions. **4. closing statement.** See different meanings under CLOSING (def. 1) and SUMMATION. **5. exculpatory statement,** a statement that, if true, tends to exonerate a suspect; e.g., "I was at home watching TV." If such a statement is shown to be untrue (a **false exculpatory statement**), a jury is permitted to look upon it as evidence of guilt, on the dubious theory that an innocent person would have no reason to lie. **6. opening statement.** Same as OPENING. **7. prior inconsistent statement,** an earlier statement by a witness which is inconsistent with the witness's testimony at a trial or hearing. It may be introduced as evidence, not for its truth (since that would violate the rule against HEARSAY), but to impeach the witness's credibility. See also *admissible for a limited purpose* (under ADMISSIBLE). **8. spontaneous statement.** Same as EXCITED UTTERANCE. **9. statement of claim,** a document, or portion of a document, formally setting forth the claim that one is making in a case. **10. statement of the case,** the portion of a brief summarizing the facts rather than arguing the law. Also called **statement of facts.**

state's evidence, 1. evidence voluntarily given by a participant or accomplice in a crime against others involved, usually in exchange for immunity or lenient treatment. A suspect or defendant who agrees to provide such evidence is said to **turn state's evidence. 2.** generally, any evidence offered by the prosecution in a state criminal case.

states' rights, a slogan invoked by those who oppose the granting of rights, benefits, and protections to people by FEDERAL LAW, and argue that the various state governments should have the right to set their own standards on such matters as civil rights, environmental protection, and care for the poor. Cf. SUPREMACY.

status quo, *Latin.* (lit. "the position in which") **1.** the way things are at the time of speaking: *to preserve the status quo.* **2.** Also called **status quo ante,** with *ante* ("before"). the way things were prior to some specific event in the past: *to restore the status quo (ante).*

statute, *n.* a written law enacted by Congress **(federal statute)** or a state legislature **(state statute).** Often called an ACT or a LAW. Cf. COMMON LAW; ORDINANCE; REGULATION; RULE.

statute of frauds, a statute requiring certain kinds of contracts to be written, or at least to be memorialized in some writing signed by the party against which the contract is to be enforced. A contract of the specified type is said to be "within" the statute, and if it is adequately memorialized and signed it is said to "satisfy" the statute. The most common kinds of contracts covered by such statutes are agreements to be responsible for someone else's debt, contracts for the sale of land, contracts for the sale of goods above a certain price, and contracts requiring performance more than a year after the making of the contract.

statute of limitations, a statute setting the length of time after an event within which a civil or criminal action arising from that event must be brought (the **limitation period, limitations period,** or **statutory period**). Cf. LACHES.

Statutes at Large, (abbr. **Stat.**) the official compilation of acts and resolutions of Congress, treaties ratified, constitutional amendments proposed or ratified, and presidential proclamations issued, printed in chronological order for each session of Congress Although this compilation reproduces federal statutes in the exact form in which Congress enacted them, the organization of the UNITED STATES CODE and the annotations added to it by private publishers make that the preferred version for legal research. *Abbr.:* Stat.

statutory, *adj.* **1.** relating to statutes or a statute: *statutory construction* (see under CONSTRUCTION); *statutory period* (see under STATUTE OF LIMITATIONS). **2.** created by or pertaining to statutes rather than the common law: *statutory crime* (see under CRIME). **3.** existing by virtue of a statute, without regard to the intent of the parties involved or any agreement or lack of agreement among them: *statutory rape* (see under RAPE), *statutory share* (same as ELECTIVE SHARE).

stay, *n.* **1.** the postponement or temporary suspension of a proceeding or of the legal effect of a statute or court order. **2. automatic stay,** a stay imposed by statute, which takes effect automatically upon the occurrence of some event. **3. stay of execution, a.** a stay preventing a person who has won a money judgment from immediately seizing the judgment debtor's assets, usually to allow the debtor time to appeal. **b.** an order that a prisoner sentenced to death not be put to death just yet. Such an order might be issued either by a court or by the governor of the state; in the latter case, it is commonly called a REPRIEVE. —*v.* **4.** to order or cause a stay.

steal, *v.* to obtain money or property by LARCENY or, more broadly, by larceny or other criminal means such as ROBBERY, EMBEZZLEMENT, or FALSE PRETENSES.

stipulation, *n.* **1.** a representation or condition spelled out in a contract. **2.** an agreement between opposing lawyers with respect to some procedural step in a case, often altering normal time limits or other procedural requirements for mutual convenience or as a matter of courtesy. Typically such a stipulation will be submitted to the judge to be so ORDERED, which turns it into a **stipulation and order.** See also CONFIDENTIALITY STIPULATION. **3.** an agreement between the parties in a case with respect to a fact or a legal issue, so as to simplify the case by eliminating issues that cannot reasonably be disputed. A fact thus agreed upon is a **stipulated fact,** which must be accepted as true by the judge and jury. See also *stipulated damages* (under DAMAGES). —**stipulate,** *v*

stirpes. See PER STIRPES.

stock, *n* **1.** a security (see SECURITY[1]) issued by a CORPORATION or *joint stock company* (see under COMPANY), representing an ownership interest in the issuer An entity may issue several classes of stock conferring on their owners (called stockholders or shareholders) varying rights with respect to participation in control of the company (through voting for DIRECTORS and on certain company matters), participation in earnings (through DIVIDENDS declared by the directors), and participation in *net assets* (see under ASSET) upon liquidation of the company. The total stock of any class is divided into equal fractional parts (SHARES), varying quantities of which may be held by different owners, who have greater or lesser rights in proportion to the number of shares that they own. **2. assessable stock,** stock whose owners may be required to make additional financial contributions to the issuer if needed. Most stock carries no such obligation, and so is **nonassessable stock. 3. capital stock, a.** broadly, any stock; the totality of a company's stock of all classes **b.** narrowly, *common stock.* **4. common stock,** the lowest class of stock in a corporation If the corporation has only one class of stock, it is common stock. In the event of liquidation, the common stockholders divide up anything that is left of the company after all obligations to creditors and preferred stockholders have been satisfied. Cf *preferred stock.* **5. paid-up stock,** stock for which the corporation has been paid in full. Also called **fully paid stock. 6. preferred stock,** stock conferring preferential rights to dividends or to assets upon liquidation of the corporation, ahead of the rights of common stockholders Cf. *common stock.* **7. publicly traded stock,** stock that is freely bought and sold among members of the general investing public; stock in a *publicly held corporation* (see under CORPORATION). **8. restricted stock,** stock that may not be transferred to a new owner except upon specified conditions. Stock in a *close corporation* (see under CORPORATION) is often restricted to prevent sale to an outsider who would not fit in with the small group of owners **9. stock with par value,** a class of stock to which the issuer has assigned a PAR VALUE. Also called **par value stock. 10. stock without par value,** a class of stock to which the issuer has not assigned a par value. Also called **no-par** (or **nonpar**) **stock.**

stock association, Same as *joint stock company* (see under COMPANY).

stock certificate, an instrument representing a specified number of shares of a specific class of stock in a particular company.

stock manipulation. engaging in *wash sales* of stock (see under SALE) or other conduct in the stock market designed to create a false impression of widespread investor interest in a stock, usually in the hope of driving up the price. Also called **market manipulation.** This is a kind of *securities fraud* (see under FRAUD).

stock option, 1. a right to purchase or sell a specified number of shares of a particular stock at a specified price some time in the future. **2.** Also called **employee stock option.** Such an option to purchase stock in a corporation, granted by the corporation to an employee as a form of compensation.

stock warrant. Same as WARRANT²

stockbroker. See under BROKER

stockholder, *n.* an owner of shares of STOCK Also called **shareholder.**

stockholder derivative action. See under ACTION.

stop, *n.* **1.** momentary detention of a person by law enforcement officials, falling short of an ARREST, as at a highway checkpoint for drunk drivers or to question a person acting suspiciously. **2. stop and frisk,** a stop accompanied by a pat-down for weapons. This may be done upon grounds falling somewhat short of PROBABLE CAUSE for arrest or a full search, if the officer can articulate a sound basis for the procedure —*v.* **3.** to make a stop of a person.

straight bankruptcy. See under BANKRUPTCY.

straight bill of lading. See under BILL OF LADING.

straight life insurance. See under LIFE INSURANCE

stranger, *n* a person with no legally recognized right or interest in the transaction, proceeding, relationship, or other matter under discussion; an outsider

street name, the name of a firm of stockbrokers acting as *record owner* (see under OWNER) of stock on behalf of one of the firm's customers Holding stock in street name rather than in the names of individual stockholders facilitates the transfer of stock when it is bought and sold among customers of the various brokerage firms

strict construction. See under CONSTRUCTION

strict liability. See under LIABILITY

strict scrutiny, the standard by which the Supreme Court assesses the constitutionality of a law that limits a FUNDAMENTAL RIGHT (such as freedom of speech) or that treats people differently on the basis of a SUSPECT CLASSIFICATION (such as race). Under the strict scrutiny test, a law will be upheld only if it is found to serve a COMPELLING INTEREST of the government and to be "necessary" to the achievement of that interest See also SCRUTINY Cf HEIGHTENED SCRUTINY; RATIONAL BASIS TEST

strike¹, *n.* **1.** a concerted stopping of work by employees in a company or industry, in support of a demand for higher wages or better conditions of employment, or in protest of some action of the employer. Cf. LOCKOUT **2. wildcat strike,** a spontaneous strike not officially authorized by a union. —*v* **3.** to engage in a strike.

strike², *v.* to delete or nullify words spoken or written or papers submitted in a case Stricken material is officially disregarded at trial, but normally remains in the record for purposes of appellate review See discussion under NONRESPONSIVE.

strike suit. See under SUIT

sua sponte, *Latin.* of its (his, her, their) own accord. Said of action taken by a court without being asked to do so by a party. Often expressed in English as **on its (his, her, their) own motion,** although technically a court cannot make a motion to itself· *The court dismissed the action sua sponte* (or *on its own motion*) *for lack of jurisdiction.*

sub judice, *Latin.* (lit , "under the judge") submitted to a judge or court (but not to a jury) and awaiting decision. See also SUBMIT.

sub silentio, *Latin.* (lit "under silence") implicitly; without saying so. *The court's holding overruled its prior decision sub silentio.*

subcontract, *n.* a contract by which a party who has been engaged to carry out a large project engages someone else (a **subcontractor**) to do some of the work. See also *general contractor* (under CONTRACTOR).

subject matter jurisdiction. See under JURISDICTION¹.

subjective test, a legal standard that depends upon what is in someone's mind. For example, legal principles phrased in terms of INTENT, KNOWLEDGE, or GOOD FAITH involve a subjective test. Cf OBJECTIVE TEST.

sublease, *n.* **1.** a LEASE granted by one who is already a lessee of the property. The grantor of a sublease on real property is called the **sublandlord** or **sublessor,** and the person to whom it is granted is the **subtenant** or **sublessee;** in the rare sublease of personal property, only the terms "sublessor" and "sublessee" would be appropriate —*v.* **2.** to convey, receive, or hold by sublease.

sublet, *v.* **1.** to SUBLEASE real property to or from someone. —*n.* **2.** a subleasing arrangement or relationship with respect to real property, or the property itself.

submit, *v.* **1.** to place a matter formally and finally into the hands of the proper body for decision; for example, to submit a case to a jury, a motion to a judge, a dispute to an arbitration panel, or a referendum to the voters See also SUB JUDICE. **2.** to present evidence and argument to a court solely in writing, without oral argument or testimony See also *on papers* (under PAPERS) **3. take on submission,** (of a judge or court) to receive or allow only written evidence and argument on a matter to be decided. Cf HEAR. —**submission,** *n.* —**submitted,** *adj.*

subordinate or **subordinated,** *adj.* lower in priority than a competing right, claim, or claimant. Also called **junior.** Opposite of SENIOR. —**subordination,** *n.*

subornation of perjury, the crime of inducing a person to commit PERJURY The person who commits this crime is said to **suborn** the witness or to **suborn perjury.**

subpoena *n* **1.** a PROCESS directing a witness to appear and give evidence in a court proceeding. **2. subpoena ad testificandum,** a subpoena requiring the person served to appear and testify. See also AD TESTIFICANDUM **3. subpoena duces tecum,** a subpoena requiring the person served not only to testify but also to produce specified documents or other physical evidence. See also DUCES TECUM —*v.* **4.** to serve a subpoena on a person.

subrogate, *v* to substitute a new person for the original claimant with regard to a right or claim For example, if A's car is damaged in an accident caused by B and A's insurance company pays the repair bill, then the insurance company may take A's place in suing B to recover those expenses; the insurance company is said to be "subrogated to" A's damage claim against B. The original claimant is called the **subrogor;** the substituted claimant is the **subrogee.** —**subrogation,** *n.*

subscribe, *n.* **1.** to sign a document, particularly a formal instrument such as a deed, will, or affidavit. **2.** to agree to contribute a certain amount of capital to a corporation in exchange for a certain amount of its stock, or to promise to contribute a certain sum to charity —**subscription,** *n.*

subsequent. See *condition subsequent* (under CONDITION).

subsidiary, *n* **1.** a corporation more than 50% of whose voting stock is owned by another corporation Also called **subsidiary corporation.** Cf PARENT COMPANY **2. wholly owned subsidiary,** a corporation all of whose voting stock is owned by another corporation

substance, *n.* **1.** the real or underlying nature of a transaction, claim, law, or other matter, as distinguished from its FORM For example, an exchange of valuable real estate for one dollar is a sale in form, but in substance a gift **2.** Also called **substantive law.** the entire body of law that establishes and defines those rights and duties that the legal system exists to protect and enforce; distinguished from PROCEDURE For example, in an automobile accident, the questions of whether a driver was responsible and should pay damages or be fined or imprisoned are matters of substance, whereas the steps that must be gone through to determine responsibility and assess damages or a penalty are matters of procedure. **3.** See CONTROLLED SUBSTANCE. —**substantive,** *adj*

substantial capacity test, the principle that a criminal defendant may establish an INSANITY DEFENSE by showing that as a result of mental disease or defect he lacked "substantial capacity" either to appreciate the wrongfulness of his conduct or to conform his conduct to the requirements of law. This test has been adopted in a substantial number of states.

substantial evidence, the STANDARD OF REVIEW usually

used by courts in reviewing administrative determinations. It requires considerable deference to the agency, whose decision will be affirmed so long as there was more than a minimal amount of evidence to support it, even if the reviewing court believes that the preponderance of the evidence pointed to the opposite conclusion

substantial performance, performance of a party's obligations under a contract that complies with what was required in all but minor respects; performance in such a way that there has been no *material breach* (see under BREACH).

substantive due process. See under DUE PROCESS.

substantive law. Same as SUBSTANCE (def. 2)

substituted service. See under SERVICE

subtenant. See under SUBLEASE.

succeed, *v.* to take over a right, interest, or duty of another; to take the place of another with respect to some matter: *When Company A was taken over by Company B, Company B succeeded to all the rights and obligations of Company A.*

succession, *n.* **1.** broadly, any acquisition or taking over of another's right, interest, or duty. **2.** narrowly, the acquisition of rights or property of another upon the other's death, especially by INTESTATE SUCCESSION.

successor, *n.* one who succeeds to the right, interest, or duty of another (the PREDECESSOR). Also called **successor in interest.**

sue, *v.* to file a SUIT against a person: *The injured passenger sued. The injured passenger sued the driver.*

sufferance. See *tenancy at sufferance* (under TENANCY).

suicide, *n.* killing oneself. Attempted suicide is a crime in some states; aiding and abetting a suicide (making the death what is commonly referred to as an **assisted suicide** or, if a physician renders the assistance, a **physician-assisted suicide**) is a crime in all or virtually all states. See also LIVING WILL

suit, *n.* **1.** a *civil action* (see under ACTION) brought by one person or entity against another. **2. collusive suit,** an improper type of suit in which the parties pretend to be adverse in order to present a hypothetical question to the court or obtain a mutually desired outcome. **3. strike suit,** a disparaging term for a large-scale *class action* or *derivative action* (see under ACTION) that is viewed by the defendants as unfounded and intended solely to induce them to agree to a settlement (usually including payment of attorneys' fees to the plaintiff's attorneys) in order to avoid the expense of litigating the case on the merits.

summary, *adj.* describing proceedings conducted in a simplified or abbreviated manner because the issues and circumstances do not require more extended or elaborate treatment; for example, *summary judgment* (see under JUDGMENT). —**summarily,** *adv.*

summation, *n.* a lawyer's address to the judge or jury after all evidence has been presented, summarizing the case and attempting to convince them to find in favor of her client. Also called **argument, closing argument, closing statement,** or just **closing.** Cf. OPENING STATEMENT.

summons, *n.* a PROCESS directing a defendant to appear in court to answer a civil complaint or a criminal charge.

Sunday closing law, a law forbidding certain otherwise legal activities on Sunday. See also BLUE LAW.

sunset law, a statute that expires automatically after a certain period of time.

sunshine law, a statute requiring that official meetings of governmental agencies be open to the public.

Superior Court, the name given in some states to the lowest court of *general jurisdiction* (see under JURISDIC-TION[1]), and in a few states to the first level of appellate court. Cf. INFERIOR COURT.

supersedeas, *Latin.* (lit. "You shall desist.") a stay of execution of a judgment to allow appellate review. See also *supersedeas bond* (under BOND[2]).

supervised visitation. See under VISITATION.

supplemental jurisdiction. See under JURISDICTION[1].

suppress, *v.* **1.** (of a court in a criminal case) to prohibit the prosecution from introducing evidence obtained in violation of the Constitution, such as evidence derived from an unlawful search and seizure or an involuntary confession. See also EXCLUSIONARY RULE; MIRANDA RULE. **2.** (of a party in a civil or criminal case) to withhold evidence that should have been produced. **3. suppression hearing,** a hearing held in advance of a criminal trial to determine whether evidence objected to by the defendant should be suppressed. —**suppression,** *n.*

supra, *adv. Latin.* (lit. "above") earlier in the same document. Used particularly in a second or later reference to an authority already cited in full: *In Doe v. Bolton, supra, the court found the law unconstitutional.* Opposite of INFRA.

supremacy, *n.* the principle, set forth in the Constitution, that FEDERAL LAW is the "supreme Law of the Land," so that any conflicting state law is invalid.

Supreme Court, 1. Short for **Supreme Court of the United States.** The highest court in the federal judicial system, with final say in interpretation of FEDERAL LAW and jurisdiction to resolve controversies between states. Unless the context makes it clear that a state court is being referred to, in American legal writing the phrase "Supreme Court" always means the Supreme Court of the United States. **2.** in most states, the highest court of the state, with final say in the interpretation of state law. In some states, the highest court has a different name or there may be more than one highest court handling different types of cases; in at least one state (New York) the Supreme Court is the lowest court of general jurisdiction, equivalent to what some states call the SUPERIOR COURT. **3.** (*l.c.*) loosely, the highest court of any jurisdiction: *The final authority on interpretation of state law is the state's supreme court.*

surety, *n.* a person who joins in a contract as a co-obligor in order to assure the obligee of an additional (usually more creditworthy) source for performance of the obligation. For example, when an automobile dealer insists that a young buyer get her father's signature on a car loan contract, the father becomes a surety; the daughter is called the **principal obligor** or **principal debtor,** or simply the **principal,** but the dealer (the **creditor** or **obligee**) may look to either the principal or the surety for payment.

surety bond. See under BOND².

suretyship, *n.* **1.** strictly, the three-way contract or relationship among a SURETY, a principal obligor, and their obligee. **2.** broadly, any arrangement or undertaking by which one becomes answerable for the debt, default, or miscarriage of another, including a GUARANTY (def. 1). See also GUARANTY (def 2).

suretyship bond. See under BOND².

surrebuttal, *n.* **1.** the presentation of evidence or argument in response to a REBUTTAL. **2.** specifically, a *surrebuttal case* (see under CASE²). —*adj.* **3.** presented in response to a rebuttal: *surrebuttal case; surrebuttal argument.*

surreply brief. See under BRIEF.

Surrogate, *n.* in some states, the title given (instead of Judge or Justice) to the judge of a probate court or other court dealing with decedents' estates.

surrogate mother, a woman who bears a child for a couple when the wife is unable to do so, having agreed to relinquish parental rights to the couple upon the birth of the child. The child is usually conceived with the husband's sperm, either through artificial insemination of the surrogate mother or through in vitro fertilization of an egg from the wife, which is then implanted in the surrogate mother's uterus. As a general rule, courts and state legislatures have not been supportive of such arrangements.

surveillance, *n.* **1.** covert monitoring of a person's movements and activities or of people and activities at a specific location, especially by law enforcement authorities; often includes EAVESDROPPING. **2. electronic surveillance,** the use of video cameras, radio transmitters, and other electronic devices in surveillance See also *electronic eavesdropping* (under EAVESDROPPING); WIRETAP.

survive, *v.* of a cause of action, to remain in existence ("alive") after the death of the plaintiff or defendant. At common law, most tort claims did not survive the death of either the injured party or the tortfeasor; most states have adopted "survival statutes" permitting most such actions to continue, with a representative of the decedent's estate substituted for the decedent as a party —**survival,** *n.*

survivorship. See RIGHT OF SURVIVORSHIP.

suspect classification, a law's CLASSIFICATION of people into categories regarded by the Supreme Court as requiring STRICT SCRUTINY under the EQUAL PROTECTION clause of the Constitution So far, the only classifications deemed to merit this highest level of SCRUTINY are those based on race, ethnicity, national origin, and ALIENAGE. Cf QUASI-SUSPECT CLASSIFICATION.

suspended sentence. See under SENTENCE

sustain, *v* **1.** to rule favorably upon *The court sustained the objection* (*the motion, the appeal*) **2.** to satisfy: *The plaintiff sustained her burden of proof.* **3.** to justify; to warrant. *The evidence sustained the verdict*

swear, *v.* **1.** to take an OATH or state under oath. Sworn statements are subject to the penalties for FALSE SWEARING and PERJURY In its narrow and traditional sense, swearing is an explicit or implicit invocation of God; in a loose sense, it is simply a solemn promise or statement (backed up by the law of perjury), and so includes affirming (see under AFFIRM¹). To avoid religious implications that are offensive both to some very religious and to some nonreligious people, the word "affirm" may always be used instead of "swear." See also SWEAR OR AFFIRM. **2.** (sometimes followed by *in*) to administer an oath to a person: *swear the witness; swear in the new Chief Justice.* **3. swearing contest,** *Slang* a situation in which the only evidence on an issue in a case is the conflicting testimony of opposing witnesses, each of whom swears (or affirms) that his version is correct and the opposing version is a lie.

swear or affirm, a phrase used to avoid the religious issues raised by the use of SWEAR alone· *Do you swear or affirm that the testimony you give will be the truth, the whole truth, and nothing but the truth?* The Constitution requires that the President of the United States take an oath or affirmation that begins: "I do solemnly swear (or affirm) that I will faithfully execute the Office of President... " See also OATH OR AFFIRMATION.

syllabus, *n.* a brief summary of the facts and holdings in a case, prepared or authorized by the court and printed at the top of the court's opinion for the convenience of readers, but not forming part of the official opinion. Cf. HEADNOTE.

symbolic speech. See under SPEECH.

T

take on submission. See under SUBMIT

take the stand. See under STAND.

taking, *n* **1.** the act of a state or federal government in depriving a property owner of the use of her property in order to serve a public purpose; an exercise of the power of EMINENT DOMAIN. This may occur through a formal proceeding to take title to the land and oust the owner, or by any law or government activity that substantially destroys the usefulness or economic value of the land or entails physical occupation of the land If a taking has occurred, the property owner has a constitutional right to JUST COMPENSATION. **2. regulatory taking,** a statute or regulation that destroys the value of land and thus amounts to a taking.

tangible property. See under PROPERTY.

tax, *n.* **1.** a sum of money required to be paid to the federal, state, or local government for the support of government activities and services to the public at large; distinguished from a fee (see FEE²) in that taxes are collected from a broad class of persons without regard to their use of a particular government service or exercise of a particular privilege. **2. flat tax,** a tax, particularly an INCOME TAX, set at a fixed percentage of the amount being taxed, so that those with low taxable incomes are taxed at the same rate as those with high incomes. Most so-called "flat tax" proposals, however, would tax only earned income (primarily wages), and make unearned income (interest, dividends, capital gains) entirely exempt from income taxes. Since the rich derive a much higher proportion of their income from investments than do people of ordinary means, the overall effect of many such proposals would actually be regressive, not "flat " **3. progressive tax,** a tax with rates that increase as the amount subject to the tax increases, so that taxpayers with more money pay proportionately higher taxes The basic design of the federal income tax has traditionally been progressive, at least in theory, although over a 30-year period beginning in the 1960's the top marginal tax rate—the rate paid on the top portion of the taxable income of taxpayers with the very highest incomes—has been lowered over and over again, from 91 percent to less than 40 percent, making the system much "flatter" than was contemplated when the current Internal Revenue Code was adopted in 1954. See also TAX BRACKET; TAX RATE. **4. regressive tax,** a tax structured so that the effective tax rate decreases as income or value of the kind subject to the tax increases (e.g , the SOCIAL SECURITY TAX), or any other tax whose practical effect is to tax the poor more heavily in proportion to their incomes than the rich (e g., the SALES TAX) —*v* **5.** to impose a tax on or by reason of. *to tax an individual or corporation; to tax income, imports, or property.* **6.** to require the losing party to pay the winner's COSTS in a court case *costs were taxed to the plaintiff* See also *ad valorem tax* (under AD VALOREM); *capital gains tax* (under CAPITAL¹), DUTY (def 2); ESTATE TAX, ESTIMATED TAX; EXCISE; FRANCHISE TAX; *generation-skipping transfer tax* (under GENERATION-SKIPPING TRUST); GIFT TAX; IMPOST; INCOME TAX, INHERITANCE TAX; PAYROLL TAX; POLL TAX; PROPERTY TAX; SALES TAX; SELF-EMPLOYMENT TAX; SOCIAL SECURITY TAX, STAMP TAX; USE TAX, VALUE ADDED TAX; WITHHOLDING TAX

tax avoidance, the structuring of transactions and choosing of options in filling out tax forms so as to minimize one's taxes by lawful means. Cf TAX EVASION; TAX FRAUD.

tax bracket, an income range to which a specific TAX RATE is applied for income tax purposes In a progressive income tax structure (see *progressive tax,* under TAX), the portion of a taxpayer's taxable income that falls within the lowest bracket is taxed at the lowest rate, and the portions in higher brackets are taxed at successively higher rates. A taxpayer is said to be "in the X% bracket" if the highest bracket into which her income reaches is taxed at the indicated rate; it does *not* mean that the taxpayer's entire taxable income is taxed at that rate See also *marginal tax rate* and *effective tax rate* (under TAX RATE).

tax credit, a reduction in a tax allowed to certain classes of taxpayers for reasons of public policy. A tax credit is a direct subtraction from the tax itself, in contrast to an income tax DEDUCTION, which only reduces the income upon which the tax is calculated and so has less impact on the actual tax bill

tax evasion, the crime of contriving in any way not to pay the amount that one is legally obligated to pay in taxes Cf TAX AVOIDANCE.

tax exempt, 1. not required to pay taxes *Qualified charitable organizations are tax exempt.* See also *qualify for tax-exempt status* (under QUALIFY¹) **2. a.** not taxable to the recipient or owner *tax-exempt interest, tax-exempt property.* **b.** producing income that is not taxable *tax-exempt municipal bonds.*

tax fraud, the crime of intentionally filing a false tax return or making other false statements under penalties of perjury to taxing authorities Cf TAX AVOIDANCE.

tax free, *Informal* Same as TAX EXEMPT (def 2)

tax lien. See under LIEN

tax rate, 1. the percentage of taxable income or of the value of taxable property that must be paid as tax **2. effective tax rate,** the actual percentage of one's taxable income that is owed as income taxes; in a progressive tax system, this is always lower than the *marginal tax rate* except for taxpayers in the lowest income bracket, because all taxable income below the taxpayer's top bracket is taxed at less than the marginal rate **3. marginal tax rate,** in a progressive income tax system, the tax rate applicable to the portion of a taxpayer's income that exceeds the threshold for that taxpayer's top tax bracket. Cf *effec-*

tive tax rate. See also *progressive tax* (under TAX); TAX BRACKET.

tax return. See under RETURN.

tax sale. See under SALE.

tax shelter, an investment or other financial arrangement that serves to reduce taxes or to generate both income and offsetting deductions and credits so as to minimize tax on the income.

taxable, *adj.* subject to being taxed: *taxable income* (see under INCOME); *taxable property; taxable gain; taxable costs.*

temporary remedy (or **relief**). See under REMEDY.

temporary restraining order (TRO). See under RESTRAINING ORDER.

tenancy, *n.* **1.** broadly, any *possessory estate* in real property, including *tenancy in fee* and *life tenancy.* (See all three phrases under ESTATE[1].) A tenancy may be designated as BY THE ENTIRETY, IN COMMON, IN SEVERALTY, or JOINT, depending upon the ownership arrangement. **2.** specifically, a LEASEHOLD or landlord-tenant relationship. See defs 3, 5, and 6 for types of leasehold. **3. periodic tenancy** (or **estate**), a tenancy which runs for successive fixed periods of time such as a month or a year, continuing indefinitely but terminable at will by either the landlord or the tenant upon reasonable notice at the end of any period. Also called **month-to-month tenancy, tenancy** (or **estate**) **from year to year,** or the like **4. tenancy** (or **estate**) **at sufferance,** the interest of a person who wrongfully continues to occupy property after the right to possession has ended; this is not a real tenancy or estate because it is not a possessory interest. Also called **holdover tenancy. 5. tenancy** (or **estate**) **at will,** a tenancy of indefinite duration terminable by either the landlord or the tenant upon reasonable notice at any time. **6. tenancy** (or **estate**) **for years,** tenancy for a specific length of time, not necessarily measured in years; for example, a one-week tenancy. Also called a **term of years.**

tenant, *n.* a holder of a TENANCY; a person with a present right to possession of real property, especially the holder of a LEASEHOLD. A tenant is designated as a *periodic tenant, tenant in common, tenant in fee,* etc., according to the nature of the tenancy; see classifications under TENANCY and ESTATE[1]. See also *holdover tenant* (under HOLD). Cf. LANDLORD.

tenantable, *adj.* (of leased premises) in sufficiently good repair to be usable for the intended purpose. In the case of a residential lease, "tenantable" is the same thing as HABITABLE.

tender, *v.* **1.** to offer something formally, in a way that makes it clear that the thing offered will be given, done, or effective immediately upon acceptance: *to tender payment; to tender performance; to tender one's resignation.* —*n.* **2.** the act of tendering or the thing tendered. See also LEGAL TENDER.

tender offer, a public offer to buy up a specified amount of stock in a particular corporation at a particular price if shares are tendered by the current stockholders on or before a particular date, made in an effort to take over control of the corporation.

tender years, extreme youthfulness: *a child of tender years.*

tenement, *n.* **1.** any property of a permanent nature, especially an interest in land. **2.** a run-down or overcrowded apartment house in a poor section of a city

tenor, *n.* **1.** the exact words or terms of an instrument: *The defendant offered a compromise, but the plaintiff seeks to enforce the contract according to its tenor.* **2.** the general meaning or course of thought in an informal communication: *The tenor of our conversation was that there is still ground for compromise.*

term, *n.* **1.** a specific, finite period of time during which an agreement is operative or an interest remains good, or at the end of which an obligation matures. *the term of a lease; the term of a bond.* **2.** (of a court) **a.** the period of time during which the court has sessions: *The October Term of the Supreme Court runs from October to June.* **b.** in some courts, a sitting of the court for a particular type of business: *trial term.* **3.** a portion of an instrument dealing with a certain matter, or the provision it makes for a particular matter· *The contract includes a cancellation term permitting either party to terminate the arrangement on 60 days' notice.* **4.** a word or phrase. See also TERM OF ART. —*adj.* **5.** lasting only for a specified term or maturing at a specified time: *term insurance; term loan.*

term life insurance or **term insurance.** See under LIFE INSURANCE

term of art, a word or phrase having a special meaning in a particular field, different from or more precise than its customary meaning.

term of years. Same as *tenancy* (or *estate*) *for years* (see under TENANCY)

terms and conditions, all of the provisions of a contract or other instrument; another way of saying "terms."

terrorem. See IN TERROREM.

test case. See under CASE¹

testament, *n.* a WILL. In previous centuries, sometimes a technical distinction was drawn between "will" and "testament." In modern usage, "testament" is almost never used except in the phrase LAST WILL AND TESTAMENT.

testamentary, *adj.* **1.** pertaining to a will or wills: *The will was declared void because the decedent lacked testamentary capacity.* **2.** established or accomplished by will: *testamentary gift* (see under GIFT); *testamentary guardian* (see under GUARDIAN); *testamentary trust* (see under TRUST) Cf. INTER VIVOS.

testator, *n.* a person, especially a man, who makes a will. When the maker of a will is a woman, it is still usual to refer to her by the old-fashioned word **testatrix.**

testify, *v.* to give evidence under oath or affirmation at a trial, hearing, or deposition.

testimonial privilege. See under PRIVILEGE.

testimony, *n.* statements made under oath or affirmation by a witness at a trial, hearing, or deposition.

theft, *n.* a broad term for crimes involving the wrongful taking or keeping of money or property of another. The exact scope of the term varies from state to state, but it typically includes LARCENY, FALSE PRETENSES, EXTORTION, EMBEZZLEMENT, and RECEIVING STOLEN PROPERTY, but not ROBBERY, BURGLARY, or FORGERY.

thing in action. Same as CHOSE IN ACTION.

third party, a person who is not a party—or at least not initially or directly a party—to a transaction, proceeding, or other matter under discussion, but who may be affected by it: *The court considered the potential effect of its injunction on third parties.*

third-party, *adj.* **1.** involving or pertaining to a third party, or to a *third-party action.* See also *third-party beneficiary contract* and *third-party beneficiary* (under CONTRACT). **2. third-party action,** an action by which the defendant in a civil case files a complaint against a person who was not initially a party to the case, claiming a right of INDEMNITY or CONTRIBUTION from that third party in the event that the defendant is found liable to the plaintiff. The third-party action is an extension of the main action, and the issues in both actions are litigated together in one big case. See also IMPLEAD.

three strikes law, a law providing for life imprisonment for anyone convicted of a third crime of a particular type; for example, a third violent crime.

through bill of lading. See under BILL OF LADING.

ticket, *n.* **1.** a piece of paper evidencing a contractual right to goods or services: *movie ticket; pawn ticket.* **2.** a simple form of SUMMONS or CITATION issued for minor traffic and motor vehicle violations.

time, *adj.* **1.** lasting until, maturing on, or payable only on or after, a specific date in the future; not payable on demand: *time loan; time instrument.* See also *time draft* (under DRAFT). Cf. *payable on demand* (under DEMAND). **2. time deposit,** money deposited with a bank which the depositor does not have the right to withdraw until a specific length of time has passed; for example, an account represented by an ordinary CERTIFICATE OF DEPOSIT. Cf. *demand deposit* (under DEMAND).

time is of the essence. See under OF THE ESSENCE.

time, place, and manner, a phrase describing the kinds of restrictions that a government may place on SPEECH without violating the First Amendment. Restrictions may be placed on the time, place, and manner of speech if they are narrowly tailored to serve legitimate governmental interests and are not based on the content of the speech. For example, to prevent chaos a city may prohibit marching in the streets without a parade permit, but the granting or denial of a permit may not depend upon the message the marchers seek to convey

title, *n.* **1.** ownership of property, or of a *possessory interest* (see under INTEREST[1]) in property; the right to possess or control possession of property. **2.** *Informal.* a document evidencing such ownership, such as a DEED or BILL OF SALE or, especially, a CERTIFICATE OF TITLE (defs. 1 and 2). **3.** a portion of a statute or codification. *Employment discrimination is prohibited by Title VII of the Civil Rights Act of 1964.* See also UNITED STATES CODE **4. defective title,** title that, because of a gap in records or for some other reason, is too uncertain to qualify as *marketable title.* Also called **bad title** or **unmarketable title. 5. equitable title, a.** the ownership interest of a person who has a right to have title conveyed to her but to whom legal title has not yet been formally conveyed, especially a person who has entered into a specifically enforceable contract to purchase land but has not yet received the deed. **b.** the right of the beneficiary of a trust with respect to trust property of which the trustee is the legal owner. Cf. *legal title.* **6. insurable title,** title that a reputable insurance company would be willing to insure Insurable title may contain minor defects that would make it unmarketable, but that are too remote to cause an insurance company to refuse to insure it. See also TITLE INSURANCE **7. legal title,** actual title to property as recognized under traditional principles of law without consideration of equitable rights, including a seller's title in land as to which a deed has not yet been delivered to the buyer, and a trustee's title to property held in trust for the benefit of another Cf. *equitable title;* EQUITABLE DISTRIBUTION. **8. marketable title,** title that is free of any reasonable risk of successful challenge by an outsider claiming *paramount title* to the same property. Also called **clear title, good title,** or **merchantable title.** If a person who has contracted to sell land proves unable to deliver marketable title, the purchaser ordinarily may cancel the deal. **9. paramount title,** as between competing claims to possession of the same property, the superior claim. A person in possession of real property may be evicted only by one with paramount title; for example, although a holdover tenant has no right to possession of the premises, he cannot be evicted by an outsider who has no better right, but can be evicted by the landlord. **10. Torrens title system.** Same as TITLE REGISTRATION SYSTEM See also ABSTRACT OF TITLE; CHAIN OF TITLE; CLOUD ON TITLE; COLOR; *covenants* (or *warranties*) *of title* (under COVENANT); DOCUMENT OF TITLE; *try title* (under TRY); QUIET TITLE; *warranty of title* (under WARRANTY).

title insurance, insurance purchased by a buyer of real estate to protect herself or the bank that is taking a mortgage on the property from loss due to previously unrecognized encumbrances on the property or competing claims to title. See also TITLE RECORDING SYSTEM

title recording system, the only mechanism made available by most state governments for keeping track of ownership of real estate. It consists of a public office in which copies of documents affecting title to land—such as deeds and mortgages—may be (but often are not) filed. To attempt to determine the status of title to a parcel, one must hire someone familiar with these records to do a TITLE SEARCH. But since the system is too haphazard to be reliable, anyone actually spending or lending money for the land must also purchase TITLE INSURANCE to be protected from loss due to unexpected claims or encumbrances upon the land. Cf. TITLE REGISTRATION SYSTEM

title registration system, an alternative to the TITLE RECORDING SYSTEM made available in a few states, under which title to land can be registered in a state or local government office and evidenced by an official certificate (see CERTIFICATE OF TITLE, def 2), which is conclusive evidence of title for most purposes. Also called **Torrens title system.**

title search, the process of searching through public records in an effort to assess the status of a claimed title to real property by tracing the CHAIN OF TITLE, noting mortgages or other encumbrances on the property, and the like See also TITLE RECORDING SYSTEM

TM, an abbreviation indicating that the word or design it accompanies is claimed or sought to be established as a TRADEMARK, although it is not a *registered trademark* (see under TRADEMARK). Cf. ®

to the order of. See under ORDER²

toll, *v.* to suspend the running of the STATUTE OF LIMITATIONS under circumstances where the law recognizes that a plaintiff or prosecutor was prevented, through no fault of her own, from commencing an action. One speaks of circumstances that "toll the statute" or "toll the limitations period."

Torrens title system. Same as TITLE REGISTRATION SYSTEM.

tort, *n.* **1.** a wrongful act, other than a breach of contract, that results in injury to another's person, property, reputation, or some other legally protected right or interest, and for which the injured party is entitled to a remedy at law, usually in the form of damages. **2. constitutional tort,** unconstitutional conduct by a public official causing injury to a private individual. The Supreme Court has held that under certain constitutional provisions—notably the Fourth Amendment ban on unreasonable searches and seizures—a person harmed by offical conduct in violation of her constitutional rights may sue the official for damages **3. intentional tort,** a tort committed by one who intends by his action to bring about a wrongful result or knows that that result is substantially certain to occur; e.g., BATTERY or TRESPASS. Cf. NEGLIGENCE; STRICT LIABILITY. —**tortious,** *adj.*

tortfeasor, *n.* **1.** a person or entity that commits a tort **2. joint tortfeasor,** one of a number of individuals or entities whose tortious conduct contributed to an injury.

total breach. See under BREACH.

toto. See IN TOTO

Totten trust. See under TRUST.

trade regulation, the body of law that deals with government regulation of competitive business activities; it includes ANTITRUST law and laws dealing with unfair competition, false advertising, and the like.

trade secret, confidential information used in a company's business, such as a secret formula or process or a database of cl'ent information, that gives the company an advantage over competitors and would be helpful to competitors if they learned of it. Trade secrets are valuable property of a company and courts are very protective of them

trade union, 1. broadly, a labor UNION of any kind. **2.** narrowly, a *craft union* (see under UNION).

trade usage. See under USAGE

trademark, *n.* a name, symbol, or other MARK used by a company to identify its products and distinguish them from goods produced or sold by others Such a mark may be registered with the United States Patent and Trademark Office, making it a **registered trademark;** unless the registrant's right to use the mark is successfully challenged within five years after registration, the registrant normally has the exclusive right to use the mark from then on. See also ®.

transaction of business, any activity of a corporation within a particular state or having an impact within the state. Such transaction of business provides a sufficient basis for a court to exercise jurisdiction over the corporation in a suit arising out of that specific activity, even if the corporation does not engage in regular activity in that state and thus is not generally subject to suit there. Cf. DOING BUSINESS.

transactional immunity. See under IMMUNITY.

travel. See RIGHT TO TRAVEL.

treason, *n.* **1.** the crime of committing acts of war against the United States or intentionally giving aid and comfort to its enemies. See also OVERT ACT. **2. high treason,** in early English law, treason against the crown, as distinguished from "petty treason," which included a wife's killing of her husband or a servant's killing of his master.

treatise, *n.* a book or, especially, a multivolume work, systematically and exhaustively discussing and analyzing an area of law, such as contracts, evidence, or federal procedure. Treatises are a major research tool for lawyers and are often cited as authority by judges See also HORNBOOK.

treaty, *n.* a formal agreement between two or more nations on matters of international concern. Treaties of the United States are negotiated by the President and ratified by a two-thirds vote of the Senate. They are part of FEDERAL LAW and thus supersede any contrary state law and any prior federal statute; but Congress may negate or abrogate a treaty simply by refusing to enact any necessary implementing legislation or by enacting a subsequent statute inconsistent with the treaty. See also EXECUTIVE AGREEMENT.

treble damages. See under DAMAGES

trespass, *n.* **1.** Also called **trespass to land.** intentional or knowing conduct that directly results in invasion of land possessed by another, such as walking on it without permission, chopping down a tree onto it, tunneling under it, shooting a bullet over it, or staying on it after being asked to leave Trespass is a tort against the person entitled to exclusive possession of the land **2. criminal trespass,** the crime of entering or remaining upon another's land, structure, or vehicle after being notified (orally or by posting of signs or enclosure with fencing) to keep out or to leave **3. trespass to chattels,** the tort of intentionally interfering with another's possession of goods, as by using, moving, or damaging the property This tort is confined to relatively minor interference, serious interference with personal property is regarded as CONVERSION —*v* **4.** to commit a trespass.

trial, *n* **1.** the procedure by which evidence is presented in court under the supervision of a judge and the ultimate factual issues in a case are decided **2. bench trial,** a trial in which no jury is present and all factual issues are decided by the judge. Also called **nonjury trial; judge trial; trial to** (or **by**) **the court. 3. de novo trial,** a new trial, granted by the trial judge or ordered by an appellate court in a case because of some error or injustice in the first trial Also called **trial de novo; retrial;** or simply a new trial See also DE NOVO **4. jury trial,** a trial in which the facts are determined by a JURY Under the Sixth Amendment (see Appendix), state or federal criminal defendants facing potential sentences in excess of six months' imprisonment are entitled to demand a jury trial The Seventh Amendment (see Appendix) gives litigants in the federal courts a right of jury trial in civil damage actions that would have been submitted to a jury in traditional common law courts; in the state courts, juries in civil actions are usually allowed by state law but are not required by the United States Constitution Also called **trial by jury. 5. public trial,** a trial open to observation by members of the public The Sixth Amendment (see Appendix) gives state and federal criminal defendants the right to such a trial, and in 1980 the Supreme Court held that the First Amendment gives the press and public a general right to attend such proceedings However, proceedings may be closed in rare cases in which a judge finds an overriding interest such as protection of a juvenile witness, and cameras may be banned from the courtroom **6. speedy trial,** a criminal trial commencing without unreasonable delay after arrest or indictment The Sixth Amendment guarantees this right, and all jurisdictions have statutes or court rules setting standards for moving criminal cases to trial in a timely fashion

trial brief. See under BRIEF

trial by ambush, *Informal* a disparaging term for trial procedures or strategies that involve withholding relevant information from the other side and then presenting it under circumstances in which the other side does not have a reasonable opportunity to investigate and rebut it. Modern procedural rules, especially those providing for DISCOVERY, seek to minimize opportunities for trial by ambush. Also called **trial by surprise.**

tribunal, *n.* any court or body established to decide disputes: *administrative tribunal; disciplinary tribunal; judicial tribunal.*

trier of fact, the person or group charged with deciding the factual issues in a proceeding; the jury in a jury trial or judge in a nonjury trial. Also called **factfinder.**

TRO. See *temporary restraining order* (under RESTRAINING ORDER).

true bill. See under BILL.

trust, *n.* **1.** an arrangement in which one person (the TRUSTEE) holds property for the benefit of another (the BENEFICIARY or CESTUI QUE TRUST), to whom the trustee owes a FIDUCIARY DUTY in regard to the safeguarding, management, and disposition of the trust property and income. See also *breach of trust* (under BREACH). **2.** broadly, any FIDUCIARY RELATIONSHIP. **3.** a cartel or other monopolistic business arrangement or enterprise. This is the kind of trust for which the ANTITRUST laws were named. **4. blind trust,** a trust in which assets of a public official are managed without disclosing to the official (who is the beneficiary) how they are invested; established to minimize CONFLICTS OF INTEREST. **5. business trust,** an unincorporated association serving the same general purposes as a business corporation and subject to the same taxes, but organized as a trust. Instead of shareholders it has beneficiaries, whose investments constitute the trust property and are usually represented by transferrable certificates. Also called **Massachusetts trust** or **Massachusetts business trust.** **6. constructive trust,** a trust that arises BY OPERATION OF LAW, without any intention by the parties to create a trust, when through fraud, duress, mistake, or the like, property, or legal title to property, falls into the hands of a person who has no right to it. Under principles of EQUITY, the person with the property is deemed to hold it in trust for the person who should have received it, with an obligation to turn it over in full and intact See also IMPRESS. **7. express trust,** a trust established intentionally (unlike a *constructive trust*) and explicitly (unlike a *resulting trust*). It may be created orally, but usually is set up in a written TRUST INSTRUMENT, by which the person setting it up (the grantor or donor or settlor) transfers property to the trustee with instructions as to how and for whose benefit it is to be managed and used. **8. grantor trust,** a trust in which the grantor conveys property to a trustee to be held or managed for the grantor's own benefit; for example, a *blind trust.* **9. in trust,** subject to a trust: *He left $100,000 to his brother in trust for his brother's children, to be distributed to them when they reach the age of 21.* **10. inter vivos trust,** a trust established and effective during the grantor's lifetime. Also called **living trust.** Cf. *testamentary*

tained by a new client or for a new matter, usually viewed as a deposit on fees to be incurred.

retirement plan, an arrangement by which money is set aside during an individual's working years for use after retirement, especially a PENSION PLAN.

retreat, v. to withdraw from a confrontation rather than fighting back In general, American law, in the spirit of the Wild West, holds that a person who is attacked need not retreat even if that can be done safely, but may stand his ground and use reasonable force in SELF-DEFENSE Some jurisdictions make an exception for situations in which it appears that the only sufficient force to avoid death or serious bodily harm would be deadly force, requiring a person to withdraw (except from his own home or place of business) if it is clear that he can do so in complete safety, rather than use deadly force against the attacker. This is colloquially called a duty to "retreat to the wall "

retrial. Same as *de novo trial* (see under TRIAL)

return, v. **1.** to submit to a court an account of action taken in a judicial matter, particularly action by an officer or official body: *The grand jury returned an indictment The jury returned its verdict The sheriff returned an affidavit of service of the writ of attachment* —n. **2.** the act of returning such an account, or the written document itself. *Return was made last week. The return of service was filed last week.* **3.** Also called **tax return.** the document in which a taxpayer reports to the government on matters having tax consequences: *income tax return; estate tax return.* **4. individual return,** an income tax return filed by a person who is single, divorced, or legally separated pursuant to a judicial decree. **5. joint return,** an income tax return filed by a husband and wife together for the purpose of reporting and paying tax on their combined income. **6. return date,** the date upon which a return is due, a motion is to be argued or submitted, or a person is to appear or otherwise respond to a court order or PROCESS See also RETURNABLE. **7. separate return,** an income tax return filed by a married person for the purpose of reporting and paying tax only upon his or her own income.

returnable, *adj.* required to be submitted to the court or appropriately responded to; a term usually used in connection with the *return date* (see under RETURN): *The summons is returnable in twenty days. The order to show cause is returnable at 9:00 a.m on Monday in Courtroom 23.*

reverse, v. (of an appellate court) to nullify the judgment of a lower court in a case on appeal because of some ERROR in the court below. Sometimes a reversal disposes of the entire case; in other situations it requires further proceedings on REMAND. Cf AFFIRM² —**reversal,** *n*

reversible error. See under ERROR

reversion, *n.* the *future estate* (see under ESTATE¹) retained by the owner of an estate in real property (or his heirs) when the owner transfers an estate of shorter duration than the one he owns and does not dispose of the *trust.* **11. resulting trust,** a trust inferred from a transaction or conduct of a sort that normally evidences an intent that property in the hands of one person be held for the benefit of another. **12. spendthrift trust,** a trust created to provide some income to the beneficiary while preventing both the beneficiary and the beneficiary's creditors from having access to the money or property held in trust except to the extent that the trustee doles it out **13. testamentary trust,** a trust established by will or taking effect only upon the grantor's death Cf. *inter vivos trust* **14. Totten trust,** a bank account in which a beneficiary is named to receive any funds that happen to be left in the account if the account holder dies. Although the account is said to be "in trust for" the beneficiary, no trust arises so long as the account holder remains alive **15. voting trust,** an arrangement by which a number of shareholders in a corporation transfer their voting stock to a trustee for a period of time to hold and vote in accordance with an agreement among them, thereby concentrating their voting power and avoiding dissension.

trust deed. Same as a DEED OF TRUST.

trust indenture. See under INDENTURE.

trust instrument, an instrument creating a TRUST, such as a *trust indenture* (see under INDENTURE), *declaration of trust* (see under DECLARATION), DEED OF TRUST, or will The instrument must identify the trust property, the trustee, and the beneficiaries and state the terms of the trust.

trustee, *n.* **1.** the person who holds the property in a trust and administers it for the benefit of the beneficiaries. **2.** very loosely, anyone with a FIDUCIARY DUTY to another. **3. bankruptcy trustee,** a person appointed by a court to administer the property of a debtor. Also called **trustee in bankruptcy. 4. constructive trustee,** the person in possession of property subject to a *constructive trust* (see under TRUST).

try, *v.* **1.** (of a judge) to conduct the trial of a case, either with or without a jury. **2.** (of a lawyer) **a.** to present or defend a case in court, through witnesses and other evidence. **b. try to the court** (or **to the judge**), to try a case without a jury. **c. try to a jury,** to try a case with a jury. **3. try title,** to test the validity of title to property in a judicial proceeding.

turn state's evidence. See under STATE'S EVIDENCE.

Twinkie defense, the popular name given to the defense raised by the assassin of two San Francisco government officials in the 1970's. The jury accepted the killer's argument that eating junk food had corrupted his mind, and convicted him of involuntary manslaughter instead of murder. The defense has become a symbol of what many regard as the inventiveness of attorneys in devising excuses for criminal conduct and the credulousness of juries in accepting them.

U

ultimate fact. See under FACT.

ultra vires, *Latin.* (lit. "beyond the powers") describing an act that is beyond the scope of authority of the actor, especially an action taken by a corporation that is not authorized by its articles of incorporation. Under traditional doctrine, any ultra vires contract or other act of a corporation was void. Modern articles of incorporation typically authorize the corporation to do "anything a natural person might do," making ultra vires corporate acts almost impossible.

ultrahazardous activity. Same as ABNORMALLY DANGEROUS ACTIVITY.

unanimous opinion. See under OPINION.

unavailable witness. See under WITNESS.

unclean hands, 1. the quality of having acted unfairly in regard to the very matter with respect to which one is seeking relief in court. Cf CLEAN HANDS. **2.** the doctrine, derived from England's courts of EQUITY, that one who comes into court complaining of another's unfairness will be denied relief unless he himself acted fairly in the matter; expressed in such maxims as. "He who seeks equity must come into court with clean hands." Referred to equally as the **clean hands doctrine** and the **unclean hands doctrine. 3.** a defense often raised in response to claims for *equitable relief* (see under REMEDY), based upon the plaintiff's own improper and unjust conduct in the matter. Referred to as the **unclean hands defense** or somewhat less commonly as the **clean hands defense.** See also IN PARI DELICTO.

unconscionability, *n.* the doctrine that a contract that is so unfair and one-sided as to "shock the conscience of the court" need not be enforced by the court. The doctrine is most often applied to consumer transactions in which the court believes that the consumer was taken advantage of. See also *adhesion contract* (under CONTRACT); BARGAINING POWER. —**unconscionable,** *adj.*

unconstitutional, *adj.* **1.** in conflict with some provision of a constitution; said particularly of state or federal statutes that violate the United States Constitution. Cf. CONSTITUTIONAL. **2. unconstitutional** (or **invalid) as applied,** unconstitutional in its impact upon a specific individual or class of individuals, but otherwise enforceable. For example, a public school dress code prohibiting the wearing of hats in class might be held unconstitutional as applied to children whose religions require head covering. **3. unconstitutional** (or **invalid) on its face,** unconstitutional in its entirety and hence not enforceable at all. —**unconstitutionality,** *n.*

uncontrollable impulse test. Same as IRRESISTIBLE IMPULSE TEST.

under color of law, (of improper conduct by a state official) with the appearance of legal authority; in actual or purported performance of one's duties as a state official In some circumstances the phrase also applies to private conduct that is specifically authorized or approved by state law. Under the Civil Rights Act of 1871, anyone who has been deprived of federal civil rights under color of state law may sue the wrongdoer

under protest, an expression signifying that in complying with some demand or performing some action one is not conceding that the action is legally required and reserves the right to contest the issue in court A particularly common example is the payment of a tax bill under protest, in order to preserve the right to question its amount or validity while avoiding penalties for late payment should the tax be upheld.

under seal. See *contract under seal* (under CONTRACT); *instrument under seal* (under SEAL¹)

under the influence. See DRIVING WHILE INTOXICATED

underage, *adj.* describing a person who has not yet reached the minimum age set by law for a specified activity, such as consumption of alcohol or engaging in sexual activity. See also *statutory rape* (under RAPE); AGE

undersigned, *n , adj.* a term used in the body of a document to designate the person or persons whose signatures appear at the end. This expression is commonly used in preprinted form contracts to refer to anyone who might sign them.

understanding, *n* **1.** an agreement, particularly a somewhat informal or preliminary one. It may or may not be sufficiently definite to be enforceable as a contract. See also INDEFINITE; *memorandum of understanding* (under MEMORANDUM). **2.** a party's interpretation of a contract term If one party's understanding differs from another's, a court may have to interpret the contract.

undertaking, *n.* **1.** a bond (see BOND²), PLEDGE, or promise given to guarantee performance or indemnify another against loss. **2.** any contractual or noncontractual promise.

underwrite, *v.* **1.** to provide insurance; to guarantee payment under an insurance policy: *to underwrite insurance; underwrite an insurance policy.* **2.** to guarantee that an entire issue of securities will be sold, either by assisting in their sale to the public and agreeing to purchase any that remain unsold, or by buying up the entire issue for resale to the public: *to underwrite securities; underwrite an issue of securities.* —**underwriter,** *n.*

undisclosed principal. See under PRINCIPAL.

undivided interest or **undivided fractional interest.** See under INTEREST¹

undocumented alien. See under ALIEN

undue influence, the use of a position of power or trust to induce a person to enter into a transaction that does not reflect his true wishes, or that he would not have entered into if given unbiased advice. This is a ground for rescinding or refusing to enforce wills, gifts, and contracts.

unearned income. See under INCOME

unemployment compensation, weekly payments made for a limited period of time to most workers who lose their jobs through no fault of their own, provided under a system of insurance **(unemployment insurance)** established by state law.

unethical, *adj.* contrary to the generally accepted standards of honesty and fairness in the conduct of one's business or profession **Unethical conduct,** also called **unprofessional conduct,** is not necessarily a crime, but is often the basis for a malpractice action or disciplinary proceeding.

unfair competition, 1. the use of product names, packaging, or other devices similar to those of a competitor so as to confuse the public about whose product they are buying. **2.** Also called **unfair methods of competition.** any improper conduct by which a business might gain unfair advantage over competitors. See also PASSING OFF

unfair labor practice, any of a long list of coercive, discriminatory, or otherwise improper activities of employers or unions prohibited by the National Labor Relations Act.

Uniform Code of Military Justice, the federal statute establishing a comprehensive system of justice applicable to members of the armed forces in their military capacity, complete with its own courts and judicial procedures.

Uniform Commercial Code (U.C.C.), a lengthy statute, adopted in substantially the same form in every state except Louisiana, establishing a uniform basic body of law governing sales of goods, negotiable instruments, bank deposits and collections, and various other commercial instruments and transactions. See also UNIFORM LAWS.

Uniform Laws (or **Acts**), a set of model statutes on a wide range of subjects, approved by the National Conference of Commissioners on Uniform State Laws (made up of representatives appointed by the governers of all states) and recommended to state legislatures for adoption. The purpose of the Uniform Laws is to mitigate the legal uncertainty and confusion that inevitably arises when fifty states adopt different and often conflicting laws on the same subjects, particularly with regard to transactions involving people and property in different states. Many of the Uniform Laws have been widely adopted, most notably the UNIFORM COMMERCIAL CODE. See also CONFLICT OF LAWS; MODEL LAW.

Uniform System of Citation. See BLUEBOOK.

unilateral contract. See under CONTRACT.

unilateral mistake. See under MISTAKE.

unincorporated association. See under ASSOCIATION.

union, *n.* **1.** Also called **labor union.** an organization of workers formed for the purpose of bargaining collectively with employers over wages and working conditions. See also LABOR ORGANIZATION; TRADE UNION. **2. craft union,** a union composed only of people in the same trade or craft, regardless of the industry in which they work. Also called **horizontal union.** See also TRADE UNION. Cf. *industrial un-*

ion. **3. independent union,** a union of workers in a particular company, not affiliated with a larger union. **4. industrial union,** a union of workers in a particular industry, regardless of their individual trade or craft. Also called **vertical union.** Cf. *craft union.* **5. local union,** a local bargaining unit of a larger union. **6. union certification,** certification by the National Labor Relations Board of a particular union as the exclusive collective bargaining agent for a particular group of employees, upon a vote of the employees. **7. union shop.** See under SHOP.

United States Attorney, the chief lawyer for the United States government within a federal *judicial district* (see under DISTRICT). Each United States Attorney is appointed by the President and is responsible for prosecuting federal crimes and representing the United States in all civil litigation within her district. Lawyers on the staff of a United States Attorney, who usually do most of the actual courtroom work, have the title **Assistant United States Attorney (AUSA).** Cf. ATTORNEY GENERAL; *Solicitor General* (under SOLICITOR)

United States Code (U.S.C.), the congressionally authorized codification of statutes enacted by Congress, organized into fifty broad subject areas, or "titles." See also ANNOTATED; STATUTES AT LARGE

United States Court of Appeals, one of the intermediate appellate courts in the federal judicial system, lying between the United States District Courts and the Supreme Court of the United States. There is one such court for each CIRCUIT in the federal system Since very few cases are accepted for review by the Supreme Court, as a practical matter the Court of Appeals is the court of last resort for most federal litigants, and since the decisions of a Court of Appeals are binding upon all United States District Courts in its circuit, these decisions are extremely important in formulating federal law

United States District Court, the federal court of original jurisdiction for nearly all civil and criminal matters that can be brought in federal courts There is one such court for each federal *judicial district* (see under DISTRICT), although each court has several judges and many have two or more courthouses located in different parts of the district.

United States Supreme Court, an informal but generally accepted name for the *Supreme Court of the United States* (see under SUPREME COURT)

unjust enrichment, any situation in which a person receives a benefit that properly belongs to another or retains, without paying for it, a benefit that in justice should be paid for; for example, receiving delivery of goods intended for another, or refusing to pay a doctor who provided necessary emergency care while one was unconscious. See also RESTITUTION.

unlawful, *adj.* contrary to, unauthorized by, or disapproved of by law. Unlawful conduct need not be criminal; the term is broad enough to include torts, or conduct such as undue influence which might lead a court to declare a transaction void. Cf. ILLEGAL.

unlawful assembly, the offense of the coming together as a group of three or more people in public for the purpose of engaging in a riot or some other openly violent activity. Cf. FREEDOM OF ASSEMBLY.

unlawful detainer. See under DETAINER.

unliquidated, *adj.* **1.** uncertain, disputed, or not yet determined as to amount *unliquidated claim; unliquidated damages.* **2.** not yet sold *unliquidated assets; unliquidated inventory.* Cf. LIQUIDATE

unmarketable title. Same as *defective title* (see under TITLE)

unnatural act, oral or anal sex or sex with an animal—acts that the law traditionally regarded as so unspeakable that courts and legislatures literally would not speak their names, but instead condemned them under such names as "unnatural act" or "the crime against nature." See also SODOMY.

unprofessional conduct. Same as *unethical conduct* (see under UNETHICAL)

unreasonable restraint of trade, business conduct which tends to reduce competition in the marketplace, and whose adverse effect is not outweighed by some permissible business justification Concerted action that unreasonably restrains trade, such as PRICE FIXING or a *group boycott* (see under BOYCOTT), is outlawed by the SHERMAN ANTITRUST ACT

unreasonable search. See under SEARCH.

unreasonable search and seizure. See under SEARCH AND SEIZURE.

usage, *n.* **1.** a practice or method of doing business that is followed with such consistency by people engaged in transactions of a certain type in a particular place, vocation, or trade that the law will normally presume, with respect to a particular transaction of that type, that the parties intended that practice to be followed See also CUSTOM **2. usage of trade,** a usage followed in a particular vocation or trade. Also called **trade usage.** Cf COURSE OF DEALING; COURSE OF PERFORMANCE

use, *n.* **1.** Also called **use and benefit.** benefit. For example, a case named *Smith for the use of Jones v. Lee* would be one brought for technical reasons by Smith although the person who would benefit from its success would be Jones. **2.** an old term for a *beneficial interest* (see under INTEREST[1]) in property, especially real property. **3.** the manner in which land that has been zoned is or could be utilized. **4. best use,** the most lucrative use that could be made of a parcel of land as currently zoned The assessed value of land for property tax purposes may be based upon this hypothetical use rather than the actual use Also called **best and highest use** or **highest and best use. 5. conforming use,** a use of land permitted by current zoning regulations. **6. nonconforming use,** a land use contrary to zoning regulations. Nonconforming uses typically exist because they were there before a zoning plan was adopted, and are usually permitted to continue for many years. **7. public use,** a use of land that benefits the public at large Under the power of EMINENT DOMAIN, the state or federal government may take private property for any public use, provided that the owner is fairly compensated.

use immunity. See under IMMUNITY.

use tax, a state tax on the purchase price of goods purchased outside the state for use within the state from a vendor who does business in the state Use taxes are imposed in an effort to make up revenue lost when consumers avoid local sales taxes by shopping out of state.

usual covenants. See under COVENANT.

usury, *n.* the crime of charging a higher rate of interest for a loan than is allowed by law. —**usurious,** *adj.*

utmost care. See under CARE.

utter, *v.* **1.** to put an instrument into circulation or offer it to someone as what it purports to be. **2. uttering a forged instrument,** the crime of passing a counterfeit or forged instrument or attempting to do so by offering it as if it were genuine

V

v., the abbreviation for *versus,* meaning "against," in case names; usually read as a letter rather than a word: *Roe v. Wade* (pronounced "Roe vee Wade").

vacate, *v.* to nullify a judgment or court order. This may be done by the court that issued the original judgment or order, or by a higher court on appeal. See also QUASH; SET ASIDE.

vacatur, *n. Latin.* (lit. "Let it be made void.") **1.** a court order vacating a previous judgment or order. **2.** Sometimes called **vacation.** the act of vacating a judgment or order.

vague, *adj.* uncertain in meaning or scope. In a contract, a certain amount of vagueness is seldom a barrier to enforceability; the court will enforce the contract in accordance with whatever it finds to be the most reasonable interpretation. Cf. INDEFINITE. A criminal law that is excessively vague may be held unconstitutional **(void for vagueness)** on the ground that it is a violation of due process to convict a person of a crime for behavior that was not clearly defined as criminal. —**vagueness,** *n.*

value. See *assessed value* (under ASSESS); MARKET VALUE.

value-added tax, a tax, used in many countries and sometimes proposed for the United States, levied upon the increase in value of a product at each stage of production or distribution. The tax at each stage is paid by the seller and added to the price paid by the buyer, having much the same effect as a SALES TAX.

variance, *n.* **1.** in zoning law, permission to use property in a particular way that is not generally allowed in that zone, granted to an individual property owner to prevent undue hardship. **2.** in procedure, a difference between what was originally alleged and what was actually shown at trial. This is seldom of much importance in civil cases. **3. fatal variance,** in criminal cases, so great a variance between what was charged and what was proved that the defendant was misled and deprived of a fair trial.

vehicular homicide. See under HOMICIDE.

veil, *n.* See *corporate veil* (under CORPORATE).

vel non, *Latin.* (lit. "or not") or the opposite; or the lack thereof: *The issue for decision is the adequacy, vel non, of notice.*

vendee, *n.* a buyer.

vendor, *n.* a seller.

venire, *n.* a group of citizens called into court at the same time for jury duty, from which a jury or juries will be selected. An individual potential juror was traditionally called a **venireman,** but today **veniremember** is preferable Also called **array** or **jury array,** or sometimes **panel** or **jury panel.** See also *jury panel* (under JURY).

venture, *n.* See JOINT VENTURE.

venturer. See under JOINT VENTURE

venue, *n* **1.** the county or judicial district where a case is maintained When courts in more than one geographic area have jurisdiction to consider a case, rules of *venue* determine where the case should be filed **2.** in an affidavit or affirmation, the part that tells where the instrument was executed. See also ss

verbal, *adj.* **1.** in words; spoken or written; expressed in words rather than implied by conduct: *An offer of contract may be accepted either verbally or by conduct manifesting agreement, such as commencement of performance.* The word "verbal" is sometimes confused with ORAL. **2. verbal act,** words (written or spoken) having legal effect; for example, a written consent or an oral contract. A verbal act is not regarded as a mere assertion of fact, and so is not excluded from evidence as HEARSAY.

verdict, *n.* **1.** the jury's decision in a case Traditionally required to be unanimous, but now in many cases permitted by a vote of 10 or 11 members of a 12-member jury or 5 members of a 6-member jury. Cf. JUDGMENT; FINDINGS OF FACT AND CONCLUSIONS OF LAW **2. chance verdict,** one reached by flip of a coin or other process of chance Obviously improper. **3. compromise verdict,** one arrived at as a compromise among conflicting views of jurors. Unless all jurors, after further deliberation, come to agree that the verdict is correct (i.e., consistent with the evidence and the judge's instructions), this is improper. **4. directed verdict,** one entered by the judge because, upon the evidence presented, the law permits only one outcome, so that there is nothing for the jury to decide. **5. excessive verdict,** one awarding damages grossly disproportionate to the plaintiff's injuries in light of the evidence and the nature of the case. A remedy for this is REMITTITUR. **6. general verdict,** one consisting of a single overall finding covering all issues; for example, "Guilty," "Not guilty," or "We find for the plaintiff in the amount of $60,000." Cf *special verdict.* **7. inconsistent verdict,** one having two or more components that, under the judge's instructions, are logically inconsistent. If this is noticed in time, the jury may be sent back to reconsider, with clarifying instructions. **8. quotient verdict,** a type of *compromise verdict* in which the amount of damages is arrived at by averaging the amounts proposed by different jurors. **9. special verdict,** one in which the jurors are required to agree upon answers to a list of questions (called **special questions** or **special interrogatories**) about specific issues in the case. Used especially in complex civil cases. Cf. *general verdict.* **10. verdict against the weight of the evidence,** one found by the judge to be so clearly contrary to the credible evidence that it would be unjust to let it stand. The usual remedy in such a situation is to set aside the verdict and order a new trial.

verification, *n.* **1.** the act of verifying a document **2.** a statement affirming or swearing to the truth or authenticity of a document, written on the document itself or attached to it.

verify, v. **1.** to swear to or affirm the authenticity of a document, or the truth of the statements it contains. **2. verified complaint,** a COMPLAINT to which a VERIFICATION has been affixed affirming or swearing to the truth of the facts alleged. (Other pleadings may likewise be verified.) **3. verified copy.** Same as *certified copy* (see under CERTIFY).

vertical price fixing. See under PRICE FIXING.

vertical union. See under UNION.

vest, v. (of a power, right, or property interest) **1.** to come into being or become certain: *Your pension will vest when you have worked here for five years.* **2.** to attach to or reside in someone (used with *in*): *Upon the death of the parents, title to the farm will vest in the children.* **3.** to grant to or endow someone (used with *with*): *The deed vests the buyer with title to the property.*

vested, adj. **1.** describing an interest in property that either confers a present right to possession, use, or enjoyment of the property or is certain to confer such a right in the future: *vested estate* (see under ESTATE[1]); *vested interest* (see under INTEREST[1]); *vested pension* (see under PENSION). **2.** (of rights generally) protected by the Constitution from being arbitrarily taken away or nullified. See also *vested right* (under RIGHT).

vexatious litigation, baseless LITIGATION commenced only to annoy and harass the defendant.

vicarious liability. See under LIABILITY.

victim impact statement, a report on the impact that a crime had on its victims, given to a judge for consideration in sentencing the convicted criminal. See also PRESENTENCE REPORT.

victimless crime, conduct not in itself harmful to the person or property of anyone but consenting participants, but nevertheless defined as criminal; for example, gambling, drug use, or prostitution.

victims' rights, rights of individuals who have been the victim of a crime to be informed of various stages of the criminal justice process concerning the crime of which they were a victim and to present their views, as by addressing the judge before sentencing and the parole board at any parole hearing. Such rights are a relatively new concept enacted into law in some states.

video will. See under WILL.

violation, n. **1.** a breach, infringement, or transgression of any rule, law, or duty. **2.** the name given in some states to an offense below the level of MISDEMEANOR, punishable only by a fine or forfeiture and not classified as a crime. *a littering violation*

visa, n. written authorization to enter a country, issued to an individual from another country and normally stamped into the individual's passport. Typically a visa states when entry may be made, how long the individual may stay, and the permitted purpose for the visit. See also GREEN CARD.

visitation, n. **1.** a visit by a parent with a child who is in the custody of someone else, in a situation in which the parent has been deprived of custody, as through divorce or because of child neglect. **2. visitation rights,** authorization by court order for regular visitation, upon whatever terms the court decrees. **3. supervised visitation,** court-ordered visitation conditioned upon there being another adult present, in cases in which there is reason for concern regarding the safety of the child.

void, *adj.* having no legal force or effect; not binding or enforceable because of a legal defect or for reasons of PUBLIC POLICY· *a void check, statute, contract, judgment, marriage,* etc. A transaction or instrument may be void from the outset **(void ab initio),** and thus never legally recognized at all, or it may become void at a later stage because of a change in circumstances. See also AB INITIO; VOIDABLE; *void for vagueness* (under VAGUE).

voidable, *adj.* describing a contract, instrument, transaction, or relationship that may be rendered VOID at the option of one party. *voidable preference* (see under PREFERENCE); *voidable contract; voidable marriage.* For example, a transaction entered into as a result of fraud would normally be voidable at the option of the defrauded party. See also AVOID, RATIFY.

voir dire, *Law French.* (lit "to say truly") **1.** questioning of prospective jurors for possible sources of bias and for other information relevant to jury selection See also CHALLENGE. **2.** preliminary questioning of a trial witness, usually outside the presence of the jury, to determine competency to testify, admissibility of proposed testimony, qualification as an expert, and the like. See also *qualify as an expert* (under QUALIFY¹)

voluntary, *adj.* **1.** done without compulsion or obligation. See *voluntary* BANKRUPTCY, COMMITMENT, CONFESSION, DISCONTINUANCE, DISMISSAL under those words **2.** done intentionally rather than accidentally or reflexively. See *voluntary* MANSLAUGHTER, WASTE under those words. **3.** gratuitous; without consideration. See *voluntary conveyance* (under CONVEYANCE).

voter qualification, a legal requirement for eligibility to vote in a public election, such as age or residence Federal voting rights legislation has outlawed many such requirements, such as passing a literacy test, that tended to prevent disadvantaged minorities from voting. See also POLL TAX.

voting trust. See under TRUST

wage earner's plan. See under BANKRUPTCY.

wait and see zoning. See under ZONING.

waiting period. See under RESIDENCY.

waive, *v.* to abandon a right, privilege, or claim, intentionally and with knowledge of what you are giving up

waiver, *n.* **1.** the voluntary, intentional relinquishment of a right, privilege, or claim that you know you have. **2. express waiver,** a waiver expressed in words. **3. implied waiver,** a waiver indicated by conduct. For mere conduct to be effective as a waiver, the circumstances must evidence the actor's awareness of her rights and intent to give them up.

want, *n.* **1.** the absence of some necessary element or prerequisite· *The application for a search warrant was denied for want of probable cause. The fraud claim was dismissed for want of evidence of reliance.* **2. want of consideration,** the lack of CONSIDERATION for a promise, without which there is no enforceable contract: *The contract failed for want of consideration.* Cf. FAILURE OF CONSIDERATION. **3. want of jurisdiction, a.** a court's lack of *subject matter jurisdiction* (see under JURISDICTION¹) over a particular case, making any decision it might render on the merits of the case void. **b.** a court's lack of *personal jurisdiction* (see under JURISDICTION¹) over a party to a case, making any decision on the merits unenforceable as against that particular party unless the party appeared in the case without raising a prompt jurisdictional objection. **4. want of prosecution.** Same as FAILURE TO PROSECUTE.

wanton, *adj.* an older term of somewhat vague scope, generally describing conduct characterized by INTENT, KNOWLEDGE, or RECKLESSNESS rather than mere negligence. (But see *wanton negligence,* under NEGLIGENCE.) The term is often thrown in to add a note of moral outrage to a description: *willful and wanton; recklessly and wantonly.* See also STATE OF MIND. —**wantonly,** *adv.*

ward, *n.* a person for whom a GUARDIAN has been appointed.

ward of the court, *Informal.* any minor or incompetent person involved in legal proceedings. The common saying that "infants and incompetents are wards of the court" signifies that judges have a duty to make sure that the interests of litigants who are unable to look out for their own rights are adequately represented and well protected.

warehouse receipt, a receipt issued by a warehouser identifying goods received for storage and evidencing the right of the person with the receipt to take possession of those goods. A warehouse receipt is a DOCUMENT OF TITLE.

warehouser, *n.* a person or entity in the business of storing goods for others: still often referred to by the more cumbersome historical term **warehouseman**—an odd linguistic artifact since the warehouser is usually a company rather than an individual of either sex See also *warehouser's* (or *warehouseman's*) *lien* (under LIEN).

warrant¹, *n* **1.** a formal document, usually issued by a court, authorizing or directing an official to take a specific action. **2. arrest warrant,** a warrant directing or authorizing law enforcement officers to arrest an individual. It is issued upon a showing of PROBABLE CAUSE to believe that a crime has been committed and that the individual in question committed it. Also called **warrant of arrest.** Cf. SUMMONS, CITATION. **3. bench warrant,** a warrant issued by a judge from the bench, directing that an individual be brought before the court, usually because the individual has failed to appear in response to a summons or subpoena or has violated a court order. **4. death warrant,** a warrant signed by the governor of a state directing the warden of a prison or another appropriate official to carry out a death sentence at a specific time on a specific day. **5. search warrant,** a warrant, issued upon a showing of probable cause to believe that items connected with a crime will be found in a particular place, authorizing law enforcement authorities to search for those items in that place and seize them if found. **6. warrant of eviction,** a warrant directing a sheriff to put a person wrongfully in possession of property (usually a holdover tenant) out of the property.

warrant², *n.* a certificate issued by a corporation entitling the holder to purchase a specified number of shares of a specified class of the company's stock at a specified price, usually good until a specified date. Also called **stock warrant.**

warrant³, *v.* to issue or become bound by an express or implied warranty.

warrantless, *adj.* performed without a warrant. See *warrantless arrest* (under ARREST); *warrantless search* (under SEARCH)

warranty, *n.* **1.** a legally binding representation made or implied in connection with a sale of goods, transfer of land, or other contract or financial transaction, ordinarily relating to the quality, integrity, or usefulness of the subject matter of the transaction (such as a product, a parcel of land, or a check); if the representation proves untrue, the person or company that made it (the **warrantor**) normally will be liable for any resulting loss or injury. Popularly called a GUARANTEE, though in legal usage that means something different. In some phrases, especially in real estate transactions, also called a COVENANT. **2.** a representation made by the purchaser of an insurance policy, incorporated into the policy and relied upon by the insurance company in issuing the policy; if it proves untrue, the policy will be void. **3. affirmative warranty,** in an insurance policy, a policy owner's warranty of existing or past fact, such as that he is 52 years old and has never been treated for heart disease. Cf *promissory warranty.* **4. construction warranty,** a warranty by the builder or seller of a new house that it is free from basic structural defects. Also called **home owner's warranty. 5. express warranty, a.** a warranty expressed in words. **b.** in connection with a sale of goods, any words or conduct of the seller amounting to a representation about the quality or nature of the goods, such as the showing of a model or sample. Cf. *implied warranty;* PUFFING. **6. full warranty,** in the sale of a consumer product, a written warranty meeting certain federal standards To qualify as a full warranty, the warranty must include a promise to remedy any defect or malfunction that occurs within a specified period of time without charge, and to permit the consumer to choose between a replacement and a refund if the product cannot be fixed Cf. *limited warranty.* **7. implied warranty,** a warranty imposed by law in connection with a particular transaction, because the law regards such a warranty as inherent in that type of transaction unless the circumstances clearly indicate or the parties explicitly agree otherwise. For example, if you buy a painting at a gallery, the gallery impliedly warrants that it is theirs to sell; therefore, if it turns out to be stolen and the rightful owner traces it and takes it back from you, you can sue the seller to recover the value of the painting. Cf. *express warranty.* **8. limited warranty,** in the sale of a consumer product, any written warranty that falls short of the requirements for a **full warranty.** Under federal law, a limited warranty must be clearly labeled as such and must clearly state the scope of the warranty. **9. promissory warranty,** in an insurance policy, a policy owner's warranty that certain facts will continue to exist, or certain acts will or will not be done, during the term of the policy; for example, that she will not smoke. Cf. *affirmative warranty.* **10. warranty of fitness for a particular purpose,** the implied warranty of a seller of goods who has reason to know that the buyer needs the goods for a particular use and is relying upon the seller to furnish suitable goods, that the goods being furnished will in fact be suitable for that use. **11. warranty of title,** the implied warranty of a seller of goods that the title conveyed to the buyer will be good and unencumbered, and that its transfer is rightful. Cf *warranties of title* (under COVENANT). See also *breach of warranty* (under BREACH); *warranty deed* (under DEED); *warranty of habitability* (under HABITABLE); *warranty of merchantability* (under MERCHANTABLE); *warranty of quiet enjoyment* or *covenant of warranty* (both under QUIET ENJOYMENT). Cf. COVENANT, GUARANTEE, GUARANTY.

wash, *n. Informal.* a transaction or set of related transactions leaving a party in substantially the same position as when he started. See also *wash sale* (under SALE)

waste, *n.* **1.** substantial permanent change, beyond normal wear and tear, in the condition of real property while it is in possession of a tenant. A tenant who causes or permits waste is normally liable to the owner for damages **2. ameliorating waste,** a substantial change that actually increases the value of the property. Normally this does not give rise to liability. **3. commissive waste,** waste caused by intentional conduct of the tenant. Also called **voluntary**

waste. **4. permissive waste,** waste that the tenant negligently allows to occur, as by failing to provide routine maintenance.

wasting, *adj* of such a nature as to be used up or dissipated over time· oil and coal are *wasting assets;* a trust in which funds are used for trust purposes faster than they accrue is a *wasting trust.*

weapon, *n.* **1.** anything designed or used to cause bodily injury **2. concealed weapon,** a weapon carried in such a way as not to be obvious. **3. deadly weapon,** anything which, either by design or by the way it is wielded in a particular case, could cause death or serious injury. Also called **dangerous weapon; lethal weapon.**

weight, *n.* **1.** Same as PROBATIVE VALUE. **2.** of all the evidence on both sides of an issue, the more convincing body of evidence, as determined not by mere quantity but by its significance, coherence, and credibility. See also *verdict against the weight of the evidence* (under VERDICT).

whistleblower, *n.* **1.** an employee who reports dangerous or illegal conduct of an employer to authorities. **2. whistleblower law,** a statute protecting whistleblowers from retaliatory firing or other action by the employer.

white-collar crime, *Informal.* any business or financial crime of a type typically engaged in by executives and professional people, often involving very large sums of money to which they have access in the course of their business. Punishments for such crimes are sometimes thought to be disproportionately light when compared with those for nonviolent crimes, involving far less money, by people of lower social status.

white slavery, until 1986, the statutory term for the federal crime of transporting a woman across state lines "for the purpose of prostitution or debauchery, or for any other immoral purpose." In 1986, the White-Slave Traffic Act was amended to sanitize it of sexist and racist terminology and make it as applicable to someone who takes a paid male companion on a trip as to one who takes a paid female companion.

whole. See MAKE WHOLE.

whole life insurance. Same as *straight life insurance* (see under LIFE INSURANCE)

wholly owned subsidiary. See under SUBSIDIARY.

widow's (or **widower's**) **election.** See under ELECTION.

widow's (or **widower's**) **elective** (or **statutory**) **share.** See under ELECTIVE SHARE.

wife abuse. See under SPOUSAL ABUSE.

wildcat strike. See under STRIKE[1]

will, *n.* **1.** a person's declaration of how she wants her property to be distributed when she dies. Because the maker of a will (the TESTATOR) is never available to testify to its authenticity, the law requires considerable formality in the execution of a will. The requirements vary from state to state, and not following them exactly will render the will invalid. **2. holographic will,** a will written out by hand, signed, and dated by the maker; recognized in a number of states as valid even if not witnessed like a normal will **3. joint will,** the wills of two people, usually husband and wife, in a single document **4. nuncupative will,** a will that is spoken, not written; allowed in a few states under special circumstances, notably when death is imminent Also called **oral will. 5. video will,** a will read or recited by the testator on videotape, sometimes augmented by explanations of the reasons for certain gifts (or nongifts) and expressions of sentiment for those left behind. Videotape cannot take the place of formalities required for a valid will, but can be a useful supplement. **6. will contest,** a challenge to the validity of a will See also CODICIL; *election under the will* (under ELECTION); TESTAMENT; LAST WILL AND TESTAMENT. Cf. AT WILL; LIVING WILL; INTESTATE SUCCESSION.

willful, *adj.* describing wrongful conduct done with INTENT or KNOWLEDGE, and sometimes RECKLESSNESS: *willful neglect* (see under NEGLECT); *willful negligence* (see under NEGLIGENCE); *willful violation of an injunction.* See also STATE OF MIND. —**willfully,** *adv* —**willfulness,** *n.*

wind up, to bring the affairs of a corporation, partnership, estate, or other enterprise to an end by fulfilling or settling remaining business obligations, liquidating and distributing any remaining assets, and dissolving the organization Cf GOING CONCERN.

wire fraud. See under FRAUD

wiretap, *n.* **1.** originally, the attachment of an extra wire to a telephone line to listen in on conversations. Now the term is used broadly and informally to cover any interception or recording of conversations or data transmissions by electronic or other artificial means without the consent of the participants. If done by a private individual, wiretapping is normally a crime, and may also give rise to a tort claim for INVASION OF PRIVACY If done by law enforcement authorities, it normally requires a search warrant In most states, however, one participant in a conversation may record it without the knowledge of the others —*v* **2.** to install a wiretap or listen by means of one.

wish, *n., v.* an ambiguous word too often found in wills, sometimes construed as a directive and sometimes as a mere hope or suggestion. See also PRECATORY LANGUAGE.

with all faults. See AS IS.

with prejudice. See under PREJUDICE.

withholding tax, a sum of money required to be held back from an employee's wages, or in special circumstances from an investor's earnings, and sent directly to taxing authorities as an advance on the imployee's or investor's taxes. Often simply called **withholding.**

within, *prep.* covered by; governed by *within the statute; within the usual meaning of the word; within the intent of the contract; within the language of Smith v. Jones.* Cf. OUTSIDE; DEHORS

without prejudice. See under PREJUDICE.

without recourse. See under RECOURSE.

witness, *n.* **1.** a person who has seen or heard something relevant to a case or an investigation. See also EYEWITNESS **2.** a person who testifies in a legal or legislative proceeding. **3.** Also called **attesting witness.** a person who formally observes the execution of a document, especially a will, and signs it as evidence that it was duly executed. **4. character witness,** a witness called to testify about the CHARACTER of a party or of another witness. **5. expert witness,** a witness qualified by education or experience to testify about and render opinions on specialized subjects beyond the knowledge of average people Unlike a *fact witness,* an expert witness need not have personal knowledge of the events or matters involved in the case See also BATTLE OF THE EXPERTS; *qualify as an expert* (under QUALIFY¹). **6. fact witness,** a witness called to testify about things she has personally done or observed. Unlike an *expert witness,* a fact witness ordinarily may not express opinions See also *opinion evidence* (under EVIDENCE). **7. hostile witness,** a witness called by one side in a case but known to be friendly to the other side or found to be evasive in answering questions If declared to be a hostile witness by the judge, such a witness may be asked leading questions even on direct examination and may be impeached even in states that normally do not allow impeachment of one's own witness. Also called **adverse witness. 8. interested witness,** a witness with an interest (see INTEREST²) in the case. That interest may be considered by the jury in assessing the witness's credibility. See also IMPEACHMENT **9. material witness,** a witness whose testimony is essential to one side or the other in a criminal case Such a witness may be required to travel from one state to another to testify, and in some circumstances may even be held in custody to assure that she will appear to testify **10. unavailable witness,** a witness whose testimony cannot be obtained at a trial, for reasons ranging from outright refusal to answer questions while on the stand to being dead. In some circumstances, prior statements or testimony of such a witness may be admitted under a *hearsay exception* (see under HEARSAY) —*v.* **11.** to see or hear an event. **12.** to act as an attesting witness to the execution of a document: *to witness a will.*

witness stand. Same as STAND

work made for hire, any of a certain class of copyrightable works, specified by statute, with respect to which the copyright is usually owned not by the creator of the work, but by the company that hired the creator to do the work The principal categories of such works are those created by an employee whose job it is to produce such works (as in the case of a newspaper article by a staff reporter), and those created by an *independent contractor* (see under CONTRACTOR) who was specially hired to produce a compilation, a contribution to a larger work, or an adjunct to a work created by someone else and who agreed in writing that the resulting work would be deemed a work made for hire. Often referred to informally as a **work for hire.**

work product, 1. Also called **attorney work product.** notes and other documents and materials prepared by or for an attorney in preparing for a case. **2. work product doctrine,** the principle that work product materials may not be demanded by the other side in pretrial DISCOVERY except upon a showing of special need, and that even then the attorney's analysis of the case need not be disclosed

work release, the release of a prisoner for a certain period of time each day to work at a job or participate in a training program. Cf HALFWAY HOUSE.

workers' compensation, payment to a worker as compensation for on-the-job injury Most employees in America are covered by a state or federal law, often called a **workers' compensation act** or **employers' liability act,** requiring compensation for such injuries regardless of who was at fault, establishing the amount of compensation for different types of injuries, and dictating a funding mechanism, such as an insurance program (**workers' compensation insurance** or **employers' liability insurance**) paid for by employers.

world. See ALL THE WORLD.

World Court. Informal name for the INTERNATIONAL COURT OF JUSTICE.

writ, *n.* **1.** any of a class of court orders derived from early English law, each having a specific name and purpose, by which a court commands a certain official or body to carry out a certain action Only a few writs are still in use in the United States Their formal names are always in the form "writ of. . " (for example, "writ of habeas corpus"), but the words "writ of" are often omitted **2. extraordinary writ,** any of a special class of writs whose effect is in some way to interfere with or open to question the proceedings of a court or other body Most of the writs that survive in America today are extraordinary writs Also referred to by the older name **prerogative writ. 3. Great Writ.** See HABEAS CORPUS **4. writ of error,** a writ issued by an appellate court to a lower court in certain kinds of cases that may be appealed as a matter of right, directing that the record of a case be sent up for review of alleged errors of law **5. writ of execution,** a writ directed to a sheriff or similar officer directing the officer to seize property of a *judgment debtor* (see under DEBTOR) or take other action to enforce or satisfy a judgment of the court. For writs of ATTACHMENT, CERTIORARI, CORAM NOBIS, HABEAS CORPUS, MANDAMUS, PROHIBITION, and QUO WARRANTO, see those words.

written contract. See under CONTRACT

wrong, *n.* **1.** the violation of or failure to perform a legal duty, or the infringement of another's legal rights **2. private wrong,** a wrong that injures or interferes with the rights of a specific person or private entity, usually a basis for a tort or contract action **3. public wrong,** a wrong that injures or interferes with the rights of the public at large, subject to civil or criminal proceedings brought by the state or its agencies or the federal government —**wrongful,** *adj.*

wrongful birth, a relatively new kind of tort action, usually brought by the parents of a newborn infant on their own behalf or on behalf of the child, alleging that the child would not have been born but for the medical malpractice of the defendant, such as an unsuccessful sterilization or abortion or bad advice that led the parents not to have an abortion. The damages sought typically include the costs of raising the child, and particularly the extra costs of caring indefinitely for a severely disabled child. Also called **wrongful life.**

wrongful death, a tort action brought by or on behalf of close relatives or beneficiaries of someone who has died, alleging that the death was caused by a wrongful act of the defendant, such as medical malpractice, reckless driving, or murder. The damages claimed include the loss of future income that the deceased would have earned over a normal lifespan.

wrongful discharge, the firing of an employee for a reason not permitted by law or in violation of contract Depending upon the circumstances, this may give rise to a tort or contract claim, a union grievance, or a civil rights claim. Also called **wrongful termination.**

wrongful life. Same as WRONGFUL BIRTH

wrongful termination. Same as WRONGFUL DISCHARGE.

X

X, *n.* a mark traditionally used as a SIGNATURE by people who cannot write their names Typically, the person's name and the words "his mark" or "her mark" would be printed near the X, and one or more neutral individuals would sign as witnesses.

X-rated, *adj.* a lay term popularly applied to sexually oriented or pornographic entertainment in any form. The label has no legal significance. Cf. OBSCENE; INDECENT; PORNOGRAPHY.

Y

year-and-a-day rule, the common law rule, still followed in many states, that one cannot be found guilty of homicide if the victim lives for a year and a day after the act. Most states have abandoned the rule in light of modern medicine's ability to prolong dying in some cases for very long periods.

Your Honor. See under HONOR.

youthful offender. Same as *juvenile offender* (see under JUVENILE).

zone, *n.* **1.** an area or district within a city, town, or county designated for a particular use or uses under a ZONING plan. **2. combat zone,** *Slang.* a zone in which sex-related businesses, such as topless bars and "X-rated" video stores, are concentrated This was once viewed as a way to allow some such businesses to exist while limiting their spread. In recent years, zoning plans which require dispersion of such businesses, rather than concentration of them in one zone, have been more popular with municipal governments **3. floating zone,** a zone definition included in a municipality's zoning law but not assigned a specific location on the map until some real estate developer proposes to put a particular tract of land to the specified use —*v.* **4.** to designate an area for particular uses under a zoning plan.

zone of employment, for purposes of WORKERS' COMPENSATION laws, an employee's workplace Any accidental injury to a worker within the employee's zone of employment entitles the worker to compensation from the employer

zoning, *n.* **1.** the division of a locality into geographic zones, pursuant to a plan under which the kinds of uses to which the land may be put, and the kinds of structures that may be built, vary from zone to zone **2. cumulative zoning,** a zoning plan in which each successive zone definition merely adds to the list of permitted uses. Thus a zone might permit residential use only, or residential and trade use, or residential and trade and industrial use. Cf. *exclusive zoning* **3. exclusionary zoning,** zoning that effectively keeps out low- and moderate-income families For example, zoning in which all residential areas are restricted to single-family homes on large lots. Cf. *inclusionary zoning.* **4. exclusive zoning,** zoning in which each zone has its own distinct use; for example, residential only, trade only, or industrial only. Cf. *cumulative zoning.* **5. inclusionary zoning,** zoning that provides for a certain amount of low- and moderate-income housing A few states have laws requiring that zoning plans be inclusionary. Cf. *exclusionary zoning.* **6. industrial performance zoning,** zoning in which the definition of permitted use depends upon the amount of noise, smoke, or other pollution generated, rather than upon general categorizations such as "industrial" vs. "non-industrial " This allows non-polluting industries to exist in zones where more polluting industries would be disruptive **7. spot zoning,** the zoning of a single lot or small tract to allow a particular use that is not permitted in the surrounding area Often attacked as political favoritism inconsistent with the general zoning plan. **8. wait and see zoning,** a zoning plan in which undeveloped areas are not designated for any use until a developer comes forward and proposes a particular use for a particular area —*adj* **9.** pertaining to zoning *zoning regulation*

APPENDIX: SUMMARY OF AMENDMENTS TO THE CONSTITUTION

The Constitution of the United States of America was written over the summer of 1787, and took effect in 1788 upon ratification by nine of the original thirteen states. The Constitution in its original form established the structure of the national government and enumerated the powers of each of its branches, but said little about the rights of the people. When Americans speak of "constitutional rights," therefore, they are almost invariably referring not to the original text of the Constitution, but to one or another of its amendments.

By one estimate, ten thousand proposed amendments have been introduced in Congress in a little over two centuries; just twenty-seven have been adopted, and they are summarized here. The year that each amendment became part of the Constitution is given in parentheses. Words and phrases in SMALL CAPITAL LETTERS refer to entries in the dictionary where more detailed information can be found; phrases in *italics* are discussed at entries indicated in small capitals.

The first ten amendments were adopted almost immediately to address the widespread concern about the Constitution's general lack of explicit protections for individual rights; these are known as the BILL OF RIGHTS. Although these amendments were originally intended only as limitations on the power of the federal government, and for most of the nation's history provided no protection against state laws that violated individual rights, most of the provisions of the Bill of Rights have now been made applicable to state governments by virtue of the INCORPORATION DOCTRINE.

The Thirteenth, Fourteenth, and Fifteenth Amendments represent the nation's effort to embody in its fundamental law the principles of equality and human dignity that emerged from the Civil War, and are often referred to as the CIVIL WAR AMENDMENTS.

I (1791)

guarantees FREEDOM OF RELIGION, FREEDOM OF SPEECH, FREEDOM OF THE PRESS, FREEDOM OF ASSEMBLY, and the RIGHT OF PETITION.

II (1791)

concerns the RIGHT TO BEAR ARMS as an aspect of the maintenance of a well regulated MILITIA.

III (1791)

prohibits the housing of soldiers in private homes without the consent of the owner, except in time of war.

IV (1791)

prohibits *unreasonable search and seizure* (see under SEARCH AND SEIZURE), and requires a showing of PROBABLE CAUSE for the issuance of any *search warrant* or *arrest warrant* (see both under WARRANT[1]).

V (1791)

requires INDICTMENT by a *grand jury* (see under JURY) before any person can be put on trial for a serious federal crime; bans DOUBLE JEOPARDY and compulsory SELF-INCRIMINATION; prohibits the federal government from depriving any person of life, LIBERTY, or PROPERTY without DUE PROCESS of law; and prohibits the TAKING of private property for *public use* (see under use) without JUST COMPENSATION.

VI (1791)

guarantees criminal defendants the right to a speedy and public trial by jury (see *speedy trial, public trial,* and *jury trial* under TRIAL; see also JURY); also guarantees them the right to be informed of the charges, the right of CONFRONTATION of adverse witnesses, the right to use PROCESS to compel the attendance of witnesses for the defense, and the RIGHT TO COUNSEL.

VII (1791)

preserves for litigants in civil damage actions in the federal courts the common law right of *jury trial* (see under TRIAL; see also JURY).

VIII (1791)

prohibits criminal courts from requiring *excessive bail* (see under BAIL[1]) or imposing CRUEL AND UNUSUAL PUNISHMENT.

IX (1791)

states that the listing of specific rights in the Constitution is not to be interpreted as suggesting that other rights do not exist or are not equally deserving of protection.

X (1791)

emphasizes that the federal government has only those powers delegated to it by the Constitution.

XI (1798)

requires federal courts to respect the *sovereign immunity* (see under IMMUNITY) of state governments.

XII (1804)

revised the electoral college system to reduce the potential for deadlocks in elections for President and Vice President.

XIII (1865)

abolished SLAVERY and *involuntary servitude* (see under SERVITUDE), except for forced labor as punishment for a crime.

XIV (1868)

extended American citizenship to people of color by declaring that all persons born or naturalized in the United States and subject to United States jurisdiction are citizens of the United States and of the state where they reside. This amendment also prohibits the states from depriving any person of life, LIBERTY, or PROPERTY without DUE PROCESS of law, and guarantees all persons EQUAL PROTECTION of the laws. See also INCORPORATION DOCTRINE.

XV (1870)

extended the vote to people of color by prohibiting the denial or abridgment of the right of citizens to vote on account of RACE, COLOR, or previous condition of SERVITUDE.

XVI (1913)

empowered Congress to institute the federal INCOME TAX.

XVII (1913)

changed the method of electing United States senators from election by state legislatures to direct election by the people.

XVIII (1919)

the Prohibition Amendment: prohibited the manufacture, sale, or importation of alcoholic beverages in the United States. Repealed in 1933.

XIX (1920)

the Woman Suffrage Amendment: extended the vote to women in all states by prohibiting the denial or abridgment of the right to vote on account of sex.

XX (1933)

revised the starting dates for terms of office of the President, Vice President, and members of Congress, and made provision for various contingencies in presidential succession such as the death of a President-elect before taking office.

XXI (1933)

repealed the Prohibition Amendment and gave the individual states the power to regulate the distribution and use of intoxicating liquors within their borders.

XXII (1951)

prohibits any individual from being elected President more than twice, or more than once if the individual has already acted as President for more than two years of a term to which someone else was elected.

XXIII (1961)

extended the right to vote in presidential elections to residents of the District of Columbia. The nation's capital still has no voting representation in Congress, even though more Americans live in the District of Columbia than in some states, and even though Congress makes most of the District's laws. A proposed constitutional amendment to allow citizens in the District of Columbia representation and voting rights on an equal footing with citizens of the 50 states was adopted by Congress in 1978 but failed of ratification.

XXIV (1964)

abolished the POLL TAX as a requirement for voting in primary and general elections for national office.

XXV (1967)

provides a mechanism for filling vacancies in the office of Vice President, provides that the Vice President will serve as Acting President during periods of presidential disability, and provides procedures for determining whether such a disability exists.

XXVI (1971)

lowered the voting age to eighteen.

XXVII (1992)

provides that no change voted by Congress in its own compensation may take effect until after the next biennial congressional election.